The Soul as Virgin Wife

STUDIES IN SPIRITUALITY AND THEOLOGY 1

Lawrence Cunningham, Bernard McGinn, and David Tracy
SERIES EDITORS

The Soul as Virgin Wife

Mechthild of Magdeburg, Marguerite Porete,
and Meister Eckhart

AMY HOLLYWOOD

University of Notre Dame Press
Notre Dame and London

Manufactured in the United States of America

Paperback printed in 2001

Library of Congress Cataloging-in-Publication Data

Hollywood, Amy M., 1963–.
 The soul as virgin wife : Mechthild of Magdeburg, Marguerite
Porete, and Meister Eckhart / Amy Hollywood
  p. cm. — (Studies in spirituality and theology series : vol. 1)
 Revision of author's thesis (Ph. D.—University of Chicago, 1991).
 Includes bibliographical references and index.
 ISBN 0-268-01769-7 (pbk. : alk. paper)
 1. Mysticism—History—Middle Ages, 600–1500. 2. Mysticism—
Catholic Church—History. 3. Mechthild, of Magdeburg, ca.
1212-ca. 1282. 4. Porete, Marguerite, ca. 1250–1310. 5. Eckhart,
Meister, d. 1327. I. Title. II. Series.
BV5075.H64 1995
248.2′2′09022—dc20   94-40479
                                                          CIP

♾ *The paper used in this publication meets the minimum requirements of the
American National Standard for Information Sciences—Permanence of
Paper for Printed Library Materials, ANSI Z39.48-1984*

TO MY MOTHER AND FATHER

Contents

ACKNOWLEDGMENTS

This book began as a dissertation, written under the exemplary guidance of Bernard McGinn. Initially, the study focused on detailed analyses of the mystics' texts. These readings remain central, but I realized that the theoretical and historical grounding for my conclusions needed to be articulated in greater detail; this led me to write chapters 1 and 2 and substantially revise the remainder. Bernie McGinn has been unstinting in his support throughout the process of revision and expansion, providing all of the postdoctoral assistance for which a former student could hope. I am glad to be able to acknowledge my debt to him here.

I would also like to thank others who have read the manuscript, offering suggestions and criticisms, and often saving me from error. David Tracy and Anne Carr read the early version with care, often clarifying for me my own conclusions. Frank Tobin's comments were invaluable for the final revision of the manuscript. I hope that Stephanie Paulsell will always be my first reader and thank her for the generosity and unflagging enthusiasm with which she greeted this and other projects. Reed Lowrie read the penultimate version with an editor's eye (and pen), making important suggestions. The book is now, I hope, much more readable. For comments on sections of the text and other forms of assistance, thanks also to Ellen Babinsky, Lawrence Cunningham, Michael Drompp, Liz Feder, Rahel Hahn, Michael McLain, Kevin Madigan, Cynthia Marshall, Charlie Poole, Michael Sells, Walter Simons, Brad Stull, and Mark Winokur.

Others, without reading or commenting directly on the present study, played important roles in its genesis. I am indebted to the members of various reading groups in feminist theory, both at the University of Chicago and Rhodes College, in particular Cathy Frasier, Susan Hill, Maggie Kim, Susan St. Ville, Susan Simonaitis, and Kathy Waller. Thanks also to my friends Maria Arbusto and Ellen Armour.

Ellen listened to me work through many of the ideas presented in the opening chapters. I hope I didn't bore her too much.

I presented portions of the present work at the International Conference on Medieval Studies, the American Academy of Religion, Rhodes College, Hamilton College, and the Medieval Colloquium of Dartmouth College. These audiences gave me not only an opportunity to try out ideas, but also many helpful comments and suggestions.

For financial support during the writing of this study, I thank the University of Chicago, the Charlotte Newcombe Fellowship Foundation, the Rhodes College Faculty Development Endowment, and the Burke Fund of Dartmouth College.

I am also grateful to everyone who made me talk about something else—especially Ken Fox. And again, thanks to Reed, who has yet to see the last of Mr. Farnear.

1

VISIONARY IMAGINATION AND APOPHASIS

In the middle years of the thirteenth century, Mechthild of Magdeburg described the genesis of her book, a compendium of visions, prayers, dialogues, and mystical accounts entitled *The Flowing Light of the Godhead* (*Das fliessende Licht der Gottheit*). From the time she first was greeted by God, through her decision to leave home, family, and friends to live as a solitary beguine, until the moment she was called on by God to write of his glory, her life was one of conflict between body and soul:[1]

> These were the weapons of my soul [sighs, tears, confession, fasts, vigils, beatings, and constant prayer] with which I so completely overcame the body, that for twenty years there was never a time when I was not tired, sick, or weak, most of all from compunction and sorrow, and also from good desire and spiritual work, and I had many difficult sick days from nature. But powerful love came and occupied me so profoundly with these wonders, that I did not dare remain silent, although in my simplicity this caused me much sorrow.[2]

Reluctant to undertake the task set for her by love, Mechthild questions God on his choice of one so unworthy as the spokesperson of his glory.

Mechthild describes herself as "a fool, a sinful and poor human being in body and in soul." She argues that God should entrust his words to "wise people" (*wisen luten*) whose lowliness will not diminish his glory.[3] God's answer, here and elsewhere in the text, is to insist on the precedence of his will over her reservations. He plays on her modesty; Mechthild uses the humility topos of Christian literature to her advantage, for God argues that his glory is more fully displayed through her lowliness than through the wise.[4] His word and

1

command, moreover, is reinforced by the cleric to whom Mechthild goes to discuss her dilemma. Mechthild inscribes within her text its official approbation by both God and man.[5]

Writing is not only an approved activity for Mechthild, then, but one demanded by the divine. She *must* write; she cannot be silent about the wonders with which love occupies her. Yet these wonders not only cure but also cause her suffering. As she writes in an earlier passage, God's wonder wounds the soul: "Lord your wonder has wounded me, your grace has oppressed me."[6] Throughout the text she reflects on the wounds of Christ and refers to the Song of Songs and the wound inflicted on the lover by the beloved; "the wounded soul" (*gewundete sêle*) thereby identifies herself with both Christ and the bride who mourns the absence of her beloved.[7] These wonders and the wounds they inflict are both the source of her writing and its subject matter. Through writing of these wonders, experienced as a wounding intensification of her suffering, she will ultimately be healed:

> Then our lord spoke: "You shall follow me and trust me in these things, and you will be sick for a long time and I will care for you, and all of those things which you need in body and in soul I will give to you."[8]

Mechthild's wounds are caused by love, the agony brought about by the apparently intermittent nature of God's presence to her soul. At first blaming this absence on the body and its physicality, experienced as a barrier to divine bliss, she comes to understand it as rooted in the will and its dispositions. Through obedience to God's will, Mechthild is eventually able to recognize and experience his continual presence. Reflection on the wounds caused by the wonders of love heals her. Furthermore, in communicating these wonders and wounds through a written text, she is able to make the divine voice present to herself and others.

The relationship between divine absence and the powers of the imagination, as well as the ambivalence of the latter for the medieval Christian author, is made even more explicit in the prologue to *The Mirror of Simple Souls* (*Le Mirouer des simples ames anienties et qui seulement demourent en vouloir et desire d'amour*) by the solitary, itinerant beguine Marguerite Porete (d. 1310).[9] In the opening of this allegorical dialogue, Love gives an exemplum explaining its genesis and function. Love tells of a young lady, the daughter of a king, who lives in a foreign country. There she hears of the "great courtesie and nobility of King Alexander," with whom she falls in love. Her love, however, causes her only sorrow and unhappiness, for Alexander is inaccessible to her, and she can accept no other love but his.

> And when she saw that this faraway love, who was so close to her within herself, was so far outside, she thought that she would comfort her unhappiness by imagining some figure of her love, by whom she was often wounded in her heart. Therefore she had an image painted which represented the semblance of the king whom she loved as close as possible to the presentation of that which she loved and the affection of love by which she was captured, and by means of this image, together with other practices, she dreamed of the king himself.[10]

Through the imagination, the princess makes what is absent present, even if only in attenuated form. In doing so, her suffering is partially overcome.

Yet unlike the image of Alexander, which is the product of the princess's imagination (and the skill of the unspecified painter), the *Mirror* is said to be given by God to the soul, who caused the book to be written. Porete underlines the "givenness" of the *Mirror*, thereby subverting any claim that it is merely the product of her own imagination.[11] Ultimately, the relationship between the soul and the divine undercuts the hierarchy and antithesis between created and uncreated by showing the roots of both in each other. The soul's work, to create a text that is a mirror of God, the soul, and their unity, is achieved only through a fall out of createdness and into her uncreated being. This occurs, as in Mechthild's *Flowing Light*, through inscribing textually the wonders/wounds and the one who brings them about, leading to the death of the self and its will. Yet for Porete, as we shall see, the desire to move beyond wonders, the suffering they engender, and the recording of this pain drives and disrupts her narrative and theology. In this nonplace of will-lessness, the soul is transformed into the divine— the gap created by time, multiplicity, and embodiment is overcome.

The German Dominican preacher and theologian Meister Eckhart (d. 1327/29) construes the relationship between pain and the work of the soul in slightly different terms. Equipped with an institutionally sanctioned mode of discourse and authorized to interpret the text of scripture, Eckhart does not need to legitimate his speech through recourse to visionary and mystical identifications. Yet despite this, "work" is a central term in his German sermons, one through which he deconstructs his own sanctioned authority.[12] Refusing to embrace absence and the suffering it entails, he points to the power of in- or trans-figuration to re-form the soul into justice and the divine; as in Porete's *Mirror*, absence is overcome not merely in attenuated form but entirely.

> The just person seeks nothing in his works, for those who seek something in their works are hirelings and traders, or those who work something for a wherefore. Therefore, if you will be in- or trans-figured into justice, then intend nothing in your works and in-figure no wherefore in yourself, neither in time nor in eternity, neither reward nor blessedness, neither this nor that; for these works are all truly dead. Yes, and if you image God in yourself, whatever works you perform therefore, these works are all dead, and you will spoil good works; and not only will you spoil good works, but more; you will also sin.[13]

Calling on his hearers to go beyond images (*bilde*) for the divine and for justice, to work without a why, Eckhart does not deny the power of figuration but rather displaces it, and with it the necessity of both wonders and suffering. One *becomes* divine, one becomes the Son of Justice to whom the soul gives birth in moments of detachment and imagelessness, therefore becoming the true image of the divine in the world. This is the work that Eckhart calls on the soul to perform. In doing so, the apparent antithesis between creature and creator is overcome and with it the interplay of absence and presence, suffering and ecstasy, that rests on this split.

THE SOUL AS VIRGIN WIFE

The great historian of the religious movements of the thirteenth century, Herbert Grundmann, argued that

> the theological system and the speculative teaching of the German mystics are precisely not the foundation, point of departure and source, but rather the intellectual justification and the attempt at a theoretical ordering and a theological mastering of that religious

experience that first arose in the mystical experience of the religious women's movement.[14]

In this book, I will both substantiate and complicate Grundmann's thesis. I hope not only to demonstrate the influence of the beguine mysticisms on Eckhart's thought,[15] but also to show how Mechthild, Porete, and Eckhart all work to subvert medieval discourses on, and practices concerned with, gender and subjectivity.[16] Eckhart's debt to the women beguines and religious of the twelfth and early thirteenth century, its consequences and implications, have been largely ignored in studies of late medieval mysticism, despite the repetition of Grundmann's assertion that the mysticism of spiritual poverty and detachment characteristic of Eckhart and the later German mystics was grounded in the experience, ideals, and, I would add, texts, of the women's movement.[17] While general claims are often made that Eckhart's speculative approach is a reaction to the highly affective and experiential mysticism said to prevail in beguinages and convents,[18] the adequacy of these terms themselves are currently being questioned, and the real similarities and differences between late medieval mystical texts analyzed.[19] Through a more detailed study of Mechthild, Porete, and Eckhart on the interrelated themes of body, will, and work and the interplay of pain, visionary imagination, and apophasis, I will assess the reasons for their desomatizing transformation of "female spirituality" and its implications for modern studies of gender and medieval mysticism.

Evidence for a direct textual relationship between Eckhart's work and Marguerite Porete's *Mirror of Simple Souls* has been established, and it has recently been shown through external evidence that Eckhart may also have known Mechthild of Magdeburg's *Flowing Light of the Godhead*.[20] Taken together, moreover, these two texts can be seen as representative of the kinds of spirituality characteristic of the women's religious movement, although the paucity of women's writings and multiplicity of meanings within those that survive should not be ignored.[21] Although much recent work on women's spirituality in the later Middle Ages has focused on hagiographical and legendary texts,[22] the writings of women must be the basis for any account of their self-understanding and the route to God that they saw open for themselves. In making this claim, I do not wish to imply that there are essential, biologically or culturally grounded differences between men and women. In fact, the evidence I will present demonstrates the contrary thesis, in that both Mechthild and Porete, to varying degrees and in different ways, reject the definitions of female sanctity expressed in the hagiographical literature and some female-authored mystical writings.[23] Yet in order to understand sexual and gender differences as they were constructed and construed in the Middle Ages, we must give attention to the ways in which textual production and experience were grounded in a culture marked by sex and gender dualisms and their profound material consequences.[24]

Furthermore, while *The Flowing Light of the Godhead* and *The Mirror of Simple Souls* are different in genre and intention from the biblical commentaries, questions, and sermons of an educated churchman such as Eckhart, they are overtly theological works, with very different aims than hagiography.[25] Hagiographical writings are an excellent indication of trends in popular piety and are also able to give insight into the ideals promulgated, predominantly by medieval men, *for* medieval women. Carefully used, these writings may yield other information about medieval women's lives.[26] Yet to compare the type of piety offered in the hagiographies with Mechthild, Porete, or Eckhart's theological formulations, without careful attention to genre, ignores central differences in perspectives and skews the modern historian's understanding of their meanings. Through attention to mystical texts we can avoid the false contrast between "experience" and "theory" used by Grundmann and others to describe the relationship between the beguines and Eckhart. We must look at women's, and particularly the beguines', own formulations of their theological and mystical teachings in order adequately to assess the relationship between their spirituality and that of Eckhart, despite the recognition that women's writings themselves internalize and are mediated through male-dominated culture.[27]

On first reading, traditional contrasts between affective and speculative forms of mysticism may seem legitimate in describing the relationship between the texts of Mechthild, Porete, and Eckhart. Eckhart clearly downplays the role of love and of extraordinary experiences of the love of God so central in the writings of Mechthild and, to a lesser extent, Porete. Although love still plays an important role for Eckhart, and is clearly the focus of a number of the vernacular sermons preached to women,[28] it is not as central a mystical term for Eckhart as it is for the beguines. In displacing love as a central name of the divine, Eckhart undercuts the possible gender implications and gender play of Mechthild's and Porete's language. On the one hand, love is feminine in both Middle High German and Old French, so that in stressing love as God's primary name, Mechthild and Porete effectively, although intermittently, feminize the divine.[29] At the same time, both Mechthild and Porete bring together the understanding of God as love with courtly images and themes in which God is represented as the male lover, in contrast to the female soul.[30] In this way, the cultural association of women with eroticism is accepted, spiritualized, and, in part, subverted. This, however, is only one strategy adopted by the beguines, for in downplaying feminine and erotic language Eckhart follows another path initiated within the beguine texts themselves.

The differing conceptions of the role of love in the accounts of the return of the soul to God are grounded in diverse views of createdness and in turn lead to diverse ethical implications for the Christian while still in this life. The relationship and tensions between the active and contemplative lives are pivotal issues in the beguine milieu, attested to by the mixed form of life itself, the hagiographical literature, and the beguine writings. Reflecting these concerns, the concepts of the body, the will, and the work of the soul become central in different ways and in different configurations for each of the three mystics. Ultimately, it is in their understandings of the experience and attitude of the mystic in this life that Mechthild and Porete most diverge. While Mechthild attempts to join action and contemplation through the "wounded soul's" divinizing identification with Christ's love, Porete's desire for spiritual liberty leads her to reject the "works" of both the active and contemplative lives. Eckhart formulates his dialectic of the soul as both wife and virgin—Martha and Mary, active and contemplative—in an attempt to unify the activity of Mechthild's loving and suffering soul with the detachment and peacefulness of Porete's.

Kurt Ruh, in his formulation of what is distinctive in the beguine spirituality, argues that while both Mechthild and Porete stress a love of God that leads to a union without distinction between the loving soul and the divine, for Mechthild this union is always transient as long as one remains in the body.[31] Both the presence of God in this loving union and the suffering engendered by God's absence from the soul are taken up as essential parts of the journey, for it is by suffering with the humanity of Christ that one is led to fuller union with his divinity.[32] Mechthild writes:

God leads his children, whom he has chosen, in wonderful ways. It is a wonderful way and a noble way and a holy way which God himself went, that a human being might suffer pain without fault and without guilt. . . . Since he wills that they be like his dear Son, who was tormented in body and soul.[33]

Ruh argues that there is a twofold understanding of love in Mechthild. On the one side is the experience of divine love (mystical marriage and union) and on the other the love that the desolate soul must, together with the suffering Christ, express for humanity.[34] The two experiences of love have a dialectical relationship to one another. Only as one accepts the desolation of the loss of the experience of divine love and makes it an expression of solidarity with the suffering of Christ and his love for humanity is one returned to the presence of and union with divine love. Evident throughout the writings of Mechthild, then, are what Caroline Walker Bynum calls "alternations between alienation and ecstasy,"[35] experiences grounded in the erotic model itself.

Marguerite Porete, as Ruh points out, goes farther in appearing to claim that a lasting essential union with the divine can be achieved on earth. Love, in fact, ultimately frees the soul from all desire and servitude, allowing her to become fully united with the divinity:

I used to be shut away in the servitude of captivity,
When desire imprisoned me in the will of affection.
There the light of ardor from divine love found me,
Who quickly killed my desire, my will and affection,
Which impeded me in the enterprise of the fullness of divine love.[36]

For Porete the soul's experience of the ecstasy of love must be surpassed, and the soul must annihilate her will and affections in order to be fully and permanently united with the divinity of God. Unlike Mechthild, Porete does not assimilate the suffering of the soul in the experience of God's "farnearness" to the suffering of Christ in his humanity and thus to the necessity of *caritas*, or concern for sinful humanity. Important for Porete is that the soul pass beyond its present troubled state to a higher level where "desire" is lost. Having become absolutely humble, the soul loses her "name" and experiences the absolute and constant presence of the divinity: "I hold him, she said, for he is mine. I will never let him go. He is in my will. Let come whatever might come, since he is with me. It would be a lack in me, if I should be astounded."[37]

While Eckhart is closer in many ways to Porete in his stress on the annihilation of the will and the role of detachment and spiritual poverty, he also attempts to bring the other moment of the dialectic—the outflowing of the soul in loving works so central for Mechthild—to play in his thought. Breaking through to the absolutely simple and unified ground of the divine nature is always tied to the birth of the Son in the soul and the fruitfulness of the soul in works of justice and goodness. The soul, for Eckhart, must always be both virgin and wife.[38] In attaining a state of absolute detachment, moreover, she comes to be truly fruitful. By surpassing all creatureliness, both images of God and the human will, human beings become one with him in the absolute union of the ground of God and the uncreated ground of the soul.[39] The metaphysical and theological underpinnings Eckhart gives to these assertions will need to be fully articulated, but I wish here to stress that Eckhart removes the twofold movement of love found in Mechthild from the emphasis on the dialectic of suffering and fulfillment in which it is embedded in her writings.[40] Where Mechthild interpreted her experiences of suffering as the absence of God and his consoling gifts and the presence of Christ's wounds on her body and soul, Eckhart attempts a dialectical solution to the problem of the presence and absence of God based on his view of detachment. The soul becomes absolutely indistinct in detaching herself from all creatureliness, and is thereby one with the absolute indistinction that is the unity of the divine. Through this she comes to experience the absolute presence of God. God, who is distinct (i.e., transcendent) due to his lack of distinction (i.e., immanence) is always present to the soul, yet in her attachment to creatureliness she is not aware of this.[41] For Eckhart, the fulfillment of both love of God and of neighbor lies in detachment, which reveals to the soul the presence of God in her ground.

While both beguine mystics stress the loss of the soul's will and the infusion of the will of God, Mechthild emphasizes the experience of love and of suffering and the absence of the divinity that brings about this loss of self-will. The disinterested love of the soul for God can be brought about only through a radical experience of his absence. For Eckhart, like Porete, the emphasis is placed on attaining a state of disinterested love, or of detachment from self-will, in which the soul recognizes the absolute presence of the divinity. Yet, as I have said, he attempts to stress detachment without doing away with the fruitfulness and work of the soul. This shift explains Porete's and Eckhart's distrust of the kind of mystical experiences that serve as the basis for Mechthild's thought and that of many other religious women. Eckhart, in bringing together action and contemplation, formulates a "mysticism of everyday life" that is not dependent on extraordinary experiences.[42] His mysticism—like Porete's—is not experiential in the traditional sense, but rather initiates a change of consciousness, a new way of viewing the relationship between the self and God in which the self is emptied so that it might become the place in which God works. While these themes can be uncovered in the *Mirror*, Porete, perhaps because of the greater constraints caused by her sex, consistently downplays action in favor of freedom.

This preliminary sketch of the issues to be discussed in the following pages might suggest that Eckhart has succeeded in combining the radicality of detachment and loss of self-will found in Porete's writings with the emphasis on continual fruitfulness found in Mechthild. However, from a modern feminist perspective the suspicion is raised that in attempting to resolve apparent conflicts within and between women's texts, Eckhart dissolves ambiguities intrinsic to their spirituality. Most importantly, we might ask if in minimizing the role of experience and the body in the mystical life he does not denigrate forms of redemptive spirituality central to many medieval women's writings.

Eckhart displaces Mechthild's characteristic emphasis on suffering, then, and also the body as intrinsic to human creatureliness. Throughout Mechthild's work are dialogues between the body and the soul that point to her more ambivalent attitude toward creatureliness. Rather than being a mere "nothing" from the standpoint of its createdness, as it is for Eckhart, the body is both clung to and fought off as a more substantial entity and adversary. At the same time, through purification of human love and desire one attains unification with divine love. The closing dialogue of Mechthild's work emphasizes that for her the self is always a composite of body and soul. The soul tells the body, which it will soon depart,

> Oh my most beloved prison, within which I am bound, I thank you for all that in which you have followed me. Although I am often troubled by you, yet you have come to my help. All your need will be taken from you on the last day.[43]

The soul's joy, she suggests, will not be complete until joined with that of the body.

Mechthild's hope for the body is based on the Incarnation, just as the necessity of bodily and spiritual suffering is illustrated by the suffering of Christ's humanity. It is the constant juxtaposition of these two elements, the body and creatureliness on the one hand and suffering on the other, that Eckhart attempts to bypass. Again one may be tempted to argue that Eckhart moves away from the particularity of the female-authored text and the kind of experiences described there, dissolving ambiguities seen by many as "essential" to women's writings. This suggests an evaluative critique of the relationship between the beguines and Eckhart, a reversal of that judgment implied in Grundmann's historical claim that Eckhart had "mastered" their thought. Evaluation may be unavoidable, but I am more interested in understanding. It is necessary, therefore, to uncover the theological and spiritual issues of concern to Mechthild, Porete, and Eckhart. This kind of contextualization illuminates their profound commonality of purpose, despite the obvious divergences within and between their texts. As a result, many contemporary feminist assumptions about embodiedness, imagination, and gender are themselves put into question by these medieval texts.

The crucial move made by Eckhart—to locate sinfulness, temptation, and detachment in the will, a will that must then be overcome—is, then, begun by Mechthild herself and taken further in Porete.[44] In deemphasizing the body, its sinfulness, temptations, and future glory, Eckhart, like Porete, underlines the fact that true spiritual poverty must be that of the will alone, and that it is the will which creates distance between the human being and God. By moving away from special experiences of God's presence and absence and showing that love as a human affection must be transcended in absolute detachment, Eckhart expresses a new appreciation of the world as sharing in both creatureliness and God. Hence the possibility that in embracing women's influence, he also attempts to resolve the tortured sense of life in this world and in the body found in Mechthild and the radical detachment from the world that makes it difficult for Marguerite to explain how the soul acts in time. He does so, moreover, in ways suggested by the beguine texts themselves. In drawing out these aspects of their work and in bringing the two strands of beguine spirituality together, Eckhart provides a new understanding of the world and of the role of the detached soul, an understanding that is—in theory— accessible to both men and women. This is not to posit Eckhart as the winner in a contest created by the historian between the three mystical theologies presented here, but rather marks an attempt to show how Eckhart situated himself in relation to his two predecessors, how his thought was significantly shaped by the mystical concerns and theologies of the women's movement, and how he might have come to his distinctive resolution of their tensions. Most important, perhaps, in bringing together the different spiritual emphases found among *women*, particularly in these two beguines, Eckhart sheds light on their thought and arrives at the formulations of it that he preached to women. Nevertheless, the viability of his position, given the material and ideological context of late medieval Europe, is called into question by his condemnation.[45] The intermittent suspicion to which Mechthild was subject in her more theologically daring moments, the trial, condemnation, and execution of Porete, and the ensuing decrees of the Council of Vienne (1311–12) associating beguines and heresy demonstrate the even greater dangers for women.[46]

The assertion of an uncreated aspect of the soul in which God and the soul are unified in their ground can be found in Mechthild, Porete, and Eckhart and is the basis for their move away from the body, suffering, and visionary imagination as central to the spiritual life; it is also a central issue in the suspicions against them. Through the unity of God and the soul in their grounds the suffering of the human being, occasioned by the apparent absence of the divine, is overcome. The interplay between suffering, visionary imagination, and embodiment are complex, however, and laden with tension. For a better understanding of what follows, and to avoid some of the pitfalls of contemporary scholarship on suffering and the body in medieval thought, an elucidation of the theoretical and philosophical issues and a decentering of modern presuppositions with regard to them, are required. Most important, the relationship between pain and the imagination must be clarified, together with my assertion that medieval visionary experience is tied to the work of the imagination. I will then turn in chapter 2 to other important aspects of beguine spirituality and the accounts of female religiosity within and against which Mechthild, Porete, and Eckhart write, before more carefully analyzing and comparing their texts.

"THE BODY IN PAIN"

Elaine Scarry argues that in the Hebrew biblical tradition the central distinction between God and humans is between one who is disembodied and those who are embodied.[47] Embodiment marks createdness. Scarry goes on to point to the centrality of scenes of wounding and images of the wounded body in the Hebrew scriptures. These episodes, she argues, identify God as a torturer who asserts his *existence* and his *power* through human flesh, himself having no materiality on which to inscribe his presence and inspire belief. In the apparent absence of God, the disbelief of the people is countered by the wounded body. God makes his presence known by painfully inscribing the bodies of disbelievers.

The wounded body is capable of signaling God's presence because it marks human immanence, limitation, and hence createdness. As Drew Leder has shown, embodiedness, while always constitutive of human being in the world, is not always present to consciousness.[48] In fact, the lived experience of the body is marked by absence; in moments of perception, concentration, and thought, the bodily organs through which we operate disappear. Other important systems and organs in the body function *best* and most efficiently as recessive and absent from consciousness, although we cannot live without them. For example, performing actively in the world depends on not having to give attention to every breath drawn. More radically, no amount of conscious attention can aid in the digestive process. Although we can learn to eat substances that are more easily digestible, we cannot will enzymes to work on the food in our stomachs. Consciousness of this process occurs only in its breakdown, as pain and/or illness.

Leder calls this form of bodily presence dys-appearance, pointing to the fact that the body is insistently and compellingly present to lived experience in moments of dysfunction and suffering.[49] Yet this presence is itself a form of absence, hence his use of the term dys-appearance, which shows that the body as experienced in pain is experienced as the absence of an absence.[50] Leder and Scarry both emphasize, furthermore, that our ability to experience ourselves as transcendent to the body is not only constitutive of embodied experience but also is necessary to overcoming pain. Although in physical suffering the body is made insistently present to consciousness, human beings attempt to separate "themselves" from the body that is experiencing pain. In doing so, the human subject is able to maintain its integrity in the face of a destructive experience *and* may be put in a position to fight against that experience.

Scarry argues, moreover, that pain is marked by its intransitive and nonintentional nature. While I experience my pain with absolute certainty— there is in fact nothing of which I am more certain than that I am in pain—for others, my pain is radically unknowable insofar as it is incommunicable. For Scarry, "the mute facts of sentience" are isolating; it is only when we generate language, ideas, and cultures around and through the facts of our embodiment that we can talk about shared aspects of human nature.[51] In cutting off lines of communication between human beings, pain is a harbinger of death. Through communicating pain a transcending movement is begun, which marks and brings about its alleviation.[52] While the wounded body might be seen as communicating pain, it does so only within the terms of culture and its shared meanings. Compassion, according to Scarry, is a function of the imagination.[53]

The imagination, broadly understood as that creative power constitutive of human culture, therefore enables us to overcome pain in at least two ways. On the one hand, it enables us to deal with *some* of our physical pain by setting it within the human community and its technologies of alleviation, themselves products of the imagination. In the Middle Ages, such technologies were often powerless in the face of disease and pain, a fact of which we must not lose sight.[54] In addition, imagination enables human beings to avoid the suffering they inflict on themselves, suffering brought about by crises of faith in the powers of the imagination and human creativity.[55] For Scarry, this is expressed in the Hebrew scriptures by the crises of belief in the God who is said to be creator of all things, including humanity.

The Hebrew scriptures, therefore, contain not only scenes in which God is shown as the torturer legitimating himself through and on the human body, scenes that in their textual form already mark an imaginative movement away from the wounding of physical bodies, but also accounts of material creation inspired by God's commands, moments that point to another, nondestructive manner in which the apparent absence of God can be overcome. In building the tabernacle, for example, God's presence is made known through the use of tools rather than weapons.[56] The Hebrew Bible, then, begins a process Scarry finds reaching its culmination in the New Testament—the celebration of material culture and the powers of imagination.[57] Through embodiment in Jesus Christ, God undercuts the absolute distinction between himself and humanity which necessitates scenes of wounding, and instead allows humanity to embrace its own creative potential. The written inscription of wounding marks the first movement in a series of displacements in which human embodiment and its fragility are transcended and the divine is embodied in texts and material artifacts. Through these works, themselves products of human embodiment, the suffering and limitation inherent to corporeality are overcome. In other words, the body is itself the source of human transcendence.[58]

Yet for Christian believers, the problem of God's absence continues, perhaps especially among those who claim to have experienced the divine presence in extraordinary ways. The popularity of the Song of Songs as an allegory of the relationship between the church or the soul and the divine points to the centrality of the problematic interplay of Christ's presence and absence.[59] From Christian thinkers, with apparently unshakable belief in the existence of God and of Christ, come accounts of suffering caused by the *dissimilarity* between the believer and God, experienced as the absence of the loved object. The products of material culture, moreover, from language to images to political systems, despite their value, are incapable of attaining the perfection the divine demands. All language falls short of naming the divine, all images and concepts are but pale reflections of its glory, and all human culture is tainted by its dissimilarity from that perfection. What Scarry reads as an unproblematic embrace of material culture is in fact always haunted by the specter of a missed perfection. The antithesis Scarry creates between wounding and creation, between torture (or self-torture) and the work of the imagination, is made infinitely complex in much Christian thought. The problems of divine absence, moreover, are now transposed onto the body of God and those *believers* who wish to follow his path. At the center of Christianity stands the cross; particularly in the late medieval period, to believe in Christ is to follow him in his suffering.[60] It is precisely within the terms of Scarry's (tension-ridden) antitheses, then, that the work of Mechthild, Porete, and Eckhart can best be understood.

While it might appear anachronistic to speak of Mechthild, Porete, and Eckhart in terms of imagination, with its modern stress on human creativity as constitutive of cultural worlds, the accounts of textual genesis given above show the importance of the term and its referent in medieval texts. For all three mystics, the relationship between pain and imagination, highlighted so brilliantly by Scarry, is laid bare. Their textual productivity is seen as transcending visionary imagination insofar as they attempt to move beyond the suffering engendering and engendered by it. While for Mechthild union with God occurs in and through the interplay between visionary experience, absence, and suffering, she will point to another route to God's presence taken up and elaborated on by Porete. Porete uses the term *ymagination* only to elide it: she highlights both the similarities and differences between her textual production and the secular work of the imagination that serves as her exemplum. Eckhart deliberately plays on the word for image (*bilde*), exploiting the transformative powers of prefix use in order to highlight the way in which detachment makes God present in radical ways (in that the soul is *in-* and *übergebildet* into the divine in becoming detached from all createdness).

THE PROBLEM OF FEMALE SPIRITUALITY
AND THE VISIONARY IMAGINATION

In their commentaries on the powers of the creative imagination and its limits, the passages cited at the opening of this chapter help to elucidate a central problem in modern studies of the mystical movements of the later Middle Ages. The distinction between "affective" or "visionary" and "speculative" forms of spirituality, and the often denigratory comments about the facile and literalistic quality of much of the former, have led many scholars to reject these modern distinctions. Yet they continue to reemerge; and, not surprisingly, they are almost always gendered.[61] While attention to the sources demonstrates that a real difference is being marked through these modern categories, it occurs not between male- and female-authored texts, but within them both. The tendency of modern scholarship to be critical of such visionary somatization also has its roots in medieval texts, although again, in ways and for reasons very different than have been acknowledged.[62]

Negative evaluations of visionary texts have their source in the classical distinction, elaborated in Augustine and repeated in varying forms by Bernard of Clairvaux, Eckhart, and others, between three divergent modes of seeing: corporeal, spiritual, and intellectual.[63] Only in the final mode does true perception and union between the

knower and the known occur. Following Pauline passages in which the
ineffability of the divine and the inadequacy of human comprehension
are highlighted (1 Cor. 2:9; 13:12), the Augustinian distinctions attempt to articulate and resolve the ambivalence that haunts Christian
discourse on and use of images and concepts. Following the lines of
Platonic philosophy, Augustine and others understand imagination
strictly according to its medieval usages. It occupies an intermediate
rank in the hierarchy between sense perception and intellect, for it
is tied to perception and the bodily.[64] Like Augustine and Bernard,
Eckhart privileges intellectual over spiritual and corporeal vision.[65]
Eckhart in fact goes beyond Augustine and Bernard, arguing that the
soul must strive for detachment from all images in order to become
fully receptive and hence united with the divine. Furthermore, the
anagogical reference to intellectual "vision" must itself be overcome.
He insists that the soul not only be "on the wall" without mediation,
but that she be "in the wall," the source from which she comes. The
soul must *be* that which she reflects.[66] His work, then, appears to be
antithetical to that of the visionary women whose lives are created
and recounted in the hagiographies of the thirteenth century, as well
as to the visionary and prophetic aspects of the women writers' texts
(evident in Mechthild, although markedly absent in Porete). Eckhart
seems to stand with those who would claim that visionary experience
marks a preliminary or even defective stage in the mystical life, one
still grounded in and tied to the senses and materiality and therefore
not truly spiritual.[67]

Yet as Jeffrey Hamburger has recently demonstrated through his
study of the *Rothschild Canticles*, a visionary handbook created in
Franco-Flemish lands around 1300, presumably for a woman religious or beguine,[68] there is substantial evidence, despite claims to
the contrary, for a relationship between art, visionary imagination,
and mysticism in the later Middle Ages. This discovery debunks the
claim that "true" mysticism operates in a realm beyond images and
hence cannot be depicted or aided by art, for within the *Rothschild
Canticles* visual images are themselves used apophatically, thereby
clarifying the interplay of imagination, vision, and apophasis.[69] While
the *Rothschild Canticles*, with its florilegia-like text and lavish miniatures representing the mystical life, is unusual, Hamburger cites central
passages in mystical writings, particularly those of the Benedictine-
Cistercian Gertrude of Helfta, that describe the use of devotional

images as aids to prayer and meditation and as constitutive of visionary experience. Many further indications of these practices can be found in the hagiographies of the early beguines and Cistercian nuns, suggesting the use of pictures and paintings as aids for meditation and as foundational images for visionary experience.[70] Attention to such texts and artworks offers new ways of understanding medieval visionary experience and its relationship to images and the imagination, elucidating the ties and tensions between visionary and apophatic mysticism.

The little known or discussed *Life* of the beguine Odilia of Liège (d. 1220) offers the closest parallel to the *Rothschild Canticles*, both in its account of the use of devotional images and in the specific content of the pictures and visions described. The text describes Odilia as a young widow, who wishes above all else to regain her lost chastity. In order to attain this goal, she gives up worldly pleasures and devotes herself to remembering the passion of Christ. Through constant meditation on his side-wound and stigmata, she is freed from her sensuality and returned to a state of chastity. Odilia's hagiographer further elaborates on this form of meditation:

> In fact, she had the image of a crucifix depicted in her psalter: trembling, she meditated with intent acuity of mind on the scars caused by his wounds and the cuts caused by the lashes and the needles of the thorns and the very wound in his side. And suddenly she completely dissolved into tears, so greatly was she afflicted with these harsh sufferings that she was not able to bear it. And the anxiety of sorrow compelled her to burst out in these words: I will hold this in my memory and my soul will melt away within me.[71]

Contemplation of Christ's wounds, made visible through the crucifix, help to engrave Odilia's consciousness with the suffering through which her innocence is regained.

The use of tools like the *arma christi* and other devotional images in order to aid meditation is well known.[72] In the *Life* of Odilia, moreover, devotional images serve as the (pre)text for visionary and locutionary experiences. Her hagiographer goes on to describe Odilia's visions of Christ on the cross in language that demonstrates their foundation in artistic images. Even more interesting is the account of Odilia's Trinitarian visions, which are almost direct verbal descriptions of the Trinitarian miniatures of the *Rothschild Canticles*.[73]

She saw a very bright star descend on the altar, which divided itself into three parts, each being as great as the first had been, although it had been divided. The separated parts were not diminished, nor would they have been increased had they come together: they remained of one and the same amount of splendor. So he wished to make known to his handmaid through an image [*figura*] the unity of the highest and individuated Trinity.[74]

As Hamburger explains, the Trinitarian images of the *Rothschild Canticles* bring together light and veil imagery, simultaneously revealing and concealing the mystery of the Trinity. The interrelationship between the three persons of the Trinity, furthermore, is conveyed by the interlocking and flowing of one into the other, represented in one image as blazing suns or stars whose flames meet to create a triangle (*Rothschild Canticles*, fol. 79r). While Odilia's vision is able to state in words aspects of the Trinitarian mystery that cannot be portrayed (the equality of the three to the whole from which they came), the image is able to convey the simultaneous revealing and concealing in a way more concise than any verbal presentation. Both, then, are at the same time visionary and apophatic, the visionary providing the matter for its own negation and transcendence.

Despite differences brought about by the resources of the two mediums, clearly some relationship should be posited between the visions described in the *Life* of Odilia and the Trinitarian (and other images) of the *Rothschild Canticles*. The early date of Odilia's *Life* suggests the existence and use of such illustrations in the southern Low Countries at a time considerably prior to the probable date of the *Rothschild Canticles* itself. The context for the use of such a book is thus further solidified, upholding Hamburger's thesis. The intensely visionary quality of the lives described in the hagiographies of the early beguines and Cistercian nuns of the thirteenth century may well have been grounded in the use of similar devotional images and meditational practices.

Central among such images are, not surprisingly, those found in the Bible. Just as visual imagery is a source for the visionary imagination, so also are the verbal images of scriptural and liturgical texts. The *Rothschild Canticles*, with its combination of textual selections and pictorial images, demonstrates their parallel use. The book, however, creates difficulties for many modern theories of mysticism and mystical experience, which view images and concepts (whether visual or verbal) as secondary to experience. Two assumptions obscure the links between art and scripture, visionary imagination, and mysticism. First is the belief that the "presence of God" and "union with God" are virtually identical experiences. Mystics' statements concerning the ineffability of God and union with him are then taken as proof that all descriptive language is secondary, inadequate, and hence not to be understood as in any way constitutive of these experiences. The testimony of medieval Christian writers, however, makes clear that this conflation is inadequate. For example, in Hadewijch's famous Eucharistic vision or Mechthild's account of the dance of the soul with the young lord, there is a movement from experience of presence imagistically described to that of merging or union in which visionary language is both used and negated.[75] The experiences are ineffable in divergent ways and differing degrees, for while "spiritual" visions are said to be only partially captured in human language, *union* leads to the apophasis of all imagery and concepts. Although in these examples, the two types of experience are viewed as being contiguous, they are not identical and cannot be talked about in the same way. For this reason, I prefer to distinguish between visionary and unitive texts; this is not to deny that the two constantly intermingle and interpenetrate, both textually and experientially. The visionary moment provides the text for apophasis, in ways parallel to Eckhart's apophatic reading of the cataphatic language of scripture. For women, with limited access to biblical texts and no official authority to interpret them, visions—often grounded in biblical, liturgical, and visual images—serve as a means of legitimation and provide a subject matter on which to speak and to transcend through apophasis.[76]

The second assumption made by those who wish to deny any causal relationship between image or text on the one hand, and visionary or mystical experience on the other is that experience and language can be separated not only analytically but also experientially, and that such experiences mark a place beyond language (and hence, so the argument goes, beyond images).[77] The growing philosophical conviction that all human experience is mediated by language-use creates difficulties for this position.[78] Yet what are we to do with many mystics' laments over the inadequacy of language to explain the experience of union with the divine. This is not, I believe, simply a modern problem with premodern texts and assumptions. Rather the paradox of mystical language lies here, for it is a discourse predicated on its own impossibility. In other words, the proliferation of "mystic speech" is a direct result of the mystic's inability to convey the truth of her or his experience and the apophatic negation of that language itself constitutes mystical experience.[79] The inadequacy of referential language is a mark both of one's distance from and proximity to God. Furthermore, the text itself, authorized by the union between the soul and God that makes God the author of the text, undercuts its own authority (and its own existence) through its claims to the inadequacy of language.[80] To take the mystic at her word, then, is to involve oneself in a continuing, and productive, paradox. Hence, the validity, I believe, of Michel de Certeau's claim that mysticism should be understood as a "modus loquendi" rather than a type of experience to be phenomenologically analyzed.[81] The evidence we have is texts, and mysticism must—and was meant to be— approached through them. By concentrating attention on the writings, one takes with utmost seriousness the mystic's own activity and her own conception of the importance of this mystical work.

Meditation on images and texts, then, is foundational for medieval Christian visionary and mystical unitive experience. The use and subversion of biblical images to describe and evoke the experience of God's presence and union with God must be understood in this context, for through meditation on such biblical images, and in particular the erotic language of desire in the Song of Songs, such experiences are brought about in the mystic.[82] This is not to deny but to underline and explain further the literary nature of mystical texts. If we accept the premise that experience is mediated through and structured by language, then we must recognize that we have no access to an unmediated experience. Acknowledging the mediated nature of mystical texts, furthermore, allows us to take into account their literary quality without denying their claims to speak out of and to particular realms of experience. We can then grasp the difficulty the medieval author herself poses as central to her writing. The bridal language of the Song of Songs, used by Mechthild and many others, is not a later addition, a vain attempt through the application of biblical images to convey the ineffable experience of God's presence and union, but rather is intrinsic to that experience in its very ineffability. Yet images are always haunted with absence; the apophatic tendencies in Mechthild, Porete, and Eckhart are attempts to overcome this absence through the transformation of language and consciousness.

Visionary and mystical experiences are grounded in meditation on devotional images and biblical texts. This is not a claim about the reality or the "givenness" of these experiences but merely highlights their "constructedness" and clarifies their often traditional quality; for the medieval thinker to recognize the role of human imagination in that construction is not to deny its divine source. The search for a *purely* divine source, furthermore, is what leads to apophasis and the constant attempt to negate images and the imagination. Mechthild, Porete, and Eckhart are attempting to create a new form of consciousness in the reader. Images, whether visual or verbal, are created and evoked. Then, through the negation of these images, other modes of being are brought into existence. The compatibility of imaginative and divine authorship is demonstrated most clearly by medieval texts themselves, in which meditative aids such as images and textual florilegia are seen as constitutive of experience without invalidating its divine referent or significance.[83] The turn to apophasis, then, is not a denial of the validity of the visionary imagination, but rather an attempt to transcend its limitations. For while such devotional practices are of great spiritual worthiness, they do not, in and of themselves, ensure the reception of more exceptional gifts, understood to be freely given by God.[84] This uncertainty, together with the continuing gap between image and divine, leads to the suffering of the devout that Mechthild, Porete, and Eckhart attempt to allay through apophasis.

The suffering of the visionary or mystic occurs on three levels, as attention to the fourteenth-century *Showings* of Julian of Norwich clearly demonstrates. Unlike thirteenth-century mystical texts, Julian's emphasizes physical, bodily suffering and its redemptive capacities, explicitly taking up central themes in thirteenth-century hagiographies of women. Despite this divergence, the parallel with thirteenth-century texts remains instructive. At the beginning of her work, Julian describes the three things for which she prayed to the divine: to *contemplate* Christ's passion with true compassion, to *share in* and *imitate* that suffering through her own illness, and to be given three spiritual gifts.[85] When she shares in Christ's passion through her own bodily illness, the cross she contemplates comes alive with the visions that form the basis of her book. Julian therefore encapsulates the threefold way in which desire to experience God's presence occasions suffering in the believer. The image she contemplates causes suffering because of its subject matter—Christ on the cross—and also because, as image, it is always at a remove from the divine presence. In order to make the divine present in his suffering, the believer *herself* must suffer in imitation of Christ's crucifixion. Central to this movement is not only the interplay between presence, absence, and the imagination described above, but also the role within the Christian tradition of the suffering and death of Christ as his redemptive "work." The body, senses, and imagination, according to a strand of the Christian tradition that reaches a high point in the thought of Julian, can only be redeemed *through* the suffering that seems constitutive of embodiment. This suffering, although primarily spiritual in thirteenth-century female-authored texts (for example, Mechthild's "wounded soul"), is occasioned by the continued link of the visionary mode with the imagination and, hence, with the body and its limitations; the desire to transcend such suffering in body and soul leads to the primacy of apophasis in Porete and Eckhart.

APOPHASIS AND TRANS-FIGURATION

The contrast between visionary and apophatic modes of mysticism and textual production can be clearly seen in a comparison of Mechthild of Magdeburg and Eckhart's descriptions of their "work" given above: Mechthild's visionary, imagistic, and erotic mysticism, highlighting the wonders of love as source for and subject matter of her text, seems far removed from Eckhart, with his emphasis on detachment and the virgin, imageless soul. As Hamburger notes, Eckhart's texts are not without images (for example, the soul as virgin and wife), which are necessary to any discourse, but he emphasizes the apophatic use of language. For Mechthild, although the "work" of writing will eventually enable the soul to overcome the gap between herself and the divine, the role of suffering and visionary imagination *in* that movement is continually stressed, particularly in the early portions of the text. Her book replaces her body as the site of wonders and wounding, but suffering at this point remains constitutive of her experience. Despite attempts to ease this pain through her understanding of the "well-ordered soul," Mechthild's love and attachment to embodiment continually erupt and disrupt her text. For Eckhart embodiment and images become suspect in that they are always inadequate to the divine, haunted by absence and pain. Imagination (*in-bildunge*, in one use of the term) becomes in- or trans-figuration (*über-bildung*), a process of self-transformation. Porete's text clarifies the profound relationship between these two apparently divergent means of dealing with absence and suffering, for it is insofar as the soul becomes uncreated, and hence unified with Love, that she is able to create/to be a mirror of the ever-present divine.

The difference is best described in terms of *how* imagination or the processes of figuration are understood to work. Rather than making the divine present through images and concepts, aspects of the thought of Mechthild, Porete, and Eckhart differ from that of many of their contemporaries in the claim that the soul herself can and must be refigured or reimagined, and as such become united without distinction in and with the divine. The radicalness of this claim, tied to the linguistic strategies of apophasis that enable it, separates the beguine mystics and Eckhart from most of their contemporaries. Where Mechthild often uses visionary images as the base for her apophasis, Porete and Eckhart eschew extraordinary experiences of God's presence. This move is tied to a shared desire to re(e)valuate the body. In order to do so, paradoxically, they must move away from (in the case of Mechthild) and reject (in that of Porete and Eckhart) the "somatic" and visionary religious experiences claimed by their contemporaries to be constitutive of women's religious experience (and of some men's).

Historians have recently argued that the language of the women mystics, with its emphasis on erotic and bodily images, reflects the ways in which women were culturally defined as more bodily and fleshly than men.[86] As such, women's references to sexuality and food, human bonds and love, in descriptions of their relationship with the divine, are based on their embrace (and partial subversion) of the views of women prevalent in their society. The argument might go further, claiming a phenomenological basis for women's language. For women, one might argue, the body is present in experiences other than those denoting illness or injury. While male experience of embodiment finds presence only in pain, women have access to other modes of bodily dys-appearance through which embodiment is embraced. Yet the limitations of eroticism as a site of resistance are often thematized within women's texts; passionate love is allied with suffering and the body and soul are still in pain. Many women, like Mechthild, may turn to erotic language as another way to revalorize their bodiliness;

yet their experience of love itself is marked by extreme suffering, engendered by the absence of the lover and the presence of the flesh.

The very grounding of medieval women's texts in some form of visionary imagination, experience that serves as the authorization of their texts, is allied as well to the problems of embodiment.[87] Women's textual production is, at least implicitly, dependent on the marking of their subjectivities by the divine in extraordinary ways. Without such experience, God is perceived as absent, and suffering ensues. By embracing that suffering—understood as the mark of Christ's wounds upon them—women are redeemed and sanctified. Yet the women writers of the thirteenth century refuse the purely bodily designation of this suffering, and with it the emphasis on physicality and physical asceticism found in the hagiographical tradition; they attempt to associate not primarily with the body of Christ but with the humanity designated by that body. Mechthild, at the close of her life, and Porete throughout the *Mirror*, question the continued need for *any* suffering as constitutive of women's religiosity. For such women, the acceptance of male definitions was not without resistance. The hagiographical texts, on the contrary, explicitly thematize the suffering bodies of women as sites of redemption. Based on the "wounding" of the body, such practice is redemptive of the body only at the cost of its suffering. By embracing the body in its dys-appearance, human salvation becomes dependent on pain.

This mode of bodily salvation predominates in male-authored lives of religious women, causing us to question whose body is being redeemed, and by whom. Women, associated by medieval culture with the body, must be redeemed and can redeem men, primarily through their suffering bodies and souls. Both bodily and spiritual suffering, moreover, are implicitly and explicitly criticized by Mechthild, Porete, and Eckhart. To see this we must read their texts with and against evidence about female—and particularly beguine—spirituality. Taking the form of overwhelmingly male-authored hagiographies, the sources must themselves be read with suspicion, as the following chapter will demonstrate.

2

THE RELIGIOSITY OF THE
MULIERES SANCTAE

To demonstrate the relationships between Mechthild, Porete, Eckhart, and the women's religious movement of northern Europe, particularly the beguines, and to show how the mystical texts emerge out of and in response to central tendencies within the beguine milieu and its hagiographical presentations by male ecclesiasts, some attention must be given to the central spiritual themes of that movement. Other than the writings of Hadewijch, Mechthild, Porete, and the related treatise of the beguine-educated Cistercian, Beatrice of Nazareth, most of the early sources for the spirituality of the beguines are hagiographical.[1] Concentrating on these texts, modern scholars have defined late medieval feminine spirituality in terms of its Christocentrism, visionary-mystical quality, and bodiliness, particularly with regard to asceticism, paramystical phenomena, and imagery.[2] The first two claims are substantiated by both hagiographical and mystical texts. Attention to the divergences between these sources, however, raises important questions about the validity and explanatory power of claims to the bodiliness of women's spirituality. Although clearly central to popular conceptions of women's religiosity, there is overwhelming evidence that in the thirteenth century women themselves were more concerned with issues closely paralleling those important to the male mendicant orders: the meaning of the apostolic life, centered on an interrogation of the roles of poverty, work, and action, and the relationship between the active imitation of Christ and the search for unity with the divine. The tension between these concerns and male hagiographical attempts to read women in terms of the body can be seen throughout the *vitae* of the thirteenth-century beguines.

26

GENDER AND GENRE:
HAGIOGRAPHICAL BODIES

Despite criticism of the tendency to distinguish between affective forms of mystical piety and the supposedly more abstract and theoretically oriented writings of men, variants of the distinction return even among its critics. The most recent formulations focus on the place of the body, both literally and figuratively, in medieval women's lives and spiritualities. Caroline Walker Bynum offers an oft-cited summation:

> Thus, as many recent scholars have argued, the spiritualities of male and female mystics were different, and this difference has something to do with the body. Women were more apt to somatize religious experience and to write in intense bodily metaphors; women mystics were more likely than men to receive graphically physical visions of God; both men and women were inclined to attribute to women and encourage in them intense bodily asceticisms and ecstasies. Moreover, the most bizarre bodily occurrences associated with women (e.g. stigmata, incorruptibility of the cadaver after death, mystical lactations and pregnancies, catatonic trances, ecstatic nosebleeds, miraculous inedia, eating and drinking pus, visions of bleeding hosts) either first appear in the twelfth and thirteenth centuries or increase significantly in frequency at that time.[3]

Bynum distinguishes female from male spirituality in three ways: with regard to harsh asceticism, paramystical bodily phenomena, and bodily metaphors. Less clear from her account is that while the first two are central to the predominantly male-authored hagiographical traditions, only the third occurs in the female-authored mystical writings of the thirteenth century, in which bodily images are often central vehicles of the visionary imagination.

Women in the Middle Ages were certainly believed to be more fleshly, or more fully identified with the body, than were men, traditionally associated with reason.[4] Grounded in Aristotelian views of women's deficiency and their material contribution to reproduction, such identifications were exploited by the misogyny of the early church fathers and medieval commentators.[5] Yet, as Bynum shows, the twofold pattern of identification between women and embodiment could be used to their advantage, for the medieval world's attitudes toward the body were much more ambiguous than one might first assume. The centrality of the doctrine of bodily resurrection is clear evidence of this fact; therefore, many medieval texts emphasize women's association with embodiment not in a negative manner but in ways that exhibit the body's power to be divinized through its share in Christ's suffering, understood as redemptive of the entire human person. Just as Christ's wounded body becomes the mark of God's presence in and redemption of the created world, so the woman saint is often depicted as sharing in the suffering and redemption of Christ.[6]

Before the fourteenth century, however, it is predominantly men who portray women in this way. Women as body, through suffering, redeem both themselves and the men around them. The extreme ambivalence of this position was clear to many medieval women, including Mechthild and Porete. While ascetic and paramystical experiences may be central to medieval culture's perceptions and descriptions of female sanctity, then, their primacy in late medieval women's *lived experience* has not been proven. There are, in fact, almost no extended accounts of bodily asceticism and paramystical phenomena in the writings of medieval women before the fourteenth century—although the language of visionary imagination can be transposed into such narratives.[7] A comparison of hagiographical and mystical texts demonstrates that the distinction made by Bynum—at least with regard to asceticism and paramystical phenomena—is not one between men's and women's religiosity, but between hagiographical and mystical writings and between the multiplicity of male paths to the divine and the uniformity of those prescribed by men for women.

Hagiographical and mystical texts differ structurally, thematically, and stylistically. Yet despite repeated warnings against conflating the two, and against taking predominantly male-authored descriptions of women's lives and experiences at face value, the practice continually reemerges.[8] In part this is because the nature of the differences between the genres and the gender implications of their authorship have not been adequately addressed. Through a demonstration of these distinctions, I believe, the dangers of unproblematically assimilating the evidence concerning "saints" and "mystics," and of taking the word of hagiographers at face value can be elucidated. I am not arguing for a simple relationship between experience and discourse; rather, given the complex interplay between them, I am suggesting that it is crucial to ask who is speaking, from what position, and with what relationship to institutions and power.[9]

A comparison of the Latin *Life* of Beatrice of Nazareth (1200–68), particularly its book 4, and the vernacular treatise "On the Seven Manners of Loving" will clarify the genre and gender dynamic underlying the divergences between hagiographical and mystical texts. Beatrice of Nazareth was, at the time of her death, a Cistercian nun.[10] She had early contact with beguines, living with a beguine community in Leau (Zoutleeuw) after the death of her mother.[11] She is one of the many thirteenth-century holy women in Liège who occupy a place between the beguine and Cistercian milieus, attesting to the interpenetration of the two. Her stay with the beguine community, however, seems to have lasted only a year or so. At about the age of eleven, she continued her education within Cistercian houses. In May 1236 she was transfered to the Nazareth foundation, where she spent the remainder of her life.

Beatrice's biography was written in Latin shortly after her death, probably by a male cleric or Cistercian.[12] The author claims to have based the text upon autobiographical writings left by Beatrice in the vernacular.[13] Those autobiographical texts, reputed to be the sources for much of books 1 through 3, are no longer extant. Book 4, however, is a Latin version of Beatrice's own short vernacular treatise on the seven manners of loving God, of which three manuscripts survive.[14] The differences between the two texts highlight the crucial distinctions between hagiographical and mystical conventions, audiences, and aims. The changes the author of the *Life* makes to Beatrice's treatise help to demonstrate what can and cannot be portrayed in thirteenth-century hagiographical writings and the different ways in which mystical experience is figured in the two genres. We can thereby uncover the methods used by the medieval hagiographer to portray mystical experience in dramatic, narrative form. In doing so, I will show the dangers threatening the historian who accepts the hagiographer's account as if it were a piece of modern historical writing, shaped by concerns and conceptions of reality identical to our own.

To begin, in book 1 of the *Life*, the traditional place for such texts to describe events preceding the turn to the internal life, Beatrice's hagiographer describes her ascetic practices. The account is traditional, however, in more than the usual sense, for it is almost identical with the description of the ascetic practices of the male Cistercian Arnulph.[15]

It includes a fairly standard description of various methods used to "master" her "frail body," including beating herself with sharp twigs, sleeping on a bed strewn with such twigs, and finally carrying the twigs in her bosom all day so that she might be continually tortured by their stings.[16] The fact that Arnulph's activities are described in almost exactly the same terms does not preclude Beatrice's having performed these acts; she is particularly likely to have participated in the monastic asceticisms common to her order and its interpretation of the rule of Benedict. Beatrice certainly fasted, kept vigils of protracted prayer, and followed a life of poverty and humility. However, it must be asked why the hagiographer uses an existing account of more radical ascetic practices to describe Beatrice's activity.

A hypothesis can be offered, although without the text of Beatrice's autobiographical writings it is impossible to prove. If the hagiographer was working from these writings, his use of passages from another text for this aspect of her life points to the absence of any description of harsh ascetic practice in Beatrice's own work. The absence of harsh asceticism is, as I have said, much more typical of women's writings before the fourteenth century than current accounts of medieval women's spirituality suggest. Angela of Foligno's (d. 1309) *Book*, arguably an "auto-hagiography," is the only nonhagiographical exception.[17] Because descriptions of ascetic practice, however, were considered a necessary part of the hagiographical genre, in particular for women and nonclerical men,[18] the author searched for a model to fill in the gap in his sources—hence his use of the *Life* of Arnulph. This not only raises the question of the historical validity of accounts of ascetic practices found here and in other saints' lives of the period, but also illustrates the ways in which genre expectations shape hagiographical texts. While there is substantial evidence that the ideal of sanctity as grounded in bodily experience, asceticism, and their mystical correlates was more prevalent in descriptions (predominantly male-authored) of female saints, this tells us very little about the actual ascetic practices of Beatrice of Nazareth or any other woman in the thirteenth century.[19]

The problematizing of modern conceptions of medieval women's spirituality and religious practices in the *Life* of Beatrice of Nazareth goes further, however, than the issue of bodily asceticism. A comparison of Book 4 with Beatrice's vernacular treatise, "On the Seven Manners of Loving," shows the tendency of the hagiographer to

translate mystical into paramystical phenomena, or internally apprehended into externally perceptible experiences.[20] The tension between
the body and the soul is exacerbated, and even made central to
the experience recounted, in a way not found in Beatrice's mystical
treatise.

The *Life*'s translation of the treatise shifts the site and tone of events
immediately. Whereas Beatrice writes an impersonal third-person narrative, the hagiographer (like most modern readers) assumes she is
speaking of her own experiences:

> *Treatise*: There are seven manners of loving, which come down from
> the heights and go back again far above.[21]
>
> *Life*: These then are the seven degrees or stages of love, seven in
> number, through which she deserved to come to her beloved, not at
> an even pace, but now as if walking on foot, now running swiftly,
> and sometimes even flying nimbly on agile wings.[22]

While Bynum argues that the female mystics tend to speak of "*my*
mystical experience" whereas male mystics speak impersonally of "*the
mystical experience*," here we see the opposite gender- and voice-
dynamic.[23] The male hagiographer, in fact, reads Beatrice's text as
autobiographical in the same way Bynum and others do, demonstrating the similarity of their gender assumptions. Beatrice's text is—while
impassioned—impersonal, distanced, and generalized in its narrative
structure. The movement described is less that of the soul (the main
actor in the treatise, which is never specified to be that of the writer or
narrator), than of the divine. The hagiographer personalizes and par-
ticularizes Beatrice's general description of the relationship between
the divine and the loving soul. This often takes the form of giving an
externally perceptible bodily dimension to her mystical account.

Despite the hagiographer's translation, Beatrice's vernacular treatise
does not recount degrees or stages so much as different manners of
loving, manners with often scarcely apprehensible differences.[24] At
issue for Beatrice is the continual movement of presence and absence
between the soul and God, a movement that parallels that between the
Lover and the Beloved in the Song of Songs. In learning to acquiesce to
this oscillation, the soul comes to experience a deepening sense of the
divine love and presence. The soul is no longer the bride or beloved
but rather the housewife of God,[25] one whose life is marked, not by a
dialectic of ecstasy and despair, but by a steady sense of the underlying

presence of God in reality.[26] In personalizing and somatizing the seven stages of loving, the hagiographer alters this mystical path.

Whereas in the first manner of loving, Beatrice discusses the soul's desire "to keep the purity and nobility and the freedom in which it was made by its Creator, its image and likeness,"[27] the hagiographer interprets this in terms of ascetic practices. Through "corporal exercises" (*corporalibus exercitiis*) she sought "to obtain that liberty of spirit we mentioned."[28] In the same way, the intense self-scrutiny demanded by love leads Beatrice, according to the hagiographer, to "bodily illnesses" by which she was "so weighed down . . . that she thought death was near."[29] Again, the humility of the second manner of loving, which desires to serve all most faithfully, is portrayed by the hagiographer in terms of Beatrice's life of service and humility in the convent.[30] In these examples, then, the hagiographer attempts to read Beatrice's life itself as an enactment of the mystical journey described in her treatise.

This movement involves a somatization of the mystical, as becomes further apparent in the fourth manner of loving. Here a mystical commonplace in which the soul is compared to an overflowing vessel is given bodily expression:

> *Treatise*: When the soul feels itself to be thus filled full of riches and in such fullness of heart, the spirit sinks away down into love, the body passes away, the heart melts, every faculty fails; and the soul is so utterly conquered by love that often it cannot support itself, often the limbs and the senses lose their powers. And just as a vessel filled up to the brim will run over and spill if it is touched, so at times the soul is so touched and overpowered by this great fullness of the heart that in spite of itself it spills and overflows.[31]
>
> *Life*: In this stage the holy woman's affection was so tender that she was often soaked with the flood of tears from her melted heart, and sometimes because of the excessive abundance of spiritual delight, she lay languishing and sick in bed, deprived of all her strength. . . . Just as a vessel filled with liquid spills what it contains when it is only slightly pushed, so it happened frequently that she, pushed as it were, would let spill out by many signs of holy love what she felt inside; or else she would undergo a kind of paralyzed trembling, or would be burdened with some other discomfort or illness.[32]

What Beatrice describes from the inside, as it were, is transposed by the hagiographer into external and visible form, making use of the commonplaces and topoi of hagiography to facilitate his translation. Where Beatrice describes the passing away of the body's faculties in the soul's ecstasy, the hagiographer underlines the *signs* on the body that such an experience is occurring. The state of the soul is made manifest in the body, in its tears, weaknesses, and illnesses in the face of intense spiritual experience.

A similar externalization of the bodily aspects of Beatrice's text can be seen in descriptions of the fifth stage, in which her writing achieves an intensity and fervor meant to evoke the madness and violence of love. The strength of divine love is felt in both body and soul, the lines between the two becoming increasingly difficult to decipher.

> *Treatise*: And at times love becomes so boundless and so overflowing in the soul, when it itself is so mightily and violently moved in the heart, that it seems [*dunct*] to the soul that the heart is wounded again and again, and that these wounds increase every day in bitter pain and in fresh intensity. It seems [*dunct*] to the soul that the veins are bursting, the blood spilling, the marrow withering, the bones softening, the heart burning, the throat parching, so that the body in its every part feels this inward [*van binnen*] heat, and this is the fever of love.[33]

While Beatrice stresses the internal bodily state, its significance, and divine referent, the hagiographer focuses on the sensibly marked body.[34]

> *Life*: Indeed her heart, deprived of strength by this invasion, often gave off a sound like that of a shattering vessel, while she both felt the same and heard it exteriorly. Also the blood diffused through her bodily members boiled over through her open veins. Her bones contracted and the marrow disappeared; the dryness of her chest produced hoarseness of throat. And to make a long story short, the very fervor of her holy longing and love blazed up as a fire in all her bodily members, making her perceptibly [*sensibiliter*] hot in a wondrous way.[35]

In the hagiographer's account, Beatrice possesses a divinely marked body, uncommonly like those found in other hagiographical accounts from Marie of Oignies (d. 1213) to Lukardis of Oberweimer (d. 1309).

For the hagiographer, Beatrice's body is the site of her sanctity— it suffers, weeps, groans, grows hot, and glows, in its progression from the first aspirations toward divine love and the final achievement of union with that God who is love. Throughout the *Life* the body and the soul are portrayed as mirroring each other, and also as in a state of conflict. This struggle exists in Beatrice's own text, but in a different place and with different repercussions. It does not provide the content or enactment (perhaps more graphically, the picture) of the ascent—the interplay of God's presence and absence as internally experienced provides that—but rather is the fruit of the soul's ascent in this life. Beatrice uses bodily language to convey her suffering—the hagiographer needs a more graphic, objectively apprehensible means of conveying her sanctity to the reader. He therefore describes the *visible* body and its markings, for only through her wounded body can the divine presence be seen.[36]

According to Beatrice, when the soul has passed through the six stages of loving, having become love itself and returned to her own nature, which is love, she laments her exile on this earth and desires to be freed from the body. Yet this very sorrow, and the internally experienced fissuring of the body that her desire brings about, becomes a part of the union between the soul and God. The hagiographer, although emphasizing the suffering *body* in his rendition of Beatrice's text, feels called on to soften her expressions of desire and their vehemence. He both literalizes and fears the audacity of Beatrice's desire to be with God.

> *Life*: The vehemence of this desire was so excessive that she sometimes thought she would lose her mind for its grievousness, or would shorten the days of her life because of her anguish of heart and great damage to her vital bodily organs.[37]

Fearing for her health, the hagiographer tells us, Beatrice avoids thinking about heaven and her future bliss when her ecstatic desire threatens the body. But for Beatrice, thoughts of heaven and their attendant *internally* experienced suffering are central to the movement of ascent to the divine:

> *Treatise*: So the soul refuses every consolation, often from God himself and from his creatures, for every consolation which could come to it only strengthens its love and draws it up towards a higher life; and this renews the soul's longing to live in love and to delight in love, its determination to live uncomforted in this present exile.[38]

As for Mechthild and Porete, the will is the locus of the conflict that leads to the experience of union and exile. The body is not the focus of battle, nor is it said to be externally marked by this struggle (either through ascetic practices, tears, illnesses, fevers, or paramystical phenomena) over the internal disposition of the will and affections.

Hagiography, however, tends to represent the state of the soul through external narrative devices. This becomes most pronounced in texts describing women's lives.[39] Various factors might contribute to the greater emphasis on the mystically marked body in hagiographies of holy women. The identification of women with the body demands that their sanctification occur in and through that body. Furthermore, women's access to religious authority was, in the thirteenth century, primarily (if not solely) through visionary and mystical experience. Linked to embodiment through its ties to the imagination and often described through bodily images and metaphors, visionary experience was also at times described in terms of its internally experienced, sensible effects. Yet the medieval hagiographer wants externally sensible *signs* of visionary and mystical experience in order to verify the claims to sanctity of the woman saint. Beatrice's hagiographer, then, transposes her accounts of internal experience into descriptions of the body in its externality. The visionary woman becomes a vision, a divinely marked body, a spectacle for the viewing pleasure of her contemporaries.[40] For this reason, the internal mystical life of Beatrice is transformed into a series of struggles between the body and the soul, of battles represented and enacted on the body of the holy woman.

The experiences described by Beatrice in her treatise might have been accompanied by physical phenomena like those recounted by her hagiographer. Yet in the thirteenth century, these physical events are not important to the female authors of mystical treatises. Anything that we know about the externally visible bodies of Beatrice of Nazareth, Hadewijch, Mechthild of Magdeburg, Gertrude of Helfta, Marguerite of Oingt, or Marguerite Porete is conveyed incidentally. Asceticism and paramystical phenomena are not intrinsic to their texts, although descriptions of the body as *experienced* (usually as languishing or breaking down in the intensity of divine union) sometimes are. Although Mechthild writes of the wounded body of Christ, she describes the movements of the wounded soul; she thereby relocates suffering from the body to the exiled soul, sparing the former in its innocence. Ultimately, through her understanding of the well-ordered soul, Mechthild attempts to spare herself spiritual suffering as well. For Porete, the body is even less in evidence, marking her rejection of the cultural identification of women with bodiliness. Her contemporaries responded by viewing her as a "pseudo-woman," (*pseudomulier*)[41] suggesting the intransigence of gender ideologies.[42] Despite the evidence of her *sex*, in refusing the *gender* assigned to her Porete defies the categorization of her society. Although valuations may change, modern commentators implicitly accept the continuator of Nangis's depiction of Porete when they repeat essentializing descriptions of women's experience and writings.

Although absent in Beatrice and Porete, visionary experience, with its odd status between internal and external, subjective and objective, *is* central to most women's writings, providing the necessary grounds for authority.[43] Most thirteenth-century female-authored mystical texts discuss visions and visionary experiences in order to legitimate the writer's authority in the face of her institutional silencing. Without such legitimation (and even with it), women were subject to suspicion and condemnation. They had no basis on which they could write or teach, nor any "text" that they might legitimately read and interpret.[44] The visionary source of authority not only has a theological basis,[45] but it is grounded in the male clerical elites' desire for some external and objective criteria by which they might judge women's sanctity. Where for the hagiographer the mystic's body is her text, for the mystic her internal *experience* (often, although not in the cases of Beatrice and Porete, her visionary experience) is her text.[46] Only in the fourteenth century, after the condemnation of Porete and the Council of Vienne's decrees associating the women's movement and heresy, do more concrete physical authorizations, in the form of bodily asceticism and paramystical phenemona, become necessary to legitimate the woman writer (as, it could be argued, they had earlier been necessary to legitimate the woman saint).[47]

Any study of late medieval mysticism, then, that works with the assumption that an easily identifiable difference exists between male and female forms of spirituality and writings is in danger of missing the complexity of these materials. I do not, however, wish to adopt the opposite approach, asserting that since authorship is always contested and gender always fluid, we should ignore the ways in which medieval texts are marked.[48] Moreover, as I showed in chapter 1, there are distinctions lying behind those described by Bynum and others; between hagiographical and mystical writings, between the ideals of sanctity prescribed for men and women, and, finally, between those texts and moments within them grounded in visionary experience and its often highly imagistic language and the drive to apophasis or un-saying in which images and concepts are negated. While thirteenth-century women's mystical texts *do not* stress asceticism and paramystical phenomena, their tendency to use often highly imagistic, bodily, visionary language leads to transpositions like those made by Beatrice's hagiographer. Yet the beguine writers also subvert their visionary images through apophasis. Radically antiessentialist, apophatic language severely problematizes attempts to characterize it in gendered terms. Neither obviously somatic nor antisomatic—for to negate images and concepts is not necessarily to negate the body— it calls into question those dualisms on which much modern textual analysis has been based. As such, it resists our categories of thought. This language enables the process of transfiguration through which the divine is incarnated continually in the world, yet it is foreign to the imagistic and narrative demands of hagiography.

The disjunctions between mystical and hagiographical writings do not require that the latter be discounted entirely, as presenting merely mainstream (and hence male) presentations of female sanctity. We can learn a great deal from hagiographical accounts, as long as we are clear about what kind of evidence they offer. Very few female-authored hagiographies exist from before the fourteenth century; those that remain are often marked by the genre assumptions described above, albeit with signs of reluctance. Gertrude of Helfta's hagiographer eschews descriptions of intense bodily asceticism.[49] Marguerite of Oingt, although clearly uncomfortable with any form of extreme asceticism, follows the demands of the genre and opens the *Life* of the Carthusian Beatrice of Orniceaux with an obligatory account of the bodily horrors to which Beatrice subjected herself.[50] The thirteenth-century life of the beguine Douceline—generally believed to have been written by a fellow beguine—although giving little attention to her ascetic practice, includes an account of her beating a seven-year-old girl bloody because she looked at a man working nearby.[51] Most prominently, the early fourteenth-century convent chronicles are replete with ascetic and paramystical phenomena, although one wonders if the increased suspicion of women's mystical piety surrounding the Council of Vienne and its aftermath might not have reinforced the exigencies of the genre in these cases.[52]

The sources, then, clearly confirm that radical asceticism was an accepted and expected aspect of female sanctity. Although similar expectations were increasingly common for all aspiring to sainthood, the burden of sanctifying the body fell inordinately on women. Through their bodily asceticisms and paramystical feats women were understood not only as sanctifying their own bodies but also as healing, sanctifying, and aiding those around them, particularly men.[53] The degree to which such legitimating strategies were internalized by medieval women can be gauged by the repetition of similar tropes within female-authored hagiographies and their incorporation within other female-authored texts. While there is evidence that women hagiographers submit to genre expectations in the thirteenth century, bodily asceticism and paramystical phenomena do not begin to emerge in women's mystical writings until the fourteenth century, when, coincidentally, persecution of beguines and other religious women in northern Europe was given new impetus by the decrees of the Council of Venice.[54] Concerned particularly with keeping control over women's religious life through enclosure and supervision, these acts culminate in an increasing "specularization" of their spirituality.[55] Before this period, women's mystical treatises found their primary form of legitimation in the depiction of visionary experience and the erotic language of the Song of Songs, both of which lend themselves to, without enacting, the movement toward externalization and somatization seen in the *Life of Beatrice*.

The hagiographical sources from the Low Countries offer highly mediated access to the lives of the early beguines and of those Cistercian nuns who had contact with them. As long as we recognize that such mediation exists, that men like the canon Jacques of Vitry and the Dominican Thomas of Cantimpré were attempting to offer a picture of female sanctity acceptable to the ecclesiastical hierarchy (of which these two hagiographers were themselves a part, a position which no doubt shaped *what* they saw)[56] and of use to that hierarchy and to the Christian church as they conceived it, these sources can offer us important information on the *climate* in which the beguine movement arose and in which Mechthild and Porete wrote.[57] Read against themselves and other sources, furthermore, they may also elicit information about medieval women's experience. To understand that experience more fully, however, we must give heed to the points of resistance and conflict within these (predominantly) male-authored accounts, to women's mystical writings, and to the tensions and conflicts between the two sets of texts. Most important, we must read the hagiographies with and against women's mystical writings and resist the desire to read the women's texts through the eyes of the medieval hagiographer.

THE ACTIVE AND CONTEMPLATIVE
LIVES IN BEGUINE HAGIOGRAPHY

Many of the women known by their contemporaries as *mulieres sanctae*, or beguines, were actively pursuing their version of the apostolic ideal through life in the world. The forms of life identified with the beguines—semireligious women living alone or in groups lives of prayer, service, and mutual exhortation—occupy a specific place in the religious map of thirteenth-century northern Europe, one distinct from that of Premonstratensian, Cistercian, and mendicant women, although with important contacts and relationships between these religious circles.[58] I will now take up the question of whether, read critically with and against mystical texts, the hagiographical tradition can elicit insight into a distinctive beguine spirituality. While Grundmann argued almost sixty years ago that semireligious women were instrumental in the development of vernacular spirituality and in the particular forms these spiritual writings took, more recently it has been argued that it is impossible to distinguish beguine religiosity from that of Cistercian and Dominican nuns.[59] I maintain that careful attention to the sources, both hagiographical and mystical, will support the insight that the beguine lifestyle is reflected in their spirituality, although in ways that increasingly converge (within the hagiographical tradition, at least) with their Cistercian and mendicant sisters.

Various attempts have been made to find similarities between the writings of the three known beguine mystics, a project in which this study takes part. I begin with the arguments made by Kurt Ruh and Bernard McGinn, that the writings of these three mystics (and also the related work of Beatrice of Nazareth) are marked by their allusions to a form of union between God and the soul that passes beyond all distinction.[60] For all of the beguines, love is the central mystical category, but the understanding of love varies according to the radicalness of their views on union. All at least hint at the existence of some uncreated part of the soul that shares an abiding and absolute union with the divine. What becomes crucial for Mechthild and Porete is how this understanding of the precreated soul transforms the relationship between the active and contemplative lives. While the theological daring and antinarrative language of union without distinction is not in evidence in the hagiographical tradition, the relationship between action and contemplation *is* a central issue in the hagiographies of early beguines.[61]

This theme is played out most obviously through allusions to two biblical pairs—Rachel and Leah, and Mary and Martha. Just as Bernard of Clairvaux took over traditional exegesis of the Lukan passage to elucidate the interrelationship between the active and the contemplative lives, the Premonstratensian Hugh of Floreff uses them in his hagiography of Ivetta, the recluse of Huy.[62] Like her more famous contemporary, Marie of Oignies, Ivetta chose as a young widow to devote herself to the care of lepers, renouncing life in the world. In her desire to be absolutely humble before God and other humans, she hoped to become a leper herself, going so far as to drink the water in which those afflicted had been bathed and taking other measures to infect herself. Hugh, however, in describing her works of charity and desire to humble herself, takes care to show that she does not forget the internal life at the expense of manual labor.

> Nevertheless, among these duties of industrious servitude and the bleary-eyedness of Leah, Rachel's beauties were not forgotten: but just like Moses, now taking care in the encampments of the people, now in the tabernacle of the covenant awaiting God's responses, whatever she did externally, within she always persevered, neither in the days nor in the nights being absent from divine colloquies and prayer.[63]

Hugh insists on the mutuality of her roles as both Rachel and Leah, or active and contemplative, at this stage in her life, but shortly after claims that in choosing to adopt the life of a recluse, Ivetta opts for contemplation over activity in the world: "And having given up the ministry of Martha, she transferred herself to the part of Mary, which is better."[64] In describing her renunciation of the unenclosed lifestyle for a more traditional one of enclosure and prayer, Hugh returns to a traditional approbation of the path of Mary over that of Martha.

Hugh understands Ivetta's move to a more traditional, enclosed lifestyle as a choice of contemplation over action, but for the hagiographers of those women who continue to live in the world the dichotomy is a cause of constant anxiety and reinterpretation, marking their anxiety over women embarking on the mixed life. In the hagiographies of holy women from the Low Countries, the figures of Mary and Martha are used to inscribe the dual nature of the beguine life, as well as to justify the movement from less to more enclosed and traditional forms of religiosity.[65] The hagiographers present those living in the world in the context of a tension between their desire to be both Mary and Martha and the traditional claim, reinforced by male misogyny and fear of uncontrolled women, that contemplation was the preferred mode of existence, especially for women.

Although the figures of Mary and Martha are not consistently named in the early beguine lives, the contrast they represent is fully exploited. Jacques of Vitry in the *Life* of Marie of Oignies emphasizes, like Hugh, her ability to be rapt in contemplation while still engaged in manual labor.[66] Like Ivetta, however, Marie ultimately abandons the active life for that of contemplation.[67] Thomas of Cantimpré tells us that Margaret of Ypres was blessed with the same twofold ability, enabling her to avoid her mother's scolding. Her preoccupation with spiritual matters, however, still got her into trouble at times with her more practical-minded family.[68] While for Marie the theme is a corollary of her desire to live a life of poverty, for Margaret it marks the tensions between her contemplative lifestyle and her life in the world. Juliana of Mont-Cornillon, who lived as an Augustinian, semireligious, and Cistercian, is described early in her *Life* as bringing Mary and Martha miraculously together in one person.[69] The theme, moreover, is almost entirely absent in the hagiographies of those women who had less active involvement with beguines and spent most of their lives in monasteries. This is particularly noteworthy given that the relationship between the active and contemplative lives is a central theme in Bernard of Clairvaux's sermons on the Song of Songs, an important text for Cistercian spirituality.[70]

The *Life* of Lutgard of Aywières is instructive, for it was written by the hagiographer of two early beguines, the above-mentioned Margaret, as well as Christina the Astonishing. Perhaps most remarkable about these three lives, written at different points in Thomas's career, is how dissimilar they are.[71] While they share a certain flair for the miraculous characteristic of Thomas, even this element is less in evidence in the more mystical hagiography of Lutgard. In the elaborately structured tripartite life, Thomas recounts Lutgard's career according to the threefold path of spirituality, based on the typology of the three books of Solomon, and culminating in the life of perfection in which the union of the soul and God recounted in the Song of Songs is achieved.[72] While Lutgard's humility is continually stressed, there is no mention of manual labor as an expression of that humility or of the conflict between the path of Martha and that of Mary. Rather, it could be argued, Lutgard is presented throughout as an aspiring and soon to be perfected Mary, pursuing and attaining the life of contemplation. The majority of the hagiography describes Lutgard's visionary, prophetic, and mystical experiences.

MENDICANCY AND MANUAL LABOR
AMONG THE EARLY BEGUINES

A second and allied concern in the hagiographies of the early beguines is the desire for mendicancy as an expression of poverty, humility, and conformity with the life of Christ. Although downplayed by most modern commentators, the fact that these incidents are mentioned in the hagiographies, given male clerical objections to such activities, suggests their historical reliability and importance. Even more than the general pursuit of the active life, mendicancy is seen by the hagiographers themselves as inappropriate activity (although the *desire* for extreme poverty is praiseworthy). Included within the texts as an approbation of the wish for *spiritual* poverty and a warning and disclaimer against actual begging by women, the practice is both recorded and curbed through the hagiographical tradition.

Marie of Oignies is shown being persuaded not to beg by her friends, who call on her spirit of charity to keep her off the streets.[73] Christina the Astonishing does beg for her bread; moreover, she is moved by the spirit to do so and is able to tell the spiritual state of the giver through her reactions to their alms.[74] Margaret of Ypres, having given all of her possessions to her mother, begs in order to have alms to give to a leper who seeks aid from her. On other occasions, her love of poverty leads her to leave her mother's house in order to beg. She is dissuaded from this activity, however, by her Dominican confessor and adviser, Siger of Lille, who assures her that it is inappropriate for a young virgin.[75] The life of the beguine turned Cistercian, Ida of Nivelles, gives another detailed picture of beguine mendicancy, one which explicitly brings together the figures of Mary and Martha, the desire for extreme poverty, and begging. Ida is described "as a new Martha," begging in the squares and marketplaces of the town, then returning home to share her takings with her companions.[76] In the south of France, Douceline also desires to follow the poverty and mendicant lifestyle of Francis, to whom the text explicitly refers.[77] As late as the mid-fourteenth century, the life of Gertrude van Oosten, a beguine primarily known for her reception of the stigmata, depicts her begging, suggesting the importance of mendicancy as a trope for beguine activity.[78]

The desire to beg is closely aligned to the emphasis placed on manual labor, highlighting the parallels and divergences between the aims and ideals of the early beguines and those of Francis and his followers in the south. The similarity was clear to contemporaries like Jacques of Vitry.[79] Yet the clerical reception of the desire to follow the apostolic life as interpreted by Francis and the early beguines with regard to poverty and mendicancy was very different. While the 1215 ban against new religious orders may be in part responsible for the fact that the beguine lifestyle—"living in the world but not in a worldly way"—never received official sanction, the acceptance of both Francis's and Dominic's new mendicant orders in the years after 1215 suggests the limitations of this explanation. Rather, the attitudes toward female mendicancy seen in the early beguine hagiographies, together with the continual problematizing of the relationship between action and contemplation, point to the more obvious explanations of clerical suspicion and indifference to women's pursuit of these ideals. Behind the denigration of female mendicancy, absolute poverty, and pursuit of the active life lies the desire to maintain enclosure as the norm for religious women.[80]

In the face of this opposition hagiographers depict women like Marie of Oignies, Margaret of Ypres, and Gertrude van Oosten as tempering their ideals, achieving compromises between their desire for radical poverty and the male hierarchy's desire for women to lead controlled and regulated lives. Mendicancy is therefore replaced by manual labor, a move praised by some contemporaries and claimed by Robert Grosseteste to be preferable to the mendicant lifestyle.[81] Many beguines and beguine communities supported themselves through their work, at times playing an important role in the local economy.[82] Their labor is mentioned only in passing, and with edifying spiritual comment, in the *Lives*. For example, Marie is praised for her ability to earn her livelihood (and that of other holy women) by the labor of her hands while still remaining rapt in contemplation.[83]

The desire to return to religious lives of simplicity, including manual labor as stipulated in the rule of Benedict, is already a feature of the twelfth-century reform movements, in particular those of the Cistercians and Premonstratensians.[84] In these cases, labor takes the form of charitable activity, the upkeep of the sisters being provided by the foundation. For example, the Premonstratensian, Oda of Rivreulle, engaged in hospice and hospital work.[85] In a similar way, Marie of Oignies and Ivetta of Huy, provided with money to live on from their own labors and from the little they retained from their husbands, minister to lepers, as Francis of Assisi will do a few years later.[86] Yet both Marie and Ivetta eventually seem to have abandoned this life in order to devote themselves more fully to prayer and contemplation and, perhaps more important for the hagiographical tradition, to avoid the crowds of admirers who begin to follow them to their hospital retreats. Just as actual poverty is displaced by a desire for spiritual poverty, so the active life of charity, necessitating minimal or no enclosure, was not the only type of labor considered worthy of note by hagiographers. In fact, they seemed to have found more saintly those women who surpassed manual labor in order to devote themselves to the central "work" of the hagiographies: praying for and, through ascetic feats and visionary advice, rescuing souls on earth and in purgatory.[87] This form of charity, in which the enclosed as well as the semireligious can easily engage, marks a central point of convergence between the beguine and Cistercian milieus and their hagiographies; it is also the arena in which corporeal and spiritual suffering most forcibly come into play. Attention to this spiritual work in the beguine hagiographies, then, further elucidates the role of suffering and of the paramystical feats of saintly bodies in these writings.

PURGATORY, SUFFERING, AND THE WORK OF PRAYER AND PENANCE IN BEGUINE AND CISTERCIAN LIVES

While Jacques LeGoff calls the Cistercian Lutgard of Aywières the saint of purgatory, the most startling example of this theme in the lives of thirteenth-century beguines and Cistercians occurs in that of Christina the Astonishing. The hagiography is cited by modern commentators as an example of the extreme bodiliness of medieval women's sanctity and religiosity, but the circumstances of and reasons for Christina's miraculous activities are rarely discussed.[88] A fuller reading of the hagiography again leads to reconsideration of the nature of the text as a historical document and the purposes of its narrative form and content. By clarifying the sometimes divergent theological claims underlying descriptions of extreme asceticism and miraculous bodily phenomena, furthermore, I hope to offer a more adequate understanding of the nature of the beguines' suffering for souls in purgatory.

The hagiographer Thomas of Cantimpré did not know Christina. He bases his claim to reliability on what he has heard of her and the fact that Jacques of Vitry mentions her miraculous activity in his *Life* of Marie of Oignies. Jacques speaks there of seeing Christina suspended in the air in prayer, impervious to the presence and touch of those around her.[89] This only scratches the surface of her abilities. She is able to withstand the pain of intense bodily torture, which does not mark or harm her physical body in any way. Unlike in many other hagiographies, in which the holy woman's body is externally marked by her internal experiences, Christina pursues an exhibitionistic and seemingly impossible asceticism without suffering external bodily harm. She puts her body in ovens, submerges it in boiling and then freezing water, turns herself on a wheel, and after each of these acts her body remains unscathed. Furthermore, when she is arrested by family and friends who fear for her sanity, she is miraculously freed by God from her restraints and her virgin breasts give forth an oil with which she is able to feed herself in her wanderings outside the town. Her body itself is of an extreme lightness, so that in prayer she floats to the tops of trees or church spires, unable to bear the weight of the earth. What is the reason for Christina's miraculous activities and her body, marked by its "wholeness" rather than by its wounds? Put simply, she occupies a resurrected body, one still subject to death yet of a spiritual nature unknown to those who have not died before. As Thomas of Cantimpré tells us in the first chapter of the life, Christina has died. Herein lies the explanation for her amazing asceticism and paramystical feats.

Born the third of three daughters to "honest" parents, after their death she was relegated by her sisters to care of the cattle. Despite the humility of her task, or rather because of it, God visited her continually with his graces, until finally, unable to sustain this internal exercise of contemplation, her body weakened and died. Christina's body in life behaved in the same way as Beatrice of Nazareth's did, according to her hagiographer. On her way to her place in heaven, Christina is shown purgatory. The souls she sees there are suffering so terribly that she believes she is in hell. After she arrives in heaven, God offers her a choice:

> Truly, my dearest, you will be with me, but now I offer you two choices: either remain with me now or return to the body, there to undergo the penance of an immortal soul in a mortal body, but without harm to that body, and to deliver by your penance all those souls who you pitied in that place of purgatory and by the example of your penance and your way of life to convert living human beings to me and repel them from evil things, and having done all these things to return to me, having accumulated for yourself a reward of such great profit.[90]

Being an incipient saint, Christina unhesitatingly agrees to the second proposal.

In describing the "work" Christina must do in order to free souls from purgatory, this passage and the text as a whole reiterate the profound ambivalence of medieval attitudes toward the body and, in particular, women's bodies. Yet, Christina's suffering is not performed in order to torture her flesh, as those with modern sensibilities might believe, but to benefit other suffering souls.[91] The desire to imitate Christ's self-sacrifice for humanity lies behind this conception of sub-stitionary atonement for souls in purgatory. Like Christ, Christina is given an opportunity to suffer for others. For one living in a world in which physical pain seems inevitable, Christina's stance becomes heroic. The question of why the body must suffer for human sinful-ness remains. The text, however, challenges modern conceptions of a dualism between body and soul, for while the acts of suffering *seem* physical and the pain is described in physical and bodily terms, in fact the body itself is not harmed. The miracle of Christina's life is not only that she is able to sustain such intense suffering but that she is able to do so without harming the body (in fact, the former miracle can be seen as depending on the latter, for if the body were harmed as it should have been by her actions, she would have died, thereby bringing her suffering to an end).[92]

A related ambivalence with regard to the body and its labors can be seen in a remarkable series of passages from the *Life* of Marie of Oignies. Early in the *Life*, Jacques tells of how Marie, recalling bodily and sensuous pleasures that she had experienced before her conversion (she had eaten meat and drunk watered wine after an illness) wishes to punish her body. She therefore takes out a little knife and cuts away a piece ("not small") of her flesh. The inclusion of this account within the hagiography suggests approbation of a morbid asceticism that demands the punishment, if not the destruction, of the body. Jacques's depiction of Marie's continual tears and fasting to the point where she can no longer eat reinforce this image. Yet he is adamant that this self-laceration is different from the other actions and is not acceptable from the standpoint of Christian orthodoxy. As he describes it, Marie immediately feels shame for her deed and attempts to hide it from all around her, with the exception of her confessor. Despite these disapproving sentiments, however, Jacques goes on to compare Marie to the ancient desert fathers, Simon the Stylite and Antony, and their heroic asceticisms.

> Why are those who are amazed at the worms that swarmed from the wounds of Simon and at the fire with which Antony burnt his feet not astonished at such fortitude in the frail sex of a woman who, wounded by charity and invigorated by the wounds of Christ, neglected the wounds of her own body.[93]

Jacques does not find fault with the impetus to her act (in fact, it is quite good for a "frail woman"), but rather with the "mistaken fervor" that leads Marie to create a wound in her own body. While hagiography demands external signs of sanctity, the conditions under which they can be brought about are strictly delimited. Only God can or should mark the female body as holy.

Despite the apparent prohibition, furthermore, elsewhere in the text Jacques relates other tales of wounding asceticism. For example, while Marie was walking through the town of Nivelles, she knew that Christ was suffering on account of the wickedness of its inhabitants. Wishing to share Christ's pain, Marie again pulls out her little knife, planning to cut the bottoms of her feet so that she will suffer as she walks through the unholy place. There is an odd lacuna in the text here; it is not clear if God allows Marie to disfigure her body or whether he causes her to feel the *pain* of the cuts without the lacerations themselves being made:

Thus did she suffer not only in mind but also (what is more mar-velous) she suffered sensible pain in her feet that walked in the aforesaid places and she could scarcely find rest when she had struck her feet many times on the ground.[94]

Either, as with Christina, Marie's physical body is saved the harm that she is called on to feel, or the narrator is uncomfortable with explicit description (and implicit approbation) of an act of self-mutilation that he nevertheless desires to include within the text.[95]

This recurring ambiguity with regard to the location of suffering and the relationship between bodily suffering and sinfulness can also be seen in medieval discussions and representations of purgatory in theological, visionary, and imaginative writings.[96] Although doctri-nally the medieval church considered purgatorial sufferings to be spir-itual, representations of them use bodily images to convey the agony of the sinful soul.[97] As in the *Life* of Christina the Astonishing the dismemberment and disfigurement of the body is precluded, affirming its basic integrity. In this way, the theological view of suffering is main-tained at the same time as it is described (and hence made "visible") in bodily terms.

But while the resurrected body is safeguarded, those on earth—particularly women—occupy a more ambiguous and ambivalent po-sition. In his fascination with Marie's self-wounding (and, given the evidence from Beatrice of Nazareth's *Life*, it is not clear we should take these accounts literally), Jacques demonstrates his own fascination with women's suffering bodies as redemptive. After her death, Thomas of Cantimpré tells us, Jacques carried Marie's finger as a protective relic.[98] Marie's dismembered body saves Jacques from drowning, a move into the realm of externality clearly paralleled by the transfor-mations between treatise and *Life* seen in the case of Beatrice.

We here reencounter both the complexity of medieval anthro-pologies, which can not be understood as simply dualistic, and the heterogeneity of medieval culture. Christina suffers the pains of child-birth without any bodily signs of this suffering and goes through flames without being burned or scarred. This suggests a realm of feeling or sensation separable from the body itself, yet not fully identified with the soul. In this way hagiographical figurations meet theological orthodoxy, for what Christina purges through her suffering is not the body, hypostasized and differentiated from the soul, but rather the will, which in turning toward what is not God brings sin into the world.[99] The language of bodily suffering is used analogically. Jacques, on the other hand, struggles between two conceptions of the relationship between the body and suffering. One, like that suggested in Thomas's text, points to the role of the will, which is not purely body or soul, in suffering and atonement. The other view elides the distinction between flesh and body found in the Pauline text, associating women as body with fallen humanity and thereby seeking salvation through and in the suffering of women's bodies.[100] While Bynum is clearly correct to argue that pain, in the Middle Ages, is understood as "the experience of a psychosomatic unit,"[101] underlining the identity of subjectivity with both body and soul, many medieval texts emphasize the will as that which brings the two realms together and therefore is the locus of suffering for sin, whether one's own or that of others. This is the theological point made at times even in the hagiographies, countering their tendency toward the objective and external with its often misogynistic overtones; the point is made explicit by the beguine mystics.

What we have in the *Life* of Christina and that of Marie, finally, are presentations of women living in the world for others, in which their actions take the form, almost solely, of ascetic and contemplative work for sinners on earth and in purgatory. Action and contemplation are brought together with only minimal contradiction. This accords with the theological visions of Hadewijch and Mechthild, for whom it is necessary to suffer with Christ in his humanity in order to be God with his divinity.[102] Although without stressing the ascetic and bodily manifestations of this imitation and union with Christ's redemptive activity, Hadewijch and Mechthild's formulations clearly parallel hagiographical presentations, such as Thomas's depiction of Lutgard of Aywières. Lutgard is able to devote continual fasts and prayers for sinners both in this world and the next while living first as a Benedictine and then a Cistercian nun. According to Thomas, she had no desire for a more active life in the world. The themes of prayer and ascetic substitutions for sinners in imitation of the life of Christ, then, unite the spirituality of the beguines with that of the Cistercian nuns.

Yet, as I have suggested, this view of female spirituality—particularly insofar as the bodily nature of redemptive suffering is emphasized—reflects contemporary male expectations and desires. While scholars have amply documented the centrality of asceticism in medieval women's *vitae* and given nuanced and sympathetic interpretations of the theological significance of these acts, the ways in which they serve to reinforce male hagiographers' views of women and their spirituality need to be constantly reiterated. Not surprisingly, hagiographies most consistently portray saintly women as renouncing their desire for extreme poverty and action in favor of spiritual poverty, contemplation, and ascetic work on behalf of sinful human beings, for these practices accord with and reinforce the kinds of spirituality the church wished women to practice. Insofar as we find these activities and ideals repeated in women's writings, the reliability of male-authored hagiographical accounts is not greatly in question. But when the hagiographical and mystical texts diverge, as they do with regard to bodily asceticism and its significance, questions must be raised about who is writing and from what vantage point.

While the beguines clearly desired to model their lives on Christ's both in his union with God and his compassion for others, the understanding of how best to imitate Christ was subject to constant reinterpretation, revision, and scrutiny. Beginning with the desire to follow Christ in his absolute poverty and service to those in need in the world, male-authored hagiographies depict *some* women (and perhaps those considered to be most saintly by male contemporaries) as tempering and internalizing their ideals in agreement with existing female monastic practices. Begging is replaced by manual labor, hospital and other work by fasts and prayers for souls in purgatory. Independent evidence suggests that some beguines embraced the extremes of asceticism described in the hagiographies in attempts to achieve union with God through the suffering of Christ;[103] yet we must question the extent to which the lives themselves reflect women's actions and to what extent they *shape* them. Just as in contemporary culture images of beauty produced by the media and other sectors of society are embraced by enormous numbers of women, so too the productions of cultural ideology directly shaped many medieval women's lives. While pervasive, however, these images did not go unchallenged. Mechthild, Porete, and Eckhart are allied in their attempts to temper hagiographical images and contemporary practices.

EUCHARISTIC AND MYSTICAL PIETY

Two final elements in the hagiographies of religious women from the thirteenth century, once again found in both beguine and Cistercian lives, must be mentioned: the emphasis placed on Eucharistic piety and the visionary and mystical life. Both have been much more amply discussed in the literature than the previous themes, and therefore require only summary comment here. Eucharistic piety, taking the form of devotion to the Eucharist itself, the feast of Corpus Christi, and devotion to the Sacred Heart,[104] is a direct extension of the Christocentrism of the hagiographies of holy women and in many female-authored mystical texts. Although the interplay between the body of Christ, his humanity, and women's associations with both are complex, the relations are signified in and through the Eucharist in hagiographical and mystical writings. The hagiographies show women combining extreme food asceticism with a desire to communicate frequently.[105] Their wish to suffer for others through fasting is directly linked to their nourishment through and by Christ's suffering body. Marie of Oignies, Margaret of Ypres, and Ida of Léau all are described by their hagiographers as reaching the point where they can eat only the Eucharist.[106] In fact, Marie is able to detect an unconsecrated host because she cannot digest it. Although representing women as focused on Eucharistic piety might be seen as a way of subordinating their spirituality to clerical mediation and control, in fact, when the clergy deny them communion, Ida of Léau, Ida of Louvain, Alice, and Lutgard (among others) are satisfied miraculously by God himself or a saint.[107] The later theme is repeated in a text authored by a woman; Mechthild of Magdeburg receives the Eucharist directly from John the Baptist—a vision that led to some controversy.[108]

In reception of the Eucharist, moreover, hagiographers depict the holy women as experiencing union with Christ not only as pleasure but also as bodily suffering. Many women's bodies were said to be marked miraculously in this identification by the stigmata.[109] Not only through food deprivation, but also through identification with Christ's suffering body on the cross and in the Eucharist, women were presented as suffering bodies redeeming themselves and humanity. Central to the hagiographical accounts of women's lives in the Low Countries, such practices most likely reflect and are shaped by women's attempts to follow Christ in his poverty, suffering, and humility within the confines open to them in the thirteenth century.

In addition, in both the hagiographies and women's writing, the Eucharist often serves as the opening for more extraordinary experiences of God's presence. As Simone Roisin demonstrates, in the Low Countries during the thirteenth century there was an unprecedented emergence of mystical hagiographies.[110] While Roisin devotes her attention to the Cistercian lives, she also shows how the particular forms of Eucharistic and mystical piety that inform those lives are found among the early beguines. The hagiographies of Marie of Oignies, Odilia, Christina, Ivetta of Huy, Margaret of Ypres, Lutgard of Aywières, Juliana of Cornillon, and the three Idas, are replete with accounts of visionary experiences, divine locutions and, although less prominently, mystical union. Hagiographers emphasize the "objective" aspects of these experiences, their locutionary and visionary content. In the hagiographies, as in Mechthild's *Flowing Light*, ample space is given to discussions between the soul, God, Mary, various saints, and demons. These dialogues serve to educate, warn, or prophesy. In many cases, the spiritual welfare of the living and the dead were made known, precipitating the saving work of the holy woman. These visionary and prophetic moments are also found in many female-authored texts. Mystical union itself, however, is most often marked in the hagiographies, as in the *Life of Beatrice*, by external signs such as swooning, levitations, stigmata, and tears. Here again the limitations of the hagiographical genre in depicting the internal experience of mystical union are made apparent. The mystical *modus loquendi* is, despite the recurrence of the visionary and mystical on a thematic level in the texts, notably absent, and with it the implicit and explicit critique of "female sanctity" inscribed in the mystical texts. Apophasis is foreign to the hagiographical genre, which depends for its existence on images of sanctity and divinity.

MECHTHILD OF MAGDEBURG AND MEISTER ECKHART

Both the Eucharistic piety and visionary-mystical fervor prevalent in the hagiographies of women religious and semireligious during the thirteenth century can be seen in the life and writings of Mechthild of Magdeburg. She integrates concern with the Eucharist as food and as body with her theological understanding of the role of the imitation of Christ and the apostolic life. Like other women known only through their hagiographies, Mechthild ties her Christocentric theology with a desire to live in spiritual poverty. Echoing another central theme of the lives, Mechthild is concerned to maintain the unity of action and contemplation, bringing together her mystical experiences with a life of charity and of discipline in the world.[111] She calls on the soul to work on behalf of others; her visions of purgatory and prayers on behalf of souls suffering there tie her directly to the beguine themes discussed above.[112] Moreover, Mechthild demonstrates a distinctively beguine approach to these issues, for her solitary, unenclosed lifestyle is crucial to her understanding of the necessity of following Christ in his suffering, loneliness, and exile.[113] Lutgard of Aywières, when elected prioress of her Benedictine convent, was forced to flee to a Cistercian convent in a country in which she did not speak the language, in order to maintain her solitude and humble position, but Mechthild chose a style of life that necessarily entailed exile.[114]

Mechthild had contact with larger communities of beguines, and her advice to them helps contextualize her own work. She criticizes some of the beguines she sees around her for their willfulness and their refusal to listen to the counsel and advice of fellow beguines and male advisers. The greatest spiritual danger, according to Mechthild, is that of false holiness, in which the body performs works while the soul is tainted.[115] Mechthild herself echoes two of the predominant criticisms leveled against the beguines by outsiders—lack of discipline and over-rigorousness, typically suspected as being hypocrisy. In all of her criticisms of other beguines, however, there is never any question of doctrinal error, and Mechthild is quick to exonerate her own teaching against claims of heresy and to defend her right to teach from the revelations given to her by God.[116] As a representative of the mainstream of the beguine movement, and one with a vested interest in keeping that movement alive as a viable alternative for religious women, Mechthild wishes to avoid the extremes of behavior suspected and prohibited by the ecclesiastical hierarchy.

There is no direct textual evidence to link Meister Eckhart and Mechthild, but there is external evidence to support the claim that Eckhart could have known Mechthild's *The Flowing Light of the Godhead*, written in Magdeburg and disseminated from there and from the famous convent of Helfta in the years between 1250 and 1274. Both Magdeburg and Helfta are fairly close geographically to Erfurt, where Eckhart received his early education and was prior of the Dominican convent from 1294 to 1302. Furthermore, Dietrich of Apolda, the author of a very popular *Life* of Saint Dominic was a member of this same community. His *Life* of Dominic, composed between 1287 and 1298, includes passages taken from the Latin translation of Mechthild's *Flowing Light*.[117] Mechthild's work, then, was being read and cited in the convent, most likely in the very time Eckhart was prior.[118]

More important, Mechthild can be taken as giving one of the clearest theological and mystical articulations of the beguine spirituality (and of the spirituality of the women's movement as a whole), which is centered on an understanding of God as love and the road through Christ's humanity to union with the divinity. Bringing together the themes discussed above, the spirituality was an attempt to understand the unity of action and contemplation in and through an imitation of Christ that leads to union with the divine.[119] This spirituality, clearly also part of mendicant religiosity, in particular that of the Franciscans, takes on a peculiarly visionary-mystical form in the north, where it is primarily disseminated by women. Eckhart would have come into close contact with the new trends in spirituality through religious and semireligious women to whom he preached and ministered.[120] Although he does not emphasize the humanity of the historical Christ, Eckhart does take up the ethical and this-worldly dimension of the beguines' thought initiated by and exemplified in the imitation of Christ. For Mechthild, as with many of the women religious and beguines, one followed the humanity of Christ through suffering and acts of charity. These acts become the locus of the divine within the world for women mystics such as Hadewijch and Mechthild, for when they follow Christ in his humanity they become one with the divinity. Their Christlike activities become that of the divine in the world. Hagiographers primarily depict the ascetic dimension of women's lives and the way in which their bodies are transformed into containers of the divine,[121] but Mechthild emphasizes the charitable dimension of her life and the way in which she is able to save souls through sharing in the compassion of Christ. She also increasingly attempts to save the suffering soul through her understanding of her union with the divine in, and as, love. Although this ties her to Porete, and thence to Eckhart, he is most clearly influenced by the aspect of her text and of the beguine spirituality that insists on the role of work and charity in the spiritual life.

MARGUERITE PORETE AND MEISTER ECKHART

So far I have looked at one aspect of the beguine spirituality, that most clearly documented in the evidence from hagiographers and the writings of Hadewijch and Mechthild of Magdeburg. Although Hadewijch and Mechthild spiritualize suffering, fourteenth-century accounts of persecutions against the beguines suggest that many women did take up the rigorous pursuit of the apostolic life depicted in the hagiographies, extending Hadewijch's and Mechthild's *imitatio Christi* to his physical suffering. Perhaps in response to this asceticism—or at least in response to the societal expectation of such pain engendered by the hagiographies—a different type of spirituality begins to emerge in Hadewijch and Mechthild, one most fully and clearly articulated by Porete. Porete shares the beguine-Cistercian milieu's emphasis on feminized divine love and with it much of the mystical eroticism of the Song of Songs found in the mystical hagiographies and the writings of the beguines. She rejects, however, not only the bodiliness and asceticism of the former but also the visionary spirituality prescribed for women in the lives and used as the basis for many women's own textual practice of mystical apophasis.

Radical asceticism, scrupulosity, and the concurrent sanctification of the body were attributed to the beguines by many of their contemporaries. Although the hagiographical accounts must be read with some suspicion, as the *Life* of Beatrice makes clear, the centrality of the hagiographical topos, together with other evidence, points to a climate in which asceticism and rigor were praised and expected. Not only are notable figures like Marie of Oignies and Christina described as being led to self-mutilation and extremes of sleep and food deprivation in their search for sanctity, but others may have attempted to imitate such "holiness."[122] When persecutions of the beguines began to increase after the Council of Vienne, a number of inquisitorial documents suggest that beguine and beghard communities followed these ascetic extremes.[123] The inquisitors link such practices to their understanding of the so-called heresy of the Free Spirit. Yet the actual source for many of the tenets of this heresy, Marguerite's *Mirror*, was an attempt to move away from male-prescribed and implicitly sanctioned extremes of physical deprivation.[124] Thus, as I will argue in the following chapters, Porete offers an understanding of the way to union with the divine that does not require over-scrupulosity and extreme asceticism, but rather mitigates the anxiety caused by those tendencies within the women's religious movement. Porete radicalizes a position first suggested in Mechthild's *Flowing Light*. Her move toward apophasis is allied with her attempt to subvert prevalent understandings of female sanctity as tied to bodiliness, asceticism, and visionary imagination. In this, Eckhart follows her.

Eckhart has the most obvious and textually defensible ties with this aspect of the beguine spirituality. Historical evidence shows that Eckhart could have known Porete's work, and there are textual parallels that clearly establish his knowledge.[125] On the historical side, Eckhart was in Paris in the year following Porete's condemnation and execution, staying in the same Dominican house as the man who condemned her, the Dominican inquisitor William Humbert.[126] Colledge and Marler point out that William Humbert had ordered all copies of the *Mirror* to be surrendered to him on pain of excommunication; yet as contemporary evidence shows, it would not have been at all unusual for copies to have been kept intact in the Dominican house at Paris.[127] Grundmann and others argue, therefore, that while it would have been impossible for Porete to have known Eckhart's work at the time she was writing, he might easily have known hers. Any explanation of textual parallels between the two, therefore, must work with the hypothesis that Eckhart did in fact know the *Mirror*. The condemnation of her book and her own execution, the fact and circumstances of which Eckhart would have been fully aware, easily account for his failure to make any allusion, direct or indirect, to her.[128] To understand and describe Eckhart's relation to the beguine piety more adequately, however, I must first give a detailed analysis of the texts of the three mystics, beginning with Mechthild of Madgeburg's *The Flowing Light of the Godhead*.

3

THE SOUL AS *HAUSFRAU*:
MECHTHILD OF MAGDEBURG'S
THE FLOWING LIGHT OF THE GODHEAD

GENRE, VOICE, AND STRUCTURE

Mechthild of Magdeburg's *The Flowing Light of the Godhead*, like many texts produced by medieval women, has been praised more often for its immediacy than for its literary style or rhetorical power.[1] Commentators generally take it to be formless, an assumption supported by the judgment that it was essentially a journal or diary of its author's inner life.[2] This interpretation gives further credence to claims for the immediacy of Mechthild's accounts, but to read *The Flowing Light* as a diary obscures the literary character of her descriptions of the soul and her own experiences. While genre theory is an increasingly problematic area in literary and textual criticism, various forms of reader-response criticism convincingly argue that the conventional categories by which a text as a whole is defined and understood significantly effect the meanings it generates.[3] As Kathryn Lynch explains, "genres are not instruments for prescribing meaning before the fact or classifying it afterward, but for interpreting and producing meaning in the moment."[4] For this reason, the claim made by Kurt Ruh and Alois Haas that *The Flowing Light* must be understood as a confession in the tradition of Augustine marks an important break with previous discussions of the text.[5] Readers should approach Mechthild's work not as a diary or even as a partial or "veiled autobiography,"[6] but as a theological reflection on the experiences of a Christian soul. The enormous differences between Augustine's and Mechthild's texts do not lie in their genre, and thus in their intentions and reception; rather, they stem from the nature of the authors' experiences, shaped, in each case, by the sex, social position, and historical time of the author. The two writers ground their descriptions of the Christian soul in their experiences and are led by them to adopt different rhetorical strategies.[7]

To explain the genre of *The Flowing Light* by means of the *Confessions* might appear to raise more questions than it answers, both because of the problems inherent in reading women's writings through male paradigms and because the structure and coherence of Augustine's text have been questioned by many critics, particularly those who wish to see in it the first example of autobiography.[8] Yet women often write both with and against male paradigms; as long as we recognize both aspects of this movement, comparisons are justified. Furthermore, autobiography is a modern category that carries with it all the truncations and expansions of the concept of the individual as it arose in the seventeenth and eighteenth centuries. For modern commentators, the first nine books of the *Confessions*, giving an account of Augustine's life, development, and conversions, from childhood to his famous vision at Ostia and return to Africa, are the heart of the book and its paradigmatic expression. Rousseau and other modern male autobiographers find the exemplar for their undertakings in these books. From their perspective, the account of memory in Book 10 and the spiritual exposition of the opening chapters of Genesis in Books 11–13 seem at best superfluous and at worst proof that a fully embraced Christianity destroys the individual. Mechthild's work, if taken as autobiographical, appears to support the latter notion, for almost all references to external circumstances and traces of her "individuality" are effaced.[9]

In response to this type of criticism of the *Confessions*, commentators have tried to show the text's unity while suggesting that it cannot be understood as autobiographical in the modern sense of the term.[10] Both Augustine and Mechthild are concerned not only with the writing of the self's life but with the interaction of the self and God. Both of their works are dialogical and can be understood only through the broader conception of selfhood that this implies,[11] for God is the life of the Christian soul and the external and psychological events, relations, and developments that most moderns identify with life have bearing only insofar as they relate to and draw the self toward its true existence in and with the divine.

Despite the similarities in form and intention between Augustine's and Mechthild's texts, there are crucial differences between them, grounded in Augustine's and Mechthild's divergent experiences and theologies. External and psychological factors play a large role in the first nine books of the *Confessions* because it takes Augustine so long to come to what he considers to be the true life. His path to Christianity and the development of his selfhood in relation to God are mediated by external events, books, and persons. The historical moment—that period of late antiquity in which Christianity was ascendant, but not yet completely dominant—together with Augustine's role as an educated man within, and yet slightly marginal to, the Roman Empire, are constitutive of his experience in central ways. Augustine's active life of striving both leads to and is questioned by Christianity. His life, furthermore, is essentially interactive and continues to be so after his conversion. God speaks to him through others and through the words of philosophers and of scripture. Even his most mystical moments are shared.

Mechthild's conversion to the religious life, on the other hand, is early, sudden, and direct.[12] Living in a predominantly Christian culture, conversion for her means not acceptance of Christian belief but the full devotion of her existence to God. For Mechthild, this occurs through immediate experiences of the divine, which continue throughout her life and are the direct inspiration of her writing. The external events of her life are of importance only insofar as they present the opportunity for her to follow the path of Christ in his life of contempt, exile, suffering, and death. After his final conversions to Christianity and the religious life, Augustine returns to philosophy, interpreting the human mind as God's image and scripture as divine revelation, and puts aside the narrative of his external life. In a similar manner, Mechthild recounts, interprets, and reflects on her religious experiences, the only sacred text directly available to her for commentary.

According to Augustine, human beings attain the eternal Word only fleetingly while on earth. At Ostia, Augustine speaks with his mother:

> And while we spoke of the eternal Wisdom, longing for it and straining for it with all the strength of our hearts, for one fleeting instant we reached out and touched it. Then with a sigh, leaving our spiritual harvest bound to it, we returned to the sound of our own speech, in which each word has a beginning and an ending—far, far different from your Word, our Lord, who abides in himself for ever, yet never grows old and gives new life to all things.[13]

Due to its transience and transcendence, direct apprehension of the Word is not sufficient to form the basis of the Christian life in this world, yet the eternal Word is mediated and made available to humans through Christ. As Eugene Vance points out, "in the *Confessions*, Augustine emphasizes his understanding of Christ more as an epistemological instrument than as a historical person in whose passion he might vicariously indulge."[14] Augustine's Christian life lies, rather, in scripture and the church, both instituted by Christ and mediating his salvific work to humans.

As a woman, Mechthild, unlike Augustine, was barred from ecclesiastical and teaching offices (although not from the mediation of the church, whose authority she accepted), and from direct access to scripture.[15] Like the great women visionaries of the twelfth century, Hildegard of Bingen and Elizabeth of Schönau, Mechthild finds a place from which to speak authoritatively of the Christian life through the presentation and interpretation of her visions and religious experiences.[16] She goes further, however, and makes the very transience of these visions and unitary experiences the basis for her identification with the passion of the incarnate Christ; her text becomes the record of this "alternation of ecstasy and alienation"[17] and of her theological reflections on the true Christian life and the nature of the divinity.[18]

To read the *Confessions* as an autobiographical work requires attention to only one facet of confession as understood by Augustine and his contemporaries. Confession was not only an admission of sins but also an act of praise and a profession of faith.[19] The relative paucity of the first type of speech-act in Mechthild's work obscures its confessional character; yet the praise of God that resounds throughout *The Flowing Light* is always coupled with the soul's expression of her own weakness and unworthiness. At times, this topos is taken to the point where the "I" no longer claims to speak; rather it is God who speaks through and to her. Here finally lies the deepest disjunction between Mechthild's use of the confession and that of Augustine, for it is in their rhetorical strategies, grounded in their different experiences, that the two theologians are the most divergent.[20] Throughout, the *Confessions* is a first-person prayer addressed to God; the crucial shifts occur when Augustine broadens the speaker of the prayer from a solitary "I" to "we" and his subjectivity expands to include all Christian people.[21] His autobiographical objectification of the self in the first part of the work is always facilitated by the double character of the pronomial "I," which can refer to the past self as well as the present self.[22] In other words, Augustine does not attempt to create an absolute disjunction between himself as narrator of the text and himself as the object of scrutiny within it, nor does he try to merge the narrating voice with that of its interlocutor, God. In this, Augustine, despite his humility before God, speaks with the authority granted men in late antiquity.

Mechthild's narrative style, however, reflects her lack of cultural authority as a woman; her choice of voice serves paradoxically both to dissolve and to multiply the speaker(s) of the text. She often writes directly in the first person, particularly in the later books when her confidence and authority have been established, yet the text is filled with dialogues and partial dialogues in which various personifications of the human faculties and virtues, the saints, and God speak in the first person to one another, and the narrating "I" is subdued. While in part grounded in the courtly tradition and its use of poetic dialogue,[23] the practice also has theological significance. The tension of this narrative style, which makes it difficult to differentiate the human narrator from the divine, is clear in the places where Mechthild suddenly shifts voices in the course of narration or only obliquely names the speaker.

Taken by many to be the first outpourings of Mechthild's soul, and hence to be marked by the most immediate expression of the experience of divine love and union, the first book of *The Flowing Light* illustrates her dialogical practice.[24] Although commentators read these sections as autobiographical and immediate, the third-person narrating voice is impersonal and distanced. Leaving aside for the present the highly ambivalent preface, most of the book is made up of dialogues between the soul and Love, God, Christ, the senses, and the body. After a dialogue between Love and the soul,[25] Mechthild tells of the true greeting of God in a detached and objectifying manner:

> The true greeting of God, which comes from the heavenly flood out of the spring of the flowing Trinity, has such great power that it takes from the body all its strength and makes the soul open to herself, so that she sees herself similar to the holy, and receives then in herself a godly glow. Then the soul separates from the body with all her strength, wisdom, love, and desire; but the least bit of life remains with the body, as in a sweet sleep.[26]

Having passed beyond the vision of the Trinity and the secret place where God plays with the soul "a game that the body does not know"[27] into "a wonderful place," the narrating "I" emerges for the first time in the text, only to express its inability to speak.

> Then they soar further into a wonderful place, of which I do not wish to speak and cannot. It is too difficult, I do not dare, for I am a very sinful human being.[28]

The "groundless soul," together with the "endless God," attains a state that the full humanity of the narrator cannot hope to speak of or reach. The common Christian belief in the inexpressibility of the divine within finite human language, so clearly expressed by Augustine in his account of the experience at Ostia, is reinforced by and conflated with the belief that the divinity cannot be apprehended by the body or senses, but only by the soul. What the soul wordlessly experiences cannot be spoken by the narrating "I," who is reduced to silence.

In the opening dialogue between the soul and Love, Mechthild describes all that the soul must renounce for the love that is God: all earthly honors, goods, and companions, as well as the health of the body, and ultimately, she suggests, the body itself.[29] While one remains in the body, the enjoyment of the divine presence is brief: "When the game is at its best, then one must leave it."[30] While lamenting the necessity of her return to the body, the soul accepts the will of God. The body, who greets her on her return, is seen as an enemy.

> Then the body says: "O lady, where have you been now? You return so lovingly, so beautiful and strong, free and full of knowledge. Your wandering has taken from me my zest, peace, color, and all my strength." Then she said: "Quiet, murderer, cease your lamenting! I will always guard myself against you. It does not trouble [us], that my enemy might be wounded; rather I rejoice in it."[31]

This enmity parallels the disjunction between the third-person narrative and the soul who experiences the divine, making it clear that the authorial persona cannot be equated with the soul, but rather with the earthly conglomerate of body, senses, and soul that is the human being. Mechthild, particularly in the first book, distinguishes between these three aspects of humanity and the narrating voice, who as a sinful human being marks their conjunction, yet is unable to contain or express the experiences of the soul. Mechthild emphasizes the disjunctions internal to the human speaker again, stating that her body is in torment while her soul enjoys high wonder.[32] Here, as in the previous passage, the narrator is able to give voice to the reluctant suffering of the body and the vigilance and joy of the soul, both of which are part of her full experience. At the same time the use of the dialogue form and third-person descriptive narration often allows the narrator to disappear or remain implicit.

The speaker in *The Flowing Light* is made even more ambiguous in those passages where his or her identity is marked only by the title of the chapter, brief external references, or oblique internal ones.[33] In the first book, for example, a series of chapters create a dialogue between the soul and God in which the speaker is marked only by the chapter titles.[34] In a later series, only the hortatory "du" and a subsequent chapter title tell us that the soul is responding to God and that he is the initial speaker.[35] Such hortatory passages are particularly ambivalent, for without the explanatory framework readers could understand them as addressed by Mechthild directly to the reader rather than by God to Mechthild, and to the reader only by extension. In other sections, only internal references allow us to judge who is speaking. Chapter 32 of Book 1, for example, opens with advice that could be given by either Mechthild, God, or Christ; only gradually does the real speaker emerge.

> If someone offers you honor, you should be ashamed. If someone torments you, then you should rejoice. If someone does good to you, then you should fear yourself. If you sin against me, then you should be troubled in your heart. If you are not able to be troubled, then see how grievously and how long I was troubled for your sake.[36]

However, the identification of Mechthild with the suffering Christ, both of whom are tormented and persecuted by those they attempt to advise and save, leads to a referential ambiguity here and elsewhere that Mechthild does not decide.

Readers encounter this ambivalence most clearly in the Prologue, which describes the nature and mission of the work:

> I send this book now as a messenger to all spiritual people, both bad and good, for if the pillars fall, then the building cannot stand, and it refers to me alone and with praise reports my mystery.[37]

Although these lines repeat words spoken by God to Mechthild later in the text,[38] some commentators have argued that the "I" refers to Mechthild or the narrator herself.[39] To say that the book refers to Mechthild alone and reveals her secrets, given Mechthild's self-understanding as one united with God and Christ, is to say that the book refers to God alone. Yet it is on the basis of this very identification that one is able to understand the speaker as God. Only when Mechthild has separated herself from all earthly things and come to nothing is she united with God and able to receive his secrets.[40]

A tension exists, however, between the collapse of the text's speaker and God and the fragmentation of the self into its constituent and conflicting faculties shown earlier. To return briefly to the comparison with the *Confessions*, Augustine speaks throughout as a human being, albeit one illuminated by the Word and praying to speak the truth garnered from the Word and not his own vain imaginings. Although Mechthild is less careful later in *The Flowing Light* to mark textually that the soul alone tastes divinity, the disjunction between the soul and the body, between heaven and earth, and hence between the human creaturely self and the heavenly inspired soul, remains throughout the text; only hopes of eschatological reconciliation point to the final union of these multiple voices and their union with God. In the book's early portions, moreover, embodiment is experienced solely as a division between the divine and the human. The conflation of the text's speaker with God is premised on the nobility of the soul and the annihilation of bodily and earthly cares and desires:

> "Where were you made, soul, that you climb so high over all creatures and mingle yourself in the holy Trinity and yet remain entirely in yourself?" . . . I was made in the same place by love, therefore no creature can comfort and free me according to my noble nature except love.[41]

Augustine turns to the human mind within which the image of God is still obscurely visible and hence is able to find a trace of the divine origin of humanity that is made clear and reconstructed through the mediation of the Word, but he maintains that the ability to return to this origin is fleeting on earth and cannot be translated fully into human speech. Mechthild claims both more and less. On the one hand, the human being in its entirety, both body and soul, is sinful, powerless, and unworthy, a "lame dog," "poor maid," and "despicable one,"[42] who is unable adequately to comprehend or voice the intimate secrets of the soul and of God. On the other hand, when the human self is brought to nothing through sharing in the suffering of Christ's humanity, the soul is released from exile, reaches her ground, and tastes the love that created her. Mechthild is able to speak as the blissful soul and the lamenting, tormented body; as the sorrowful, exiled soul and as God in his Trinitarian and incarnate forms.

Such considerations show the reflective and rhetorical nature of Mechthild's text and dispel the illusion of its immediacy and artlessness. Increasingly Mechthild unproblematically adopts the first-person narrative voice, displaying both her growing sense of authority and the normalization of her discourse. The highly traditional, allegorical, and glossed nature of the later books' visions of heaven, hell, purgatory, and the last days of the world add to our sense of Mechthild's rhetorical sophistication.[43] Mechthild's text, however, opens itself even more emphatically than does Augustine's to the charge that it lacks a coherent overall plan. The *Confessions* are highly structured, as becomes apparent when the work is viewed not solely as an autobiography in the modern sense but as a highly personal theological reflection on the life and development of a Christian and his relationship with God. Any such developmental pattern is very difficult to discern in *The Flowing Light*.[44] Written over a thirty-year period, the text shows certain shifts of emphasis and style, but the basic movements of the soul and the theological understanding that they engender are laid out in the early parts of the book. The oscillation between experiences of ecstatic union and divine presence and the lamentation of the exiled soul in the experience of divine absence remain the driving force of the work and a central structuring pattern. Although there are important shifts in Mechthild's understanding of the nature of human sinfulness and the true meaning of spiritual poverty, her reconciliation of these two experiences through "sinking love" and the imitation of Christ is present already in the earliest books. Mechthild does not work with a developmental pattern or a progression of stages, but rather models her book on the constant oscillation she finds in the Song of Songs, in which the beloved is continually lost and found again in the interplay of desire and fulfillment.[45]

In attempting to show *The Flowing Light's* self-conscious use of voice and other rhetorical strategies and to argue for a kind of coherence in its structure, I wish to give further support to the claims first put forward by Jeanne Ancelet-Hustache that the teaching in the book cannot be seen as a pure and entirely unsophisticated expression of the writer's experiences.[46] Like the fourteenth-century English mystic, Julian of Norwich, in the second version of her *Showings*, Mechthild has reflected on these experiences and given them theological shape and significance.[47] She offers what Marianne Heimbach calls a "theology of experience,"[48] which must be distinguished from the learned theologies of both monastic and scholastic teachers, yet still recognized as providing a distinctive teaching about God, creation, the fall, salvation history, and the relationship of the soul with God.

As I suggested in chapter 1, the relationship between "experience" and "language" in mystical texts is complex and problematic. Mechthild writes that the soul passes through visionary experience into the ineffable consciousness of union and that the latter is not "seen" by the eyes of the soul, but "tasted" in a more direct and inexpressible manner.[49] In the traditional visionary language inherited from Augustine, Mechthild here describes experiences that pass beyond even the "senses" that apprehend "spiritual" or imaginative visions.[50] She provides an apophatic moment in which her often highly imagistic language (whether understood literally or spiritually) is itself found to be inadequate. Furthermore, the allegorical and often traditional symbolism of the visionary accounts themselves (experienced by the spiritual senses) demonstrates the self-consciousness with which Mechthild describes her experiences, although without thereby obviating their claims to authenticity.

After this preliminary account of the nature of Mechthild's book and the best ways to approach it, I now turn to an exposition of its primary themes, beginning with the central role of love in both the initial act of creation and the return of the soul to God. I will then consider Mechthild's understanding of the nature of the union between the loving soul and God. This will lead, finally, to a more detailed examination of the role of the body and of the will in her thought, and the way in which the work of the soul on earth serves to mediate between two differing conceptions of human sinfulness and suffering. The analysis of Mechthild's writings will lay the foundation for my conclusions. Here we find first articulated the central theological problems concerning the body and the will that are developed and responded to in Porete's work and are the source for Eckhart's revisions of Porete's mystical theology with his renewed emphasis on the place of work in the mystical life. While Mechthild attempts to resolve the conflict between Mary and Martha through her suffering identification with Christ, Porete elides them both to free the soul. Eckhart, as I will show, in a very nontraditional reading, gives Martha the greater part.

LOVE AS THE GROUND OF THE DIVINE, OF THE SOUL, AND OF THEIR UNION

At the close of Book 4, which may mark the end of the book as it was first circulated in Mechthild's lifetime,[51] the reader is told the primary message of *The Flowing Light*:

> This book was begun in love, and it should also end in love, for there is nothing so wise or so holy, so beautiful or so strong, and so perfect as love. Our lord Jesus Christ said: "Speak father, I will now be silent as you are silent in the mouth of your son, enflamed on account of the weakness of the people; and thus my humanity spoke fearfully, because of the falsity of the world, for it rewarded me with bitter death."[52]

Here Mechthild succinctly delineates her conception of God, the soul, and salvation history, for the power of love drives the narrative of that story and the work of Christ, which serves to mediate God's love to weak and sinful humanity. Through her identification with Jesus Christ, who remains silent and suffers so that the Father's word might be heard, Mechthild comes to understand her own mystical life and prophetic mission.

Following 1 John 4:8, Mechthild identifies God with love: "That I love you greatly, I have from my nature, for I myself am love."[53] In the vernaculars of northern Europe, love is feminine; writing in one of these vernaculars, Mechthild establishes a central relationship with a feminized divine. Although God is experienced predominantly through the model of heterosexual love found in the Song of Songs, in which the feminine soul relates lovingly to Jesus Christ, Ulrike Wiethaus has argued that by identifying Christ with love, Mechthild figures Christ as a composite of masculine and feminine genders.[54] This language may reflect nothing more than the vagaries of grammar; yet, as we will see, the gendered nouns of the vernaculars are played on with great frequency by Mechthild and Porete, while apophasis and the negation of imagery is often accompanied by an attempt to find more neutral or neuter names or concepts for the divine.

As Margot Schmidt has shown, furthermore, Mechthild's nomination of the Trinity as a "playful flood of love"[55] brings together images conveying the force of the divine Trinity and the erotic exchange between it and the soul.[56] The phrase adds to traditional Trinitarian conceptions by highlighting the soul's ability to take part in the unceasing play of divine love within her, while at the same time bringing the feminine term "Trinity" to prominence along with those of "Father" and "Son."[57] The soul becomes a fourth feminine pole in the loving interchange between the persons of the Trinity, an interchange in which gender as well as being is fluid.[58]

It is for this reason that God created humanity:

"We wish to become fruitful so that humanity might love us in return and know our great nobility a little. I will myself create a bride for myself, who should greet me with her mouth and wound me with her appearance; then first will love occur."[59]

Although the Son foresees great suffering, he must eternally love humanity and by his words brings about its creation. With the fall of the soul, the Trinity remains true to her beloved, for in choosing the soul of Mary as his bride, God prepares the way for humanity's salvation.[60] In her discussion of Mary's soteriological role, Mechthild conflates the figure of Mary with that of the church; she assigns to Mary's soul the appellations and duties of the preexistent church as upholder of the Old Testament prophets and wise men and as nourisher and mediator after the ascension of Christ.[61] Once again, a female figure is divinized, for Mechthild suggests that Mary preexists in the Father just as the Son does. Mechthild thereby underlines God's faithfulness in love, for in choosing a new bride God works toward the dead bride's revivification and salvation, which the Son offers to secure on account of his love for humanity.[62]

The mission of love is to bring about this union between the soul and God: O blessed love, that was your mission without beginning and is still, that you bind God and the human soul together; that should be your mission without end.[63]

The work of love is twofold, both compelling the divine downward toward humanity and causing the soul to turn away from earthly things and desires upward to God. Love is able to perform this work, for she is herself God and able to compel him; at the same time love is the ground of the soul herself. Created by and for love, the soul's life truly consists in loving love.[64]

What should have been an effortless and unceasing flow of love between God and the soul, however, is destroyed by Adam's fall. Mechthild never gives an explicit account of the cause of this fall, although its origin becomes clear in her vision of hell. Just as love is the principle of unification, discord is brought about by hate: "I have seen a place whose name is eternal hate. It is built in the lowest abyss with the many stones of capital sins. Pride was the first stone, as is very apparent in Lucifer."[65] To the sin of pride, Adam adds disobedience, evil desire, gluttony, and unchastity.[66] These sins, however, all have their root in the misdirection of the love and desire owed to God toward oneself and external goods. Only by stripping the soul of these unworthy attachments and desires can the right relation of love for God be restored, and with it the soul as the image of God's love. The touch of divine love draws the soul to this act of renunciation and return. Once she has been wounded by the love of God, no created thing can satisfy her desire.[67]

The path toward true love, then, lies through the renunciation of the pleasures and beauties of the world. In the opening dialogue of Book 1, as I have said, Mechthild describes all that the soul has renounced for love, who promises the soul that her reward will be far greater than any of her sacrifices.[68] The soul claims that love has taken from her all worldly goods and honor, her childhood and her youth, friends and relatives, and the comfort and health of the body. The extent of this act of renunciation is vividly evoked later in the book when Mechthild describes the great sorrow that accompanied her first greeting by God:

> Whenever I saw anything that was beautiful or dear to me, then I began to sigh, and after that to cry and after that I began to think, to lament, and to speak in this way to all things: "Oh no, now look out! for this is not your beloved, who has greeted your heart and has illuminated your senses and has so wonderfully bound your soul, so that this manifold sweetness of earthly things does not draw you from him; moreover the nobility of

creatures, their beauty and usefulness, therein I will love God and not myself."[69]

The comfort and pleasure of the soul cannot lie in these creaturely things, for her birthplace is with divine love and her true beloved lies within the flowing Trinity.[70]

In her descriptions of the union of the soul and God, Mechthild at times suggests an essential union between them or, more accurately, a union without distinction, which is more radical than the language of the union of wills found in patristic, monastic, and other early mystical authors.[71] Yet in a passage cited previously (*FL*, bk. 1, ch. 22), she explicitly states that the soul, while unified with God, remains distinct in herself. Furthermore, the conjugal motif drawn from the Song of Songs, the motif that governs Mechthild's descriptions of union, requires the maintenance of two identities, although they are joined in the most intimate manner conceivable. I will show that while Mechthild offers the first glimpse of a union without distinction (and with it the stress on apophatic language necessary to such union), her concern is less with the "oneness" of God and the soul than with the fact that the soul in her barest ground is of the same nature as God, that is, love. In her insistence on the Trinitarian nature of the union between the soul and the divine, Mechthild avoids some of the theological difficulties faced by Porete and Eckhart, both of whom seem to take the union of the ground of the soul with God as the basis for a movement beyond the Trinity; when Mechthild suggests such radical moments, she also was criticized by her contemporaries.[72]

Mechthild's longest and most paradigmatic description of the soul's union with the divine takes the form of an allegorical dialogue between the soul, the senses, and God, represented as a beautiful youth. Following the Song of Songs and courtly traditions, the soul is represented as a bride arrayed in the virtues and awaiting her beloved.[73] On his arrival, the youth leads her in a "dance of praise."[74] The soul cannot take part in this mystical experience without being led by Christ:

> I cannot dance, lord, if you do not lead me. If you wish me to leap high, then you yourself must sing along. Then I might leap into love, from love into knowledge, from knowledge into fruition, from fruition over all human senses. There I will remain and yet I will circle further.[75]

The path from love through knowledge, fruition, and beyond human senses must be initiated by God and thus is dependent on grace. Yet the soul, Mechthild implies, has the right to demand the direct apprehension of God without any mediation.

While the senses offer the soul the cooling consolations of the intermediaries of the church to comfort her in the absence of her beloved, the bride refuses them all. Not even the mediation of Mary and the infant Christ is sufficient to her: "That is a childish love, that one suckles and rocks a child. I am a full-grown bride. I wish to go after my beloved."[76] The senses fear this full-grown union, for they cannot share in it and are blinded by the fiery heat of the Godhead. To remain in that place for too long leads to the death of the body and the senses, yet the soul is unconcerned, for her true nature lies there. To the lament of the senses, she replies:

> The fish cannot drown in the water, the bird cannot sink in the air, gold cannot be destroyed in the fire, for it receives there its clarity and its shining color. God has given this to all creatures, that they tend to their natures; how then could I oppose my nature? I must go from all things into God, who is my father by nature, my brother through his humanity, my bridegroom through love, and I am his bride without beginning.[77]

At the height of union, the shared nature of the soul and God is fully laid bare, as God tells the soul; "you are so strongly en-natured in me, that nothing can be between you and me."[78] In this experience of shared being, neither the soul nor the divine can be named or apprehended by the human, created realm of the senses and understanding.

The exchange between the soul and the divine continues unceasingly, implying that Mechthild does not envision or experience a complete loss of the soul into the divine, but rather an interchange of being between two persons. The soul shares everything in common with the Trinity except her uncreatedness. Even this is only partially true, for, insofar as the soul has her true nature in the divine, she exists before creation. The ceaseless exchange between the soul and the divine, then, might be understood as the interplay between the soul as precreated and her creation out of the loving interplay of the Trinity. Like a fish in the water, the soul is at home in the Trinity and experiences the world itself as an arid beach of exile.[79]

Such an interpretation of the passage accords with Mechthild's reply to those critics who claimed that in calling God the soul's father by nature, she denied the operation and necessity of grace in reunifying the soul with her creator. These critics, Mechthild claims, are correct to say that humans are God's children by grace, but she is also correct to say that they are his children by nature. The soul comes to know this through the illuminating grace of God. Grace, Mechthild implies, is made necessary by the fall and by human sinfulness, which clouds the eyes of the soul through which she recognizes that God

> has formed her after himself, he has planted her in himself, he has unified himself with her the most among all creatures. He has enclosed her in himself and has poured out so much of his godly nature into her that she cannot say anything else, but that he is, with all unifying, more than her father.[80]

Mechthild goes on to suggest the preexistence of all things in God before creation, writing that before God had become the creator he was like "a cell, and all things were enclosed in God without a key and without a door."[81] Creation itself, then, appears to share in a certain "uncreated" being in the divine. Furthermore, the impersonality of Mechthild's language here and the commonality of the image work as a form of apophasis; the highly eroticized and gendered language of union, which marks earlier passages, is superseded in order to uncover the realm beyond essence and difference in which the precreated soul shares her nature with the divine.

This passage, together with that cited earlier in which Mechthild claims that love is the birthplace and true home of the soul (*FL* bk. 1, ch. 22), point clearly to a differentiation between the soul and her ground in *The Flowing Light*. The distinction, which will prove crucial to the mystical theologies of Porete and Eckhart, allows for an understanding of the soul as always in part unified with the divine. Despite the fall and the present sinfulness of humanity, there is a preexistent aspect of the soul that remains one with God. Although the fall makes grace necessary, if one recognizes the natural affinity between the soul and the divine, one knows that the nature of that kinship and unity is never destroyed. By virtue of her lineage, the soul is one with the Father by nature, and as Mechthild will argue increasingly throughout her life, the recognition of that lineage makes unnecessary any special gifts or experiences of the Godhead.

THE SUFFERING BODY AND THE SUFFERING CHRIST

Given Mechthild's understanding of a preexistent aspect of the human soul, the role of the body and senses as constitutive of human nature becomes problematic. In the earliest sections of *The Flowing Light*, as we have seen, Mechthild argues that the embodiedness of humanity is a hindrance rather than a help on the road to union with God. Furthermore, she implies this is not only true on earth, but also after death. In a paradoxical image, Mechthild conflates Good Friday and Easter when, Love tells the soul, all her sufferings will be made good;

> But when your Easter comes, and your body receives its death blow, then I will go all over you and I will go all through you, and I will steal your body, and I will give you your beloved.[82]

The same disjunction between the fate of the body and that of the soul is found in a chapter entitled "God's curse in eight things":

> I curse you: your body must die, your word must perish, your eyes must close, your heart must flow, your soul must climb, your body must remain, your human senses must pass away, your spirit must stand before the holy Trinity.[83]

As if to reiterate the body's worthlessness, it is cursed twice—it must both die and remain on the earth. The human senses and speech are also left behind by the soul, spirit, and heart. These three terms are virtually synonymous in Mechthild's text, the heart being granted equivalence with the soul because it is the seat of love, the site of the kinship and equality between the soul and God.[84]

A pair of dialogues between the body and the soul, one of which was quoted earlier, reinforce the dichotomy, portraying enmity between the desire of the body for comfort and earthly goods and that of the soul for God. Both cannot be satisfied, but rather the fulfillment of the one's desire destroys the other's and causes torment.[85] The soul's anguish, however, is twofold. Not only must she fight the desires of the body and senses, but due to her embodiedness, the consolations of the experience of God's love and presence can only be fleeting. To keep the soul alive in her imprisonment, God grants her brief periods of unification with him, which Mechthild has Love describe as bread and water that keep the soul alive in the prison of the body.[86] Her true joy, however, can only come with the death of the body.

Mechthild comes to understand the necessity of this suffering in body and soul through her identification with Christ and his saving work.[87] For Mechthild, Christ's soteriological acts both repay the debt owed to God by humans for their disobedience[88] and show humans the path of purifying suffering and pain that they must follow in order to return to the unifying embrace of the Trinity. If, as Haas and Heimbach have argued, Mechthild works toward a reconciliation of the conflicting experiences of God's presence in ecstasy and the alienation of his absence, through her conception of sinking humility or love,[89] the roots of this rapprochement lie in her understanding of the necessity of following the path of Christ. The identification of the soul with the suffering Christ is repeated throughout the work, Christ's historical way being seen as an exemplar of the way of the loving soul:

> God leads his children whom he has chosen in wonderful ways. It is a wonderful way and a noble way and a holy way, which God himself went, that a human being might suffer pain without sin and without guilt. On this way the soul, who pines for God, rejoices, for she rejoices naturally in her lord, who on account of his good deeds suffered many pains.[90]

Mechthild's entire beguine way of life as she describes it in Book 4 reflects her desire to follow the steps of Christ, who suffered in lonely exile on this earth in order to make humanity worthy of the loving embrace of the Father.

Having received her first greeting from God when she was twelve years old, Mechthild later decides to leave her family and friends:

> I had long before desired that I might be despised through no fault of my own. Then I went, on account of the love of God, into a city, in which no one was my friend except one person alone. I feared that because of this person, holy contempt and the purity of God's love might not be given to me. But God nowhere deserted me, and brought me into such loving sweetness, into such holy knowledge, and into such ungraspable wonder, that I could barely use earthly things.[91]

By choosing to leave family and friends in order to dwell in a city in which she was unknown, Mechthild not only acts negatively—renouncing all earthly goods and pleasures for the love of God—but also positively, in responding to the example of Christ. Her deepening conception of what it means to follow the way of Christ also leads to an increasing, although never complete, ability to follow his path without lamentation.

When the soul's lament has freely turned to praise, she receives a vision showing the nobility of a life of consolation mixed with pain.

> Then our lord lifted up two golden chalices in his hands, which were both full of living wine. In the left hand was the red wine of pain and in the right hand the white wine of overpowering comfort. Then our lord spoke: "Holy are those who drink this red wine, for I alone pour both out of godly love. Yet the white is nobler in itself; and the noblest of all are those who drink both the white and the red."[92]

The way of pain is necessary because of the embodiment of humans, which can not sustain the eternal embrace of God without suffering and death, and because of their sinfulness, which must be purified in love and suffering. The relationship between these two causes of pain, however, human embodiment and sinfulness, is one of the most difficult aspects of Mechthild's work, and, as I have suggested earlier, the point about which she shows the most ambivalence and apparent changes of position over the course of her life.

THE LOCUS OF SINFULNESS: FROM THE BODY TO THE WILL

In Book 7, thought to have been written at the end of Mechthild's life while she was living at the convent of Helfta, appears a dialogue between the understanding and the conscience in which the former pities the latter, burdened with the guilt of all sinners and imperfect people. "They have free wills, so that they can go to the kingdom of heaven or to hell, or into a long purgatory: that is a great burden to you."[93] This passage not only demonstrates Mechthild's increasing identification with the mediating function of Christ and those who follow him, but also makes explicit where she locates sinfulness at the end of her life. The will sins and a good will makes up for the inadequacies and weaknesses of the body.[94] The point is made implicitly in an earlier chapter in which Mechthild disagrees with the common Christian teaching that it is human to sin, pointing to the example of Jesus Christ, who did not sin despite his humanity.[95] Mechthild calls her body sinful, but she goes on to claim that sinfulness is not natural to humanity or to bodies:

> This is human; hunger, thirst, heat, cold, pain, sorrow, temptation, sleep, tiredness. These are things which Christ suffered in himself, he who was a true human on account of us and with us. Moreover, if sin were merely human, then he should also have sinned, for he was a true human being in the flesh and an upright human being in wisdom and a constant human being in virtues and a perfect human being in the Holy Spirit, and in addition he was an eternal God in eternal truth and not a sinner.[96]

Mechthild does not conceive of the weakness brought about in humans by their embodiment as intrinsically sinful or as leading humans inevitably into sin. Only the weakness of the will, which cares more for earthly and bodily things than for God, causes human sin. What appears in Book 1 as a battle to the death between the body and the soul is now understood as an attempt to bring about the proper ordering of the human faculties and the human will. Due to the weakness of the will and the body, this process is painful to both, yet Mechthild increasingly offers hope of their eschatological reunion in a new, well-ordered and purified state.[97]

The growing respect for the human body accompanies an attempt to understand how, if at all, it might also share in the enjoyment of the divine presence as it is forced to share in the painful way of Christ. Mechthild explains that the revelations of the divine recorded in her text are experienced in all of her limbs: "I do not know how to and cannot write, unless I see it with the eyes of my soul and hear it with the ears of my eternal spirit and experience in all the limbs of my body the power of the Holy Spirit."[98] While the passage is primarily concerned with showing that the Holy Spirit enables her writing, it also suggests the involvement of her entire embodied being in this process. Whether this power is experienced as pain or pleasure is not clear, but in a later passage Mechthild explicitly speculates on whether the body might not receive some pleasure and strength through sharing in the divine embrace.[99] Physical suffering, moreover, is often said to be necessitated by the recalcitrance of the will rather than by the body's own evil. For example, God replies to Mechthild's prayers on behalf of a spiritual person who insists on following her own will that he will make that person sick, lame, dumb, and blind, thereby forcing her to turn her will to his sweetness.[100] God still makes his presence known and discplines the will through the human body, yet he names the will explicitly as object of that action.

The closing dialogue of *The Flowing Light* must be understood in relation to the ambivalence marked by such texts:

> Thus the tormented body speaks to the exiled soul: "When will you fly with the feathers of your desire into the blissful heights, to Jesus, your eternal beloved? Thank him there, lady, for me, that although I am despicable and unworthy, he nonetheless wished to be mine and came into this exile and took on himself our humanity. And pray, that he might keep me without guilt in his pure protection until a holy end when you, most beloved soul, turn from me."[101]

The body, though tormented and unworthy, is able to offer its thanks to the Lord for having taken on a body and hence human nature. Through the Incarnation, he opened the path by which humanity might be saved and bodies as well as souls kept from guilt. By empowering the will, Christ frees the body from guilt as well, for the body is only able to sin with the active direction of the will. The body still suffers, but in hope for the entire human being rather than in self-loathing.

The truly allegorical nature of this dialogical exchange is highlighted by the personification of the body, which appears itself to possess a will enabling it to follow the direction of the soul.[102] To give the will its own voice in the dialogue would perhaps lead to a clearer expression of Mechthild's theological perspective, yet that would deflate the allegorical movement, making the figures mere abstractions. This, in turn, would undermine the experience of conflict intrinsic to Mechthild's thought, for while allegories grounded in personification thrive on conflict, rigid personification creates stasis.[103] The complexity and ambivalence of Mechthild's attitudes toward the body is fully expressed in the soul's reply.

> "O my most beloved prison within which I am bound, I thank you for all that in which you have followed me. Although I am often troubled by you, yet you have come to my help. All your distress will yet be taken from you on the last day. Then we will no longer lament, then everything will please us well that God has done with us, if you will just stand fast now and have sweet hope."[104]

Unlike the soul, the body must wait until the last day for its full restoration; yet Mechthild's use of the first person plural to describe their joy at that time suggests that the soul's rapture will not be complete until the body is able to share it with her.[105] Furthermore, Mechthild maintains her Trinitarian center, for she writes that through obedience the soul is bound to God, the body to Jesus, and the senses to the Holy Spirit; in their refurbished state the body and the senses will participate in the full union with the divine Trinitarian flow of love.

THE WELL-ORDERED SOUL

With the displacement of the body as the locus of sinfulness, there is a corresponding shift toward concern with the will and its role in the imitation of Christ. Just as the will is not given a separate voice in the allegorical dialogues, however, it is also not generally the subject of special discussion; rather it is often the implied theme bringing together a number of strands in Mechthild's work. As we saw above, Mechthild does discuss the importance of free will and the power of the good will, in both cases using the same Middle High German term (wille). Throughout the text, furthermore, she speaks of the "desires" (gerunge) of the soul in both a positive and a negative sense.[106] However, there are many passages in which the will is not explicitly named despite the fact that the theological message might easily be conveyed in terms of volition. Mechthild's understanding of the way of Christ, sinking humility, and the well-ordered soul are all grounded, although implicitly, in an understanding of the importance of the will and its pivotal role in human sinfulness and salvation.

In her understanding of the path of Christ that the soul must follow, Mechthild speaks of the necessity of spiritual poverty and humility; the human will must empty itself in order to accept the will of God. Such elements are in evidence from the beginning of her work, when she writes that the soul must become nothing in order to achieve union with the divine.[107] A similar idea is expressed in God's injunction to the soul that she should "love the nothing" and "flee the something."[108] The soul's willingness to suffer God's absence for his honor also finds early expression when she claims that she would willingly go to hell to further the praise of God.[109] This conception is most fully expressed, as Haas and Heimbach have shown, in Mechthild's description of sinking humility, which hunts the soul up into heaven and draws her again into the abyss. She leads the soul to all creatures individually and says: "Now see, all of this is better than you are!" And she brings the soul then to the place from which she can go no further, that is, under Lucifer's tail. If the soul could then in her desire, according to her will, be there for the honor of God, then she would not be drawn away.[110]

In what Heimbach calls Mechthild's mysticism of ascension and descension, both the presence and absence of God are given meaning as part of the mystical life. Like the pilgrim, who after ascending the mountain with great desire always climbs down the other side with fear lest he fall over, the soul must take care to accept the descent from God with fear and humility.[111] The soul who is capable of experiencing this oscillation with indifference and unabating love has no more need to fear than do souls in heaven.

Despite this consoling claim, Mechthild is careful to differentiate between the state of souls on earth and those in heaven. The distinction is twofold:

> Moreover the poor body must feel both fear and shame in light of the darkness of its heart and the weakness of its external senses, for it is still untransformed by death. Although the soul is as beautiful in her body as in the heavenly kingdom, yet she is not so certain. . . .[112]

The body is still not transformed and the soul, although beautiful, daring, powerful, loving, gentle, holy, and sufficient, does not yet have the perfect certainty, strength, and constancy that will come to her with death (*FL*, bk. 5, ch. 4). The untransformed earthly body keeps the soul from enjoying her full heavenly state on earth, as does the continuing possibility of the will's reassertion of itself and rejection of the divine.

A growing concern with the problem of constancy is found in Mechthild's text alongside the emphasis on the good will. The primary danger for the soul, as expressed in the allegory of the pilgrim rising and descending the divine mountain, is that the oscillation between ecstasy and alienation will lead her to despair and loss of faith in God. In Book 2, the loving soul prays for the gift of fidelity.

> O lord, since you have taken from me all that I had from you,
> Allow to me still by grace the same gift
> Which you have given to a dog by nature,
> That is, that I might be faithful to you in my need
> Without any discontent:

This surely I desire
More intensely than your heavenly kingdom.[113]

The appelation "dog" or "lame dog," which Mechthild uses for herself on numerous occasions, refers both to her weakness and lowliness and to the fidelity the soul requires in order to remain true to her beloved in his absence.

In response to this lament, God gives one of several similar replies to the question of why the soul must suffer this oscillation.

My godly wisdom is so great on your behalf,
That I so order all my gifts in you
That you can bear them in your poor body. . . .
Your wounded heart's sighing and trembling
Has driven my justice from you,
Which is very just to you as to me.
I can not be alone away from you.
No matter how far we are separated
We still can not be divided. . . .
If I should give myself to you at all times according to your desire
Then I would have to lose my sweet dwelling place in you on earth,
for a thousand bodies could not survive the desire of one loving soul.
Therefore, the higher the love, the holier the martyrdom.[114]

The soul experiences God only intermittently because the body cannot bear his might and he wishes to maintain a sweet dwelling place on earth. More important here, however, God tells the soul that, despite their apparent absence from each other, they cannot be separated. Beneath the experience of his apparent absence lies the unperceived presence of God to the soul.[115]

The final goal of the soul on earth is to be well ordered and able to greet the experience of God's presence or of his absence with equal praise and love. This is the way of Jesus Christ, who came into the land of exile to suffer and die in apparent estrangement from the Godhead, while secretly sharing constantly in the undivided divinity. On this basis, Mechthild draws a contrast between the responses of Mary the mother of God and Mary Magdalene to the absence of the earthly Jesus.

Maria, our lady, spoke with her thought to our lord as often as she wished, and so his Godhead sometimes answered her. Therefore she bore her suffering in a seemly manner. For this, Mary Magdalene was unprepared. When she did not see our lord with fleshly eyes then she was uncomforted, and her heart bore all the while great sorrow and discomfort. She burned greatly in simple love, without the high knowledge of heavenly things, until the hour when the apostles received the Holy Spirit. Then for the first time her soul was wounded with the Godhead. But our lady was very still, when our lord rose up from the dead so nobly. Her heart had in godly knowledge the deepest ground of all humans.[116]

Unlike Mary Magdalene, who without the physical presence of Jesus becomes lost and inconsolable, Mary has developed her sense of the internal presence of God. While Mary Magdalene is wounded both by God's absence and his return, Mary is at peace in the ground of the human and the divine. This historical remembrance can be transposed to the situation of the loving soul, who imagines that God is absent when his presence is not seen and felt by the spiritual senses. Although God only at times directly responds to Mary's internal dialogue, she knows that he is always with her in the unity of the ground of the soul with the divine, whether his presence is apparent or not.

Mechthild calls the soul that approaches a likeness to Mary "well-ordered": "Love, your departure and your arrival are both alike welcome to the well-ordered soul."[117] The soul in this state prays not for God's extraordinary gifts but for constancy. She bemoans not God's apparent withdrawal from her but her own sinfulness and unworthiness, which draw her away from the recognition of God, her Father by nature.[118] Even these lamentations, however, are tempered by the possession of a good will, one directed toward the love of God and his praise. When Mechthild's soul mourns that on account of her weakness and that of the body she has not been able to accomplish all the good that she would desire for God and his honor, the Lord assures her that her will and desire will be the measure of her reward rather than what she has actually been able to accomplish.[119]

THE WORK OF THE SOUL

This brings us to the role of work in Mechthild's theology, and its relationship to the theological movement from the body to the will as locus of sinfulness. There is a decidedly ethical aspect to Mechthild's text; she laments not only over her incapacity to subsume her will to that of the divine, but also over her inability to do all the good she might. Out of Mechthild's mystical and visionary experience spring positive tasks and services that she desires to fulfill for God, and the neglect of these duties is experienced as sinfulness. For Mechthild, the mystic's or contemplative's struggle with the relative value of action and contemplation, traditionally understood as the conflict between Martha and Mary, is almost entirely absent.[120] Rather, the active life is seen as having its roots and impetus in the contemplative. But first we need to understand what, for Mechthild, constitutes the active life.

One of the first references in *The Flowing Light* to the active life exhibits its inextricable relationship to Mechthild's Christological mysticism.

> You should love the nothing.
> You should flee the something,
> You should stand alone
> And should go to no one.
> You should [not] be untroubled
> And free from all things.
> You should release the prisoners
> And compel the free,
> You should comfort the sick
> And yet you should not possess yourself.
> You should drink the water of pain
> And ignite the fire of love with the wood of virtue,
> Then you will live in the true desert.[121]

The roots of this teaching lie in the conception of the religious life as an imitation of the life of Christ on earth found among the early beguines and mendicant orders. Mechthild juxtaposes the ideal of spiritual poverty, in which the will renounces all creaturely goods for the one good that is uncircumscribed and unfathomable by the human senses, with the life of active service to others in imitation of the earthly mission of Christ; she ends with a reference to the way of pain and persecution suffered by Christ and those who follow him. The desert is no longer understood literally, but rather lies in the cities and urban centers where the believer follows a life of spiritual solitude while attending to the earthly and spiritual needs of others.[122]

Although there are other references to external acts of charity in *The Flowing Light*, particularly to care of the sick, as in the hagiographical tradition Mechthild presents her mission primarily as a spiritual one.[123] Her activity is twofold. The first practice is prayer, by which she attempts to draw sinners on earth and in purgatory back to God. In two places, Mechthild tells of visions in which the soul's tears and lamentations for sinners in purgatory lead the Lord to release them before their time.[124] She continually prays for those on earth in need or sin and for those just departed from the earth. In Book 5, Mechthild describes her three spiritual children, over whom she suffers and laments. The first are those in mortal sin, whose only hope lies in the fact that being still in the body they have a chance for true repentance. The second are souls suffering in purgatory, and the third and most difficult are imperfect spiritual people, those who outwardly appear good and wise but who have only a superficial grasp of God and care for their own words and their own wills more than for his.[125] Mechthild envisions herself as a mother to these children, dragging them before God and praying that he might bring about their repentance and forgive them.

The second pole of Mechthild's mission, as Heimbach has convincingly shown, lies in the writing of the book itself and the spiritual warning and counsel it offers Christianity.[126] Commanded by God and speaking his words to the people, Mechthild takes on an ecclesiastical-prophetic role otherwise inaccessible to someone without teaching office. The work in its entirety as an expression of a specific theological position is made possible by this visionary authority. In addition, individual visions and discussions with divine, saintly, or recently deceased persons allow Mechthild to offer more specific and practical injunctions to the church. She tells her readers, on behalf of God, what are the seven virtues necessary to all priests and describes the false virtues that most plague the church, among a host of other suggestions surrounding the sacraments and ecclesial life. Many of these passages, like some of those discussed earlier in this chapter, do not clearly mark the speaker, pointing to the pervasive and empowering ambiguity between the divine and human voices in the text.[127] In a more markedly prophetic vain, she recounts her visions of the last days and the coming of Enoch and Elias in which a new, more perfect mendicant order will arrive on earth.[128] Foretelling the future, Mechthild offers a subtle indictment of the comparative laxity of the Franciscan and Dominican orders.[129]

Despite her powerful use of the authority granted to her by vision-ary and mystical experience, the disparity between her status within society and the church and the task assigned her by God is felt and lamented by Mechthild herself. God's reply when she asks why he has chosen an unlearned woman like herself to speak his word mirrors the movement of Mechthild's mystical thought:

> . . . where I gave especially my grace, there I sought ever the lowest, smallest, most secret place. The highest mountains on earth cannot receive the revelations of my grace, for the flood of my Holy Spirit flows naturally to the valley. One finds many a master wise in the scripture who in himself, in my eyes, is a fool. And I say to you still more, that it is a great honor to me before them and strengthens holy Christianity in them very much, that the unlearned mouth teaches learned tongues of my Holy Spirit.[130]

Mechthild's lowly status becomes the justification for her lofty role, and the intensification of her humility creates a place where the divinity can speak to humans on earth. Mechthild is not only the bride of Christ but also his "housewife."[131]

Such metaphors elucidate the dual understanding of love found in Mechthild's text.[132] On the one hand, there is the experience of divine love in mystical marriage and union, and on the other there is the love that the desolate soul must, together with the suffering Christ, express for humanity. As we have seen, these two experiences of love have a dialectical relationship to one another. When the soul accepts the desolation of the loss of the experience of divine love and makes it an expression of solidarity with the suffering of Christ and his love for humanity, she comes to recognize her ground in divine love and returns to the presence of and union with the Godhead. Implicit in the later parts of *The Flowing Light* is the belief that God is always with the soul, regardless of her awareness of his presence in the ecstatic embrace; one comes to this realization by following the path of Christ. The suffering of the soul is first experienced as purely negative, the loss of divine presence. However, acceptance of this suffering as a necessary part of the way of Christ, of his love for humanity, transforms suffering into an expression of the unity, as loving, between the ground of the human being and of the divine. Suffering is not dissipated or treated as an ontological nullity, but is seen to be the necessary consequence, and hence marker, of love or charity when found on earth. But by turning one's unavoidable suffering into an occasion of loving imitation of Christ, the path from human to divine love, and the intrinsic relationship between the two, is made clear. Central to this movement is the redirection of the will away from the body and its conflicts toward submission to the will of God. The necessity of suffering is thus spiritualized, partially transcended, and given central theological significance. Even as she evokes the well-ordered soul, Mechthild continues to chide those who wish to be God with God without suffering with his humanity.[133] The ethical activity of the soul, moreover, her work in imitation of Christ while on this earth, is absolutely necessary to the movement of the soul back to her source and home in the divine.

Despite this resolution of the tensions within Mechthild's text, the complete integration of the human being and the divine will come about only with death and the resurrection of the body.[134] The final book of *The Flowing Light* is full of Mechthild's prayers for a good end, for as long as body and soul are in this world, their salvation and adherence to the will of God cannot be assured. Mechthild wrestles with this orthodox Christian view. She finally resolves her desire for assurance of the soul's steadfastness with Christian orthodoxy through God's promise to her that while the soul's constancy cannot be guaranteed, his can be. The greatest sin is "unfaith," the inability or refusal to believe that God will be faithful.[135] Despite this, the number of prayers for a good end throughout the work, but particularly in Book 7, suggests Mechthild's lingering fear that she will be reluctant to leave the body.[136]

For, as the closing dialogue quoted above shows, while Mechthild fears and distrusts the body, she also loves it and understands it as intrinsic to her humanity; it must share in the eschatological hope of the human being if she is to remain a substantial entity in her relationship with God. While Mechthild is willing to humble herself below the lowest of all created things for the praise of God and to annihilate her own voice in order to allow God to speak through her, she is not, ultimately, able to renounce her humanity or her embodiedness. For Mechthild, all of her humanity—body, soul, and senses—is created by and in the image of the divine, all exists precreated in the divine ground, and all must have a share in the final union of the human being with God brought about by the love that is the true nature of them both. This attitude toward humanity's bodily nature is typical of much late medieval spirituality,[137] yet Mechthild's text differs from hagiographical accounts of women's lives in that the will increasingly displaces the body as an adversary who must be quelled, closed off, and reshaped through ascetic acts. The body is redeemed by the will, through which it is linked to the soul. Marguerite Porete, however, wishes to transcend not only these extremes but the very association of women with the body, humanity, and their limitations, in order to achieve a lasting union with the divine on this earth, and hence the kind of absolute assurance of salvation that Mechthild was unwilling or unable to vouchsafe herself. Before exploring these comparisons more fully, however, we must turn to Porete's text, *The Mirror of Simple Souls*.

4

THE PROBLEM OF THE TEXT: MARGUERITE PORETE'S *THE MIRROR OF SIMPLE SOULS*

THE TEXT AS MIRROR AND AS ALLEGORY

The recurring ambiguities of Marguerite Porete's work, *The Mirror of Simple and Annihilated Souls and Those Who Remain Only in Will and Desire of Love*[1] are in evidence already in this long title, for it is not immediately clear whether the genitive article is objective or possessive. In other words, does the text promise to give a reflection or representation of the two kinds of souls named in the title (objective genitive), or is it a mirror or representation of some other entity that has been given to these souls (possessive genitive)? The ambiguity is deepened by the use of the term *mirouer* itself. While arguing that Porete uses the term only in its technically accepted sense, to designate that her work offers ascetical or mystical teachings and hence to mark its pedagogical purpose, Margot Schmidt shows that various other understandings of the term and its Latin equivalent, *speculum*, were available to medieval audiences.[2] The most obvious definition is that familiar to modern readers: "a smooth surface that reflects the images of objects."[3] In medieval usage, as in modern, the term is tied to conceptions of self-reflection and self-knowledge. But for the medieval reader the deceptive quality of mirrors plays a notable role in the understanding of the term. Perhaps a result of the poorer quality of mirrors generally available before the Renaissance, always implicit in the image was the idea that the mirror offered only the illusion of reality and that the reflection seen in it was deformed.[4] The myth of Narcissus, unknowingly in love with his own reflection, popular in both the classical and medieval periods, offers a cogent example of this aspect of the mirror image.[5] Throughout the *Mirror*, Porete describes the process by which the soul is clarified, thereby becoming a mirror without blemish or obscurity.

The Latin *speculum* also refers by extension to all painting or representation, whether reflexive or not. The term is therefore used to designate instructional works that attempt to give complete factual accounts of the divinity or the world, often taking the form of encyclopedias, or exemplary works representing every existing category of person or Christian.[6] Although Schmidt argues that Porete's *Mirror* is not a representation of the divinity, this is one meaning of the term suggested by the dialogue's own central interlocuters.

In the Prologue, Love, one of the main personified speakers in the ensuing dialogue, gives an exemplum in which she shows the purpose of the text about to be read. Love relates how a young princess, who lived in a strange land, came to hear of the great courtesy and nobility of Alexander the Great and thus began to love him. Her love caused her pain, however, because of the distance separating her from her beloved, and

> when she saw that this far away love, who was so close to her within herself, was so far outside, she thought that she would comfort her unhappiness by imagining some figure of her love, by whom she was often wounded in her heart.[7]

The princess takes this imagining a step further and has a picture painted that portrays the image of the king that has presented itself to her thoughts, so that by means of this image she can in some way make the king present to herself. The peculiarity of this story is only in part undercut by the fact that it appears to have been taken by Marguerite from an Old French romance based on the legends of Alexander, the *Roman d'Alexandre* by Alexander of Bernay.[8] The question of how it is possible to portray a person one has never seen is implicitly answered by the assertion that the painter produced a likeness of the image by means of which the princess had come to love the king, the interior picture found in her heart. The princess loves the semblance and reputation of the king, not the king himself. Yet this should not discount the reality of her love, for in the courtly ethos image and reputation are important extensions of the person.[9]

After telling the exemplary story of the princess, Love cedes the floor to the Soul, who applies the exemplum to the book in hand. Through the story, Porete not only shows her knowledge of the contemporary romance traditions, but also clearly situates her own text in relation to them.[10] The Soul's application of the exemplum affects a transposition of the values of the secular world, as found in the romance and courtly tradition, into the sacred realm. Her beloved, she says, is also a king of "great power, who was by courtesy and by very great courtesy of nobility and generosity a noble Alexander."[11] Like Alexander, the Soul's king is very far away from her and she from him; she has only heard his greatness spoken of and has never seen him. But unlike the princess, who must have a painting made according to the image of her beloved that was presented in her heart's imagination, the Soul's king gives her the image of his love:

> but he was so far from me and I from him, that I did not know how to comfort myself, and so that I might remember him, he gave me this book, which represents in some manner his love itself.[12]

The use of ambiguous phrases and fluid references, which begins with the title and runs throughout Porete's work, is strikingly in evidence here. While she is pointing to a crucial difference between the portrait made by the princess and the book as images of the beloved, the exact nature of the distinction is difficult to locate. Both are images or representations, less of the beloved himself, who is and remains beyond the reach of the lover, than of the love felt for him or of the image of the beloved found within the heart or soul of the lover. Yet the ambivalence of Porete's French allows *l'amour de lui mesmes* to designate both the love the Soul feels for God and God's love for the Soul, opening a dimension not found in the Alexander legend.[13] There is no evidence in the legend of mutual love or that the image of the king internal to the princess's heart is given by him. Although the great courtesy and generosity of the king would make him responsive to all those who love him, his love is not assumed to exist. The Soul, on the other hand, is confident that her subjective experience of love for the great king about whom she has heard is reciprocated and that this king has given to her an image of his love. Furthermore, because in Porete's mystical theology, as in traditional Christian thought, God is identified with love, a representation of his love is a representation of God him/herself.[14]

In the passage cited above, the book's authorship is pushed away from the human pen and onto God because he gives the internal image to the Soul that is externalized in the form of the book. The power of God insures that the image interior to the Soul truly portrays God, not just her subjective fantasy. Because of this, any deficiencies in the representation lie not in the artificer (as is implied in the story of the princess, whose representation of the image of her beloved can never be true to the original she has never seen), but in the one for whom the image is necessary, the Soul. The cause of this inadequacy is the same—the distance between the lover and the beloved—but because God is the creator of the internal image in the Soul and hence of the book, he is able to overcome this gap insofar as that is possible. In other words, the Soul is assured that the image of God's love given by the book is not purely subjective (as the princess's may be), yet the distance between God and the Soul is still maintained, thus making an image or representation necessary. The ambiguities of imagination remain. The Soul admits

> But although I have this image, it is not that I am not in a strange land and far from the palace where the very noble friends of this lord dwell, who are all pure, refined, and free by the gifts of the king with whom they dwell.[15]

The Soul has not fully attained her goal, which is to be with the beloved, for when that goal has been reached there will no longer be any need for the image or mirror. Only an empty and pure mirror can reflect the simplicity of the divine and of the Soul, leading to the difficulty and ambivalence of the text.

The question underlying these varied layers of ambiguity is now brought to the fore, for if God is the author of the book, and the Soul who speaks in the allegorical dialogue is, by her own confession, still in a distant land and far away from the divine king, the relationship between the divine author and the human, generally associated with this Soul, is uncertain. Porete is not claiming that a human author has been miraculously superseded. On the contrary, the following speaker in the dialogue is the Author, who clearly differentiates herself from God, while at the same time pointing to the hand of God or Love in the creation of the work:

> And thus we will tell you how Our Lord is not entirely freed from Love, but Love is from him for us, so that the little ones might be able to hear it by means of you: for Love can do everything without any misdeed.[16]

The author here speaks of God as another while also suggesting that God's love compels her to speak the liberating words of the dialogue through the human voice or pen.

Moreover, while the passage above clearly distinguishes the author, God, Love, and the projected reader, in the following chapter Love declares that she herself is the author of the work and explains why she has caused the book to be written in slightly different terms than those given previously:

> As for you little ones of Holy Church, says Love, for you I have made this book, so that in order to be more worthy you might hear of the perfection of life and the being of peace, to which a creature can come by the virtue of perfect charity, to whom this gift is given from all of the Trinity; which gift you will hear explained in this book by the intellect of Love in response to the questions of Reason.[17]

While the obliquity of the language allows this passage to be interpreted along the lines of the exemplum, where the book is seen as a representation of the king's love and the perfection and peace of those who share fully in it, the lines point more directly toward an understanding of the *Mirror* as a portrait of those souls who dwell with the beloved and carry his image within them. This conception of the work is often repeated. Love thereby returns us to the initial ambiguity caused by the use of the genitive article in the title of the work. Intimately tied to the question of who writes the dialogue is that of who, or what, it describes.

The answer to both of these questions, which becomes apparent as one reads further and comes to see more fully Porete's conception of God, the soul, and their relationship, is that both God and the Soul are the dialogue's subject and author.[18] The dialectic underlying Porete's account of the soul's return to God grounds this conflation, while at the same time allowing her to avoid the theological accusation of pantheism. Only insofar as the soul is and recognizes herself to be absolutely nothing can she begin to participate in the all that is God. The movement is also reversed, for insofar as the soul is something, she cannot be united with the divine no-thing. Porete's theological dialectic, which will be described more fully below, is augmented by the rhetorical and linguistic strategies of referential ambiguity to which I have pointed. This does not completely answer, however, the question of the *Mirror*'s authorship; the position of the effaced narrating "I" or "author" and her relationship to the allegorical dialogue that makes up the text remain obscure, as does the extent to which the Soul who takes part in the discussion, usually understood as representing the authorial voice, is herself simple and free.

Interpreting the text is complicated by an unreflective identification of the allegorical figure of the Soul with Marguerite Porete and an insistence on viewing that Soul as a static figure. Such oversimplifying readings are caused in part by the modern reader's unfamiliarity with the allegorical genre and its conventions. Therefore, a brief digression on medieval allegory and the nature of the *Mirror* as a personification allegory will be helpful. First it should be said that, even among those familiar with medieval genres, there is a tendency to view medieval women's religious writing as autobiographical.[19] I have discussed some of the dangers of this assumption in relation to Mechthild and her *Flowing Light of the Godhead*, while also showing in what way it is correct to view that work as grounded in Mechthild's experience. In the case of Porete and her *Mirror*, the problem becomes more complicated, for she takes further than does Mechthild the use of certain writing strategies, rooted in personification allegory, which create distance between the text and the writer's own experiences. While, as we have seen, Mechthild undercuts and masks the narrating "I," Porete eschews the narrative voice through her use of a continuous allegorical dialogue.[20] The almost complete effacement of any external narrating voice, however, causes difficulties with her use of the allegorical genre itself, for without a narrating subject to frame the dialogue, dramatic tension and plot are undercut and confused. This, I think, accounts for some of the difficulty involved in interpreting the text and finding a consistent narrative pattern within it.

In his study of medieval allegory, W. T. H. Jackson argues that for a literary work to be truly allegorical, it requires a frame that will control its development and plot. He further argues that in a full and complete allegory, "all characters should be personified abstractions and no human beings should intrude,"[21] the persona of the author often in practice becoming a character within the allegory itself. But Jackson misses the points of conflict involved in this description, for while plot and development require the possibility of change in at least some of the work's characters, the full personification of all the actors stifles such movement. As Jon Whitman shows in his study of ancient and medieval allegorical techniques, there is in all allegory a central tension between correspondence and convergence:

> The more allegory exploits the divergence between corresponding levels of meaning, the less tenable the correspondence becomes. Alternatively, the more it closes ranks and emphasizes the correspondence, the less oblique, and thus the less allegorical, the divergence becomes.[22]

In other words, the more fully a character is identified with what it is meant to represent or, conversely, the more literal the personification, the less room there is for movement, both of character and plot. Yet the more scope one allows the characters for development and action, the less tenable the allegorical identification becomes.

Writing of the twelfth-century Platonic cosmological allegory of Bernard Silvestris, Whitman demonstrates the importance of the development of certain liminal figures to help cope with the ambivalence of allegory. The *Cosmographia*, for example, requires a figure who can generate the action of the poem—the creation of the universe—and at the same time be able to judge that action. As Whitman puts it, there is the need for a figure who is both inside the narrative (generating action) and outside it (judging this action).[23] What remains implicit in Whitman's discussion is that the one who begins an action must in some crucial way lie outside the allegory, because of this very capacity to generate change and activity. Nature, who plays the dual role in Bernard's poem, is able to mediate between Silva (uncreated matter) and Noys (the shaping intellect) without dissolving into one or the other, precisely because she is capable of change in a way the other personifications in the poem are not. This very liminality, brought about by her capacity for change and development, allows Nature to function as an external perspective, a judging consciousness in the allegory. Furthermore, it is the combination of all these factors that makes her more "human" and less rigidly allegorical. As Whitman points out, the greater concern for this external perspective in medieval allegory leads increasingly to the presence of vaguely articulated "I's" within them, for example, the Lover in the *Romance of the Rose* and the figure of Dante in the *Divine Comedy*. Only when this "I" becomes "the source of narrative action, controlling events under the guise of merely responding to them," does "medieval allegory finally pass into more diffuse forms."[24] In other words, when the narrating "I" becomes the primary center of interest we leave allegory behind; yet without some intimations of the narrating "I," whether as the viewer of an allegorical pageant or contest, or the consciousness within which a psychological allegory takes shape, allegory is unable to articulate itself as a full-blown literary genre.

Unlike Jackson, who wishes to differentiate allegory as a genre that has already accomplished its own allegorization and hence almost defies further interpretive activity, I contend that if such a pure genre exists it is solely didactic and lacking in narrative movement.[25] For an allegory to be anything other than a gallery of static personifications it requires the possibility of change and development that a narrative frame alone cannot give. The progress of Knight A from point X to point Y cannot give satisfactory plot development without some change being caused within the characters by this movement and without some consciousness within the text able to register that change. The problem from this perspective, of course, becomes how to maintain continuity of allegorical characterization if such change is to occur.

The shift from didactic moral allegory to psychological allegory endowed with plot is traced by Charles Muscatine. He emphasizes the need to look for the antecedents of the allegorical mode of Guillaume of Lorris's *Romance of the Rose* not only in the didactic forms of classical allegory exemplified by Prudentius' *Psychomachia*, but also in the love monologues of Old French romance, which use common techniques of personification to dramatize internal conflict.[26] More explicitly, internal debates are often represented as arguments between two voices, given names such as *Amor* and *Raison*. Of course, Love and Reason are the two central combatants or debators in the *Mirror*, pointing to the possible influence of Old French romances on Porete's work.[27] The question of direct influence, however, is not crucial, for as Muscatine points out, the tendency toward representing psychological indecision as a debate between vying allegorical figures or personifications of psychological traits is part of many common and shared characteristics of the age: the trend toward self-reflection begun with the mystical theologies of the twelfth century; the predilection for debate found throughout the schools and in secular culture; and the general tendency toward personifying or dealing concretely with psychological or moral abstractions. Porete, like Guillaume of Lorris, shares in the general tendencies of her age.

Muscatine's study is helpful, however, in that it supports the reader's intuition that the Soul is not only an interlocuter in the dialogue, but also the arena within which the drama takes place. The *Mirror*, like the *Romance of the Rose*, brings the genre of personification allegory in its macrocosmic dimension together with the tradition of psychological personification found in the romances. The Soul is both a character in a larger drama, that of the movement of created beings to the divine, and the arena where that drama takes place. The outcome of the debate between Love and Reason will affect the Soul, who is not only a passive observer of their interaction but also the initiator of the argument and the final judge of its outcome. Like the liminal figure of Nature in Bernard Silvestris' poem, the Soul will ultimately be changed and transformed by the debate given in the *Mirror*. The other characters, due to the rigidity of their definitions or personifications, must either conquer or be vanquished.

One must avoid any reading of the *Mirror* that assumes a consistent allegorization in which all of the dialogical figures are static. The obvious point of change in the text is the Soul. Porete underlines this point by giving voice in the text to many human faculties and attributes—Reason, Intellect, the Understanding of Faith and that of Reason, even Love at times is understood as human—only once allowing the will to have its own voice. The will, seat of volition and change within the human being, must be subordinated to the Soul, for its abnegation and self-destruction enact the dialogue's central mystical moment. By making the volitional faculty a part of the Soul, the dialogue exhibits her development through the stages about which she, Love, and Reason speak. The importance of this strategy is shown by the impossibility of adequately representing the death of Reason. Since Reason is a vital interlocutor of the Soul and Love, asking for those explanations and clarifications needed by human souls who have not ascended to the heights of simplicity, the dialogue cannot continue without her input. Love is forced to take over Reason's voice after her demise, and eventually Reason merely reappears.[28] The death of the will, however, occurs near the close of the text, for without it further change and development are impossible.

Therefore, while it may be legitimate, given medieval textual conventions, to associate Porete with the voice of the Soul, we must keep in mind the distance she intentionally creates between herself and her text and ask why she creates this distance and how it challenges any easy identification of the Soul's experience with her own.[29] Furthermore, we must recognize the way in which this elision allows the authorial voice to pervade *all* of the interlocuters within the drama. These multiple identifications may be, in part, why all of the main speakers in the text are feminine. While all creative thought and writing may be grounded in personal experience, the current danger in reading women's texts is to deny the highly mediated nature of this relationship and subsequently to denigrate the philosophical, theological, or literary profundity of the writer in favor of claims to spontaneity (certainly not highly in evidence in Porete), naturalness, or subjective force.[30] In provisionally identifying the narrating "I" with the Soul, moreover, it is important to remember that the Soul is not a fixed entity, but is endowed with a will and is open to change and development. The Soul lies both inside and outside of the text, a central participant in the drama of ascent and transformation that is being enacted and the primary observer of this drama, which represents her proper relationship with God.[31] The many ambiguities that still remain are a direct result of the disjunction between Porete's view of the final state of the simple soul and the needs and demands of a changing and ever-fluctuating world.

The *Mirror*'s primary program appears early in the dialogue. Although a portrait of God, it is also a portrait of the simple soul who has attained an almost transparent unity with God. The first description of the soul takes the form of nine points:[32]

> [*Love*]. For there is another life, which we call the peace of charity in the annihilated life. Of this life, says Love, we wish to speak, in asking where one could find
>   1. a soul
>   2. who is saved by faith without works
>   3. who is only in love
>   4. who does nothing for God
>   5. who leaves nothing for God to do
>   6. to whom nothing can be taught
>   7. from whom nothing can be taken
>   8. or given
>   9. and who has no will.[33]

In a sense, the entire work can be taken as Love and the Soul's extended commentary on and explanation of this initial description, for each of its statements represents a deliberate provocation of Reason and the church's traditional understanding of the way of salvation. The teachings of what Porete calls Holy Church the Little[34] can be superseded only by these kind of shock tactics. Reason, jolted into attention, is driven to demand from Love and the Soul explanations of their seemingly paradoxical account of the simple soul. Throughout the text, Love or the Soul add new analogies and images meant to elucidate the absolute purity and simplicity of the soul unified with God. Through such shocks and ensuing dialectical explanations, Reason is led to renounce herself.

The *Mirror*, then, cannot be understood as static and descriptive. There is movement in the dialogue, not only in its account of the soul's transformations through the stages of being to the perfection of divine life, but also in its enactment of this transformation through the dramatic interaction of the personifications themselves. The difficulties involved in this dramatization result in many of the peculiarities of the text, for the change involved in the stages of being and the goal of absolute changelessness are in conflict. Before analyzing this tension, however, I will offer an account of the developmental scheme laid out in the dialogue, together with the understanding of the nature of the union between God and the soul that is its goal. I will then turn to a discussion of the place of the body, the will, and of works in Porete's thought, approaching the tensions evoked here from a new direction.

Mechthild struggles with the problem of how to reconcile love of and care for the body with the demands of the soul. She was able to overcome this dilemma by shifting the burden of sinfulness onto the will and emphasizing the centrality of human love and createdness as intrinsic to the path of return to the divine. Porete begins with a much more radical negation of human creatureliness, including the will itself. Given this rejection, we will need to uncover the place of the human body in her thought and of the works of the human being while on earth. The central problem for Porete becomes how to reconcile the simple soul's static peace with the continued movement and change of the world in which she lives, a difficulty that endangers the work of the text itself.

THE SEVEN STAGES OF THE SOUL

In Chapter 118, the Soul gives her most detailed and orderly description of the stages through which she must pass before attaining

simplicity and freedom. These include the ascetic, churchly, and contemplative practices advocated by the majority of thirteenth-century
religious and semireligious. In her description of these lower stages,
the Soul indicates with great specificity the degree to which she rejects
those forms of ascetic, ecstatic, and mystical piety particularly associated with women. She argues that the soul must move through seven
stages, marked, as we are told earlier, by three deaths; those of sin,
nature, and the spirit.[35] Subsequent to each death are two stages, one
characterized by a certain complacency and the other by a sense of
dissatisfaction that leads to the next death.

After the initial death, the soul is given divine grace and freed of
mortal sin. She follows the twofold command to love God and her
neighbor.[36] When this minimal Christian life seems inadequate, she
moves to the second stage, in which she abandons all riches and honors
in order to follow the evangelical counsel of which Jesus Christ is the
example.[37] This precipitates her death to nature, leading to the third
stage. Here she possesses an abundance of love and desires to do good
works. This leads, paradoxically, to her attempt to give up all external
works in order to be capable of greater love for God; this is the life
of contemplation and ascetic piety, marked by spiritual poverty, fasts,
prayers, devotions, ascetic practices, and martyrdoms.[38]

> The fourth state occurs when the Soul is drawn up by the height of
> love into the delight of thought through meditation and relinquishes
> all labors of the outside and of obedience to another through the
> height of contemplation. . . . So the Soul holds that there is no higher
> life than to have this over which she has lordship. For Love has so
> greatly satisfied her with delights that she does not believe that God
> has a greater gift to give to this Soul here below than such a love as
> Love has poured out within her through love.[39]

The soul is so inebriated and blinded by love that she falsely believes
no higher fate is possible.

Mirroring the hagiographical accounts of many holy women in
the thirteenth and fourteenth centuries, Porete suggests that many
of her contemporaries are stuck on this level.[40] Such "lost souls"
are incapable of attaining freedom because of their refusal to see
that asceticism, contemplation, and spiritual delight do not represent
the soul's highest perfection.[41] Rather than taking the divine absence
as an intrinsic part of union with the divine, they attempt to elicit

experiences of divine sweetness through suffering, asceticism, and internal works. They are "merchants" who believe that one can barter with Love, and as such are unable to merit her courtesy.[42]

Freedom is attained only through the death of the spirit, which requires the rejection of both internal and external works. The first step toward simplicity is to become "bewildered"; although still "merchants" and "servants" possessed of will and works, these souls are no longer lost, for they recognize that there is a better being than nothing.[43] Recognition of their previous deceptions leads to the renunciation of the will in the fifth stage, engendering fleeting experiences of the complete transparency of the soul in her union with God in the sixth.[44] This marks the death of the spirit, which is twofold, involving both the death of reason and of the will. The relationship between these two deaths, represented dramatically in the text as separate moments yet described in the accounts of the stages as simultaneous, is unclear. According to Love's and the Soul's accounts, both reason and the will must die in order for the death of the spirit to occur and for the soul to move from the fourth to the fifth level of being. This may help account for Reason's inability to die completely, for as long as the soul clings to the will, the transition to complete union and simplicity is not possible. The seventh stage, finally, is that which awaits the soul on her departure from the body.[45]

The difference between the levels of being in the first two ways of life is between those souls who are satisfied with their present state and those who are striving to surpass their present level despite the fact that they are not yet sure how this is to be done; that between the fifth and sixth stages lies less in the attitude of the soul than in the way in which God is actively present to her. The Soul strains language to its utmost in her attempt to describe the "opening of the aperture" or the infusion of divine radiance into the soul that occurs at the sixth stage as a foretaste of the continual glory after death that is the seventh.[46] Although in the fifth stage the soul is freed of all things and transformed into divine Love, still there is no comparison between the simplicity and perfection of that stage and the radiance of the sixth. As Christ, the soul's spouse, explains to her:

> This does not hold in her [the free soul], says the spouse of this soul;
> I have sent you the betrothal gifts by my Farnearness, but no one
> may ask me who this Farnearness is, nor his works that he does and

works when he shows the glory of the soul, for nothing can be said of this except: The Farnearness is the Trinity herself and shows this manifestness to her that we call "movement," not because the Soul moves herself, nor the Trinity, but because the Trinity works in this Soul the showing of her [the soul's/the Trinity's] glory.[47]

Rather than representing a movement of the soul, the shift from the fifth to the sixth stages marks the (non)movement of the unified Trinity into her, by which she is shown her eternal glory, that of the Godhead itself.

Ellen Babinsky argues that the shift from the fifth to the sixth stages is a movement from union with the differentiated Trinity, manifest as Love (who is feminine), to that with the Father as the undifferentiated ground of the Trinity.[48] In places, however, Porete's language and its gender implications work in the opposite direction. Paralleling the distinction between the ground of the divine and the Trinity in Eckhart, the *Mirror* is more traditional and yet also more daring with regard to gender. Porete moves beyond the distinctly Trinitarian nature of Mechthild's understanding of union, yet does not postulate a distinctly non-Trinitarian ground as Eckhart does. While the persistence of Trinitarian language in Porete's formulation of the nature of the union between God and the soul in the sixth stage should be noted, furthermore, it must not be overemphasized. Like Eckhart, Porete stresses the oneness of the Deity over the persons, in keeping with her desire for an absolute unity between the soul and the divine. Unlike Eckhart, however, her language remains traditional, with little suggestion of a "God beyond God" such as is found in his work. Her emphasis is on the absolute unity of the Trinity in its source.[49] When this union is achieved the soul is not made masculine, but rather the divine is feminized.

Michael Sells suggests there is an alternative Trinity in Marguerite's text: Love (who is feminine), the Farnear (who is male and does not speak), and the soul (who is again feminine). In this way, Marguerite offers the possibility of a more gender-balanced Trinity alongside the traditional Father, Son, and Holy Spirit. While maintaining the language of erotic desire, with its stress on a male deity, she subverts this language through the relative silence of that male God and the prevalence of female-gendered voices throughout the dialogue.[50] Only when a state of complete passivity has been attained, however, do the soul and God become so united that no distinction can be made between her glory and that of the Trinity. As in many other places in the *Mirror*, Porete's use of referential ambiguity reflects the undifferentiated union of the simple soul and God. Where the masculine Farnearness represents the divine in its separateness from the soul, God in union with the soul is called *Trinité*, thereby effectively feminizing the divine and highlighting the soul's divinization.[51]

The soul paradoxically moves from striving and seeking after salvation and virtue to complete passivity with regard to these final goods and all other things. Central to Porete's text lies the dilemma already posed by Mechthild. In light of the counsel of perfection preached by the religious movements of the thirteenth century, the question was how much virtue, how many good works, and how pure an imitation of Christ was necessary to achieve salvation.[52] This becomes particularly pressing when extraordinary mystical and visionary experiences are understood to be marks of sanctity. In the absence of such experiences, the soul is desolate, as the writings of Hadewijch and Mechthild demonstrate. For Mechthild, the dialectic of God's presence and absence becomes a controlling theological principle; the absent and sought-after lover of the Song of Songs and courtly love traditions is used to express the interplay of ecstasy and desolation that marks her life. Porete's understanding of God as Farnearness derives from these same traditions.

As in Mechthild's *Flowing Light*, an ever greater awareness of sinfulness and of the inadequacy of human effort comes with increasing age. The inability ever to do all the good one is capable of becomes itself a block to God. Where Mechthild ultimately comforts herself with the belief that the will to do good is sufficient and that the Christian is not held accountable for the weakness of his or her body, Porete reaches for a more radical solution with her claim that the will must be completely annihilated, creating an even greater certainty for the soul. Evidence that these concerns lie behind Porete's mystical theology can be found in Love's advice against feeling anxiety over sinfulness, the persistent tirades against those "merchants" who think that they can achieve perfection and salvation through their own works, and the insistence that the soul must pass beyond the virtues and their dominion under reason.[53]

Porete argues against the "peasants" of the life of grace and the "merchants" of the spirit, the former being those who are satisfied with external works and mere salvation and the latter those who believe that a rigorous adherence to the virtues, internal works, and the laws of Christianity will make them perfect. She uses courtly motifs and ideals in a religious context and thereby suggests the need for suffering and works as well as the necessity of surpassing them. The use of courtly images is far-reaching, providing a model for the universe based on hierarchical social structures. They are also the source or the means of expression of much of the apparent elitism and esotericism of Marguerite's worldview. All medieval views of heaven were essentially hierarchical, but the exclusionary nature of this conception is not generally stressed. For Porete, on the other hand, hierarchy is all that will appease the Soul when she learns that even the "merchant" or "peasant-minded" soul will share in the kingdom of heaven:

> But I will tell you, says this Soul, what appeases me concerning such people. I am appeased in this, lady Love, that they are kept outside the court of your secrets, just as a peasant is from the court of a gentleman in the judgment of his peers, where no one can be, if he is not of the lineage—at least not in the court of the king.[54]

Those who forget or refuse to imitate the works of Jesus Christ's courtesy, "the rejection and the poverty and the insufferable torments"[55] that he suffered for humanity, are deemed unworthy of a place in the inner court, although orthodoxy insists they have a place in heaven. Although necessary, these works represent a trial that must be gone through and ultimately transcended.

At one point, then, the Soul expresses surprise and sorrow that those souls who are unable to understand the secrets of God and the simple souls, because reason and works still govern them, are allowed into heaven at all. Although according to Porete's conception of the stages of the soul these types of people should be higher than those who are satisfied only with salvation, her distaste for their striving after works leads to extreme statements.

> [The Holy Trinity].—I pray you, dear daughter,
> My sister and my love,
> For love, if you will,
> That you would speak no more of these secrets,
> Which you know:

The others would damn themselves with them,
There where you save yourself
Since Reason and Desire govern them
And Fear and Will.
Know, however, my chosen daughter
That paradise is given to them.
The Chosen Soul.—Paradise? says this chosen one, would you not accord to them something other? Thus also murderers will have it, if they would cry mercy. But I will keep silent in spite of this, since you wish it.[56]

We seem to be in a different world than that of Mechthild, whose concern for the honor of God does not lessen her mercy for sinners, but rather increases it. For Mechthild, any sin against God is an affront to the right order that she seeks to redress, hoping by her tears and repentance to bring souls to paradise. For Porete, the social elitism of the age, whereby only those who through arduous testing exhibit the correct and worthy lineage, makes such vicarious atonement appear meaningless. Her perfectionist stance increases the anxiety caused by any failure to imitate perfectly the life of Christ and to live according to the virtues. Yet it is this unbearable anxiety that the soul wishes to transcend, together with her enslavement to reason and the virtues. Paradoxically, Porete subverts the traditional hierarchy of Christian and noble perfection, that very hierarchy her own talk of the soul's seven stages seems to accentuate, for those who learn *not* to strive after virtue are the "highest" and closest to God.

THE PLACE OF THE VIRTUES,
THE SACRAMENTS, AND CHRIST

The theme of taking leave of the virtues is found in the early parts of Porete's text and is one to which she often returns. It is also one of the sources of her condemnation, excerpts from the work dealing with this issue appearing in at least two of the passages chosen for censure.[57] The earliest discussions appear in commentaries on the nine points quoted earlier. In the chapter following that description of the simple soul, such a soul who is saved by faith without works is shown taking leave of the virtues:

Virtues, I take leave of you forever,
I will have a heart most open and gay;
Your service is too constant, you know well.
One time I placed my heart in you, without any disservice,
You know that I was entirely abandoned to you;
I was thus a slave to you; now I am freed.[58]

As the Soul goes on to explain, she is now no longer subservient to the virtues, but rather they freely serve her. She has left the dominion of reason and the virtues, the life of the law, for that of Love. Only then, according to Love, are such souls free.

Here Love elucidates her purpose—to free souls from their suffering servitude to works, asceticism, and the cycle of ecstasy and alienation.

> *Love.*—When Love dwells in them [and] the Virtues serve them without any contradiction and without the work of such souls. Oh, without doubt, Reason, . . . such souls who have become free, have known for many days what Dominion usually does. And to the one who would ask them what was the greatest torment that a creature could suffer, they would say that it would be to dwell in Love and to be in obedience to the Virtues. For it is necessary to give to the Virtues all that they ask, whatever the cost to Nature. For it is thus that the Virtues demand honor and goods, heart and body and life. It is to be expected that such souls leave all things, and still the Virtues say to this Soul who has given all to them, retaining nothing in order to comfort Nature, that the just one is saved by great pain. And thus this exhausted Soul who still serves the Virtues says that she would be assaulted by Fear, and torn in hell until the judgment day, and after that she would be saved.[59]

Such souls, who live according to the demands of Love rather than of reason, cannot bear to live in subjugation to the virtues, for the demands of Love are too great. The relationship between suffering and the way of the virtues is stressed; Porete's theology has its impetus in her desire to surpass such torment in order to attain freedom. Suffering is also the source of the dilemma faced by Mechthild, for the greater her love for God, the more glaring her faults and omissions seem to her; the greater her ecstasy in the divine embrace, the more unbearable his absence. Against these agonies, Porete teaches that the will must be annihilated. To save "heart and body and life" and free the soul from the "great pain" demanded by the virtues, Love must free the soul from Love. In annihilating the will, paradoxically, the soul is restored to her nature.

As we saw earlier in Mechthild, the soul's pain both in the embrace of love and in its absence is understood as the result of human embodiment and of human sinfulness; a central difficulty in her work is the relationship between these two sources of suffering and distance from God. For Mechthild, suffering, although it can be mitigated through the attainment of a "well-ordered" soul, is inevitable as long as one dwells on earth. While early in the *Flowing Light* she conflates human sinfulness with embodiment, thus jettisoning all weakness and inadequacy from the soul, her work is marked by an increasing awareness of the spiritual nature of sin and the dignity of the human body as intrinsic to one's humanity. Yet the body's weakness—together with the dangers of the soul's inconstancy—endanger the peace of even the well-ordered soul. Unwilling to accept the orthodox Christian teaching about the inevitability of human sin, Mechthild is also pessimistic (one might, depending on one's view, say realistic) about the actual conditions of human beings in the world.

Porete repeats the claim that final perfection cannot occur until the body and the world have been left behind, but she still suggests that sinlessness or absolute innocence (and hence the end of suffering) can be attained by the soul on earth.[60] Sin is spiritualized and not identified with embodiment, although the body is accorded no greater stature by this admission of its innocence. On the contrary, it could be argued that Porete's position is predicated on a rejection of the body and its place as an intrinsic part of the human being, evidenced in her attitude toward the historical figure of Jesus Christ, his sacraments, and the visible church. Some commentators attribute the hostility toward Porete among her contemporaries to this aspect of the *Mirror*.[61] Not the claim, bordering on what later authorities termed antinomianism, that the free soul "gives to Nature all that is necessary to it without any remorse,"[62] a claim that seems to give too much to bodily human nature, but the preceding assertion that such a soul "neither desires nor despises poverty or tribulation, masses or sermons, fasting or prayers,"[63] leads to her condemnation. The positions, however, are linked, for insofar as attachment to createdness and the need for mediation is overcome, nature is freed from its servitude. Sin and the mediation it necessitates are, implicitly, "unnatural."

Only by renouncing the will and its works (including sacramental and contemplative practices) is the soul's true nature restored. This requires a rejection of all mediation, including the humanity of Christ.

As modern defenders have been quick to point out, the condemned clause implying antinomianism and an apparent subservience to the desires of nature and the body is followed by the qualifying claim that in such souls nature is "so well-ordered" that "it demands nothing that is prohibited."[64] Because the soul's will has become God's will, she is incapable of willing to do or of doing anything that is prohibited by the law and virtue. In her reading of Proverbs 23:16 where Truth says that one can fall seven times and still be forgiven, the Soul reiterates the assertion that the will controls sinfulness. She contradicts traditional interpretations of this scriptural passage, which read it as an assertion of the unavoidability of sin; rather, according to the *Mirror,* the text describes the will's ability to stand firm and unmoved by the lower impulses of the flesh.[65] What is implied here is a disjunction between the soul and the body, whereby the impulses of the latter have little or no effect on the will once it has annihilated itself and been taken over by God's will. In renouncing the reason and the will, the soul overcomes her only ties to the fleshly or bodily aspect of human nature and is no longer touched by their demands (except, the soul cautions, as they are necessary to maintain life).

Mechthild moves from placing the locus of human sinfulness on the body to placing it on the will, thus pointing to the necessity of correctly ordering the will and subordinating it to that of God; Porete goes even further. By calling not only for the unification of the human will with the divine, but also for its annihilation, she asserts the possibility of complete innocence while on earth. In other words, one passes beyond the stage of attachment to things of the body because one has destroyed the will that would wish to turn to these things. The body itself, since it has no agency, cannot reassert itself once the will is gone and replaced by that of God. The *Mirror* implies that those bodily aids to religion found in this world and instituted by Jesus Christ are also no longer necessary, for the annihilated soul does not need bodily support for her union with the divine.

The Soul and Love give an important role to the sacraments of the church, the works of the faithful, and the humanity of Christ in the lower stages of ascent to divine life. Yet the *Mirror* continually insists that the truly disencumbered, free, and innocent soul has passed beyond the need for such intermediaries between herself and God. In this regard, Porete's attitude toward the body and the humanity of Christ becomes particularly interesting, for in deemphasizing the body as a locus of sinfulness, she also deemphasizes it as the locus of salvific work. Christ's cross is curiously absent in the *Mirror*, and with it the idea of necessary suffering this image carried to late medieval audiences.[66] Suffering is transcended and the soul transfigured into the divine. This claim is implicit in Porete's insistence, expressed by both Love and Reason, on the doubleness and ambivalence of language, particularly when used to refer to the simple soul or to God. These "double" words cause trouble for Reason, who is able to understand them only in their literal sense and is thereby led into error.[67] Yet the simple soul not only must pass behind the corporeal, literal level of language, but even beyond language itself, both to describe God and to describe herself. Not only is all that can be said of God nothing and inadequate to him, but so also is everything said of the innocent and transparent soul.[68] Porete points to the necessity of an apophatic use of language for both the soul and the divine.[69]

UNION THROUGH THE ANNIHILATION OF THE WILL

The identity between God and the soul is purely spiritual. The likeness of her humanity to that of Christ, which plays so central a role for Mechthild, is unimportant to Porete. For Porete, the traditional Christian understanding of the human being as formed in the image of God is not a positive expression of similarity but rather of a radical dissimilarity that paradoxically leads to the identity of the soul with God. Central to Porete's understanding of the path of return is this dialectic of "the all" and "the nothing."[70] In a move followed by Eckhart, she takes the traditional image of the soul as wax, which receives the imprint of the seal who is God, to its logical extreme, emphasizing the passivity and negativity of the soul before she has been shaped by the divine image.[71] Rather than gradually re-shaping and re-forming the initial imprint, lost through sin and the fall, Porete demands that the soul return to this primal state of negativity in order to receive the divine imprint anew and perfectly. Only when the soul achieves full humility, recognizing her own nothingness in the face of the divine, can she be united with him and receive "the all."

Love.—It is fitting, says Love, that this Soul should be conformable to the deity, for she is transformed into God, says Love, through whom she has retained her true form, which is confirmed and given to her without beginning from one alone who has always loved her by his goodness.

The Soul.—Oh, Love, says this Soul, the meaning of what is said makes me nothing, and the nothingness of this alone has placed me in an abyss, below less than nothing without measure. And the knowledge of my nothingness, says the Soul, has given me the all, and the nothingness of this all, says the Soul, has taken litany and prayer from me, so that I pray nothing.[72]

Love and the Soul, then, continually undercut any positive statements made about either God or the simple soul. Both are without essence and hence unnameable. The language of the all and the nothing, furthermore, while grammatically masculine, may represent an attempt to move beyond gender differences. Porete moves to a realm of abstraction in which the apparent conformability of the soul to God becomes paradoxically the source of her absolute humiliation, which, in turn, is the grounds for her true conformity with the divine and her possession of "the all." The central implication for the corporeal life, however, is made apparent even in this passage, for when the soul has reached the stage of absolute negativity and passivity, prayer, spiritual exercises, and the use of words themselves become impossible.

Porete uses a variety of other traditional metaphors and analogies to express the unity of the soul and God at the fifth and sixth stages of being. She often takes the traditional image to its extreme in order to express her belief in the union without distinction of God and the soul.[73] For example, Love insists that fire consumes the entire substance of wood, which thereby becomes fully united with it, there being nothing left that is not fire.[74] In the same way, the soul is compared to a stream that on entering the sea is entirely lost in the larger body of water. Here again the smallness of the soul, her nothingness in comparison to the divinity, leads to her annihilation and absorption into the all. The tie to language is made explicit by Porete, for when the stream enters the sea it loses its name; its individuality and its designation are seen as reflections of each other.[75] Similarly, the soul loses her name and individuality when she becomes one with the divine.[76]

Porete occasionally uses more traditional formulas to describe the union of the soul and God, apparently maintaining that they remain two separate natures even while possessing one will.[77] She makes the traditional distinction between the human being who becomes God through grace and God who is divine by nature and emphasizes love as that which makes one out of two.

> [Love] This soul has within her the mistress of the virtues, who is called divine Love, who has transformed her completely into herself and united her to herself, which is why this soul belongs neither to herself or to the virtues.
> Reason—To whom then does she belong?
> Love—To my will that transformed her into me.
> Reason—But who are you, Love? Are you not one of the virtues with us? How can you be above us?
> Love—I am God, for Love is God and God is Love, and this soul is God by the condition of Love. I am God by divine nature and this soul is God by righteousness of Love.[78]

As with Mechthild, however, the traditional language carries the seeds of new teachings, for union through love leads to the discovery of the union of the ground of the soul or the virtual existence of the soul within the divine source. But where Mechthild combines her discussion of the ground and preexistence of the soul with use of the language of union of wills and the well-ordered soul, Porete eschews the latter with her insistence on the annihilation of the will. For Porete, union is not a *unitas spiritus* grounded in the will, but a transformation of the soul into the divine through its annihilation. By transcending the will, substance, and essence, Porete frees herself from the limitations of gender and created being.

THE BODY IN THE *MIRROR*

The question now remains to what extent this conception of radical union between God and the soul is predicated on a dismissal of the human body and of the sacraments and the bodily manifestations of the church's mission. This requires an analysis of the place of the body in Porete's anthropology and theology. Her position is difficult to ascertain fully, however, because of her reticence. Unlike Mechthild, who occasionally, and at crucial moments, allows the body to speak, Porete's allegorical debate never includes the body. Rather the Soul occasionally mentions the body (together with the soul herself) as an enfeebling encumbrance.

> The Soul.—Truly, says this Soul, my body is weak and my soul is fearful. For I often have care, she says, whether I wish it or not, from these two natures, which the free no longer have nor are able to have.[79]

There is an apparent confusion of terms in Porete's book. She uses soul as the general or common name for humanity's spiritual nature,[80] but also to mark the second of the three aspects of human nature. Porete seems to differentiate three aspects of humanity that parallel the three deaths the soul must die in order to become free: the body or nature, the spirit, and the soul. In the schema that governs the soul's ascent, the first stage is the life of grace corresponding to the body, the second the life of the spirit, and the third the divine life corresponding to the soul. The second spiritual life will end with the death of the spirit when the soul has renounced reason and the will. In the passage above, Porete is clearly referring to this death while discussing the problematic aspect of the human being as the soul rather than the spirit. It is unclear whether Porete's language is simply confused or whether we should take her literally to mean that all of the creature's human nature—body, spirit, and soul—is a burden and must be killed. From this perspective, the soul in her entirety must be renounced insofar as she is created and other than God. The problem then becomes how to speak about the human being or the soul once it has been annihilated in its specificity as a created being. This difficulty leads Porete to call the soul by that name even after the appellation is no longer strictly appropriate.

To return to the issue of the body, the soul in the fourth stage—the bewildered soul living according to reason, the virtues, and the will—is at the mercy of the feebleness of the body and her own weakness, for she is striving after good works as the way to salvation. For Porete, as we have seen, only when the soul renounces the will and the attempt to attain salvation through works can she control the body. The relationship between these two events is left unarticulated. Love is matter-of-fact about the connection. When the soul is freed from the encumbrance of reason and the will, the Sun of the Deity will illuminate her.

And when such a sun is in the soul, and such rays and such re-
splendence, the body no longer is weak, nor the soul fearful; for the
true Sun of Justice never salved or healed any soul without healing
the body, when he did his miracles on the earth; and often still he
does it, but he does not do it for anyone who does not have faith
in him.[81]

The passage points to a new respect and concern for the body, although
the ways in which its welfare is safeguarded are obscure. The passage
implies that when the soul has become united with God through
the annihilation of the will, the needs of the body are "healed" or
automatically taken away. If the will is the locus of sinfulness and it
alone feels the importunities and weaknesses of the body, it would
follow that without the will, the body will no longer cause difficulties
for the soul.

Although Porete here uses a reference to the earthly miracles of
Jesus Christ to support her position, later in the text she states more
explicitly that the human Christ and his sacraments are stages in the
progress of the soul that must be surpassed; the corporeal level of
love for Christ must be transcended. In this way, she subverts her
previous reference to the miracles of the historical Christ and their
lasting importance to the human being.

And the one who would be courteous should love only what he
ought to love. One does not love the Humanity, who loves temporality. And those who love the Divinity feel little of the Humanity.
One would not be joined nor united nor divinely filled who feels
corporeally.[82]

In a similar passage, Porete argues that in heaven there will be no
semblance of bread in the Eucharist, through which the humanity of
Christ is seen on earth, for it will not be necessary.[83] In other words,
the Eucharist is only for those on earth who need some corporeal
mediation between the human and the divine realms.

The general claim that humans must overcome the corporeal level of
love for God is not unusual. Bernard of Clairvaux argues that human
beings must surpass corporeal love for the human Christ in ascending
to spiritual love of the divinity with Christ.[84] Mechthild makes a
similar argument when she compares Mary Magdalene with Mary
the Mother of God. In The Flowing Light, the Virgin was praised for
her ability to recall and bring about the sweetness of God's presence

without needing his corporeal or physically sensed presence. Porete makes similar claims about the superiority of the Virgin Mary to Mary Magdalene and the other saints. Mary Magdalene is criticized for seeking God in the desert, for in doing so she shows her ignorance of the existence of God, without intermediary, within herself and everywhere.[85] The primary difference between Mechthild and Porete is that the latter explicitly argues that on this earth the soul is able to surpass permanently the need for any corporeal mediation between God and the soul, not only in the form of special gifts of God's grace, but also in the form of the sacraments and rites of the church. Moreover, Porete includes the works of what is considered the contemplative life— prayer, fasting, Eucharstic devotion—among those forms of mediation no longer desired or needed by the free soul. Only by annihilating the will and becoming disencumbered of all creatureliness can the soul and the body be freed.

Porete's intensified perfectionism subverts itself and frees the human being from the anxieties it engenders. Mechthild's ambivalence toward and respect for creatureliness, marked by her attitude toward the human body, keep her from making such radical claims; as long as the body is understood as having a share in salvation, its needs on earth must be met and can be dangerous. Such considerations are absent from Porete's work, in which no mention is made of a promised resurrection of the body. This again differentiates Porete's position from that of more traditional figures, such as Bernard, who despite repeated denigration of the body insist that the soul's happiness will not be complete until she is joined by her body at the final judgment. Greater danger, however, lies for Mechthild in the continued presence of the will. Porete, in demanding that all creatureliness be annihilated, overcomes Mechthild's fears of inconstancy.

It may be premature, however, to claim that Porete completely rejects the body, corporeality, createdness, and with them, the use of language. The *Mirror* itself witnesses to Porete's need for and drive toward language and mediation between God and other souls. Her continued dissemination of the work demonstrates its importance.[86] Yet unlike Mechthild, for whom work—preeminently, the writing mission given to her by God—is seen as a direct outgrowth of her mystical experience of union and loss, Porete's quest toward and claims for permanence of union create difficulties not only for human corporeality but also for the corporeality of her book.[87]

THE TEXT AS WORK AND
THE NEED TO SURPASS THE WORK

We are now in a better position to untangle further the set of issues concerning the subject matter and author of the text with which our discussion of the *Mirror* began. If, as I have suggested, one can at least in part identify the authorial persona with the Soul, the problem is still not entirely solved, for the Soul is not static, nor even clearly singular. In fact, the Soul shifts positions radically through the course of the dialogue. At one moment she appears to have reached the security of the unencumbered only to be found lacking in simplicity and detachment a moment later. For example, after the death of Reason in Chapter 87, there are a series of chapters in which the speakers are not always clearly labeled, pointing to a new fluidity of identity between Love and the Soul.[88] At the same time the claim is made that Reason, having been put to death, can no longer disturb the Soul. Objections, however, continue to be heard, for Love speaks for Reason so that the imperfect might come to have a better understanding of the way of return. It seems inevitable that Reason will reassert herself, for she clearly has not effectively been silenced.[89] If the trial of love, resulting in the death of the will, is more successful, it is only because the book ends shortly after this scene. Throughout the *Mirror*, then, the author's voice — whether identified with the Soul or, more accurately, seen as running through the various figures in the drama — is multiple and conflicting; when this multiplicity is overcome, the book is complete and all voices are silenced.

The central dilemma for the author is the necessity of explaining a state of being and of union with God that those who experience it recognize without words and those who do not cannot understand because of the distortions of reason and the will. In other words, how can one create a mirror or representation of that which cannot be represented?[90] Porete tends to describe the situation in terms of a dichotomy between love and reason, but there is a higher reason or understanding, the intellect of love, which is capable of understanding the glosses or second and hidden meanings of her words and of comprehending how they are not merely paradoxical or contradictory. For Porete, ultimately, as for many of the Christian mystics, love itself is a kind of understanding. But because of the necessity of demonstrating this double sense, or of attempting to show Reason the way away from reason, the book is filled with words that seem useless to those who live in the peace and freedom of simplicity. With the annihilation of the will, not only do the human body and the corporeality of Christ and the sacraments seem to become superfluous, but so does the work Porete has been called to do.

Toward the close of the book proper, marked by the song of the Soul, the "Soul who caused this book to be written" asks pardon of the simple souls for her prolixity. But, she claims, it is necessary because she is speaking to those governed by reason.

> Now I understand, on account of your peace and on account of the truth, that this book is of the lower. Cowardice has given refuge to it, which has given its perception over to reason through the answering of Love to Reason's questions. And so it has been created by human reason and human judgment; and human science and human judgment know nothing about the deepest love, deepest love from divine knowledge. My heart is drawn so high and fallen so low at the same time, that I cannot complete it. For everything that one can say or write about God, or think about him, God who is greater than what is ever said, is thus more like lying than speaking the truth.[91]

Despite her admission that the book is ultimately inadequate to its purported subject and speaks only of human things according to reason and its abilities, the Soul still maintains that it was brought about by Love.

> I have said that Love caused it to be written by human knowledge and the will of the transformation of my intellect, with which I was encumbered, as it appears in this book. For Love made the book, in unencumbering my spirit by her three gifts, of which we have spoken. And thus I say that it is of the lower life and very small, however large it seemed to be at the beginning of the demonstration of this being.[92]

The tense in which this claim is made is important, for the Soul implies that she has now arrived at that higher place and that the activity by which Love has caused her to write the book has itself brought about her freedom.

The process of writing the book transforms or transfigures the author in the same way that the Soul is transformed in the text, and the same transfiguration is meant to be brought about in the reader. This is the work that the author/the Soul/Porete has been called to perform. When the Soul completes that work, she is united with Love and it is possible to speak of Love herself as the author. Although the soul who has learned to live "without a why" might be unfit for or unable to carry out such a mission, Love is not. And it is precisely the simple soul who provides the space in which Love can operate in the world.

For Porete, once the task of unification between God and the soul has been accomplished, in theory the book is no longer necessary—it is an empty husk to be discarded and forgotten.[93] It is the means for other souls to come to union, but the Trinity asks the Soul not to disseminate freely the secrets that have been revealed to her, for such mysteries might lead lesser souls to their damnation.[94] The text itself, however, belies this injunction and the hierarchies on which it is based, for in it Love attempts to explain herself to Reason, albeit only in order to facilitate Reason's destruction. This contradiction points, I think, to the ways in which the *Mirror* continually undercuts its own hierarchies, for it is insofar as the Soul is nothing that she is all, insofar as she is liberated that she is perfect, and in that moment what is most hidden and distant becomes most clear. The text is only a partial and veiled rendering of that which is known by simple souls, but it also is instrumental in bringing others to this state. When liberation is achieved, the text has effectively subverted and annihilated itself.

As the Soul's song in Chapter 122 and the trial of love recorded in the appended chapters of the work (123–40) show, the final transformation of the Soul depends on the annihilation of all creatureliness within her. Love herself, insofar as she is created and human, must be overcome. Like Mechthild, the Soul is willing to be nothing and achieve full humility if that is the will of God. Yet again Porete goes further than Mechthild in her account of the trial of love by which the will is finally destroyed.

> Then in my meditation I considered how it would be if he might ask me how I would fare if I knew that he could be better pleased that I should love another better than him. At this my mind failed me, and I did not know how to answer, nor what to will nor what to deny; but I answered that I would ponder it.

And then he asked me how I would fare if it could be that he could love another better than me. And at this my mind failed me, and I knew not what to answer, or will or deny.

Yet again, he asked me what I would do and how I would fare if it could be that he would will that another love me better than he. And in the same way, my mind failed, and I did not know what to answer, any more than before, but again I said that I would ponder it.[95]

In assenting to these demands of the beloved, the Soul kills both the will and its desire.

If I have the same as you have, with the creation that you have given me, and thus I am equal to you except in this, that I might be able to exchange my will for another—which you would not do—therefore you would will these three things that have been so grievous for me to bear and swear. . . . And thus, lord, my will is killed in saying this. And thus my will is martyred, and my love is martyred: you have guided them to martyrdom. To think about them leads to disaster. My heart formerly always thought about living by love through the desire of a good will. Now these two things are dead in me, I who have departed from my infancy.[96]

Like Mechthild in her understanding of the soul as the "housewife" of God, Porete here claims that the soul must mature beyond the stage at which she needs the sweetness of love as sustenance. Porete goes further, however, in demanding that the soul surpass human love itself. Mechthild argues that in her maturity the soul must be well-ordered, subordinating her will to that of God; Porete calls for the complete destruction of the will, whereby the soul learns to live "without a why" as God does.[97] In this movement beyond human love and the human will, the necessity for works, either external or spiritual, is at an end. As the soul loses her agency, divine Love works in and through her.

Porete, in her insistence on the annihilation of the will and its goal-directed activity and the primacy she places on the *freedom* of the soul, speaks only fleetingly about the divine work in which the disencumbered soul shares. I have already discussed her claim that the simple soul takes leave of the virtues and has no need for masses, prayers, or devotions. While this claim is tempered by her assertion that such a soul never desires anything contrary to the virtues or to the will of God, thus freeing her from the charge of antinomianism leveled against her by contemporaries, she is still open to the somewhat anachronistic charge of quietism.[98] Despite her assertion of divine agency, Porete's reticence and emphasis on the lack of anxiety such souls will and should experience weakens her claim that the perfection of the annihilated soul is compatible with continued acts of charity and love in the world.

Early in the book, for example, Love argues that the annihilated soul would give to anyone in need all that she had.

> If such souls possess something . . . and should they know that others might have greater need than they, such souls would never withhold anything, even if they were certain that nothing would grow on earth any more, neither bread nor grain nor other sustenance.[99]

Yet this statement is preceded by one that, in emphasizing the perfection and peace of simple souls, subverts any claims for the charitable activity of the annihilated.

> But if this soul, who is at rest so high, could help her neighbors, she would aid them with all her power in their need. But the thoughts of such souls are so divine, that they are not detained by passing or created things, because they might conceive anxiety within themselves, and God is good without bounds.[100]

Because the simple soul is fully united with God and cannot know any lack, she cannot be troubled by the need of her neighbors and thus seems unable to work actively in the world. In stressing the freedom from anxiety of the simple soul, Porete downplays her related assertions that divine Love is able to and does, through the simple soul, respond to others' needs. Yet, as I will show, Eckhart elaborates on this second aspect of Porete's text and its alliance with central aspects of Mechthild's work in his understanding of the soul as virgin wife.

For Porete there are two loves, paralleling the double sense of all language; yet they are different from the two loves of Mechthild. This twofold love clarifies the Soul's paradoxical statement that love has saved her from love, for divine, uncreated love saves the soul from bondage to her created will and desire.[101] This is in marked contrast to Mechthild's views in *The Flowing Light*, where human love and the love one has for fellow human beings together with Christ provide a bridge to one's greater union with divine love. Mechthild implies that insofar as the soul is allied with love she preexists in the Godhead who is love.[102] Porete demands that the soul return to the state she was in before creation; the created nature of human love rules out any kinship it might have with divine love. Only such a radical negation of creatureliness will make possible the complete transformation of the soul into God which she desires.

Throughout the *Mirror*, there have been suggestions by the Soul and Love that there is a preexistent soul, since God has loved the soul without beginning;[103] the point is made explicit late in the text, particularly in the penultimate chapter where Porete describes the transformation of the soul from her threefold nature discussed above into the absolute simplicity of union with God as a return to her "first being."

> Now this soul is in the stage of the first being, which is her being, and she has left behind three and has made of two one. But what is this one? This one is when the soul is placed again in the simple Godhead, who is one simple being of overflowing fruition, in fullness of knowledge, without feeling, above all thought. This simple being does in the soul through charity whatever the soul does, for the will has become simple.[104]

Here Porete shows her greatest affinities with Eckhart, for she proposes a grounding of the soul's security in her precreated being in the source of all creation and of the Trinity. Love demands that the soul strip away all of her createdness, thereby enabling her to return to the pure passivity and receptivity of her precreated state. Once this nothingness has been attained, she can be transformed anew into the divine likeness. Through this transfiguration—the unification of the soul and the divine without distinction—she herself becomes the place in which the divine works in the world.

Although the sin that brought about the deformation of the divine image in the soul was one of the will, namely, its turn away from the divine,[105] the place of the created physical world in the divine plan remains ambivalent. Porete is generally indifferent and occasionally hostile to embodiment, and to those external and internal religious works she associates with it. This rejection, however, is a result of her desire to free "the heart and body and life" (*Mirror*, ch. 8) from the torments engendered by the life of the virtues and servitude to divine love. Yet while she attempts to describe a state of innocence in which both body and soul are free, Porete also describes the earth as a school through which the soul must pass on her way to salvation. These narrative stages necessitate that one pass through suffering works and transcend them, creating recurrent ambiguities within the dialogue.

The disjunction between the radicality of Porete's goal and her educational and progess-oriented scheme exacerbates the ambiguities and confusions within the *Mirror* and explains the difficulty many readers have in discerning any orderly narrative within it. Although I clearly disagree with those who claim that Porete's text does not represent a sustained narrative,[106] her attempt to compose one is constantly (and perhaps intentionally) undermined by the desired goal, a state of timeless and transparent union with the divine on this earth. Such a state is difficult to achieve while one is involved with the things of the world, or at least difficult to describe in narrative terms, as is suggested by the *Mirror*'s fluctuations and inconsistencies. Porete suggests that the free soul becomes the place in which Love operates, yet a certain ambivalence with regard to embodiment remains, an ambivalence perhaps brought about by her relationship as a woman to the contemporary culture's expectations about female spirituality.[107] In rejecting these prescriptions, with their valorization of suffering, Porete both rejects the mediation of the body and attempts to free it from pain. By elaborating the new relationship toward the things of this world suggested by Mechthild and Porete, Eckhart is able to follow Porete's radical vision—in which essences, as well as gender differences, are overcome in union with the divine—and reemphasize the demand for works of justice so intrinsic to Mechthild's dialectic of divine presence and absence. He thereby makes the detached soul the site of divine justice in the world, without destroying her freedom.

5

LANGUAGE AND ONTOLOGY IN MEISTER ECKHART: THE THEORETICAL FOUNDATIONS OF HIS MYSTICISM

To present Eckhart's mystical theology as a reconciliation of the mystical theologies of Mechthild and Porete, I begin with his Latin works, which elucidate and theoretically ground the ideas elaborated more fully in the German sermons and treatises. Like most contemporary commentators on Eckhart, I believe that both groups of texts demand careful attention, although the sermons have a certain primacy in that they express those aspects of his teaching he judged to be of the greatest and most widespread importance. As studies of mendicant preaching show, however, it is crucial not to distinguish too sharply between the orders' academic and more "popular" missions, for both are inextricably united in their understanding of the apostolic goal.[1]

In recognizing the centrality of the German sermons to any study of Eckhart's thought, we must admit the more uncertain nature of these texts. The Latin works that survive—the few questions, the biblical commentaries, and the prologues—are textually quite secure; they represent Eckhart's professional output and most certainly were produced in their final form by his own hand. The sermons, on the contrary, both Latin and German, are most likely the product of professional copyists, students, or women who had heard and transcribed them.[2] The authenticity of the primary themes and images found in the sermons is attested to by their repetition and elaboration throughout the corpus.[3] While this may be, in part, a function of the conservative nature of textual criticism and of the sermon form, it is also no doubt grounded in the relative consistency of Eckhart's thought during the period in which he preached the sermons. Although often quite novel in the presentation of themes and theological nuances, medieval preachers did not self-consciously strive for originality; rather, their practice was governed by pedagogical aims. Eckhart's sermons undermine the conservative and authoritarian nature of this tradition, yet they share its tendency to play variations on a few select themes.

Seen in this context, Eckhart's sermons are exceptional for the daring of their language and the radicalness of their mystical themes.[4] I am arguing, however, that a part of Eckhart's much-discussed originality is a result of his dependence on traditions within the church of his time that have not been adequately studied by most historians of Christian thought and mysticism. In particular, with the identification of *The Mirror of Simple Souls* as the work of Marguerite Porete, a reassessment of Eckhart's relationship to the women's movement and to the spirituality of the beguines becomes necessary. Of course, this influence alone cannot explain Eckhart; his distinctive voice arises out of his attempt to articulate the continuities of beguine thought and to give his own philosophical shape to these spiritualities through Neoplatonic and scholastic principles. Nor do I wish to weaken my own claims for the coherence and vigor of Mechthild's and Porete's work. I intend to show, rather, how Eckhart sought to place their ideas within the philosophical vocabulary he had at his disposal as a schoolman. In doing so, he gives the beguines' thought the semblance of scholastic legitimacy while radically subverting the language of the schools. The scholastic influences, moreover, have been uncovered and exhaustively studied by many commentators; the role of the beguine spirituality has yet to be fully assessed and integrated into readings of Eckhart's corpus. This and the following chapter will show the results of Eckhart's synthesis of beguine, scholastic, and Neoplatonic sources through an account of his mystical theology and the themes and linguistic practices he inherits from the beguines, develops, and brings to distinctive form in his evocation of union without distinction between the soul and God. Given the length of these chapters, and the complexity of the issues to be discussed, it might be helpful to give a preliminary account of what will be covered within them.

After an initial discussion of the understanding of language and gender that will govern my reading of Eckhart, I will turn to the account of religious language given in his more technical Latin works. Keeping in mind the deep interpenetration of language and ontology in Eckhart, I will then describe that ontology, focusing on the twofold structure of emanation that emerges in the biblical commentaries. Following the threefold Neoplatonic structure of emanation, remaining, and return,

I will then discuss the cosmic role of the Son and the nature of virtual existence in Eckhart's thought, before turning, in Chapter 6, to the German works and the two differing and complementary accounts of the return of the soul to God given within them. Here I will analyze the role of the will and its annihilation and of the "work" of the just human being, or the birth of the Son in the soul, in the return. Finally, while the discussion of ontology will offer a preliminary basis for understanding Eckhart's views on creation and creatureliness, it will be necessary to return to these issues, in particular exploring the way in which the "nothingness" of creation is played out as a mystical theme in the German works and the way in which a new relationship with creation is brought about through Eckhart's teaching on detachment. Only then will we be ready to return to the comparative project in Chapter 7.

MEISTER ECKHART AND GENDER

Eckhart repeatedly reverses traditional misogynistic language, which leads Jeanne Ancelet-Hustache to claim that he in some ways overcomes the prejudices of his age. While Ancelet-Hustache recognizes the many places in Eckhart's work where the common identification of femininity with matter, creatureliness, the senses, and other denigrated categories are found, she argues that the primary symbolic structure of his mysticism subverts his own assumptions.[5] Many feminist historians of thought, however, are moving away from the study of images of women toward that of the lived relationships between men and women, insofar as they can be recovered.[6] I wish to take up both historical projects, for when images and lived relations are juxtaposed they yield very different results than when they are examined separately.[7] Eckhart's gender imagery is worthy of note even without reference to the role of women in his ministry and as influences on his thought, but attention to the latter makes the imagery more striking and helps explain it. Before proceeding to the main reading of Eckhart's texts, then, it may be helpful to say a little more about the methodology that governs my study of gender within them.[8]

Any analysis of gender and its role in shaping thought and experience must distinguish between three different ways in which gender assumptions affect both texts and our responses to them. In her study of the images and experiences of women in twelfth-century France, Penny Schine Gold shows the necessarily complicated interaction of image, or ideology, and experience, and the care that must be taken in reading texts to recover the latter.[9] I think that a third level of understanding should also be taken into account, one made apparent by contemporary feminist debates in which there often exists a conflict between utopian conceptions of gender and the more practical demands of day-to-day political action.[10] Although far from identical, Christian eschatologies and modern Western utopias serve parallel functions in society;[11] hence it is useful to distinguish between the prevailing ideological constructions of gender, the lived relationships of men and women, and the eschatological or utopian conceptions of gender that may be uncovered in a given text or artifact.[12] What is important to remember with regard to the Christian Middle Ages, as with any period and place, is the enormous impact the eschatological ideal can have on the actual lives of men and women. Without making claims for the revolutionary potential of images or language, we must recognize that language does have some power to shape one's conception of self, others, and the world.

We should not, then, take Eckhart's occasional reversals of traditional misogynistic images as removing him entirely from the culture in which he lived, with all of its assumptions and prejudices, but it is equally misguided to assume that the ideology of gender in the Christian Middle Ages was monolithic and unassailable. Not only is the ideology itself multifaceted and diverse,[13] but there were also many ways in which previous discussions were transcended and subverted. There is constant slippage between the three levels I have delineated above; yet keeping such distinctions in mind can help us avoid distorting medieval texts, their meanings, and their implications. When Eckhart challenges traditional views on gender, for example, he does so in the name of his eschatological and religious views, not with an eye to political change in the world. Just as his seemingly radical mystical teaching has little or no bearing upon his attitude toward the church and its power structures, his idealization of the figure of the widow and the virgin probably has no direct bearing, in his mind, on sexual power relations. That said, it must immediately be qualified, for while there is no evidence that Eckhart intended to challenge prevailing conditions or conceptions of gender, his work has great potential for that effect. This is because of the ease with which his eschatological conceptions of gender can be seen as challenges to current ideologies and thus as reshaping and recasting prevailing gender differentiations.

It might be useful at this point to give an example of how I see Eckhart's work as more potentially revolutionary than he may have intended. In a sermon characteristic of his exegetical and preaching style, Eckhart shows his ability simultaneously to accept and reject prevailing cultural definitions and norms. In Sermon 43, one of two he preached on the Lucan passage in which Jesus raises a widow's son from the dead, Eckhart plays on a twofold definition of the term "widow."[14] As in many other sermons, he begins with the more traditional understanding of the term, telling his audience that "widow" signifies the soul whose husband is dead. This reading follows the traditional identification of the soul as feminine, based on the grammatical gender of *sêle*, or soul.[15] It also follows traditional tendencies in personification in that the husband of the soul, according to Eckhart, is the intellect. The grammatical marriage further reflects hierarchical conceptions of gender difference common in the medieval period, in which the privileged intellect, the ruler of the soul, is masculine. Eckhart refers to the higher intellect, that part of the soul through which she shares in the nature of the angels and in their timelessness, as masculine, the man or husband of the soul. By playing on the twofold meaning of *man* in Middle High German—the term signifies both man and husband (as well as serf or low vassal)—Eckhart extends the traditional understanding of the subordination of a wife to her husband to a gender identification common at the time. Eckhart subsumes the common misogynistic identification of the intellect with masculinity into his mystical teaching, for only when the soul has a husband, i.e., lives in her intellectual part and not in the lower parts that have commerce with the world of time and change, does she share in the gifts of the Holy Spirit and become fruitful. Fruitlessness is signified, according to Eckhart, by the widow's son; his death marks her barrenness. Eckhart thereby gives an allegorical and mystical interpretation of an event in the historical ministry of Jesus.

This account, however, takes up only the first fifth of the sermon. In a characteristic move, Eckhart reverses the tenor of his reading by offering a new understanding of the term "widow": " 'Widow' in another sense denotes one who is abandoned and has abandoned. Thus we must leave and depart from all creatures."[16] The widow no longer represents the soul who is misguided and rejects her higher nature, but rather is exemplary—one who has detached herself from all creatures and images. The death of the widow's son now signifies the spiritual nature of her fruitfulness rather than its loss. Those who give birth spiritually, Eckhart explains, have no need of children. He thereby compresses and slightly alters Isaiah 54:1, proclaiming that the barren woman has more children than she who is fruitful.[17]

Before explaining this paradoxical statement, I want to accent the reversal on which Eckhart's mystical teaching is founded and some of its implications. Eckhart uses the traditional conceptions of masculinity and femininity found in the Christian West, but his more radical language and insights are reserved for that part of the sermon governed by a less traditional definition of the term "widow," and the less traditional gender conception on which it is based. In this language, the soul who has given up all things, who has been abandoned and has abandoned her husband, is most truly fruitful. Nothing is said here of a masculine part of the feminine soul to which she should bow or submit herself. Rather the soul without a man, the widow or, in other sermons, the virgin,[18] is the highest ideal and the most fruitful. The virgin, furthermore, is praised for her wifeliness, for mothering the Son in the soul, in a gesture that revalidates a commonly denigrated female role in ways available to all. Even though these reversals can easily be seen as part of Eckhart's general desire to shock and surprise his audiences,[19] we must be aware that such strategies would easily lead his hearers to question common gender conceptions and the hierarchies they support, as well as their assumptions about religious belief.

Where Eckhart's first use of the feminine image clearly identifies the intellect with masculinity, and the lower reason and the senses with femininity, his second elaboration of the widow image is not so much a reversal as a recasting of the entire dualism. The intellect is no longer pitted against the senses, masculine against feminine, but rather the feminine soul is understood as one who has radically detached herself from all creatures, images, names, and the dualisms that govern creation and language. In becoming widowed or virgin, the soul becomes truly fruitful; in giving birth to the Son in the soul, the feminine soul actually becomes the Son. This may be simply a revalorization of the masculine, but Eckhart's continued insistence on feminine imagery suggests a subversion and transcendence of the very dualism of gender differentiation. This position is consistent with the Christian belief, stated succintly in Galatians 3:28, that all will be one in Christ without regard to class or gender distinctions. Eckhart accomplishes this, however, not by effacing difference, but by simultaneously using feminine and masculine language for the soul and the divine.

Eckhart forcibly states that the soul must empty herself not only of those things associated with the feminine, the senses and lower soul, but also those associated with the masculine, the intellect; the soul accomplishes this as feminine. The feminine is given a valuation within Eckhart's mystical vocabulary equalled only by that of the Son; moreover the virgin/widow soul is the site of the union between herself and God. Again, this may seem to leave the earthly hierarchies intact, in that the soul is feminine and God masculine, yet by insisting that the soul as virgin wife is divine, Eckhart attempts to overcome all dualisms in his effort to describe the return to the source in the Godhead. He strongly suggests that all earthly dualisms and hierarchies are in some essential way without meaning. Such a reading is made more plausible by the *consistent* valorization of the feminine achieved through Eckhart's use of images.[20] While he generally avoids bridal and love imagery for the divine, with its emphasis on eroticism and heterosexual relationships, his language for the soul is consistently feminized even in and through her divinization. Although God is spoken of as Father and Son, these masculine terms themselves are primarily important in their relational aspect and are surpassed by the breakthrough to the more neutral divine ground in which the soul becomes the divine mother of the Son. By downplaying the centrality of God as feminine love, Eckhart highlights the primacy of the feminine soul in the divine interaction.

Whether Eckhart's mysticism was understood as subverting gender hierarchies and essentialist definitions of gendered identity by anyone other than some of his modern commentators—generally seen as anachronistic interpreters—will be discussed briefly in Chapter 7. For present purposes it is enough to acknowledge the central role feminine images play in his work. Eckhart occasionally uses the image of the widow derived from biblical texts, but he most effectively conveys his understanding of detachment through the image of the virgin, again biblically derived and central to the entire Christian tradition.[21] Through this image, together with that of the soul as fruitful wife, he brings together the two dominant strains of beguine spirituality we have seen exemplified by Mechthild and Porete, offering a new resolution of the beguine dilemma of the relationship between action and contemplation. Again, although these aspects of Eckhart's thought are most fully articulated and given their most characteristic expression in the German works, the theoretical and philosophical grounding for them are expressed, often in different terms, in the Latin commentaries. Before I can adequately address the mystical themes of the German works, then, I must give an account of the linguistic and ontological principles that structure them.

DIVINE PREDICATION

Eckhart gives the fullest statement of his technical understanding of religious language and of the relationship between language and divine reality in the Latin commentaries. The central problem, for Eckhart as for the entire Christian tradition, is stated by Augustine in *On Christian Doctrine*:

> Have we spoken or announced anything worthy of God? Rather I feel that I have done nothing but wish to speak: if I have spoken, I have not said what I wish to say. Whence do I know this, except because God is ineffable? If what I said were ineffable, it would not be said. And for this reason God should not be said to be ineffable, for when this is said something is said. And a contradiction in terms is created, since if that is ineffable which cannot be spoken, then that is not ineffable which can be called ineffable. This contradiction is to be passed over in silence rather than resolved verbally. For God, although nothing worthy may be spoken of him, has accepted the tribute of human voice and wished us to take joy in praising him with our words.[22]

Stated succinctly, the problem is how humans are able to speak about that which is beyond all comprehension and language. Augustine introduces an aporia into this already vertiginous problem by demonstrating that in the very moment of calling God ineffable— unspeakable—one in fact speaks about him. As I suggested in discussing Augustine's *Confessions* in Chapter 3, this problem is made most apparent in the mystical experience of the divine, an experience that is said to be beyond language and description.[23]

As Bernard McGinn has shown, it is useful to look at Eckhart's peculiar response to this difficulty in light of the traditional modes of divine predication known to medieval schoolmen. Following Harry A. Wolfson, McGinn describes the five methods of speaking about the divine distinguished by scholastic theologians: (1) the way of univocation or equivocation in which terms used of things can be used of God in exactly the same sense or in a completely different sense; (2) the way of negation in which the terms used of things must be denied of God; (3) the way of causality in which the terms used to describe things can be used to describe God insofar as he is the creator of these things; (4) the way of eminence in which the terms used to describe things can be applied to God in a higher or more eminent sense; and (5) the way of analogy in which terms used of things and of God are used in a sense partly the same and partly different.[24]

Eckhart most fully articulates his theory of divine predication in the commentary on Exodus, beginning with a discussion of Exodus 15:3, "Almighty is his name." After preliminary remarks on the subject of God's omnipotence, Eckhart outlines the four-part treatise on the divine names that is to follow:

> The first is what some philosophers and Jewish authors think of this question and of the attributes which name God, such as when God is called substance, or good, caring, generous, and the like. . . . Second, there is a brief summary of what Catholic writers think of these predications or names. Third, why do Boethius and the theologians generally teach that only two kinds of categories, substance and relation, can be used of divinity? Fourth, we will speak about the name more proper and especially particular to God, that is, the "Tetragrammaton," below under Chapter 20 on the verse "You shall not take the name of your God in vain" (Ex. 20:7).[25]

Although the first part, dealing with the opinions of the philosophers and Jewish theologians, begins with a discussion of the way of eminence, when Eckhart summarizes Maimonides' position, the way of negation comes to predominate, leading to some of Eckhart's most radical apophatic statements.

In his analysis of Maimonides, Eckhart argues that only the way of causality can be understood as applying to God, for humans can talk only about what God does, not about his essence. In Eckhart's view, the way of causality does not name God in himself any more than do other modes of predication. He argues;

> all things that are positively said of God, even though they are perfections in us, are no longer so in God and are not more perfect than their opposites. For example, mercy, devotion, and the like, are perfections in us, while anger, hatred, and the like, are imperfections. Just as saying that God is angry or hates, since these things are nothing, posits nothing at all in God save that he performs certain external actions which proceed from anger or hatred in us, so too the same is true of their opposites.[26]

The passage introduces the dialectic of all and nothing that runs throughout Eckhart's work. While at times he makes an exception for the attribute of existence (*esse*) and one-ness (*unum*), insofar as they name God's perfect self-sufficient being and the source of all being, these terms apply only when they are able to point—through their apophatic negation—to the unity of divine attributes and lack of limitation within the divine.

After showing why Maimonides and other non-Christians favor the way of negation, and arguing, together with the *Guide for the Perplexed*, that no dispositions can be added to God, Eckhart analyzes what Christian thinkers have taught about the divine names. He delineates the four essential principles for understanding the Christian teaching, the last of which is the Aristotelian and Thomistic axiom that all knowledge arises from the senses. For Eckhart, this axiom is taken as evidence that the way of negation is the most adequate method of attribution for God, who is absolutely one and united, unlike the multiple world of creation. Any human cognition or method of signification dependent on the senses and the created realm is inadequate for comprehending the divinity. Eckhart's emphasis on the principle of God's absolute unity necessitates his turn to the question of whether there is a distinction of attributes in God or whether the multiplicity of attributes is merely a result of the human mind's method of apprehending reality and the divine. Characteristically, Eckhart argues for the latter solution in opposition to Aquinas. Although attributes are not false and point to something real in God, Eckhart argues that "no distinction can exist or be understood in God himself."[27] He maintains the absolute unity of the Godhead.

At this point, Eckhart moves to the third section of the treatise, where he deals with Boethius' contention that the first two of Aristotle's categories—substance and relation—can both be applied to God. The arguments have to do with the peculiar nature of relation, whereby it is not understood as an accident applied to a substance and does not add anything extrinsic to the divinity. Such claims are important for Christian thinkers who wish to maintain the Trinity and the absolute unity of the divinity; but again, despite Eckhart's predominantly traditional position, his emphasis on the unity of God leads him to cite statements that seem to remove the language of relation from the substance of the divine.[28] This points to an ambiguity that runs throughout Eckhart's discussion of substance and relation, for he goes on to argue for a distinction between the idea of God as substance and the Father as relational, thus implying a distinction between the Godhead and the persons of the Trinity inadmissible to Christian orthodoxy. Yet as McGinn argues,

> the conceptual distinction between substance and relation is legitimate in thinking about God as three-who-are-one, but is not in any way applicable to the hidden Godhead. Certainly, the conceptual distinction accepted here in no way suggests any distinction in being. Since the concept of relation in itself does not connote either *esse* or *inesse*, but is defined solely by what it is related to (*adesse*, e.g., a father as father is a father only insofar as he has a son), relation creates no distinction of essence and existence—the existence of the Father is not other than the existence that is identical with the divine essence.[29]

The distinction between substance and relation allows Eckhart to suggests a distinction in the divinity, that between the Trinity and the ground of God, without arguing for any distinction in being or ontological status, for relation adds nothing to being.

Eckhart proceeds to add a sixth principle to those necessary for understanding the Christian teaching about predication, the apparently commonplace statement originating with Aristotle "that the truth of an affirmative proposition always subsists in the identity of terms, but the truth of a negative one subsists in the difference or distinction of terms."[30] This leads to the much less commonplace statement of the "negation of negation," which plays a central role in Eckhart's language of attribution and in his mystical thought.

Truth, according to Eckhart, who follows the Aristotelian dictum, "is that which is,"[31] and that which is supremely, without any lack, is God.

> Therefore, no negation, nothing negative, belongs to God, except for the negation of negation which is what the One signifies when expressed negatively. "God is one" (Deut. 6:4; Gal. 3:20). The negation of negation is the purest and fullest affirmation—"I am who I am."[32]

McGinn argues that the dialectic of the "negation of negation" reverses the Maimonidean assertion that negative propositions are alone legitimate for God, for it points to the ultimate fullness of predication.[33] Eckhart follows Aquinas in objecting to the statement drawn from the Pseudo-Dionysius that only "negations about God are true, but affirmations are unsuitable." Like Aquinas, Eckhart states that this is true "about the mode of signifying in such sentences" but not of the affirmation itself.[34] Yet for Eckhart, the mode of signification is the central means by which consciousness is changed and the divine apprehended. While Eckhart can be seen as upholding a way of eminence as the most suitable to the divine, in that apprehension of God is possible through apophasis (in a way more radical than one would ever find in Aquinas), it is described and arrived at by different theological and philosophical paths than those argued for by Thomas. In Eckhart's differences from Aquinas the path of apophasis is inscribed, and with it Eckhart's understanding of the way in which the divine inhabits the world.

In the fourth and final part of Eckhart's treatise he discusses the Hebrew names for God, particularly the Tetragrammaton. He then turns to a general statement of the proper way to apply the divine predicates that appears to contradict the ultimate positivity of the "negation of negation" discussed above. Eckhart gives various arguments about the improper use of positive attributes, the most pertinent to his mystical theology being that one which is based on the idea of the virtual existence of all things in God. He argues that

> the perfections in exterior things are not true perfections, and to attribute them to God is to apprehend him imperfectly and as not being totally pure Intellect himself, but as being something external, at least with some part of him, as is the case in created intellects.[35]

It might seem that the idea of the virtual existence of all things in God would lead to some commonality between human and divine attributes, but Eckhart argues that the opposite is the case, for the distinction between the virtual and the actual is absolute.

In turning to negative attributions, Eckhart contends that they have two advantages over affirmations. In sections 181–82 he argues that since every negation includes an affirmation, they all lead to some positive statement and hence give some information about the divine. Furthermore, the process of negation leads to greater knowledge of God.

> The stronger the argument by which a person removes these attributes from God, the more perfect he is in divine knowledge. The same holds for one who knows how to deny many such things of him by means of the removal that happens through negative names.[36]

In other words, the more one denies of God, the more one recognizes one's ignorance, the more one knows him.[37] While such arguments seem to place Eckhart once again in the camp of those who unequivocally favor the way of negation, this does not imply that God cannot be apprehended by the soul. Furthermore, as McGinn has shown, a comparison with Aquinas on these issues can be instructive in showing their similarities as well as their differences. Aquinas, in the *Prima Pars*, in article 2 of question 13, rejects Maimonides' arguments for the way of negation as well as those for the way of causality, and argues for the way of eminence, grounded in his understanding of analogy.[38] Many recent commentators have underlined the role apophasis plays in Thomistic analogy, making plausible the argument that, while Maimonides, Thomas, and Eckhart have distinct positions, all can be seen as "subtle combinations of the *via negationis* and the *via eminentiae*."[39] Yet in Eckhart, the very rigor of apophasis is the root of his claims to apprehend and be transformed into the divine.

Eckhart never explicitly rejects the *via eminentiae* and seems to argue for its preeminence in the treatise.[40] In the Exodus commentary, for example, he affirms the term *esse*.[41] Other texts single out *unum*, or absolute unity, which is described as the "core" of *esse*[42] and is also the term for the "negation of negation." Although he may thus be seen as similar to Aquinas in arguing for the combination of the ways of negation and eminence in naming God, by explicitly affirming only *esse* and *unum* as properly divine attributes, Eckhart moves in a different direction from Aquinas, for the very imagistic emptiness of these terms makes them alone fitting for God.

Furthermore, while Eckhart, like Aquinas, makes use of analogy in his thought and language, he uses the term in a sense almost diametrically opposed to that of Aquinas. For Aquinas the term points to similarity in difference; for Eckhart analogy is an extrinsic relation based on dialectical opposition between God and creatures.[43] For Eckhart, analogy divides virtual existence (the aspect of creation that shares in and remains within the divine) from formal existence (the aspect of creation that becomes actual and existent in the world). Because of this understanding of analogy, Eckhart is able to affirm a form of the *via eminentiae* while at the same time claiming, together with Maimonides, that those things that are perfections in creatures are no more true of God than their opposites.

The dialectical use of analogy underlies almost all of Eckhart's language for God and creatures, leading to some of his most audacious statements. It is grounded on his understanding of predication, another example of a technical distinction in which Eckhart uses the same language as Aquinas but with a very different meaning. Aquinas uses the distinction between two-term and three-term predication in order to differentiate ways of referring to created reality. Two-term predications (*secundum adiacens*), such as "Socrates is," refer to actual events in the world. Three-term predication (*tertium adiacens*), in which "is" serves as a copula connecting the subject and the predicate, marks only a logical relation, without making any claims about the actual state of affairs in the world.[44] Eckhart uses the same distinction to differentiate statements made about God from those made about creatures, rather than between statements that refer to actual events and those that refer to logical relations.

The predication language, then, parallels Eckhart's well-known distinction between *esse simpliciter* and *esse hoc et hoc*, which he uses through the Prologues and the other Latin works to distinguish between God and creatures.[45] Whereas God exists simply in himself, and thus being and the other superlative attributes can be predicated of him absolutely and without limit (two-term predication), creatures are limited by time, space, and number, and thus only possess such predicates in a limited way. They must be spoken of, according to Eckhart, by means of three-term predication:

For when I say that something exists, or I predicate one, true, or good, these four terms feature in the predicate as the second term [*secundum adiacens*] and are used formally and substantially. But when I say that something is this, for instance a stone, and that it is one stone, a true stone, or a good this, namely a stone, these four terms are used as the third term [*tertium adiacens*] of the proposition. They are not predicates but the copula, or they are placed near the predicate.[46]

Eckhart takes over terminology used by Aquinas while changing the meaning of the terms in order to satisfy his own desire to emphasize the radical dissimilarity between God and creation.

The pecularities in Eckhart's understanding of predication are repeated in his understanding of analogy discussed above. He goes on to show how dialectic follows on predication and analogy as three levels of increasing penetration through which he deals with the nature of the divine and its relationship to reality.[47] Eckhart's doctrine of analogy is itself dialectical. Furthermore, the dialectic of transcendence and immanence found in his exegesis of Wisdom 7:27, "And since Wisdom is one, it can do all things," exhibits the real meaning of two-term predication for him and the primacy of *unum* as a predicate for the divine.

He begins by stating that the One is the same as the " 'indistinct,' for all distinct things are two or more, but all indistinct things are one."[48] From the beginning of the exposition the indistinct is associated with being, pointing to the centrality and interrelationship of these three terms for Eckhart. He argues that the nature of created things is to be limited and determined and therefore multiple. "Therefore," he continues, "saying that God is one is to say that God is indistinct from all things, which is the property of the highest and first existence and its overflowing goodness."[49] After having given three proofs that God is one, Eckhart moves to the second pole of the discussion; he asserts that although the term One appears to be negative, it is in fact affirmative.

The second stage of the argument, in which Eckhart demonstrates the affirmative nature of the One, hinges on an extended discussion of the "negation of negation," already encountered in the *Commentary on Exodus*. Here Eckhart argues that

the One descends totally into all things which are beneath it, which are many and which are enumerated. In these individual things the

One is not divided, but remaining the incorrupt One, it flows forth into every number and informs it with its own unity. So, the One is necessarily found prior to any duality or plurality both in reality and understanding. Thus the term "one" adds nothing beyond existence, not even conceptually, but only according to negation. This is not so in the case of "true" and "good." For this reason it is most immediately related to existence in that it signifies the purity and core and height of existence itself, something which even the term "existence" does not do.[50]

Eckhart establishes the preeminence of the term One as a predicate for God on the basis of its ability to denote the source of all things and all being, while at the same time retaining purity and distinction from all things.

In the third stage of his argument Eckhart demonstrates the dialectical unity of the negative and affirmative aspects of the One. He claims that "nothing is so distinct from number and the thing numbered or what is numerable (the created thing, that is) as God is. And yet nothing is so indistinct."[51] The first two arguments for this proposition are based in the radical dissimilarity between God and creation, but the third is thoroughly dialectical and points to the real meaning of this opposition for Eckhart:

Everything which is distinguished by indistinction is the more distinct the more indistinct it is, because it is distinguished by its own indistinction. Conversely, it is the more indistinct the more distinct it is, because it is distinguished by its own distinction from what is indistinct.[52]

As McGinn has shown, the passage becomes clearer when put in terms of transcendence and immanence.[53] Everything that is distinguished by transcendence is the more immanent the more transcendent it is, because it is made transcendent by its own immanence. In other words, God is absolutely transcendent because he is totally immanent to all creatures, or in language appropriate to Eckhart, he is *esse indistinctum*. Moreover, the more immanent to creatures God is, the greater is his transcendence, because the distinguishing feature of the One is its indistinction from all things. The radical dissimilarity between God and creatures stressed by Eckhart's understanding of predication and of analogy is here dialectically related to the radical immanence of God to creation.

ONTOLOGY: *BULLITIO* AND *EBULLITIO*

We are led, increasingly, to an awareness of the way in which Eckhart's theories of language and attribution are always intimately involved in his ontology.[54] In other words, the way one talks about God, creation, and their relationship is a direct reflection of and result of the actual ontological status of these beings and their relationship. Perhaps a commonplace in discussions about medieval theologians and philosophers, this intimate connection between language and ontology is further heightened for Eckhart because of his insistence that one must break through normal linguistic practices in order to apprehend that God who is beyond being in any limited sense. To explore this relationship further, I now will turn to Eckhart's understanding of the Trinitarian self-creation of God and his creation of the universe, what he calls *bullitio* and *ebullitio*, as they are explicated in the biblical commentaries and sermons, particularly in the commentary on John.[55] Through an understanding of Eckhart's conception of the ontological status of God and creation, we will gain further insight into his view of language and of the mystical path of return to the Godhead.

In the Preface to the *Commentary on John*, Eckhart tells the reader that he wishes "to explain what the holy Christian faith and the two testaments maintain through the help of the natural arguments of the philosophers."[56] As in the treatise on the divine names in the *Commentary on Exodus* discussed above, Eckhart has full confidence in his ability to reconcile the wisdom of the philosophers with that of the Christian faith and scriptures. His discussion of *bullitio*, the self-birth of the Godhead into the Trinity, or the reflexive movement by which the One emanates into the three self-identical persons of the Godhead, can thus be understood as an attempt to clarify the traditional Christian understanding of the Trinity as one of interrelationship and absolute equality, as well as to set up the circumstances in which creation can be viewed as capable of sharing, at least in part, in that equality.

The discussion is centered around the opening phrase of the Gospel of John, and Eckhart characteristically plays on the multiple meanings of the Latin *principium*, using it interchangeably to mean both temporal beginning and principle. As Michael Sells observes, this ambiguity allows for Eckhart to deal with a variety of interrelated themes simultaneously: the self-birth of the Godhead, the external emanation of creation, the word as expression of the Godhead and as exemplar of creation, the Trinity as unity and as differentiated into the persons.[57] Eckhart moves through an explanation of the relationship between that which proceeds and its source or principle, following Neoplatonic logical principles taken over from Proclus, later Jewish and Arabic sources, and also possibly from Boethius.[58] Using these Neoplatonic principles, Eckhart elaborates his threefold conception of the flowing forth, remaining, and return that structures Neoplatonic ontology.

Eckhart opens with the assertion that what "is produced or proceeds from anything is precontained in it" and "it is preexistent in it as a seed in its principle."[59] Yet he goes on to explain that once anything has proceeded from another, it is distinguished from its source. This leads to a distinction between univocal, equivocal, and analogical relationships. Because the Word is said to be with God, according to Eckhart, it is in a relationship of equality with its source:

> In things that are univocal what is produced is always equal to the source. It does not just participate in the same nature, but it receives the total nature from its source in a simple, whole and equal manner. Thus, the sixth point says that what proceeds is the son of its source. A son is one who is other in person but not other in nature.[60]

Here we see the traditional Christian view of the absolute equality of the Father and the Son. In contrast to the Son who proceeds from the Father, what is created is in an analogical, not univocal, relation to its source and hence inferior and unequal; this prepares for the distinction Eckhart will make between the divine *bullitio* and the act of creation or *ebullitio*.

In these statements Eckhart uses traditional Trinitarian language to describe the equality and identity of the Father and the Son, and through his use of Neoplatonic principles he gives new coherence to the coequality and coeternity of creatures in relation to God. Since that which proceeds not only preexists in its source, but also remains in that source "just as it was in the beginning before it came to be"[61] even after its procession from the source, a new dimension is added to creation's claims for coeternity and equality. Because all of creation has both a virtual and a formal aspect, it has corresponding coeternal and temporal relations to the divine production—coeternal as always virtually produced in the *bullitio* of the production of the three divine Persons and temporal insofar as it is the product of *ebullitio*.

Eckhart uses the traditional Platonic metaphor of the craftsman's work in his discussions of the principle and the flow of emanation. In divine *bullitio*, unlike in the work of the craftsman who makes an object other than himself that is removed in space and time, the generation of the divine "is without movement or time but is the goal and limit of movement. . . . Therefore, it follows that generation does not fall into nonexistence or sink into the past."[62] Insofar as creation occurs virtually with the act of divine *bullitio*, it shares in this equality, whereas the craftsman's creation is distinguished by time and space. For the Godhead, which is beyond time and spatial movement, generation is always in the principle and the Son "is always being born and always being brought forth. It must either never happen or always happen, because the principle or 'In the principle' always exists."[63] The Son is always being born, for only through being generated is he distinguished in the unity of the Godhead. Through the birth of the Son in eternity, Eckhart is able to "make sense" of the Trinitarian mystery of the distinction of the persons and the absolute unity of the Godhead. Further, the eternal recurrence of the birth of the Son lays the foundation for Eckhart's teaching on the birth of the Son in the soul, so central to the German sermons.

All humans share in God's being in that they have life, for God's being is life, which flows without medium from God to the soul. Here we see Eckhart's notion of *ebullitio*, the flowing out of all things from the divine. Human beings have "real" life virtually, i.e., in God as principle.[64] They have actual, or deficient life, insofar as they have come forth from God, the source of all life, by means of *ebullitio*. In German Sermon 6, Eckhart makes this idea explicit: "If my life is God's being, then God's existence must be my existence and God's is-ness is my is-ness, neither less nor more."[65] In the creative act of *ebullitio*, while God's being flows without medium, the relationship between the creator and the created is not univocal, but rather analogical.[66] A relationship of inferiority exists between creator and creature because life is given to the creature from that which is other than itself, God. There are two kinds of *ebullitio* according to Eckhart—the making (*factio*) of one thing from another and the creation (*creatio*) of something out of nothing. Both of these types of flowing out, however, are in the realm of efficient and final causality and as such produce something different in reality and number from their source.[67] As Eckhart argues in the John commentary, "everything that has its principle from another insofar as it is other does not live in the proper sense."[68] Therefore human beings, insofar as they are other than God—insofar as they are created—do not live or have their being in the proper sense, but only analogically and in an inferior manner. Eckhart thus states the radical dissimilarity between God and creation. To be taken up into a univocal relationship with the divine, the soul must become nothing and empty herself of all createdness, making herself indistinguishable and undifferentiated from God and therefore equal to him. In doing so, she is taken up into univocal relationship with the divine. The soul returns to her principle. She must come to share the identity with the Father found in the Son, and it is, in part, through the Son's peculiar relationship to humanity that this return is made possible. The return, therefore, is grounded in the proceeding-out or the creation, for the crucial role of the Son or the Word in the act of creation serves as the basis for the soul's ability to return to the divinity.

THE ROLE OF THE SON

Just as the Son preexists in the ground in the same way that the seed preexists in its source, Eckhart argues that the Word serves as the exemplary cause through which all other entities are created. If the Trinitarian movement of procession, remaining, and return occurs continually and without change in number or nature, the same Neoplatonic movement is repeated in a less perfect way in the creative movement of *ebullitio*. The Eckhartian theme of the continued virtual existence of all things in the Word, then, plays a crucial role in his mysticism.[69] This teaching, as we have seen, is also found in Mechthild's *Flowing Light* and in Porete's *Mirror*. It is pivotal to any mystical theology that wishes to argue for an absolute return of the human soul to the divine source and for a union without distinction between God and the soul.[70] Eckhart argues that the most real aspect of creation, its virtual existence, has never departed from the divine but preexists in the Word and remains with it even after creation. Virtual existence is the condition of possibility for the return of the soul to the divine. Furthermore, because the Son ultimately is one with the

Father, or the ground of the Trinity, the soul is able to return through the Son to the absolute ground of the divine. (Yet, as we will see later, it is through her unity with the divine ground that the soul shares in the self-birth of the Son out of the divine Trinity.)

Eckhart's distinction between univocal and analogical relations and the way creation is able to share in both of these relations through the Son become most clear in his discussion of Begotten and Unbegotten Justice. Having elucidated the manner in which the persons of the Godhead are differentiated and distinguished from each other and from creation, he is able to make statements concerning their radical equality. He does this in his discussion of the just human being (*iustus*), who "proceeds from and is begotten by justice and by that very fact is distinguished from it. Nothing can beget itself."[71] The just human being, insofar as he is just, is in Unbegotten Justice (the Father) as his principle, just as he is brought forth by Begotten Justice (the Son). Here we see operating what Eckhart calls the *inquantum*, or "insofar as," principle.[72] When he discusses the equality and identity that lie between the divine persons and the just human being, he qualifies his assertions with this phrase, thereby signifying that he is referring to the just human being in his virtual existence, within the Son or the second person of the Trinity.[73] The just human being has formal and virtual existence in the Son, who is Begotten Justice, and insofar as he has this virtual existence in the Son, he also is one with Unbegotten Justice as his principle, just as the Son is one with the Father who is the principle of the Son. The just human being is continuously one with and generated from the Father, who is Unbegotten Justice.

> It is clear that justice and the just human being as such are no more subject to movement and time than life or light are. For this reason the just human being is always being born from justice itself in the same way that he was born from it from the beginning of the time he became just. It is the same in the case of the generation and conservation of light in a medium. It must be continuously generated because it is not continuously possessed.[74]

Again we see the central role relation plays in distinguishing the persons of the Godhead, the nonstatic nature of this relationship, which must be continuously renewed in order to maintain itself, and the way in which creation shares in it.

Here we come to a double movement in Eckhart's Trinitarian understanding and his teaching on *bullitio* and *ebullitio* that makes dynamic the sometimes static traditional understandings of the Trinity and inextricably ties the just human being to both Begotten and Unbegotten Justice and to the ground of the divine that begets the persons of the Trinity. Nothing just can be begotten or continue to exist without Begotten Justice, the Son, for "Begotten Justice itself is the word of justice in its principle, the justice that gives birth."[75] All things are created through the Son, who is the principle of all creation. Yet insofar as the just human being is Justice in its principle, he is also Unbegotten Justice, for the principle of the Begotten lies in the Unbegotten source. As Eckhart concludes; "The just human being in justice itself is not yet begotten nor Begotten Justice, but is Unbegotten Justice itself."[76] The just human being, insofar as he is just, is both Begotten and Unbegotten Justice, united to both persons of the Trinity.

For Eckhart, the just human being, insofar as he is just (i.e., virtual and not actual) exists without principle because he is his own principle or "principle without principle."[77] As Eckhart explains:

What is without principle lives in the proper sense, for everything that has the principle of its operation from another insofar as it is other does not live in the proper sense.[78]

The just human being, therefore, must be radically equal to his source insofar as he lives in the proper sense. His source, the ground of the divine, cannot be in any way other; the distinction of the process of begetting is thus subverted by its eternal recurrence. The just human being shares in the entire Trinity, both as Begotten and Unbegotten, and hence shares in the equality that exists between the persons. This is the nature of univocal relations in Eckhart's thought, and it is the basis for his understanding of the return of the soul to the divine, the movement from analogical to univocal relations in and through which the soul takes part in the *bullitio* of the Trinity out of the divine ground.

VIRTUAL EXISTENCE AND THE "SPARK" OF THE SOUL

Before analyzing how these themes develop in the German works, it will be helpful to look more carefully at the idea of the virtual existence of all creation in the Godhead, the relationship of this idea to various ideas about the "spark" (*vünkelîn*) or "ground" (*grunt*) of the soul in the vernacular works,[79] and the clarifications of this idea given by Eckhart in his defense. The first and third of the propositions condemned in the papal bull *In agro dominico* (1328) are drawn from a passage in the *Commentary on Genesis* that repeats a teaching found throughout the Latin and German works. Eckhart argues for the coeternity of the Son and the world:

> In one and the same time in which he was God and in which he begat his coeternal Son as God equal to himself in all things, he also created the world.[80]

As McGinn and others argue, Eckhart was convinced that this idea was supported by the writings of Augustine, and therefore had patristic warrants.[81] His critics, however, judged the statement to be heretical; this was a result of the different theological and philosophical perspectives from which they were arguing. Eckhart clearly places this idea within the context of the Neoplatonic schema of emanation and return, where creation's primary mode of existence is in its exemplar or principle *virtualiter* (i.e., in its power to produce), and thus can be said to be coeternal with it. His critics, with their Aristotelian understanding of the distinction between *actio* and *passio*, in which potentiality and action always coincide in one movement that is formally in the thing moved, assumed that he was arguing for the eternity of creation.[82] On the basis of his distinction between virtual and formal modes of existence, Eckhart believed that it was possible to hold both that the world was created with the procession of the Son *and* that it was created in time.[83]

Human beings play a central role in Eckhart's theory of creation and have a special relationship to the Word that is expressed in a number of different ways throughout his work, in particular in his teaching about the uncreated aspect of the soul. He stresses the fact that all of creation is *one* and unified in its principle,[84] but he also consistently argues for the primacy of intelligence (*intellectus*) in the universe. All creation shares in the lowest of the three levels of being, existence; but only some share in the second, life; and even fewer in the highest level, intelligence.[85] God himself, according to Eckhart, in his principle is an intellectual being, and hence through human beings' intellects they are closest to the divine, although, as we have seen, Eckhart continually uses the movement of apophasis to subvert the intellect itself. The theme, however, runs throughout the sermons, both as part of a general argument with those who would give the will primacy over the intellect and, in a stronger form, through his teachings on the hidden power or spark in the soul.[86]

The first issue, concerning the relative primacy of the will and the intellect, is a recurring theme in Eckhart's work; he repeatedly argues for the importance of the intellect over the will in the return of the soul to the divine.[87] His arguments are based in the belief that human beings are like the divine through their intellectual natures; therefore intellect makes them capable of union and identity with God.[88] Finally, Eckhart often invokes the intellectual nature of the soul to signal her nobility. He claims that this aspect of the soul shares in the divinity, at times arguing that the highest part of the intellect is the soul's ground.[89] The character of the intellect as that which must fully empty itself in order to receive leads Eckhart to posit this aspect of the soul as the source of her nobility and identity with God.[90] Furthermore, the primacy of the intellect is tied to the claim, shared with Porete, that the will and attachment must be annihilated in order for the soul to be virgin and wifely. Once again, Eckhart's apparently metaphysical assertions are made in the name of his apophasis of all names for the soul and the divine. Eckhart uses many metaphors to describe the "hidden power" in the soul, or the ground of the soul where God's ground and the soul are one. Most often he calls it the "spark" (*vünkelîn*) or the "little town, or castle" (*bürgelîn*).[91] Yet beneath these various metaphors lies the idea of the spark or ground of the soul that is the root of Eckhart's apophatic anthropology, in which human beings in their ground are understood as beyond images and language in the same way that the Godhead is.

Like its conceptual parallel in the Latin works, the idea of the spark or ground of the soul becomes most dangerous for Eckhart when he claims that there is an uncreated aspect of the soul:

> There is something in the soul which is uncreated and not capable of creation; if the whole soul were such, it would be uncreated and not capable of creation, and this is the intellect.[92]

Although the statements condemned at Avignon concerning the eternity of the world are taken from the Latin works,[93] this suspect passage concerning the uncreated aspect of the soul is very close to formulations found in the German sermons.[94] A puzzle for students of the condemnation and Eckhart's various defenses, however, is that Eckhart claims he never made such an assertion.[95] The question then becomes why Eckhart denied having said that there is something uncreated in the soul, while at the same time accepting responsibility for other statements that were found heretical or suspicious.

As McGinn has argued, and the documents support, Eckhart disavows the claim because of the reading given to it by his accusers. Where Eckhart does speak of an uncreated "aspect" of the soul, namely, its virtual existence, he eschews any language that divides the soul into created and uncreated "parts," for the soul is not divisible in this way. This is the reading, apparently, that Eckhart was at pains to repudiate.[96] Where in Sermon 13 Eckhart speaks of a "power" (kraft) in the soul that is uncreated, the Latin translation prepared for the investigations and subsequently found in the bull used the indefinite pronoun "something" (aliquid), thereby implying a part of the soul rather than an aspect.[97] In the process of translation, the precreated aspect of the soul is made substantial and essentialized in a manner antithetical to Eckhart's apophatic practice. Although the question remains why Eckhart was not more explicit in his defense about his actual teaching concerning the virtual existence of the soul in the divine Word and hence the uncreated "aspect" of the soul, the existence of such teachings in his work is clear.[98] What is important to remember as we turn to the German works is that these arguments, whose mystical sources are the beguine texts, have their philosophical basis in the Neoplatonic ontology of emanation and remaining that Eckhart delineates in the Latin commentaries and prologues. The "spark" and "ground" of the soul, so important to understanding the return delineated in the German sermons, must be read in light of Eckhart's teaching on the virtual existence of all of creation in the Word. In this way, Eckhart takes a Neoplatonic principle found in Augustine, among others, and uses it as a central metaphorical structure for the mystical theology explored in the vernacular works, to which I will now turn.

THE CENTRAL MYSTICAL THEMES OF MEISTER ECKHART'S GERMAN WORKS

In order to uncover the significance of the virtual existence or uncreated aspect of the soul for Eckhart's mystical teaching, I will now give more concentrated attention to the sermons, in which he describes the paths human beings must take in order to return to the divine. Given the much less systematic nature of the sources for this chapter, various themes and images will be analyzed in a sequential manner foreign to the style of the sermons themselves. While it is almost impossible to separate the image of the virgin soul and the breakthrough into the divine ground from that of the wife and the birth of the Son in the soul, such a division will provisionally be made for the sake of clarity.

I begin with an acccount of Eckhart's related teachings on detachment, the virgin soul, and the breakthrough into the ground of the Godhead and of the soul that mark one moment of the return to the divine source. This will be followed by a discussion of the wifely soul and the birth of the Son in the soul as her "work." I will then explain the paradoxical nature of this twofold path of return, in which each element must occur simultaneously and without primacy being placed on either. After a brief discussion of Eckhart's language as a part of the work of the detached soul, I will describe his conceptions of creation and embodiment. I will conclude with an explication of the unity of action and contemplation in the sermons, a theme that links Eckhart directly with his beguine predecessors and audiences.

DETACHMENT, THE VIRGIN SOUL,
AND THE BREAKTHROUGH

Eckhart gives his fullest elaboration of the image of the virgin soul in Sermon 2 in the course of an exposition of detachment (*abegescheidenheit, gelâzenheit*) and how the soul attains it. The person whose soul is virgin "is free of all alien images, as free as he was when he was not."[1] Eckhart recognizes the paradox involved in this assertion, for it seems impossible for one who knows all of the things that an average person knows, to be free of all images and knowledge. He does not mean, however, that one should be literally without any images or knowledge; rather he is concerned with the attitude one has toward them.

> If I were so rational that there were present in my reason all the images that all human beings had ever received, and those that are present in God himself, and if I could be without possessiveness in their regard, so that I had not seized possessively upon any one of them, not in what I did or what I left undone, not looking to past or to future, but I stood in this present moment free and empty according to God's dearest will, performing it without ceasing, then truly I should be a virgin, as truly unimpeded by any images as I was when I was not.[2]

Like Mechthild and Porete, Eckhart stresses the importance of the attitude toward images, or, in other words, the disposition of the will. In letting go of possessiveness toward images and knowledge, one becomes "free and maidenly" as Jesus himself was.[3] Ultimately, one must become detached from one's will and very self, as Porete also argues. Like Mechthild and Porete, Eckhart inveighs against those who wish God to will according to their wills, for truly detached people "have no will at all; what God wills is all the same to them, however great distress that may be."[4] Herein lies the true freedom of the soul.

Reiner Schürmann and others have demonstrated that Eckhart's understanding of the necessity for detachment is grounded in an Aristotelian epistemology in which the mind's receptiveness depends on its blankness.[5] In a movement that closely follows the dialectic of something and nothing governing Porete's mystical theology,[6] Eckhart contends that the soul must become as "nothing" in order to achieve equality and union with God, "for the divine being is equal to nothing, and in it there is neither image nor form."[7] In the same way, in his short treatise *On Detachment*, he argues that it is necessary for human beings to practice complete self-abandonment. "You must know that to be empty of all created things is to be full of God, and to be full of created things is to be empty of God."[8] Since all created things are a mere nothing from the standpoint of their createdness (i.e., in actual existence), the soul must detach herself from all createdness, including her own, in order to become one with the divine. The soul must abandon herself in all knowing, willing, and being, and thus in all of her createdness.

These ideas are developed in the famous Sermon 52, believed by some to be a homage to Porete's *Mirror* composed after Eckhart's failed defense.[9] The sermon begins with a discussion of the ideal of poverty, so crucial to the beguine and mendicant movements. To be poor, according to Eckhart, is to want nothing, know nothing, and have nothing. The detachment of the soul from all knowledge and from the will parallels the description of the virgin soul given in Sermon 2, but Eckhart radicalizes these statements by pointing to something uncreated and self-sufficient in the soul, the ground of the soul, her uncreated spark in which her ground and God's are one.[10] He exhorts his audience to break through to the ground of the soul and thereby to the ground of the Godhead. The soul's ground exists before God, for God is only God insofar as there are creatures to call him God.[11] God does not exist until the soul receives her created being. The ground of the soul must break through even the idea of God to reemerge with the divine.

In describing this movement beyond God himself, Eckhart calls on his audience to abandon all will and desire, the necessary prerequisite to achieving this breakthrough.

> So therefore let us pray to God that we may be free of God, and that we may apprehend and rejoice in that everlasting truth in which the highest angel and the fly and the soul are equal—there I was established, where I wanted what I was and was what I wanted. So I say: If a man is to become poor in his will, he must want and desire as little as he wanted and desired when he did not exist. And in this way a man is poor who wants nothing.[12]

In the same way, the human being must be as free of all knowing as she was before she was born.

Eckhart at times says that God is being (or, to be more exact, that being is God), or that God is understanding or intellect.[13] Yet in discussing the ground of the soul and the divine, he argues that true blessedness does not consist in knowing, being, or loving.

I say that God is neither being nor rational, and that he does not know this or that. Therefore, God is free of all things, and therefore he is all things. Whoever will be poor in spirit, he must be poor of all his own knowledge, so that he knows nothing, not God or created things or himself. Therefore it is necessary for a person to long not to be able to know or perceive God's works. In this way a person can be poor of his own knowledge.[14]

If the ground of the soul has no will, knowledge, or being, then the ground of the divine must also be devoid of these predicates, for here the soul and the divine achieve their greatest unity.

Finally, the soul must have nothing. According to Eckhart, this is the most intimate kind of poverty.

Poverty of spirit is for a person to keep so free of God and of all his works that if God wishes to work in the soul, he himself is the place in which he wants to work; and that he will gladly do.[15]

The Godhead is so united with the soul that he works in himself when working in her. When a human being clings to place she clings to distinction. The soul must "pray to God that he may make [her] free of God,"[16] for in breaking through to the ground of the soul and the divine the soul is above all created things, even God. As the creator of human beings and all creatures, God becomes distinct and reified; he becomes other. The ground of the soul and of the divine is the source of pure activity and as such is pure, undifferentiated movement. Here Eckhart claims that the breaking through is nobler than the flowing out, for in the breaking through the soul becomes higher than all created things. In breaking through she is neither God nor creature, but as God in his ground is what he is, the soul is what she is and "shall remain, now and eternally."[17] The soul becomes one with the divine Godhead, for her ground and the divine's are one. She is called on to return to this "Oneness":

You should love him as he is—a non-God, a non-spirit, a non-person, a non-image. I say more: you should love him as he is, a pure, unmixed, bright "One," separated from all duality; and in that One we should eternally sink down, out of "something" into "nothing."[18]

In the breakthrough the soul becomes completely one and undifferentiated from the Godhead. Both are equal to nothing and contain no images, forms, or will. This is the virgin soul who lives without a why.

Eckhart is not simply conflating the human and the divine, as many of his critics certainly believed to be the case, for only when the soul becomes nothing and gives up her will and creatureliness is she transformed into equality and oneness with the godhead.[19] Only when she has become detached from all will and images is she assumed into a univocal relationship with God and united with him without distinction. When the soul has attained this unity she cannot ask anything from the divine, nor is it possible, for that would be to resume the analogical relationship of servant to master.[20] Therefore, Eckhart says, one should not esteem God as something outside of the self to be loved or known, but rather should become one with God by becoming nothing. As one, God works and the soul becomes, just as fire works on wood and transforms it into itself.[21] Eckhart thus maintains the radical dissimilarity between God and the human being while he also maintains their radical similarity or equality. Only when the soul becomes one with God can she truly know him: "So we are changed into God, that we shall know him as he is."[22]

Such statements substantiate John Caputo's claim that Eckhart cannot be understood as offering an objectivistic theology that gives referential knowledge about the divine and its being.[23] As we saw earlier, Eckhart maintains that the divine names show only the contours of what God is not, or at the most what God does. His essence cannot be known in this way, as Eckhart reminds his listeners:

> Some simple people think that they will see God as if he were standing there and they here. It is not so. God and I, we are one. I accept God into me in knowing; I go into God in loving.[24]

Like Porete, who argues against those who believe that one can bargain for God, or that he can be known according to human reason,[25] Eckhart denies that God can be apprehended by human senses or understanding. The "knowledge" that brings one to unity with the divine is not engendered by created reason, but rather by the uncreated ground of the soul through which she is unified with the divine and thus knows him.

The affinities of this ideal with that of the pure, simple, and free soul found in Porete's *Mirror* are readily apparent and will be discussed further in Chapter 7. For Eckhart, moreover, the fruitfulness of the soul is explicitly thematized: the virgin soul is also a wife, showing Eckhart's debt to the other side of the beguine tradition, that represented by Mechthild of Magdeburg, in which identification with Christ and his activities within the world is crucial.[26] Eckhart, however, completes the spiritualization or desomatization of the imitation of Christ suggested at times by Mechthild. The work of the divine, the just act, is both the mark and fruit of identity with the Son and the divine ground. Paradoxically, the process of desomatization allows the human being to incarnate the Son through the birth of the Son in the soul. The soul becomes one with the Son when she, insofar as she is equal to the Godhead, takes part in the birth of the Son in eternity. In this act of self-birth, differentiation and relationship do occur, although all are equal and all are divine, for the soul takes part in the act of formal emanation and in the univocal relationship that exists between the Father and the Son.[27] The soul takes part in what could be called a nondualistic differentiation, a form of differentiation that avoids the fall into duality and dualistic reference by reason of its univocity and eternal repetition. Where the Latin works discussed in Chapter 5 stress the mediation of the Son in the assumption of the soul to the divine ground, the dialectic of the soul as virgin wife is governed by a double paradigm, elaborated below, in which the equality of the ground of the soul and of the divine is *also* and *simultaneously* understood to be the ground for her share in the process of divine *bullitio*.

THE BIRTH OF THE SON IN THE SOUL

In Sermon 6, Eckhart again describes the process of letting go or detachment that leads the soul to share in a univocal relationship with God, here understood as participation in the birth of the Son in the soul.[28] He focuses on the theme of the just human being (*justus/gereht*). The just human being, insofar as he is just, is the Son, or Begotten Justice (*iustitia/gerehticheit*). When a human being commits a just act, he or she is the Son. In this process a human being becomes the Son and is assumed into a univocal relationship with God, such as that described by Eckhart in the *Commentary on John*.[29] Human beings take part in the one work of the divine, *bullitio*, its ever-ocurring self-birth. In the opening of the sermon, paralleling his discussions of the virgin soul and poverty, Eckhart describes the just human being as he who gives God what belongs to God. Honor belongs to God, and people give honor to God by abandoning everything that is theirs. "You ought to go wholly out from your own will,"[30] Eckhart writes, for the just human being has no will at all, but what God wills is his will. To be truly detached and virgin, the soul must let go of all images, attachments, will and selfhood.[31] When the soul is completely empty, wholly one, simple and free, she is equal to and undifferentiated from the divine.

The virgin soul, or in terms of Sermon 6, the just human being, who is nothing, completely empty and devoid of all images, attachments, and creatureliness, is one with the divine. But Eckhart also maintains that only through the birth of the Son in the soul, her participation in the divine self-birth, or *bullitio*, is she taken up from an analogical to a univocal relationship with God. In foreaking self-love, she abandons the world of creatures and becomes virgin. The soul becomes nothing and as nothing is equal to the divine. To the soul, insofar as she is equal with God, God gives everything that he can achieve. He must do this, according to Eckhart, for he and the soul are one, and therefore, in complete detachment she compels and forces God to give her everything he possesses.[32] The Father who gives birth to his Son in eternity gives birth to his Son in the soul. The virgin soul is made wifely and fruitful through the work of the divine as/within her.

Insofar as the soul is nothing and equal to the divine, she is also the Son to whom the Father is giving birth and the mother of that divine self-birth.

> Not only is the soul with him, and he equal with her, but he is in her, and the Father gives his Son birth in the soul in the same way as he gives him birth in eternity, and not otherwise. He must do it whether he likes it or not. The Father gives birth to his Son without ceasing; and I say more: He gives me birth, me, his Son and the same Son. I say more: He gives birth not only to me, his Son, but he gives birth to me (as) himself and himself (as) me and to me (as) his being and nature.[33]

Just as the Son is absolutely equal to the Father, the soul also is identified with both the Father and the Son. Eckhart radicalizes the traditional Christian belief in the sonship of all believers and creates an absolute identity between the Father, the Son (and the Holy Spirit, as a few texts remind us),[34] and the soul insofar as she is devoid of all creatureliness. The soul gives birth to herself when she participates in the divine self-birth. Eckhart's use of shifting and ambiguous pronouns enacts this identification and self-birth in language.[35] He directly addresses his audience, furthermore, in order to highlight the shifts in identity made possible through detachment.[36] Eckhart himself is the Son, the Father, and the soul in and through whom the divine self-birth occurs. All are one and all speak in the sermon.

The notion of self-birth is further radicalized in those passages, some of which were pointed out above, where Eckhart speaks of the profound unity between the ground of the soul and the ground of the divine.[37] As we have seen in the *Commentary on John*, it is very difficult to distinguish between the Father and the ground of the divine, that which lies behind the distinctions between the persons of the Trinity and is the source of the eternal *bullitio* or overflowing that generates the Son. The soul becomes equal to the divine in the breakthrough into her ground that is also the divine ground, yet only through participating in the work of the Father—the birth of the Son in eternity—can she take part in the univocal relationship of the Trinitarian persons. The virgin soul is made a wife and is fruitful, becoming the empty space in which the Father gives birth to the Son.

> A virgin who is a wife is free and unpledged, without attachment; she is always equally close to God and to herself. She produces much fruit, and it is great, neither less nor more than is God himself. This virgin who is a wife brings this fruit and this birth about, and every day she produces fruit, a hundred or a thousand times, yes, more than can be counted, giving birth and becoming fruitful from the noblest ground of all—or, to put it better, from that same ground where the Father is bearing his eternal Word, from that ground is she fruitfully bearing with him.[38]

The soul becomes the mother of the Son, and in doing so the mother becomes divine. Eckhart reverses traditional readings of this biblical passage, which insist that the virgin receives a hundredfold, while lay people, among them wives and mothers, are said to be less fruitful.[39] The imagery recurs and is personalized when Eckhart describes a waking dream in which he "became pregnant with nothing as a woman does with a child, and in this nothing God was born."[40] When human beings bring themselves to "nothing," they give birth to the divine.[41]

THE SOUL AS VIRGIN WIFE

In many of the sermons I have discussed, in particular 2 and 6, there is an apparent contradiction between the virgin and wifely soul.

This incongruity, however, is only a problem for Aristotelian logic, grounded in the rule of noncontradiction, and not for the mystical or "dialectical" logic of the sermon. The contradiction creates an aporia, a breakdown of logical categories and human reason, and provides a glimpse into the mystery of nondualistic reality which Eckhart is trying to engender. Interpretations of Eckhart's thought must not place priority on either the virgin or the wifely soul, on either of the two moments of return, for they are always implicated in each other. They cannot be separated as Christian and Neoplatonic strands of influence and then ordered, as some commentators have attempted to do, without subverting the complex movements of Eckhart's thought.[42]

John Caputo, for example, argues that "[I]n the one, the breakthrough of the Godhead is *more radical* than the birth of the Son and indeed the ground and basis for it. In the other, the birth of the Son *crowns* and *perfects* the unity with the Godhead as fruitfulness perfects virginity."[43] This explanatory scheme is based on the assumption of a Christian-Neoplatonic rift in Eckhart's thought: the dialectic brings the radical unity of the Godhead together with the personal loving God and Son of the Christian tradition. Through reading Eckhart with and against Mechthild and Porete, however, another contrast lying behind his thought is uncovered, one which clarifies the essential unity of the two moments of birth and breakthrough. Eckhart uses the Neoplatonic philosophical principles as another means of explaining and making apparent through language the insights of beguine spirituality, giving the legitimation of the "philosophers" to the beguine theologies. In so doing, however, he also subverts the predominant scholastic philosophy of his contemporaries and radicalizes Christian Neoplatonic thought. Moreover, Eckhart uses the apparent contradictions between his scholastic, Neoplatonic, and beguine sources to subvert and break apart normal logical categories and linguistic usages, which are profoundly implicated in each other, in order to create a new mode of consciousness. Eckhart's use of wordplay, referential shifts, logical contradictions, and double paradigms further blurs the distinction between the soul and the divine, helping to bring about the change of consciousness he demands.

In his refusal to give priority to either of the two moments of return described above, Eckhart creates a double paradigm. Once the birth of the Son occurs in the soul, she is able to break through into the undifferentiated ground of the divine, but at the same time the birth of the Son in the soul cannot occur without the unity of her ground and that of the divine. These two paths reflect the two forms of emanation from the divine discussed in Chapter 5, further emphasizing the identity of God and the soul. Yet unlike the act of creation or *ebullitio*, neither the birth of the Son in the soul nor the breakthrough to the divine ground yields an inferior relationship.

The double paradigm may be further elucidated in the context of the Christian language of grace, for there is an originary grace of creation and also the grace given by the Son and the Holy Spirit for the salvation of human beings.[44] The first corresponds to the notion of the ground of the soul and her union with the ground of the divine before creation; the second to the notion of the birth of the Son in the soul as that which creates a union between the soul and the Godhead.[45] For Eckhart the Incarnation is the central work of redeeming grace, for it is the source of humanity's divine sonship.[46] In the Incarnation, Christ takes on human nature and reforms it so that it can reattain its ground in the divine. The originary grace of creation is both common to all humanity and at the same time the site of greatest possible identity with the divine. Unlike the rest of creation, which was made according to an image that God had within himself, Eckhart writes, God

> made [the soul] according to himself, in short, according to all that he is in his nature, his being, his activity which flows forth yet remains within, and according to the ground where he remains within himself, where he constantly gives birth to his only-begotten Son, from where the Holy Spirit blossoms forth. God created the soul in accordance with this out-flowing, inward-remaining work.[47]

While the Incarnation and divine sonship bring about the breakthrough into the divine ground, the unity of the ground of the soul and of the divine is the basis for the work of the Son in the soul. Eckhart thus undermines the very scholastic distinction between originary and salvific grace with which he begins.

Through the consistent use of both sides of the double paradigm, Eckhart pushes logic to its limit and forces the reader to attempt to think beyond the confines of an Aristotelian logic grounded in the rule of noncontradiction and the excluded middle. The procession and the return are one, *bullitio* and the breakthrough are one, the role of nature and grace in the return are equal and undecidable, and Eckhart refuses consistently to favor one path over the other, for to do so would be to think in linear, logical terms and to lose the mystery of nondualistic mystical thought. The soul cannot be taken up without the breakthrough to the ground of the divine and it cannot be one with the divine ground without being taken up through the birth of the Son in the soul. The identification of human nature in its virtual existence with the existence of the Son as realized in the birth of the Son in the soul makes unity possible. Yet this unity preexists the self-birth of the Trinity and is its ground. Eckhart refuses to decide. The truth of the Incarnation lies within this paradox; Jesus Christ takes on human nature and thus through his constant self-birth is in continued relation with the world and the divine. The singular historical event itself is consistently downplayed in favor of a cosmic and spiritual reading of the Incarnation—one that makes it an experience obtainable by every human being in any historical moment. Insofar as the soul or the human being strips herself of her createdness and particularity, she is one with the ground and with the Son: central to this paradoxical interplay is the continued and continual activity of the divine in and through the world in acts of justice.

To understand the breakthrough as "foundational," then, although superficially warranted by some of Eckhart's claims, is to apply temporal and spatial categories to that which lies beyond all such dualistic frames. In superimposing such order on Eckhart's conception of the return, the mystical aporia that he creates through logical self-contradiction, double paradigms, and referential shifts is explained away.[48] Further, this view does not take into account the true nature both of the ground of the divine and of the work of the divine and soul. Accounts like that given by Caputo ignore the paradox that the soul becomes a wife *while still* a virgin.[49] If we understand the relationship of breakthrough and birth in light of the roots of the two conceptions in the mysticism of the beguines, we gain new insight into why Eckhart insists on their mutual necessity *and* simultaneity.

Before looking further at the implications of this teaching, I would like to give some attention to Eckhart's understanding of the "work" of the soul and mystical language as part of that "work." I will then explore further the place of the body and of creation in Eckhart's theology, first as they are understood negatively in the movement of detachment, and then as they are given more positive valuations in his understanding of the unity of action and contemplation. These themes, marking a central point of divergence and commonality with the work of Mechthild and Porete, will lead to Chapter 7.

THE WORK OF THE SOUL / GOD AND LANGUAGE AS WORK

As I have shown, the idea of the identity of the ground of the soul and of the divine is pointed to in the discussion of the birth of the Son in the soul found in Sermon 6. This identity is intrinsic to the self-birth, for only through its identity with God's ground is the soul able to participate in the divine *bullitio*. The ontological claim is, not surprisingly, allied with an epistemological and linguistic one. Eckhart thus argues that the soul must not name the divine, but must reject all referential language, for the divine ground, like that of the soul, lies beyond such language:[50]

> You should perceive him without image, without a medium, and without comparisons. But if I am to conceive of God so, without a medium, I must just become him, and he must become me. I say more: God must just become me, and I must just become God, so completely one that this "he" and this "I" become and are one "is," and, in this is-ness, eternally perform one work, for this "he," who is God, and this "I," which is the soul, are greatly fruitful.[51]

God is perceived and named only through the identification of the soul and the divine, marked in Eckhart's text by pronomial shifts and referential ambiguity. In the experience of identity, the work is brought forth. Or conversely, acts of justice, rooted in equality and detachment, *are* the work, the birth of the Son in the soul and in eternity.

As I argued in Chapter 5, Eckhart claims that only being (*esse*) and one (*unum*) can be predicated of the divine, and these only in an eminent sense that negates their meaning insofar as it is attached to creatures. The most adequate means of divine predication occur through the self-referral of the birth of the divine Word out of its ground. Meaning with reference to the divine exists most adequately when the soul participates in the divine self-birth of the Word, for the divine cannot be named, referred to, or imagined within human, delimited, and dualistic language since language can convey only that knowledge given through the senses.[52] As such it is marked by human embodiment and separation from the divine. Only in subverting imagistic language can God become radically embodied in the just work of the soul. The rift between embodiment and disembodiment is overcome, as the divine is shown to be radically immanent in its transcendence. Detachment, then, is both an epistemological and an ethical movement; to know God is to share in the divine being, marked by equality and justice. The fruitfulness of the virgin soul in the birth of the Son within her is the mystical corollary of the "negation of negation," for the negation of all creatureliness in detachment gives birth to the fullness of divine being.

The image of the virgin soul is a response to this apophatic understanding of the essential inability of creatures to know the creator or the ground of the divine. It is also required by the Aristotelian aspects of Eckhart's epistemology. The soul that seeks to realize the divine must participate in the birth of the Son in the soul, the process of divine self-naming. Not only is it impossible to know the undifferentiated ground of the divine within delimited logic, it is also impossible to know or comprehend the Word, the differentiated aspect of the Godhead that is the archetype of creation, without participating in the divine work. The fact that this self-naming does not lie within normal linguistic structures is pointed to by the use of the term "work" (*werk, werc, gewurke*). Eckhart's terminology subverts traditional forms of divine predication and traditional understandings of the relationship between works and contemplation. The birth of the Son in the soul is exhibited or revealed in the world through the just actions or "works" of men and women. When human beings are just, they are the Son who is born in the soul and is equal to the soul. The sign of the divine in the world is not a normal linguistic signifier, an entity, or a suffering body, but the just act, which is the fruit of the work of the divine and the soul, for it alone is the expression of the fullness of divine being.

Whereas Mechthild and Porete understand their "work" in the world as the propagation of the Word of God and of Christ as it is given to them to speak, Eckhart emphasizes that the Word, insofar as humans comprehend it, is always a "work." Although often taking linguistic form—for example, Eckhart's preaching and linguistic creativeness—the work is irreducible to referential language and narrative structures. Rather it "works" through the latter's subversion. Eckhart uses traditional Christian language as symbols for the flow of emanation and return; the "dialectical" logic and paradox of mystical philosophy, as well as the kind of pronomial ambiguity seen in the preceding passages, subvert and break apart language to reveal the mystery of a reality not governed by dualities such as creator/creature, transcendent/immanent, and male/female. Only in this way can he be said to support in a qualified way a teaching on divine predication that upholds the way of eminence; what can be said of the divine is said only in light of Eckhart's teaching on analogy and dialectic, which undermines the canons of Aristotelian logic.[53] Meaning lies in the just act, which is the manifestation of the divine in the world. These actions are not described by Eckhart, for justice is irreducible to referential language; like the divine, who is justice itself, it is neither this nor that. While the mystical awareness of the work stands as a meaningful event of divine self-naming and manifestation, it can only be named by that "un-naming" that is apophatic language.[54]

Eckhart, then, creates a mystical symbolic system to describe the union of the soul and the divine and the way in which they may be mystically apprehended. Yet the source of mystical insight lies primarily in the subversion of this symbolic vocabulary and theological system through the use of logical self-contradiction, double paradigms, and referential shifts in which God and the soul become indistinguishable. Through this language, Eckhart attempts to create a nonreferential discourse, a form of speech that breaks through reified and delimited language and thought in order to demonstrate its limitations and to allow it to function in new ways. This is one aspect of the "work" of the soul unified with the divine—one outcome of that union. Through contradiction and paradox, Eckhart sets language in motion; the signifier of the Son, for instance, is never allowed to become static and objectified, for it describes an action, process, or movement, its own eternal birth, rather than a figure or entity. Through this constant flux, dualities are subverted in Eckhart's speech.

The same occurs conceptually. Eckhart goes beyond the dualistic concepts of transcendence and immanence by asserting and subverting them both in his discussions of God as the One, or "negation of negations," discussed above in Chapter 5. By positing the unlimited, absolutely transcendent, and unspeakable nature of God, Eckhart negates all predication and claims that God is absolutely one and simple. In making God radically immanent through the birth of the Son in the soul and the equality of the ground of the soul and of the divine, however, he not only gives himself a way to speak about the divine, but also paradoxically secures its transcendence. That which is most indistinct (i.e., immanent) and most inaccessible to language is most distinct, and thus most transcendent. One must think of God as simultaneously distinct and indistinct, and the more distinct insofar as he is indistinct. The less one can distinguish one's self from the

Godhead, the more one is stripped of createdness, the more immanent is the Godhead. But the utter lack of distinction of the Godhead is its distinguishing mark, and therefore that by which its transcendence is secured. The soul "knows" the transcendent only by becoming one with it,[55] utterly indistinct; yet it "knows" the divine as different and transcendent even when it is radically immanent. The radically immanent and the radically transcendent are both maintained, and through their movement the identity and difference of God and of the soul are constituted.

Eckhart uses what he calls the "negation of negation" to maintain the absolute transcendence and absolute immanence of the divine.[56] As that which is distinct by its utter lack of distinction, God is *unum* or One. The advantage of this predicate is that it is both negative *and* affirmative: it both negates limitation and affirms the fullness and plentitude of the term under consideration. The culminating movement in Eckhart's apophasis, is, then, positive. *Unum* is the privileged term because it adds nothing to *esse*, the one term predicated of the divine, except for its absolute affirmation. As McGinn argues, Eckhart defines God as absolute self-presence and purity of being through the negation of negation.[57]

This claim, however, together with the meaning and significance of being in Eckhart's work, must be closely scrutinized if we are to avoid anachronistic readings, while recognizing Eckhart's originality within the context of medieval ontology and language. Eckhart is neither traditionally theistic nor is he atheistic or nihilistic. His language consistently subverts substantialist ontologies, and in doing so emphasizes the unity of the divine in the work that actuates it—the just act or the self-birth of the divine in the soul. This at times leads to the claim that God is nothing; but the meaning of this "nothing" must be interrogated, for modern atheism substantializes the divine just as traditional theism does. In the early *Parisian Questions*, for example, Eckhart argues for the priority of the attribute of intelligence over that of being. The act of understanding or intellection, a negative capability in its Aristotelian usage, is the foundation of being, and thus the Godhead is defined as nonbeing. Eckhart at times goes even further:

> And if I say: "God is wise," that is not true. I am wiser than he. If I say: "God is being," it is not true; he is a being transcending being and a nothingness transcending being.[58]

God is here described as both being and nothingness—in both cases transcendent to being.

At issue here is Eckhart's distinction between *esse simpliciter* and *esse hoc et hoc*, by which he is able to argue that insofar as creatures have being, God does not, but insofar as creatures are nothing, God is pure being.[59] This insofar as (*inquantum*) is central to Eckhart's linguistic practice, for by means of this principle the gap between God and creation, between being and being this or that, between univocal and equivocal relationships, is both maintained and subverted. In other words, God is the source and absoluteness of being, but being can be used of God only if it is absolutely differentiated from that being possessed by creatures.[60] God is neither some-thing or no-thing, for God cannot be delimited as an entity in this way. Hence the dialectic of "the all" and "the nothing" found in Porete's *Mirror* is repeated in Eckhart through his dialectic of being and nothingness. Through this dialectic, traditional ways of thinking about and naming the divine are undermined and the gap between being and nothing is, paradoxically, overcome. Once again, Eckhart's insistence on the radical disjunction between God and creatures raises the issue of what place the created world and human nature have in his mysticism.

CREATION

Like Porete in her dialectic of all and nothing, Eckhart appears to deny all positive valuation to creation, potentially undercutting his own claims for the importance of the "work" of justice in the world. In the same way, having spiritualized the Incarnation to the extent that it is reenacted by each believer who experiences the birth of the Son in the soul, Eckhart might seem to have lost the historical, corporeal, and created basis for charity and the imitation of Christ. Before turning in Chapter 7 to some of the possible reasons for Eckhart's spiritualization of the imitation of Christ (a movement begun by Mechthild and continued in the work of Porete), we must look more closely at the place of creation and corporeal reality in his thought.

As Alois Haas demonstrates, it is impossible to write about Eckhart's understanding of creation without reference to the theories of analogy and of dialectic considered in the previous chapter. Because Eckhart's statements about creation are always formulated in terms of his analogical and dialectical methods, furthermore, his views cannot be discussed without reference to his understanding of the divine.[61] Just as we can only interpret Eckhart's assertion that God is a "nothingness transcending being" by understanding it in connection with his formulation of the relationship between God and creatures with regard to being, in the same way his statement that all of creation is nothing makes sense only in the light of these same methodological principles.

Eckhart's most radical statements about the negative ontological status of creatures are made in the context of pleas to his audience to seek nothing but God. Eckhart's discussions of prayer, for example, continually stress that one must not ask anything from God or in any way make him a means to an end.

> You are seeking something along with God, and you are acting just as if you were to make a candle out of God in order to look for something with it. Once one finds the thing one is looking for, one throws the candle away. This is what you are doing. Whatever else you are looking for in addition to God, it is nothing, no matter what it might be—whether it be something useful or reward or devotion or whatever it might be. You are seeking nothing, and so you find nothing.[62]

Such statements, expressing distrust of and warning against the possible idolatry of works, rewards, and special experiences, are found throughout the sermons.

Eckhart goes on to explain why, given his ontology, people are seeking nothing when they desire rewards and extraordinary experiences.

> All creatures are a pure nothing. I do not just say that they are insignificant or are only a little something: They are a pure nothing. Whatever has no being, *is* not. Creatures have no being because their being depends on God's presence. If God were to turn away from creatures for an instant, they would turn to nothing.[63]

Here we are reminded of Eckhart's claim, made in his commentary on the Gospel of John, that anything that has its principle from another does not have being in the proper sense of the term. God, understood as the source and font of all being and existence, alone has being; all else is nothing.

As the commentaries on Genesis make clear, for Eckhart creation is a sharing of being, that act by which God bestows his own being on creation.[64] Yet because of the radical dependence of creation on God as its source, it is nothing in itself.

> I once said (and it is true), if someone were to have the whole world and God, he would not have more than if he had God alone. All creatures have nothing more without God than a gnat has without God—[they are] just the same, neither less nor more.[65]

This ontology insures that, with relation to formal existence, God alone has being and value; it also underlines the equal dependence of all creatures on God and points to their equality in nothingness. This equality is the ground of justice as well as of the breakthrough and birth of the Son in the soul. Equality of creatures is predicated upon their nothingness, and yet paradoxically leads to their oneness with the divine.

As in Porete's *Mirror*, the idea that the soul must comprehend her own nothingness is tied to an idea of her absolute receptivity to God. For Porete, the soul can only be reformed in the divine image when she has lost all of her own characteristics and her own will.[66] Eckhart points to a similar view with regard to the nothingness of creation when he tells his audience about the difference between human making and divine creating. His comments occur in a discussion of the relationship between the just human being and his works and the necessity for all works being done in a spirit of detachment, or without a why.

> Even if you form God within yourself, whatever works you perform for a [specific] purpose are all dead, and you ruin good works. . . . And so, if you want to live and want your works to live, you must be dead to all things and have become nothing. It is a characteristic of creatures that they make something out of something, while it is a characteristic of God that he makes something out of nothing. Therefore, if God is to make anything in you or with you, you must first have become nothing.[67]

If the soul wishes to become one with the divine and thereby become the site of his activity, all createdness must be removed and she must become detached and virgin. This language, again, is tied to the dialectical relationship between God and creatures, for only insofar as he or she is a creature, a particular being (*esse hoc et hoc*), and thus other than and dependent on God, is the human being nothing. In the very next lines of the sermon, Eckhart suggests another level of reality on which the human being dwells when he enjoins his audience to return to that aspect of their souls in which their nobility lies: "Hence go into your own ground and work there, and the works that you work there will all be living."[68]

In many places Eckhart reminds his readers and listeners that the human being is possessed of this nobility, thus subverting his own claims concerning the nothingness of all creatures.[69] The two statements, however, are not simply contradictory, as our understanding of Eckhart's dialectical ontology shows. Again the *inquantum* principle is crucial to Eckhart's thought, for insofar as human beings are created, they must be brought to nothing in order to become one with God: "No creature can reach God in its capacity as a created thing, and that which is created, must be broken, so that the good might come out."[70] Only after the human being has detached itself from its created nature, including the will, is his or her true nobility, the ground of the soul where God and the soul are one, uncovered. Yet Eckhart appeals to this nobility in order to demand detachment. Once more, a double paradigm is at work, for creatures are both all and nothing, noble and debased.

All of these statements are based on another central tenet of Eckhart's mystical theology: "God loves nothing but himself and what is like himself, insofar as he finds it in me and me in him."[71] Rather than undermining the goodness and generosity of the divine, this claim is coupled with an assertion of God's need to love human beings: "If God were deprived of loving us, that would deprive him of his being and his Godhead, for his being depends on his loving me."[72] This is true because, in conformity with traditional Christian teaching, Eckhart argues that God's being and his nature demand his love, for he is love. Without the emphasis on divine feminization found in Mechthild and Porete, Eckhart nevertheless follows them and the tradition in his reference to this attribute. It parallels the claim made in Sermon 52 that God only becomes God with the act of creation, an assertion reminiscent of Mechthild's account of creation as the outflowing of divine love.[73] For Eckhart, again in ways prefigured in Mechthild, the very Godness of God is something that the human soul must strive to surpass, returning to her precreated state before God was God and the soul was a creature distinct from the divine. The goal of the return, ultimately, is to become absolutely like the divine ground or Godhead, for according to Eckhart, only that which is like can become one. In this state of detachment, God is no longer compelled by love, but rather by the identity in nature and equality between the soul and the divine; he must give his all to the soul.[74]

Eckhart claims that by becoming nothing, the soul makes herself like to God and therefore capable of union with him; again, Eckhart might be seen as making the claim that God is nothing.[75] Yet such interpretations are tempered by a thorough understanding of Eckhart's use of analogy and dialectic. Like Porete with her dialectic of all and nothing, Eckhart consistently maintains the disjunction between human beings, insofar as they are created, and God.[76] By "nothing" in these formulations, Eckhart is referring to the fact that creatures insofar as they are creatures and have their principle from another (thereby existing in an equivocal relationship with the divine) do not share in the being that is God. When they strip themselves of all of that which is nothing from the perspective of eternity, thus making themselves nothing from the perspective of creation, souls become one with God.

This might be put in terms of a distinction between statements made from the perspective of God and eternity and those made from the perspective of time and creation. Yet this underestimates Eckhart's divergence from traditional theistic language, for insofar as God is hypostasized as a particular being (a tendency endemic to referential language) he himself partakes of the nothingness of the created realm. From this perspective, it is necessary to assert that God is nothing, therefore marking God's radical alterity from those things that make up the created world. Eckhart prays to God to free him from God in all the radicality that such language suggests, undermining the scholastic distinction, which operates within the duality between God and creatures.[77] Insofar as the soul has been taken up into an univocal relationship with the divine in the birth of the Son in the soul, she partakes in the constantly begotten eternal now, a place in which God himself both does and does not exist. Out of the nothingness of this divine ground, which is also the ground of the soul, the birth of justice takes place. Eckhart subverts theistic and atheistic language, both of which partake in referential reification.

I have stressed the centrality to Eckhart's mysticism of his distinction between virtual and formal existence and the concomitant claim that there is an uncreated aspect of the soul. This point marks his greatest theological and philosophical elaboration of Mechthild's and Porete's thought with regard to the absolute union of the soul and the divine.

As we have seen, Eckhart denied making the latter claim, but it can be found in the German sermons.[78] Furthermore, given his understanding of the relationship between the principle and its source discussed in Chapter 5,[79] the implication that an aspect of the soul is uncreated follows naturally from his claims about the virtual existence of all creatures in the Word. If all creation exists virtually in the Son and the Son is identical with the Father in the divine ground, then the soul also must have a place in the undifferentiated ground of the divine. Hence his claim that the ground of the soul and of the divine are one.[80] Even the mediation of the Son is denied in the breakthrough. Eckhart stresses the continued self-birth of the Son out of this divine ground, the self-birth through which the detached soul becomes fruitful in the world *as* the Son.

What exactly, and more concretely, Eckhart means when he distinguishes the created aspect of humanity from its uncreated aspect is in part elucidated by his distinction between that aspect of human nature Jesus assumed in the Incarnation and that from which one must detach oneself in order to become one with the divine. While Eckhart never explicitly argues with traditional and historical understandings of the Incarnation, they are certainly secondary in his estimation to its cosmic and spiritual ramifications. Like Porete, Eckhart here diverges from Mechthild's concern with the physical and human characteristics of Jesus Christ. With regard to the cosmic function of the Incarnation, Eckhart makes a distinction similar to that between *esse simpliciter* and *esse hoc et hoc*, differentiating between general humanity or human nature and the particularity of this or that human being.

> The masters say that human nature has nothing to do with time and that it is completely untouched, being much more within and closer to a person than he is to himself. Therefore God assumed human nature and united it with his Person. At this point human nature became God because he took on human nature and not a human being. Therefore, if you want to be this same Christ and God, abandon all of that which the eternal Word did not assume. The eternal Word did not assume *a* human being. Therefore, leave whatever is *a* human being in you and whatever you are, and take yourself purely according to human nature. Then you are the same in the eternal Word as human nature is in him; for your human nature and his are without difference. It is one, and whatever it is in Christ, that it also is in you.[81]

Central to this distinction is the claim that in eternity, and by extension in the eternal now in which those who are one with God dwell, there is no number and hence no individuation.[82] Individuation and multiplicity mark createdness and thus obstruct unity with the One. Eckhart makes this point explicitly in the defense documents written at Cologne, where he shows the connection between the two kinds of grace and the Incarnation. Here Eckhart again insists that Christ takes on human nature and not a particular human person in the Incarnation; therefore humans should not love what is distinct, the will, but rather the general human nature shared by all.[83]

In Sermon 25, Eckhart tells his hearers that three things keep human beings from hearing the word: corporeality, multiplicity, and temporality.[84] These three obstructions to the word are intimately related and define createdness for Eckhart.[85] Despite passing references to the resurrection of the body and the unity of the human being as body and soul,[86] the main tendency of Eckhart's thought denies the body as constitutive of human nature. Embodiment brings about and marks individuation. Eckhart suggests that this aspect of humanity must be released in order to attain unity with God. Only general human nature is essential, that which is taken up by the Son in the Incarnation and which is united in its ground with the divine source, in whose image the soul was made. If the soul is to achieve identity with the divine she must become detached from all of her own creatureliness, which includes the body as well as the personality and all other forms of particularity. Eckhart, then, insists that creation is a pure nothing, and should be treated as such.[87] Yet at the same time, he opens the possibility for a new relationship toward and understanding of corporeality attained by the detached soul; here he formulates his "mysticism of everyday life" in which activity and contemplation are one. When the soul has become detached from all individuation and the possessiveness implied in that individuation, a new relationship to corporeality (as well as to time and multiplicity) is made possible.

THE UNITY OF THE ACTIVE AND CONTEMPLATIVE LIVES

Eckhart's account of the unity of contemplation and action is the key to understanding his second conception of corporeality. This unity is symbolically expressed in the image of the virgin wife and discussed most fully in his reinterpretation of the story of Mary and Martha given in Sermon 86. He begins by contrasting intellectual satisfaction with that of the senses, marking the importance he places on the nonaffective aspect of the contemplative life; it grounds his teaching on the unity of contemplation and action:

> God satisfies our senses and feelings by granting us comfort, pleasure, and fulfillment; but to be pampered in this with regard to the lower senses is not something that happens to God's dear friends. But intellectual satisfaction is a matter of the spirit. I call that intellectual satisfaction when the highest part of the soul is not drawn down by any pleasure, so that she does not drown in pleasures, but stands sovereign above them. A person is only then intellectually fulfilled when the joys and sorrows of creatures cannot pull the highest part [of the soul] down. I call "creatures" everything that one feels and sees lower than God.[88]

When the wise and mature Martha calls lovingly on Christ to bid Mary to get up, Eckhart—having given this peaceful interpretation of the altercation between Mary and Martha—voices the suspicion that Mary was sitting more in enjoyment of the senses than to gain true spiritual profit. According to Eckhart, Martha asks Christ to make Mary get up so that she will not become stuck in a life that demands pleasure rather than spiritual progress. Christ's response (which seems in the biblical story to be a reproach to Martha) is read by Eckhart as a promise that Mary will receive the fullness of her desire and then will begin to work. This carries with it an admonishment of those who hope to escape action.

> Now some people want to go so far as to achieve freedom from works. I say this cannot be done. It was not until after the time when the disciples received the Holy Spirit that they began to perform virtuous deeds.[89]

In the same way, Eckhart continues, not until after Mary has been taught by Christ does she go out into the world to serve—preaching, teaching, and being a servant to the disciples.

These are all bodily activities, pointing to the existence in Eckhart's thought of a new relationship toward corporeality that is established when one has become detached from all created things, both corporeal and incorporeal.[90] In this sermon, furthermore, Eckhart again makes

clear that his understanding of detachment cannot be taken too literally, as signifying an insensibility to the surrounding world. Rather
the disposition of the will is at issue.

> Now our dear people imagine they can bring things to a point where
> their senses are utterly unaffected by the presence of sensible objects.
> They cannot achieve this. That a painfully loud racket be as pleasant
> to my ears as the charming tones of a stringed instrument—that I
> shall never achieve. This, however, one should attain, that one's will,
> formed to God in understanding, is free of all natural pleasure, and,
> whenever insight on the alert commands the will to turn away, that
> the will say: "I do it gladly."[91]

The body and its sensation cannot be destroyed; rather the attitude
of the soul toward these created things must be transformed through
loss of self-will and detachment.

In the sermon Eckhart describes three possible paths to God, showing that the goal is a relationship without any mediation between the
human being and the divine. Although the language of the sermon is
difficult, Eckhart places a higher valuation on the third path, in which
all mediators between the human being and God, even the humanity of
Christ, are overcome. Eckhart argues that in the first path to the divine,
"[o]ne is to seek God in all creatures through all kinds of activity and
with flaming love."[92] While this path bears the sanction of Solomon
and of Eckhart himself, he implies that it still represents a mediated
relationship, for creatures play a role in the relationship between God
and the human being. It is the way of actions and virtuous deeds. The
second path, according to Eckhart, is "a pathless path, free yet bound,
raised aloft and wafted off almost beyond self and all things, beyond
will and images. However, it does not stand firmly on its own."[93] This
is the path taken by the apostle Peter, one on which he confronts the
Son in his incarnated nature, not yet God in his pure divinity. Clearly
associated with the life of contemplation and mystical ravishment,
Eckhart insists Peter's path is not the highest, for mediation still occurs.

Only the third path is without mediation. This was the way followed
by Paul when he was lifted up into the third heaven. Eckhart argues
that it is a "path and yet is a being-at-home" where God is seen
"immediately in his ownness."[94] Eckhart places Martha here, for
despite the occasional perturbation of her spirit by created things,
she shares an unmediated relationship with God that allows her to

be "in the midst of things, but not *in* things."[95] In the vocabulary of the sermon, she has risen above "works," or external deeds of virtue, and attained to a pure "activity" in which true justice lies. Although Eckhart emphasizes the necessity of becoming like Christ, he goes further and claims that one should *be* Christ. He insists that the highest path is to share the same relationship with the Godhead as the Son does, rather than to have a relationship mediated by the Son. The Incarnation is the model for the human being, but in a different way than for many of Eckhart's contemporaries. The soul should strive to be united with the Father as the Son is united to him. Through such a union, Eckhart says in uncharacteristically explicit language, every part of the body will "practice its own proper virtue," just as they did in Christ.[96] Not only is the soul reunited with that spark of herself that exists in the Godhead, but, Eckhart also implies, the body shares in this virtual existence in the divine.

This sermon on the classical Christian contrast between the figures of Mary and Martha, representing the contemplative and the active lives, reverses the traditional reading of the text in order to demonstrate the unity of the two ways of life in Eckhart's mystical theology.[97] The sermon clearly evokes what Dietmar Mieth calls Eckhart's mysticism of everyday life.[98] Against those spiritual writers who stress special, individual experiences and inactive contemplation, Eckhart claims that the highest contemplation is compatible with, and in fact brings about, a state of heightened activity. The sermon gives clear evidence that when Eckhart discusses the birth of the Son in the soul as a "work" he does not use the term only metaphorically. Rather, in reaching a point of identification with the Son, the Father, and the ground of the Godhead, the human being becomes capable of truly just and efficacious activity in the world. Or, putting it in another way, in achieving detachment and union with the divine ground, justice, equality, and the birth of the Son in the soul are effected. The implication of the final lines of the sermon, furthermore, is that through this "work," the entire human being—body and soul—is sanctified. To understand this position, it is necessary to remember the other side of Eckhart's dialectic of the transcendence and immanence of God, for insofar as one recognizes God's absolute immanence to the world one truly sees his transcendence or indistinction. Eckhart proclaims the sanctity of the whole created world while he simultaneously maintains divine transcendence and the nothingness of creation in itself.

Another distinction must be made at this point: to say that the work is meaningful does not mean that the Son provides a purpose, goal, or end to human and divine activity, in the normal understanding of these terms. As in Porete's *Mirror*, a central theme of Eckhart's mysticism is the idea that the soul must live "without a why," as God does.[99] He argues that all creaturely things are possessed by a why; the divine is that which exists and acts without a why, merely for its own sake.[100] In a similar way, Eckhart insists that God not be understood as useful. The truly just human being performs works without intention or hope for reward.

> The just person seeks nothing in his works, for those that seek something in their works or those who work because of a "why" are servants and traders. And so, if you want to be informed by and transformed into justice, have no [specific] intention in your works and form no "why" in yourself, either in time or in eternity, either reward or happiness, either this or that. Such works are, in fact, dead. Even if you form God within yourself, whatever works you perform for a [specific] purpose are all dead, and you ruin good works.[101]

In a sense, the divine and its manifestation in the world are meaningless, in the same way that God is nothing, for they are without purpose and cannot be explained within referential language and logical categories. The birth of the Son in the soul does not give meaning, but rather opens access to the divine in the created world. Any attempt to capture the work within the matrix of purpose and intention kills, regardless of the worthiness of the goal, for according to Eckhart all that is sought for a specific purpose belongs to the realm of accidents and thus of the inessential and unequal.[102] One receives the all that is God by "living without a why," recognizing the nothingness of all things insofar as they are created and other than God and their equality insofar as they are divine.

In a similar way, Eckhart's understanding of the relationship between the interior and the exterior work underlines both the unity of action and contemplation and his denial of any "utilitarian" understanding of the "work" of the soul and of the divine. Dietmar Mieth clarifies these points in his reading of a sermon in which Eckhart cites Aquinas, only to put his teachings to much different use than the one intended.[103] Aquinas argues for the superiority of the contemplative to the active life, yet claims that acts of love further the final goal of heavenly contemplation that will occur after death. He offers the possibility of a union between action and contemplation while on earth, based on the superiority of the latter.[104] Eckhart uses this Thomistic claim to make his own quite different point about the unity of the two types of life for the detached person. For Eckhart the "works" of the active life are one with the birth of the Son in the soul, which is both the fruit and the cause of divine contemplation.[105] As with Mechthild, action does not simply aid in the final goal of heavenly contemplation, but is intrinsic to contemplation itself.

Eckhart goes so far as to insist that the interior intention, sparked by the union of grounds and the birth of the Son in the soul, is alone important, thereby further altering the traditional conception of the active life.[106] This claim was cited in four of the articles condemned in the bull *In agro dominico*, pointing to the suspicion any such assertions were under at the time due to the so-called heresy of the free spirit and its apparent quietism. Eckhart's defense again cites Aquinas in apparent support of his teaching. Yet his reference to Aquinas is based on a serious subversion or misreading of the text.[107] Although, according to Aquinas, the will's lack of completion in an external action is not subject to punishment if it is involuntary, the perfection of the will demands such completion, for that is the end or goal of the will. Eckhart, on the other hand, uses the language of interior intention paradoxically to argue that one should strive to have *no will, no end,* and *no goal.*

Despite appearances, then, the appeal to interior intention is not incompatible with Eckhart's attempt to unify the active and contemplative lives but rather reinforces the mystical themes on which this identification is based. He argues that there are four reasons why the interior act alone is important: because the exterior act can be hindered; because only the interior act is properly commanded by God; because the interior act is never oppressive; and because the interior act praises God directly as its author.[108] The unity of the interior act with the free movement of the birth of the Son in the soul guarantees its primacy over the exterior act, which is subject to outside constraint and hindrance. Through the interior movement that is the birth of the Son in the soul true justice is brought into being; the interior intention is not the created soul's, but God's. To admit that the absence of an exterior work can diminish or alter the goodness or justice of this movement would be to admit the limitations of the created world into the conception of the divine and its work, for the soul shares in this work of self-creation.[109]

So just as Eckhart downplays the historical Incarnation and the particularity of the person of Christ in favor of the cosmic dimensions of the event,[110] he also deemphasizes the exterior act in favor of the interior to show that the divine work is not subject to the particularities and constraints of the created world. Where the first move allows him to show how the divine is radically immanent in the eternal now, rather than only in one historical moment, the second speaks directly to the scrupulosity endemic to Eckhart's culture. Both moves must be seen against this climate. On the one hand, Eckhart insists that the soul must become detached from good works, for as particular acts they are involved in the world of intentions and goals—in sum, they are part of the created realm.[111] At the same time he extols the interior act, insofar as it is done without attachment and in absolute purity of intention:

> To give a hundred marks of gold for God is a noble deed . . . yet . . . if I have the will that I should give a hundred marks if I had them— if the will is perfect, then in fact I have paid God and he must give account to me as if I had really given him a hundred marks.[112]

While interior and exterior are one in the movement of the divine,[113] Eckhart insists that creatureliness and its limitations have no power to affect the detached soul's divine intention, although the exterior act might be deterred. The body, experienced as present primarily in its pain and limitation, does not deter transcendence, although it shares in it.[114] Before God, all createdness is nothing and equal, not just the will and intellect, but the body as well. The equality of the divine ground is founded on this recognition. The justice that ensues subverts the very dualisms between creator and creature, and also between body and soul, whose radicalization gives rise to new consciousness. Before further discussion of this innovation, however, it will be useful to spell out the commonalities and divergences between Mechthild, Porete, and Eckhart in order to see better how his understanding of corporeality and of the relationship between the interior and the exterior act is derived from and responsive to the theological issues outlined in their texts.

7

The Transformation of Suffering in Mechthild of Magdeburg, Marguerite Porete, and Meister Eckhart

DETACHMENT AND LOSS OF WILL IN MEISTER ECKHART AND MARGUERITE PORETE

The most obvious point of connection between Meister Eckhart and the beguine mystics lies in the understanding of the nature of the union between God and the soul found in the work of Eckhart and Porete. Colledge and Marler show that some of Eckhart's most profound and daring statements on the nature of this union without distinction, those found in German Sermon 52, are directly paralleled by statements made by Porete in the *Mirror*. Porete's radical interpretation of the beguine ideal of spiritual poverty leads her to claim that the soul must annihilate her will in order to be united with God. The truly simple soul does not even will to will according to God's will, for even this level of independent volition is an impediment to perfect union.

> Thus the soul does not will nothing, says Love, unless she is free, for no one is free who wills anything by the will within him, whatever he might will. For then he is a servant to himself since he wills that God accomplish his will to his own honor. The one who wills this only wills that the will of God be accomplished in him and in another. For such a person, says Love, God refuses his kingdom.[1]

Those who attempt to do God's will, according to Love, are "merchants" who believe that they can barter with God for his love, a commercial metaphor used also by Eckhart, who calls those who seek to will the good in order to attain salvation "hirelings and traders."[2]

173

Like Porete, furthermore, Eckhart distinguishes between those who understand true spiritual poverty and the "donkeys" who believe that poverty lies in the works of the active and contemplative lives. Like Porete, Eckhart seems here to resolve the beguine dilemma of how to be both Mary and Martha by equating *both* with the realm of works that the soul must surpass. Freedom from such activity is elsewhere described as a disencumbering, again directly paralleling Porete's language.

> As long as a person has this as his will, that he wants to fulfill God's dearest will, he has not the poverty about which we want to talk. Such a person has a will with which he wants to fulfill God's will, and that is not true poverty. For if a person wants really to have poverty, he ought to be as free of his own created will as he was when he did not exist. For I tell you by the truth that is eternal, as long as you have a will to fulfill God's will, and a longing for God and for eternity, then you are not poor; for a poor person is one who has a will and longing for nothing.[3]

Eckhart uses the same threefold description of poverty as wanting, knowing, and having nothing found throughout the *Mirror*,[4] and similarly follows Porete's description of those things for which the naked soul has no need: "possessions or honor or ease or pleasure or profit or inwardness, holiness or reward or the kingdom of heaven."[5]

Colledge and Marler also show the way in which ideas from the *Mirror* elucidate Eckhart's somewhat cryptic statements about the poor soul being the place in which God works. Even more radically, the soul who has embraced absolute poverty is so poor that God would choose to work not in the soul but in himself. This is because the soul ultimately has no will with which to will even God's will, as both Porete and Eckhart argue. The use of spatial language to describe the union of God and the soul is found in the *Mirror* and is tied to Porete's use of courtly images and tropes. The soul who is completely annihilated or unencumbered is without a proper place, and is taken to God's "place," far from her own being.[6] Porete thereby evokes the image of the soul transported to God's faraway court, where she finds her proper place and true being in the divine.

Perhaps the most important parallel between Porete and Eckhart, however, first uncovered by Bernard McGinn, is that between the idea of the virtual existence of the soul, alluded to in the passage from Sermon 52 cited above, and suggestions of such a pre-created being found throughout the *Mirror*. Both Porete and Eckhart suggest that, insofar as the will is annihilated and the soul lives without a why and without imagistic or other mediations between herself and God, she has attained her true nature in the divine. The idea of a precreated soul is thus tied to the central themes of the annihilation of the will and of living without a why and without mediation between God and the soul. Some of Porete's formulations directly correspond to those found in Sermon 52. In Chapter 91, for example, the state of the annihilated soul is likened to the time before her creation:

> Now he [God] possesses the will without a why in the same way that he possessed it before the soul was made a lady by it. There is nothing except him. No one loves except him, for nothing is except him, and thus he alone completely loves, and sees himself alone completely, and praises alone completely by his being itself.[7]

The annihilated soul returns to her precreated state. The claim implies that the soul in some way preexists within the Godhead, a suggestion found in Mechthild as well and one on which rests the beguines' attempt to allay the suffering of body and soul.[8] Through the regulation and/or annihilation of the will the soul is able to attain the innocence of her precreated being. All works, then, whether of action or contemplation, become unnecessary and the body and the soul are freed from the arduous demands of Love.[9]

As I have demonstrated, in the Latin works Eckhart provides a metaphysical context for this claim that the soul preexists in the Godhead. Through his appropriation of Neoplatonic ontology, he argues for the virtual existence of all things within the Godhead, providing a philosophical setting for the idea of the precreated spark of the soul found in the sermons. The idea of all things preexisting in the divine Idea or Logos is Augustinian, yet Eckhart develops its implications in radically new directions. The theme has its genesis, moreover, in the idea of union without distinction found in Mechthild and elaborated on by Porete.[10] Here, in the experience of union without distinction that exists before creation and to which the soul desires to return, the soul lives together with/as the divine; and, of course, it is in living divinely—without a why—that this precreated state is attained. Eckhart, in adopting this language from Porete, again marks his knowledge of her text and their commonality of purpose.[11] Like Porete, he calls on his listeners to reject the path of works, both active and contemplative, and its mixture of alienation and ecstasy, in favor of the life of detachment through which the divine is made present in its absence or made absolutely immanent in its very transcendence.

These parallels between Porete's *Mirror* and the work of Eckhart have been pointed out and discussed. What has not been adequately addressed is the divergences in emphasis, language, and tone between Eckhart and Porete and the way in which Eckhart's work shows the influence, although less directly, of other strands in the beguine movement, represented more fully in Mechthild's *Flowing Light*. I argued in Chapter 4 that a central tension runs throughout Porete's *Mirror*, a tension fueled by her attempt to bring together the realms of time and eternity, changelessness and movement, the divine and the human. Porete clearly wishes to move away from the continuing uncertainties that plagued Mechthild at the end of her life by arguing that the simple soul has achieved a state of permanent union with the divine. This state of perfection and changelessness, however, conflicts with the realm of change and movement where the soul still lives. God lives and works through her, but aside from the cogent evidence of Porete's own life and work, the ways in which this occurs and the centrality of the soul as the site of divine action in the world are downplayed. Primary in Porete's account is the call for freedom, in particular freedom from Love's demand for virtue, perfection, ascetic and mystical works. In rejecting "bodily" and "creaturely" practices, Porete's Love attempts to free human beings from suffering and anxiety. Yet *all* works and discussion of works then become difficult. Eckhart, in his appropriation of Porete's thought, addresses this tendency toward what was later called quietism[12] and its implicit devaluation of the body and the created world. Through the birth of the Son in the soul and Eckhart's understanding of the just act, the "work" of the free soul is explicitly thematized. Eckhart therefore clarifies and draws out more fully an otherwise obscured feature of Porete's text. Through his understanding of the "virgin who is a wife," he elucidates how the soul becomes the place in the world where God acts.

THE "WORK" OF THE SOUL: MEISTER ECKHART AND MECHTHILD OF MAGDEBURG

In this light, we can understand the continuing influence of the type of spirituality represented by much of Mechthild's work. On the one hand, *The Flowing Light* clearly spiritualizes the idea of poverty and emphasizes the will, not the body, as central to human sinfulness; thus it diverges from much (although not all) of the beguine hagiographical tradition. In rejecting bodily suffering as a primary means to sanctity, Mechthild, like Porete, rejects a central feature of the path to holiness prescribed for women. While Mechthild does not go so far as to call for the annihilation of the will and the centrality of apophasis, her movement away from the body as the locus of human sinfulness and her subsequent teaching on the well-ordered soul mark an important stage in the progression that will lead to such claims.[13] Her understanding of mystical union, although expressed in a variety of more traditional formulas, suggests the idea of a union without distinction grounded in the preexistence of the soul within the divine. Her stress on the visionary imagination and its ties to suffering embodiment are, then, countered within *The Flowing Light* by suggestions of a union without distinction and of apophasis. Although her early expressions of these ideas occur in contexts in which the body and the soul are pitted against each other, struggling for control over her being, they lead to and resurface in later sections, which emphasize the continual presence of the divine to the soul.[14]

Central to Mechthild's text, however, is how the contemplative, mystical life and the active life reinforce each other and become one. By loving and suffering with Christ's humanity through her work in the world the soul becomes God with his divinity and achieves union even without the benefit of special experiences of his presence.[15] What is necessary for salvation and its rewards, Mechthild argues, is for the believer to follow the way of the suffering Christ as much as she is able and to desire to do good, or possess a correctly oriented will.[16] Mechthild thereby attempts to diminish the over-scrupulousness to which she was prone.[17] God, she claims, loves the good that is in one, and that good is Jesus Christ.[18] Her use of personification in *The Flowing Light* suggests the growing importance of the will to her thought and its role as mediating a new relationship between the body and the soul. Mechthild never gives the will an independent voice. By allowing the body and the soul to speak to each other, both are portrayed as if they are possessed of volition, and thus the onus of sinfulness is shared and no longer associated primarily with corporeality.

For both Mechthild and Eckhart, identification with the figure of Christ or the Son is given primacy, although the emphasis on suffering and exile in that identification, together with the continuing problem of constancy, are downplayed by the latter. Just as for Eckhart the breakthrough into the divine ground is always accompanied by the divine work, the birth of the Son in the soul, so for Mechthild union and action are intimately related. For both, the idea that the loving or detached soul compels (*twingen*) God and forces him to give his gifts is a recurrent one.[19] Not surprisingly this theme plays a large role in one of the few sermons in which Eckhart uses the metaphor of the soul as the bride of Christ, a sermon, furthermore, which appears to have been preached to nuns or religious women.[20] Devoted to Luke 1:28 "Hail, full of grace", the sermon centers on an understanding of the Incarnation as God's making himself like humanity so that humanity might become like God. The Incarnation occurs not only, and perhaps not even primarily, in the historical person of Jesus Christ, but also in the soul of each believer who humbles him or herself and achieves true detachment. As in Mechthild's work, then, the "lowness" or humility of the detached soul compels God, for that which is on high must flow out to that which is below.

> If I were up here, and I said to someone, "Come up here," that would be difficult. But if I were to say, "Sit down there," that would be easy. God acts like that. If a person humbles himself, God cannot withhold his own goodness but must come down and flow into the humble person, and to him who is least of all he gives himself the most of all, and he gives himself to him completely. What God gives is his being, and his being is his goodness, and his goodness is his love.[21]

The soul, free of all images and creatureliness, compels God's presence, reenacting the birth of the Son to the virgin in the birth of the Son in the soul. Here the dialectic of all and nothing, found throughout the *Mirror* and Eckhart's sermons, is transposed into Mechthild's language of humility, highlighting the links between these two dialectical movements. Like Mechthild, Eckhart calls on his listeners to place the love of God over fear, and in this love and detachment to accomplish all of the works that the Son does.[22]

In exhorting his listeners to become detached so that they might enter into the "chamber" where God exists in his ground, Eckhart makes one of his few allusions to the Song of Songs tradition and the soul as the bride of Christ so important to Mechthild. The link with themes from women's religiosity is underlined by a rare reference to the suffering of Christ. Discussing the good of the Incarnation, Eckhart tells the story of a rich husband and his wife. When the wife lost an eye in an accident, she grieved that she would no longer be worthy of her husband's love. To prove the constancy of this love, the husband gouged out his own eye, thereby becoming like his wife. So Christ, in becoming flesh, metaphorically gouges out his eye so that he might become like humanity. Eckhart characteristically focuses not on Christ's suffering, but rather on his transformation of himself into the likeness of humanity so that humans might be like the divine. Human suffering is not demanded to perfect that likeness; suffering is a misfortune, one that is made good and overcome through Christ's taking on flesh both historically and in the birth of the Son in the soul.[23] Christ's action transforms suffering into union rather than demanding further pain. If God is the soul's suffering, as Eckhart puts it in his early treatise on divine consolation, then suffering itself is here transformed into God.[24] Eckhart thereby echoes Mechthild's theological formulation of the divinizing power of the soul's suffering while partially subverting it and hence addressing the problem of constancy so central to her later writings. The soul's suffering is displaced by that of the Son, just as her constancy is insured by his.

Evoking Mechthild's understanding of the detached or humble soul as one who compels God's presence, and radicalizing her claim that this humble soul is Christ with his humanity and thus God with his divinity, Eckhart's sermon suggests a debt to the kinds of spirituality found in her work.[25] This reinforces the external evidence that Eckhart could have known *The Flowing Light*. Although direct textual influence cannot be firmly demonstrated, clearly Eckhart had this kind of religiosity in mind when composing this and other thematically related sermons. He is indebted to the tradition represented by *The Flowing Light* while mitigating its tensions in ways Mechthild herself suggests without thoroughly exploiting. As with the *Mirror*, a reading of Mechthild's work with and against Eckhart's highlights important themes and elucidates provisional resolutions of its tensions. Such a reading clarifies the role of the well-ordered soul as a means of tempering the oscillation between ecstasy and alienation experienced by the "wounded soul."

To understand better the interrelationships between the texts of Mechthild, Porete, and Eckhart, however, we must turn to the place of greatest apparent divergence between them—their attitudes toward the human body, creatureliness, and visionary imagination. As I said in Chapter 1, there is a tendency in many studies of gender issues, particularly with regard to medieval writings, to "discover" distinctions between male- and female-authored texts, usually by highlighting the greater somatic, emotional, and spontaneous nature of the latter.[26] The assumption is an old one, although the valuations have changed,[27] and it is one that I clearly wish to avoid. Although late medieval culture stressed the ties between women, embodiment, and the visionary imagination, we can trace the problematizing and rejection of these kinds of claims in Mechthild, Porete, and Eckhart. They do not, however, deny the body, as I will show. Rather, they reject the emphasis on suffering—the wounded body and the wounded soul—as the central means of overcoming the distance between the human and divine. In the apophasis of visionary imagination, the suffering "heart and body and life"[28] is spared and embodiment reevaluated. Through a discussion of the multiple views and valuations of the human body in the later Middle Ages, I would like to contextualize the discussion of Mechthild, Porete, and Eckhart and offer further explanation of *why* their texts move away from certain conceptions of and relationships with the human body. This will allow a reevaluation of the sources and the intentions of these mystical theologies, as well as a critique of some of the predominant paradigms that have governed feminist descriptions and judgments of medieval women's writings and their relations to those of men. As a result, better, more historically grounded explanations for the divergence in emphasis and tone between Mechthild, Porete, and Eckhart can be given. I will conclude, then, with a discussion of the problem of authority for women in the Middle Ages and how it may point to new explanations for the characteristics of some women's religious writings.

THE BODY AND GENDER IN THE LATER MIDDLE AGES

The paucity of reference to the body, its salvation, and its salvific function in Porete and Eckhart becomes worthy of note when put into the context of thirteenth- and fourteenth-century religious and theological writings that are particularly concerned with the present and future status of the human body.[29] As I demonstrated in Chapter 2,

hagiographical writings routinely locate miraculous power in the body
(particularly among women saints).[30] Some mystical texts, moreover,
describe ecstatic events as they are experienced by the languishing
body.[31] Many writers show explicit concern for the future welfare
of the body.[32] In addition to the closing dialogues between the body
and the soul (*FL*, bk. VII, ch. 65), Mechthild has a vision in which
the fully enclosed body of John the Apostle is seen as if sleeping,
waiting its heavenly reward. Because of the great love and esteem in
which John was held, his body is granted the privilege of a heavenly
home even before the second coming, although it is not yet reunited
with the soul and hence conscious.[33] The nonverbal testimonials of
popular religion, particularly the cult of relics, further emphasize the
importance of the body as a locus of the divine within the world;
questions about the practice demonstrate the lively concern of medieval people that the soul be reunited with her physical body in the
final resurrection.[34] Finally, theological arguments reflect and reinforce evidence from popular religion. Thomas Aquinas was just as
convinced of the physicality of the resurrected body as were more
"popular" audiences; his education allowed him to specify the exact
form this body would take.[35] This varied evidence demonstrates an
intense concern among late medieval Christian people and theologians
with the nature and salvific role of the body both in this world and
in the future. Belief in the Incarnation of Christ and the resurrection
of the body augments and is reinforced, moreover, by the prevalent
philosophical belief in the unity of the body and the soul as constitutive parts of the human being.[36] The doctrine of the resurrection
of the body grounds Christian belief in the personal survival of the
individual.[37]

There is evidence, furthermore, that the later Middle Ages saw an
increased emphasis on personal immortality conjoined with the growing interiority of religiosity brought about by the mysticism of Bernard
of Clairvaux and his followers. Where in the late antique period and
the early Middle Ages resurrection was generally understood as that
of the corporate church following the final judgment, increasingly the
last judgment was placed after the death of the individual, who was
seen as rising again *as* an individual.[38] Intense concern for personal
salvation and a critique of that concern appears in the work of the
beguines, and with it comes increased tensions about the place of the
body in the resurrection. Mechthild, Porete, and Eckhart all maintain

that the well-ordered, annihilated, or detached soul cares neither for heaven nor hell, thereby exposing the spiritual dangers of the focus on personal salvation, while also attempting to allay the anxiety it engenders. Mechthild remains committed to the resurrection of the body, but she does so at the risk of continuing anxiety over a good end—her attachment to the body makes her fear death.[39] Porete and Eckhart, in their attempts to quiet such anxieties, seem to denigrate, bypass, and ignore the body. Given the identification of embodiment with women in the later medieval period, they might seem, then, to denigrate the feminine.

This suspicion is raised when one recalls that the identification of women with the body was not always as constricting and problematic as modern feminist criticism would have us believe. For many medieval thinkers the body was seen as the locus of both sinfulness and holiness; it is, therefore, the site of both greater ambivalence and of higher valuation than many modern commentators recognize.[40] In first making this argument, Caroline Walker Bynum offered an essential corrective to the false picture of medieval Christianity as unqualified in its denunciation of the body and of femaleness insofar as it is tied to bodily nature. Yet the picture requires shading in order to capture the complexities of late medieval religiosity and of women's bodies and voices within it. Bynum stresses the difficulty of women's lives and their search for religious self-expression in the later Middle Ages, but she downplays essential factors in her evidence, for while the links between women and embodiment *do* occur, they are prevalent— before the fourteenth century—in (predominantly male-authored) hagiographical writings. Within these texts, moreover, bodies and souls are redeemed through the suffering of women. In emphasizing the redeemability of the body, we must not lose sight of how its salvation was effected. Bynum's argument, moreover, although seeming to explain the nature of women's religious experience in the later Middle Ages, tells more about how the men who controlled that society viewed the human person, the body, and women and shaped larger cultural expectations. Even though many women appear to have shared these views, they took on a significantly different character and meaning when advanced by women.[41] In the hagiographies and other accounts of female saints and religious women written by men, women serve as figures for the male writer or viewer's bodiliness, rather than as autonomous female subjects.[42]

Of course, medieval women were influenced, shaped, and constricted by the cultural and religious beliefs of the world within which they lived; yet to treat hagiographical writings about women and their own mystical treatises without distinguishing between the sources obscures crucial features of the texts. Some aspects of the ideologies of women and the body were internalized by some women at some times, but resistance did occur. Accounts of intense ascetic activities in women's mystical texts before the fourteenth century are extremely rare. Mechthild and Porete use the language of eroticism and suffering to describe the experience of the soul, but alternative conceptions of the soul, the divine, and their relationships, which challenge these prevailing forms of "feminine spirituality" and the suffering it entails, are introduced and elaborated on by both. Eckhart demonstrates that resistance also occurred among men; yet the power of medieval culture to maintain dominant ideologies is evidenced in his condemnation and in Porete's execution.

THE BODY IN MECHTHILD OF MAGDEBURG, MARGUERITE PORETE, AND MEISTER ECKHART

The association of women with the body and suffering led Mechthild to identify herself with the humanity of Christ on the basis of her very femininity and humble status. While appearing to embrace the culture's ideal, she does so in ways that subtly alter and resist it. Rather than equating herself as female merely with the *body* of Christ, Mechthild takes his corporeality as an emblem for his humanity and identifies her femininity with it.[43] She argues that one attains to divinity by following Christ in his humanity.[44] This includes accepting disease and bodily suffering, but does not entail the extreme asceticism and discipline of the flesh found in the hagiographical tradition. Whereas through beatings and starvation these holy women are presented as overcoming the porousness of female flesh and inhabiting enclosed and redeemed bodies, bodies with healing and salvific power for those around them, Mechthild stresses loneliness and exile in the absence of the divine and acts of charity in prayer and deeds. God wounds Mechthild's soul, not her body.

All of this is accomplished, as I have shown, by shifting the onus of sinfulness and the fallenness of human nature away from the body and toward the will.[45] Not only is the will the source of evil in the world, it also primarily defines one as a human being, although the possibility remains open in Mechthild—and is clearly argued by Porete and Eckhart—that there is an uncreated aspect to humanity that is without any will other than God's. This view enables Porete and Eckhart to argue for the complete annihilation of the will through which evil is entirely overcome. Although Mechthild suggests the preexistence of the soul in early sections of *The Flowing Light*, and elaborates on it later in the text in her description of the continued presence of the divine even in his apparent absence, tension remains between this claim and her patent concern over sin and desire for a "good end." Reading Mechthild with Eckhart can help to elucidate the ways in which she suggests a resolution of this dilemma, one that is given greater prominence and clarity by Eckhart's philosophical vocabulary. We might thus appeal to Eckhart's "insofar as" principle— the distinction between virtual and actual existence—whereby the soul is both nothing and subject to sin insofar as she is created, while also divine insofar as she is nothing or detached. Mechthild's continued humility—and the anxiety it engenders—grounds her union with the divine and is necessary to it. Mechthild, like Eckhart, holds together the reality of multiplicity, division, and even sin, with that of the unity between the soul and God. For her, this is clearly tied to the body, as the closing dialogue of *The Flowing Light* demonstrates. Together with her emphasis on the well-ordered soul, Mechthild insists that the body must and will be redeemed.

Mechthild's most daring comments about the nature of union and her suggestion that an aspect of the soul has always been with God are made in the course of descriptions of the soul's religious experiences and her defense of the content of these experiences against critics.[46] The intensity of these ecstasies and the fact that they cannot last long when one is embodied lead to her early distrust of the body.[47] Mechthild's attempt to resolve the dangers caused by this constant oscillation between ecstasy and suffering leads to her formulation of the "well-ordered soul," for whom God's absence and his presence are both equal. By arguing that the soul must give up her pleasure, Mechthild emphasizes the importance of the properly ordered will in the religious life. In this movement toward the will, moreover, the body comes to be associated with those special experiences rather than viewed in opposition to them.[48] Visions and the loss of self in the Godhead as they are experienced ecstatically by Mechthild come to be associated with embodiment.[49] While Mechthild does not fully overcome this attachment, her problematizing of visionary imagination and suffering embodiment lead in the direction of the critique found in Porete and Eckhart of those religious who depend on extraordinary experiences.[50] For Porete, such experiences represent a dangerous stage on the path to freedom. While it has been argued that there is a place for rapturous experiences in Eckhart's thought, particularly insofar as they are nonvisionary moments of union, even narrowly defined in this manner the extraordinary is secondary in his mysticism and treated by him with suspicion.[51] In Porete and Eckhart there is a critique of special experiences, accompanied by a lack of concern with and deemphasizing of the body. Mechthild's text both records and resists this movement; she can again be seen as a point of departure for a line of thought later developed by Porete and Eckhart.

Porete both follows and diverges from the pattern of development of Mechthild.[52] She too consistently works toward a spiritualization of Christian teaching. The will is the central human faculty in her work, and for the soul to become one with the divine, the will must be annihilated. All other religious and ethical activities—both those of the active and contemplative lives—are subordinated to this final moment in which the soul becomes free and simple, absolutely united with the Godhead. For Mechthild, action and contemplation are joined through the suffering soul's imitation of Christ and attainment of good order, but Porete desires to transcend the necessity of even this spiritual suffering. Active and contemplative works, together with the mediations of the visionary imagination, are transformed through the annihilation of the will. This spiritualizing movement leads her critics, both medieval and modern, to suspect that Porete's work is antinomian and gives free rein to the desires of the body.[53] Yet, as I argued in Chapter 4, such claims rely on at least partial misreadings of the text. Porete clearly says that the soul who has been unencumbered is now governed by the will of God and hence incapable of doing anything contrary to his law.[54] The charge of antinomianism is easily countered. The charge of quietism, however, remains.

The secondary role given to the sacraments, the visible Church, the human Incarnation of Christ, and the "works" of prayer and contemplation demonstrates Porete's desire to move past the body and createdness as mediators between the soul and the divine. Apophasis is given primacy in her work, negating the mediation of the body and everything associated with it. Romana Guarnieri's argument that Porete seeks to return to a pre-Adamic state, one of innocence before creation itself has occurred, appears to have ample warrant.[55] Although Love's stated intention is to give relief and comfort to the human being in "heart and body and life,"[56] Porete is in danger of losing any point of contact between the simple soul and the world in which she still lives. Porete argues that the unencumbered soul will give to her neighbor anything he or she might need or desire, yet because of the soul's absolute simplicity she is without means of communicating with this neighbor or understanding any lack he or she might experience. For the simple soul to comprehend need in her neighbor would itself be an experience of lack and an encumbrance.[57] For Mechthild, love in its essence *must* flow out and fill that which is empty. Eckhart, following this strand of the tradition, argues that the virgin soul compels God's self-creative act to occur within her, engendering justice. By reading Porete with Mechthild and Eckhart, we can see how her text also contains the idea that the annihilated soul is the place in which and through which the divine acts in the world. Porete very clearly argues this; but her concern for absolute freedom, rooted in her resistance to prevalent prescriptions for female religiosity, causes her to leave this teaching obscure and undeveloped.

Eckhart's ideas about the body share much with Porete's, both in his claim that all createdness is a pure nothing and in the lack of attention he gives to the bodily mediation of the Incarnate Christ.[58] Like Porete as well, but much more explicitly, he teaches that there is an aspect of humans or souls that shares in the fullness of being that is the divine—an uncreated spark that is *virtualiter* identical with the divine ground. Despite first appearances, however, Eckhart's thought is not other- or anti-worldly. On the contrary, while arguing that creation is nothing, Eckhart shows that it is not evil. Like Mechthild and Porete, he locates human sinfulness and evil in the will, and only insofar as the will is attached to the things of this world do they appear to be evil. In actuality, the world is not evil but rather the will that is unable to detach itself from creation.

By reading Eckhart with Mechthild and Porete, then, two different conceptions of corporeality or createdness can be distinguished in his work. On the first level, seen from the perspective of the undetached will, creatureliness is a mere nothing that must be renounced. Once this movement of detachment has been made by the will, however, creatureliness or corporeality is itself transformed and recognized as sharing in the being of the divinity. By focusing on the relation between the created and the creator, Eckhart displaces the dualism between body and soul. Unlike those for whom the body becomes emblematic of createdness, Eckhart insists on the creatureliness of the intellectual and spiritual as well. Through the dialectic of all and nothing, moreover, the dualism between creature and creator is itself overcome. Eckhart therefore teaches an inner-worldly mysticism[59] or a mysticism of everyday life,[60] which, through the understanding of the virtual existence of all things in the divine, shows that created things are both all and nothing.

Like Mechthild and Porete, Eckhart emphasizes the will in order to resolve the tension-laden relationship between the Christian and the world. Like Mechthild, he argues that the intention is more important than the act, both in the case of good and of evil.[61] He does not thereby free human beings from the obligation to do what they are able under the cover of a supposed good intention. Rather he saves overscrupulous souls from lamenting their inability to do all the good they would like to do. As Porete argues, the will itself must be annihilated in order to free the soul. We should not blame our inability on the evil of corporeality and creation, the beguines and Eckhart argue; that inability is the result of limitation and weakness, and ultimately is of little significance. The created world is not the locus of evil, nor does it partake of evil; it merely has or lacks value on the basis of the disposition of the soul who apprehends it.

Despite the commonalities between Mechthild's, Porete's, and Eckhart's final positions, however, there are enormous differences in the paths by which they are attained and the degree of struggle encountered and depicted on those paths. The reevaluations of createdness and the body and the move beyond visionary imagination are fraught with ambivalence and tension in Mechthild and Porete, but for Eckhart createdness is all a mere nothing from which the soul must become detached. Eckhart argues that once you are detached, the body is fully available to the soul and worthy of attention. Throughout the German sermons and treatises, he calls for detachment, attending to the struggle involved in the process of letting go only on the intellectual level, or the level of consciousness; it is not depicted as a struggle between the body and the soul or the body and the will. In other words, the texts imply that with a proper understanding of the ontological relationship between God and created things, the will can renounce itself with little trouble. In Sermon 66, for example, he argues that if his listeners could realize the joy and truth lying within them, they might leave the church transformed on that very day.[62] At other times, however, he notes the inability of many to *understand*, acknowledging the difficulties of detachment.[63] Yet the struggle is never expressed in terms of the body, its desires and pleasures. Furthermore, the difficulties of detachment are not expressed in a first-person voice; rather, the impersonal speaker in the sermons and treatises acknowledges that there are those in his audience whose way to detachment may be blocked by lack of understanding or by an intransigent will. Eckhart does not *dramatize* these difficulties, as do Mechthild and Porete. Rather, he demonstrates through his use of the first-person, direct address, and pronomial ambiguities the way in which the detached soul (the speaking "I") *is* the divine (also the speaking "I").

The differing emphases placed on the difficulties in attaining detachment might be the result, in part, of the kinds of texts produced by the three mystics. In writing a confessional work over the course of many years, Mechthild was bound to emphasize the struggles involved in the fight against evil and in the taming of the will. Porete's work, while not confessional in form, is an allegory, a genre that thrives on conflict and ambivalence. Mechthild and Porete introduce narrative elements into their works, moreover, that are in some tension with the goal-less goal of the mystical life. While Mechthild, in part, accepts the gap between future resolution and present tension, Porete desires to overcome it fully and attempts to narrate just such a transcending movement. Eckhart, on the other hand, whose works are theoretical, pedagogical, and essentially non-narrative, would be less likely to feel constrained by his genres to emphasize the ambivalence and struggles of the soul. Moreover, in eschewing the language of stages to mystical union, he rejects narrative and attempts to give voice to the soul/divine speaking out of the eternal *now*.

An appeal to genre, although it helps to explain tendencies within Mechthild's and Porete's work, cannot fully explain the greater sense of conflict expressed in their texts. There is an element of choice involved in the genre in which one writes. Many pedagogical works, particularly sermons, *do* stress precisely the dangers and pitfalls of the soul's path toward God, using small narratives to dramatize them.[64] Eckhart explicitly argues that there is no path to God, no levels of being such as those found and subverted within Porete's text.[65] For Eckhart, the act of breaking through into the circle of divine activity brings the soul into union with the divine and this very activity lies outside of time.[66] It is intrinsic to the mystical consciousness he describes that no account be given of a road leading to final apotheosis. The transformation is fundamentally internal, marking the acquisition of a new state of awareness that is both one of detachment from all created reality and of identity with the divine nothingness. Mechthild accepts the soul's present involvement in time and in bodily activity as a necessary part of her path to union, although the well-ordered soul and her preexistence partially allay the tensions this immersion in the world creates. Porete and Eckhart take such conceptions further, arguing that the eternal *now* can be reached in the midst of time and in the body. While Porete uses a dramatic and narrative mode problematized and partly subverted by her own mystical project, Eckhart rejects such devices—although the sermon genre allows them—and with them any dramatization of the soul's conflicts. Porete works with and subverts narrative and allegorical genres in which conflict is primary, creating an apophatic moment through the text as a whole; Eckhart uses and subverts the sermon tradition, focusing his attention on apophasis at the level of the sentence and sermon.

Mechthild, Porete, and Eckhart are all responding to situations of great anxiety and struggle, and to a moral rigorism that threatened to destroy what they believed to be true religiosity. Mechthild clearly displaces the wounded body with the wounded soul. Her work, however, based in the powers of the visionary imagination, only begins to suggest how the tensions and suffering it engenders might be allayed. Porete's desire for a pre-Adamic state reflects her attempt to escape the demands of rigorous asceticism *and* of the visionary imagination— both expected particularly of women—for the demands of the former could never fully be met and the reception of the latter could never be ensured. I will turn to the importance and ambiguities of visionary imagination for medieval women at the close of the chapter, but first I would like to give more detailed attention to the evidence that Mechthild, Porete, and Eckhart spoke in reaction to the asceticism prescribed for women by their contemporaries. As I showed in Chapter 2, evidence for asceticism and moral rigor can be found in a variety of sources. Some of the most notorious accounts come from beguine communities questioned during the persecution of beguines and so-called heretics of the free spirit that followed the Council of Vienne and its decrees.[67] In one such inquisitorial transcript involving a community of beguines in Schweidnitz, in Silesia, the early stages of the religious life are described as filled with extreme asceticism and deprivation, in imitation of Christ, the desert fathers, and the saints—perhaps in particular those featured in the male-authored hagiographies of the early beguines or new "desert mothers" discussed earlier. The transcripts then report that asceticism was followed by complete license and loss of restraint, thereby giving a picture of the antinomianism the church most feared.[68] To what degree these accounts are to be trusted is open to question, but I agree with Robert Lerner when he argues that they most likely reflect the extremes of bodily asceticism and rigor to which many were willing to go in their pursuit of the spiritual life.

Further evidence for the *expectation* of ascetic extremism can be found in the lives of the early beguines. These texts most likely served as models for communities like that at Schweidnitz. The lives of these women, usually written by male clerics and confessors, depict acts of rigorous asceticism and deprivation as well as bodily miracles.[69] The same tendency can be seen in the lives of nuns from the thirteenth and fourteenth centuries, many written by sisters within the community for devotional use.[70] Although these accounts cannot, and were perhaps not meant to be, taken literally, and while careful attention must be given to possible differences between male- and female-authored hagiographies, and between hagiographies and other female-authored writings, the former do give a picture of the *ideals* put forward for women by male ecclesiastical leaders, ideals that again involved rigorous asceticism and the body as a site of sanctity and religious power.

Evidence for such ideals can also be found in the criticisms leveled by Mechthild, Porete, and Eckhart against the religious they saw around them. Central to this critique is the claim that asceticism and moral rigor become good deeds done not for the sake of God but for some reward in the form of extraordinary religious experiences.[71] The divine is made visible and embodied for the believer through her marking the body with acts and ascetic practices. Here Mechthild diverges from Porete and Eckhart, for her relationship to the visionary imagination is much more complex. Although her claims to transcend the mediations of the visionary imagination through the well-ordered soul who experiences God's presence even in his absence moves in the direction followed by Porete and Eckhart, her public voice remains dependent on visions and the extraordinary, ecstatic experiences grounded in them. Porete and Eckhart refuse all mediations between God and the soul, including those of the visionary imagination. They reject ascetic and visionary enactments of divine presence. While Porete castigates those who are tied to works in language drawn from the tradition of courtly love and nobility, Eckhart adopts the language of the towns and commerce. In both cases, villainous or merchant souls are depicted as desiring to work in a relationship of inequality and exchange with the divine; as such they show that they are not free and equal with God. By stressing equality, furthermore, Porete and Eckhart implicitly subvert the very hierarchical language used to describe souls dedicated to the works of action and contemplation.

Eckhart's sermon on Mary and Martha highlights the dangers of spiritual consolations experienced by the senses and stresses the necessity of not becoming trapped at the stage of spiritual sweetness and inactivity, one believed by many to be brought about through acts of asceticism and bodily deprivation.[72] This parallels Porete's understanding of the dangers of the fourth stage of being, for the "lost" souls believe that no higher experience of the divine is possible.[73] Even Mechthild argues that although there is a time for the consolations of religious experience, the danger exists that one might become a slave to spiritual pleasures and become headstrong in one's pursuit of them, regardless of the consequences for health and the body.[74] The will that remains steady in sorrow and in joy becomes fully united with God and is able to achieve works in the world; she has no need to seek further punishment for the body. At the same time, together with Porete, Mechthild claims that the soul is able to stand firm in her union with God because she has completely renounced attachment to the will and all created things. The fully articulated doctrine of the virtual existence of all things in the divine allows Eckhart to bring together these two emphases and to show the goodness of corporeality, insofar as it has being and shares in the divine, at the same time as he calls on his listeners to detach themselves from it, insofar as it is created and nothing.

In Sermon 86, Eckhart warns against two related dangers—the claims to insensibility, or the transcendence of all sensible experience, and to freedom from works; both, as I have said, were areas in which Porete was subject to misunderstanding. Eckhart deals with a number of related "dangers" to which the mysticism of at least some beguines, represented by Porete, seemed subject.[75] In a characteristic manner, Eckhart seems to ignore the issues of asceticism and possibly over-rigorous attitudes toward the body, but they are addressed by his very reticence.[76] Just as it is impossible completely to transcend affective bodily experience, so it is not necessary to torture the body, for the will is the locus of human action and of human sinfulness.[77] Eckhart's stance throughout his sermons avoids precisely the kind of prescriptions and exhortations generally understood as intrinsic to the genre; asceticism has meaning only in the context of works done for the sake of some greater good. By rejecting the "works" of both action and contemplation in favor of the one work of the birth of the Son in the soul, or the just act, Eckhart implicitly rejects asceticism.

Eckhart seeks to escape some of the tensions and misunderstandings he found in positions like those of Mechthild and Porete, while drawing out and combining their strengths. He maintains Mechthild's emphasis on the necessity of activity and work in the world as a constitutive part of the spiritual life, together with Porete's insistence on the annihilation of the will in order to reach an unmediated relationship between the soul and God. Eckhart avoids the overemphasis on asceticism and suffering, special experiences, and individualism that can be seen especially in the early sections of Mechthild's work. Although Mechthild moved away from her early rejection of the body, her later position is predicated on a life of suffering in union with the humanity of Christ. From an Eckhartian perspective, her continued ambivalence with regard to the body and the large role of visionary and special experiences in her work carry dangers not fully equalized by her theological formulations of the centrality of the will and of the well-ordered soul.[78] For Mechthild, the soul learns to become "detached" through following the path of suffering taken by Christ. Eckhart teaches detachment in order to save humanity from continual struggles with and ambivalence about corporeality and the created world.[79] Yet he clearly wishes to guard against the possible quietism of Porete's position. Even though Porete offers a formulation of how Love works through the free soul, her concern for freedom leaves this aspect of her work relatively undeveloped. As I have suggested, Eckhart elaborates on this position through his understanding of the soul as virgin wife, the just act, or the birth of the Son in the soul creating a place for the body and for the "work" in the world. He thereby suggests the relationship between mystical apophasis and ethical thought. Reading Eckhart with the beguines uncovers this implicit aspect of his work and raises once again the nature of the divergences between them. After describing his ethical insights as they are articulated against popular and scholastic texts, I will turn to the question of how Eckhart's ethics tie him to—and may explain further his divergences from—the texts of Mechthild and Porete.

AN ETHICS OF DETACHMENT

Eckhart's response to the central beguine ethical dilemma—the relationship between action and contemplation—depends on his distinction between those who are in the midst of things and those who are in them[80] and is grounded in his understanding of detachment. As Herbert Grundmann has shown, the beguine ideal of spiritual poverty was the basis for the distinctive spiritual ideal of detachment:[81]

> [O]nly in the movement of female piety in Germany did the idea of poverty expand in the direction of its original religious meaning, not into the organizational and dogmatic and not into the polemical, but rather into the mystical—the striving after inward, spiritual poverty.[82]

Although, as I suggested in Chapter 2, this spiritualizing movement may be in part a response to the demands of ecclesiastical leadership, it also *mirrors* the theological tendencies found in Mechthild and Porete. Eckhart takes the original conception further through his elaboration of the idea of detachment, thus providing an ideal of the soul who lives in the world without being of the world or attached to it for its own sake. The resulting position, grounded in his apophatic theology and anthropology, could be called an apophatic ethics.[83] Just as Eckhart's attitude toward the human body is remarkable for the relative paucity of references to it, in the same way his ethical reflections are distinctive in their almost complete lack of applications and directives. Eckhart does not argue against prescriptive ethics, yet he quite clearly does not offer one. His one command is to become detached; in the sermons he continually demonstrates for his audience how *not* to pray, how *not* to overemphasize the external aspects of religion, and how, through apophasis and detachment, to reformulate their internal nature.

The call for detachment, however, cannot be taken as solely negative. The detached soul, being completely empty and free, is able to compel God and the activity of God within her.[84] The birth of the Son in the soul marks not only the mystical union or identity between the soul and the Godhead, but also the fruitful activity of the divine in this world.[85] The importance of the idea of work and its relationship to the mystical birth of the Son in the soul justifies discussion of an ethical moment in Eckhart's thought, despite the fact that Eckhart, unlike Mechthild, gives no concrete directives for action.

Just as the term *esse* is capable of cataphatic or positive referentiality (although within the terms of Eckhart's apophasis) with regard to the Godhead, justice (*iustitia*) might be the one fixed point of reference with regard to ethical activity. While stressing and enacting the unity of divine attributes through his apophatic language-practice, justice, rooted in equality, is central for Eckhart. He goes so far as to claim that justice takes precedence over divinity (although they are one); "for just human beings, the pursuit of justice is so imperative that if God were not just, they would not give a fig for God."[86] Eckhart often speaks of the Son and the birth of the Son in the soul under the name of Begotten Justice and the just human being (*iustus*). The just human being is the one who gives to each his or her due, therefore the one who gives all to God from the perspective of religion, and the one who gives to each human being that which is his or her due as a human creature endowed with being by God.[87] Perhaps even more strongly, Eckhart insists that one should love one's neighbors not for God's sake, but as oneself—love for God and love of neighbor, like the soul insofar as she is just and divine, are equal.[88]

In extending his theological and anthropological apophatic approach to ethics, Eckhart makes another departure from the standard position of theologians and religious of his age. The rise of the mendicant orders in the thirteenth century, with their emphasis on the act of confession, led to the dissemination and study of collections of typical moral "cases" through which confessors might learn to judge actions and assign suitable penances for sinful behavior.[89] This practical approach to ethics, centrally concerned with distinguishing good from bad acts, is the root for what became known as casuistry among sixteenth-century Jesuit moral philosophers.[90] Eckhart directly opposes this kind of ethics, primarily concerned with the value of an action and its outcome. Furthermore, his disregard for particular cases and their relative moral values might be seen as a direct response to the growing moral apprehensiveness brought about by an emphasis on confession and penance. Again, by arguing for the centrality of the disposition of the will, Eckhart attempts to ease the religious tensions of those around him.

An act-oriented approach to ethics, of course, is not the only kind of moral philosophy available in the thirteenth century, yet Eckhart seems equally removed from the more theoretically based positions of a figure like Aquinas. Bringing together a concern with the practical problems of moral philosophy and his own theological and philosophical system, Aquinas, in the *Summa*, focuses on the human person as the locus of moral behavior rather than on actions themselves.[91] Thus he moves away from an act ethics and toward what could be called a rule-based ethics and an analysis of the virtues as central to proper character formation. Both of these poles of Thomistic thought seem equally alien to Eckhart, for even discussions of justice, love, and other "virtues" take on a new character in his work. Justice and love, for example, are not virtues that can be enumerated and separated from being (*esse*); they are different aspects of being or modes of being, and hence are made manifest when one has achieved a new mode of awareness, grounded in one's unity with the ground and/or Son.

Eckhart makes a further move away from Aquinas in his controversial teaching on the primacy of internal over external acts, or of intention over action. Ignoring the various distinctions made by Aquinas in his discussion of intentionality, Eckhart insists on the primacy of the interior. While this might seem to be in opposition to his teaching on the union of action and contemplation, the grounding of this union in the interior act of detachment and the birth of the Son in the soul makes the primacy of intention not only possible but necessary, for through this interior movement comes all true justice. To make ethical judgments only, or primarily, on the basis of external acts would be to deny the primacy of detachment and the birth of the Son in the soul in the ethical life.[92]

Eckhart's rejection of Thomastic ethical thought parallels his disagreements with Aquinas with regard to the divine being. Just as

Eckhart argues for the unity of predication within the divine and maintains a rigorous apophasis, allowing the terms *esse, unum,* and *intellectus* only insofar as they are subject to apophatic delimitation, he also avoids a discussion of human character in terms of virtues, showing rather that justice and love are unified with being and can be applied to the human being insofar as he or she is one with the Son. The equality between the soul and the divine that occurs when the soul comes into a univocal relationship with the Godhead is the ground for her equality with all things, and hence of justice. Thomistic ethics can be read as an attempt to bring together a rule-based account of the moral law and practical applications.[93] Although in a formal sense justice and the good are universal and immutable, in the material sense the enormous variety of circumstances and conditions in which humans must act bring about a situation where justice and the good are not always the same. For this reason, the movement from the universal rule to the practical application is complex; it is the work of morality to articulate the relationship.[94]

Eckhart's emphasis on the birth of the Son in the soul as the root of justice and goodness bypasses the distinction between the formal and material senses made by Aquinas, and insists that justice and goodness are everywhere one and the same and as such fundamentally unknowable according to created reason. He avoids any description of laws and actions or of applications, calling only for detachment, that state in which the divine can work in the soul and thus in the world. His response to the vagaries and hindering circumstances of material existence is not to create a system of morality in which particular cases can be discussed and judged, but instead to insist on the primacy of the interior act which is free from all such circumstances. Like God, the just act or the work of the soul cannot be named within human language and is not subject to the constraints of human created existence. Recognition of the equality of all things engendering, and engendered by, detachment gives birth to justice.

MEISTER ECKHART AND FEMINIST ETHICAL THEORY

Many contemporary feminist philosophers and theorists have also argued against rule-based ethical systems because they are judged to be incompatible with female ethical and moral development and represent a male bias toward rationality, disembodiment, and justice. In the most famous formulation of this supposed disjunction in moral development, the psychologist Carol Gilligan argues that because the childhood development of girls is more oriented toward interrelationships, interdependence, and feelings, they appear to be less developed on moral scales devised by men according to male norms.[95] Gilligan has been open in admitting the local and nonuniversal nature of the studies on which her claims are based, but she and other writers have often suggested parallels in different historical periods and cultural settings.[96] Eckhart, on first sight, might seem to offer a classic example of male emphasis on disinterestedness, rationality, and the principle of justice. One might be tempted to explain his differences from Mechthild and Porete in this way. Yet Mechthild and Porete also argue, to differing degrees, for detachment and loss of will. Furthermore, as I have attempted to show, Eckhart's ethics is *not* rule-based or rationalistic, and his conception of justice carries only the "prescription" of radical equality.[97] Despite this reservation, the claim still can be made that there is an element in the psychological development of men and women that might explain the disjunction between Mechthild, Porete, and Eckhart and their mystical and ethical visions. The argument might be made that Eckhart's insistence on detachment is male, and undermines female ideas of ethical action. Furthermore, it might be argued that these ideals may be held by women yet be difficult for them to attain because of the differences in their psychological development. In this way, the tensions within Mechthild's and Porete's texts might be explained.

I do not believe that such an argument, however, is possible given the nature of the textual evidence available. Differences between Mechthild, Porete, and Eckhart in their attitudes toward the human body and its createdness can be and, I believe, have been demonstrated, but it is impossible for us to uncover the "psychologies" of the authors and thus to posit a developmental cause for these differences. Furthermore, the tendency of some feminist historiography and literary criticism to universalize claims made with regard to particular historical places, times, and evidence, is dangerous both to scholarship and to feminist political and ethical aims, for it works to obscure crucial differences between women themselves, as well as between men. What we *can* learn by looking at the relationship between Mechthild, Porete, and Eckhart in light of contemporary psychoanalytic theories of gender development is that many of the lines of division taken for granted in the twentieth century are meaningless in other cultural situations. There is no necessary connection between disinterestedness and rationality, or between the ideal of justice and a rule-based ethical system. By the same token, there is no necessary disjunction between embodiment and rationality or justice.

Most important, it cannot even be argued that Eckhart saw a disjunction between embodiment and justice, for it is precisely by *embodying* Christ on earth that the work is performed. That Eckhart wished to downplay the role of the human body in the initial movement of the soul away from the will and all creatureliness is clear. In his Neoplatonic ontology, furthermore, the body has a place only insofar as it is the site of God's gift of being. Although his use of this ontology might imply that in the final return the body and particularity will be overcome, Eckhart says little about any such final return, concentrating instead on existence in this world.[98] After detachment is achieved and while one remains on earth, embodied activity is crucial to the mystical and religious life. There are, as we have seen, important ethical and spiritual reasons—apparent to Mechthild and Porete as well—for Eckhart's initial downplaying of the body, for only by emphasizing that all creatureliness, including, most importantly, the will and the intellect, must be let go of, is the moral neutrality of corporeality clearly established. The body, Eckhart implies, is only a problem as long as it is granted unwarranted ethical importance; his mystical thought ignores and downplays the role of the body in the inital movement of detachment, while at the same time it clearly shows that embodied activity, the work of the soul in the world, is central to the fulfillment of that life. He does not deny the body in itself but recognizes it as intrinsic to human nature and most present to consciousness in its suffering. Transcendence is not a denial of immanence but is its extension and fulfillment.

Scarry argues that empathy is a function of the imagination (and by extension that all imagination is empathetic), but Eckhart, like Mechthild and Porete, recognizes the limitations of the body, the root and ground of imagination. To experience the limitations of the body—pain, suffering, and the irreducible particularity of embodiment—marks for all three of them the subversion of empathetic imagination and the breakdown of human communities. In response to this situation, Mechthild, Porete, and Eckhart attempt to transcend imagination and transform their souls into the divine. For Eckhart, insofar as one recognizes the equality of all things, an equality grounded in the absolute immanence of the divine that is the source of its transcendence, imagination becomes transfiguration and the limitations of being are overcome. Through this process the created world is sanctified, not in some future time, but in the eternal and always occuring *now* of the birth of the Son. Through this eternal rebirth, time is transcended *and* sanctified. Rather than depending on the suffering of women—marked by the visible wounds and dismemberment of their bodies or by their suffering souls—to provide escape from death and a sign of the divine presence, Eckhart sought to relieve the anxiety and suffering of his listeners, calling both women and men to a new relation with the divine and/in oneself and others. God, immanent in his very transcendence, is made present not through wounds and suffering but through justice. In his freedom and authority, Eckhart was in a position to experience and understand a detachment clearly constitutive also of the experience of Mechthild and Porete, although ultimately subversive to female authority within the medieval context.

Although clearly their experiences are in part shaped by the associations of women with the suffering body, both Mechthild and Porete reject the wounded physical body as a mark of female sanctity. Through her conception of the well-ordered soul, moreover, Mechthild suggests the limits of the visionary imagination. Porete's annihilated and free soul entirely rejects the demand for visionary imagination as the necessary basis for a woman's religious voice. This is not to reject the body but to attempt to allay its suffering—both as externally marked and internally experienced. Yet women's religious authority was most effectively grounded during the later Middle Ages in the visionary imagination; their public voices, then, are endangered by the thoroughgoing apophasis of Porete and Eckhart.

Philippe Ariès argues that it was intense love of this world and the body that led late medieval men and women to their gruesome evocations of the dance of death and bodily putrefaction.[99] The medieval saint's (or perhaps better, hagiographer's) great attachment to the body led to the extremes of asceticism recorded in their lives. Through asceticism, human beings and their bodies are made whole and sanctified. In a world with little practical means of allaying pain and disease, ascetic suffering is a heroic act of bodily empowerment and healing. But clearly the burden of ascetic sanctification did not fall with equal weight on all. Hagiographical traditions portray women as disproportionally responsible for such suffering, the bodily sanctification it enabled being shared by the men around them.[100] Similarly, the writings of women in northern Europe during the thirteenth century demonstrate that their experiences of divine sweetness, their love and enjoyment of such experiences, necessitate and justify the suffering brought about when these fleeting moments pass. The pain of the exiled and alienated soul is understood as salvific, not only for the soul herself, but also for spiritual children on earth and in purgatory. Unlike the hagiographical traditions, moreover, Mechthild's spiritual children are both male and female.

While Mechthild's great enjoyment of special experiences leads to her early rejection of and battle with the body, her greater understanding of the relationship between embodiment, suffering, and pleasure causes her to temper this enthusiasm and its enmities. For the "well-ordered soul," God is present in his absence. Yet her attachment to the body—that beloved prison—remains strong, and with it her fears about constancy and a good end. Mechthild desires the sanctification of the body as well as the soul. Porete, in her desire to free the soul, seems to leave the body behind. Eckhart, through his dialectic of immanence and transcendence, attempts to achieve both the soul's freedom and the body's sanctification. In their efforts to decrease the tension and ambivalence with which Mechthild ends her book, and to point toward what was for them the true source of religiosity and ethical activity, Porete and Eckhart come together with Mechthild in their focus on the will, although the path toward its annihilation is thornier for the beguines.[101] Insofar as they reject or question bodily asceticism, paramystical phenomena, and special visionary and unitive experiences, Mechthild, Porete, and Eckhart attempt to allay women's pain.

Eckhart, in particular, tries to do away with the ambivalence still so prevalent in Mechthild and also the source of Porete's absolute insistence on freedom, by downplaying the body in the *initial* phase of the mystical life, to the point that it and all of creation insofar as it is created, become ontologically null. While Porete clarifies the *stages* of mystical life beginning to emerge in Mechthild, arguing for the importance of bodily mediations and extraordinary experiences of the visionary imagination in the lower moments of this path, Eckhart takes further her subversions of this schema. Without the stages, the role of the visionary imagination is further diminished, and with it the conflicts it engenders.

In displacing the dualism between body and soul with that between creature and creator, a movement again anticipated by Porete, Eckhart avoids the traditional identification of the body as feminine and of women with the body. Where such traditional imagery plays a role in his sermons, Eckhart almost immediately undermines this gender ideology. He then offers new readings that show one must become detached not only from the sensual and bodily but also from the intellectual insofar as it is part of the created realm. When Eckhart speaks of detachment, it is not only or even essentially the corporeal realm from which the soul must become detached, but the whole created realm, including the intellect and the will. He stresses the unity of intellect, will, and corporeality as created, subverting the dualism between the soul and the body. The ontological nullity of the created realm insofar as it is created is established without any particular negative connotation being put on embodiment. Eckhart's discussions of detachment lay the groundwork for and make possible a new positive relationship between the detached soul and the corporeal realm. Furthermore, insofar as the soul is both a virgin and fruitful, she is united with the Godhead, thus bringing female imagery to the center of Eckhart's mystical thought. The openness of Eckhart's ethics is true to the spirit of the beguines, particularly Mechthild with her overt ethical concerns, in that he encompasses even the most humble and unassuming of human activities into the divine ethical life; yet there is a crucial way in which Eckhart's work inadvertently undercuts Mechthild's teaching and, to an extent, Porete's as well.

THE PROBLEM OF AUTHORITY

Eckhart, speaking as a part of the established teaching order and as a representative of the church, has no need for further authority with which to legitimize his writings or his sermons. He is, moreover, free to subvert the very authority on which his pedagogical role rests.[102] Mechthild and Porete, like almost every woman who wrote in medieval Europe or who was in any way taken as authoritative, had need of some legitimation, and this legitimation came primarily through claims to special experiences of the divinity.[103] Although Mechthild might use her lowly status to explain in paradoxical fashion why God had chosen her as a receptacle of his teachings and prophecy, the initial source of her writings and the authority for them lies in her assertion that they were experiences vouchsafed to her alone.[104] She becomes, like the prophets, a messenger of God on the basis of her own individual religious experiences.[105] Through her visions she is able to denounce the church of her day and its clergy, as well as offer spiritual counsel and warnings to individuals. The importance of the visionary mode becomes explicit in the contrasting styles and rhetorical strategies found throughout her work. Like Eckhart, she often does not bother to mark the speaker, thereby underlining her mystical identity with the divine. When the text voices a condemnation, however, or approbation of Mechthild's own work and mission, the divine speaker is clearly marked.[106]

Porete, one of the few medieval women to write a religious text without making direct claims for special visionary experiences, was condemned to death as a heretic by male authorities. In adopting the more impersonal and literary genre of the allegorical dialogue throughout her work, she attempts to attain a neutral voice of authority that stands in agreement with her theological and mystical teachings and their distrust of special visionary gifts and spiritual consolations. At the same time, this impersonal voice often claims to be that of divine Love, speaking out of the unity between the simple soul and God.[107] Porete maintains one of the two predominant rhetorical strategies adopted by Mechthild and taken up by Eckhart. Yet since she was without claims to particular visionary and mystical experiences (sanctioned, of course, as genuine by ecclesiastical leaders), contemporaries saw her as speaking without authority. While there are clearly many reasons for Porete's condemnation, reasons both conscious and unconscious to her judges, this factor must have been crucial in their action. The "pseudo-woman,"[108] in rejecting culturally defined gender prescriptions, loses all sanction for her public voice. Even if her hearers had accepted her assertions of identification with Love, thereby acknowledging Love as the author of her book, that claim itself would be questionable without the warrant of visionary or ecstatic experience.

The historical record illustrates that claims to extraordinary visionary and mystical experiences are not sufficient to lend authority to any text, whether male- or female-authored.[109] The fact, however, that the vast majority of female-authored religious writings have their source in some kind of extraordinary religious experience has too often been seen as telling us something about the nature of women, rather than about the nature of the power structures in which they found themselves and in which they attempted to find a voice.[110] Porete and, to a lesser extent, Mechthild, by undercutting the place of the human body and special experiences in the mystical life, undermine the main avenue of religious authority and expression open to women in their culture. Eckhart displaces visionary imagination entirely, further subverting women's public voices. In a world governed by the principles and experience of apophasis, special visionary experience would not be necessary to grant the authority to speak publicly. Rather, the right to speak would be shared and authority constantly subverted through one's depth of detachment and unity with God. All speakers, whether male or female, would have "authority" insofar as they were detached. However, in the hierarchical and male-dominated world of the medieval church, for women other modes of legitimation were necessary.

The traditions influenced by Eckhart—and, indirectly perhaps, by Mechthild and Porete—clearly reflect the ambivalence created by this situation. Some demonstrate the liberating appeal Eckhart's teachings had for women, its power to subvert traditional authoritative structures, and the ability for women, in theory, to be granted enormous spiritual prestige on the basis of the identification with the divine that underlies his thought. In the work known as the "Schwester Katrei" treatise, for example, the title character is depicted as a perfectly detached soul who ultimately has authority over Eckhart himself.[111] Yet the convent chronicles of the fourteenth century, which also show direct signs of Eckhart's influence, are full of accounts of ascetic, visionary, and ecstatic experiences. This return to and continuation of earlier forms of mystical expression, as well as the incorporation of elements from thirteenth-century hagiographical writings, is seen not only among women but also among some of Eckhart's male followers, most notably Heinrich Suso. Within his "auto-hagiographical" text, he is shown following a rigorous asceticism.[112] At the same time, he urges his women followers to mitigate their own suffering.[113] In a fascinating reversal of thirteenth-century norms, Suso offers his suffering body as a replacement for the female bodies of the early beguines. By attempting to decrease women's suffering, he seems to claim he makes a better model for Christ and his humanity, inadvertently usurping a central salvific role open to women. Where the convent chronicles offer communal accounts of female sanctity that bring together Eckhart's mysticism of everyday life with the bodily demands of female spiritual authorization, Suso claims his own singularity as a replacement for suffering female flesh. The choice seems to be women's suffering or their silence. Yet Suso encouraged the work of his female followers; like many fourteenth-century women he may merely have understood the culture in which he lived and the dangers of mystical teachings that did not have a basis in the human body and human sensual experiences. In the wake of Eckhart's condemnation, the need for such grounding extended to men.

In and through her visionary imagination, Mechthild, like Porete and Eckhart, claims to speak the word of God or to speak "as" God. By reading Mechthild, Porete, and Eckhart together, we have come to see that they all claim a transfiguration that moves with and against visionary and imagistic language, pointing to the embodiment of God in the empty place that was the human agent. Yet these assertions are pursued and grounded in different ways. For a visionary such as Mechthild, the claim is based both on mystical union between the "suffering soul" and God and on visions in which he tells and shows her things that he commands her to tell others. It could be argued that the former position is more important to Mechthild theologically, but the latter type of experience grounds her authority in the eyes of her contemporaries. In response to her critics, Mechthild writes that God appears to her directly and commands her to overcome such doubts, thereby marking her as his chosen vessel.[114] The same legitimating moves can be seen in the works of most medieval women religious writers. Even those cloistered women who wrote primarily for other women within their communities made frequent reference to visionary experiences, providing both the subject matter and the legitimation of their teaching.[115] The only notable exceptions, other than Marguerite Porete, are Beatrice of Nazareth and Clare of Assisi. Beatrice does not seem to have disseminated her texts, many of which appear to have been destroyed. Clare's writings are sparse and of a private and pedagogic nature. In both cases, hagiographers immediately after their deaths described them as visionaries and ascetics.[116]

With Porete and Eckhart we move to styles of mystical writing that often claim to speak from the place of the divine, but do so without recourse to visionary authority. The shift in person is made possible through the union of the soul and the divine. Although it could be argued that Porete's allegorical dialogue represents a visionary experience in which she is taught by God, it is read much more plausibly as an account of divine wisdom, which she is able to give because of her increasing unity with Love. Eckhart at first sight might seem to speak merely with the priestly authority invested in him as a teacher and preacher. Yet throughout the sermons, through the use of logical paradoxes, chiasmus, pronomial ambiguity, and referential shifts,[117] he gives voice to the absolute identity between the soul and the Godhead, and hence speaks as the divine. He eschews priestly authority and speaks in his own voice, for which he claims divine empowerment, insofar as he is one with the Godhead in his virtual existence. Eckhart is able to claim that the Father gives birth to him, and that he *is* the Son who is unified with the divine, and as such he himself is divine.[118] Just as Mechthild and Porete claim to give the direct words of God, Eckhart claims to be that Word, and he does so without benefit of what could only be an obstruction to this union—visions and other forms of extraordinary experience. They are no longer needed, for the divine is present in/as/through the transfigured soul.

Many commentators note that Eckhart's mystical teachings only began to be viewed with suspicion when he preached them publicly. Seen in this light, the authorities distrusted less his teachings themselves than their dissemination among women and laypeople. But it was to a great extent among these laypeople, especially women, that the ideas had their genesis. By following Mechthild on the "well-ordered soul" and Porete on the annihilated, free, and unencumbered soul, Eckhart became "guilty" of divorcing the experience of mystical union with the divine, and the authority that union gives, from special experiences and visions, and hence making them available to any man or woman able to achieve detachment. Not only are there no external marks of the divine presence and hence no easily available means of validating and judging mystical experience, but that presence is available to all in a way visions and ecstasies could never be.[119] While Eckhart does not explicitly attack ecclesiastical structures and hierarchies, his teachings have a revolutionary potential clear to his enemies, if not to Eckhart himself.

The well-ordered, annihilated, or detached soul is free from the constraints of embodiment and herself becomes the divine embodied within the world. Women and men, then, mark the divine presence, not on their suffering flesh, but in acts of love and justice. Yet without changes in the dominant social structures of late medieval Europe, women were only partially able to advance the insights of Mechthild, Porete, and Eckhart. Indeed, we might well ask, together with Mechthild, whether attachment to the body and hence the constraints of embodiment can ever be overcome. Clearly, in the face of hierarchical power structures, individual projects of detachment reach an impasse. Porete's silence throughout her imprisonment and trial speaks powerfully of her belief in a path of freedom and detachment, despite an uncomprehending and intransigent male ecclesiastical world. Eckhart, at his defense, seems surprised by the church's rejection of his teaching. In the face of that rejection, many women were forced to seek access to the divine and to public voices by inscribing their bodies and souls with suffering, with wounds marking the presence of God and the limits of the imagination.

NOTES

CHAPTER 1

1. The term "beguine" is used to designate semireligious women who lived alone or in groups, dedicating their lives to God, although without taking formal vows. The first signs of the movement are found in the hagiographies of late twelfth- and early thirteenth-century women—often solitaries—from the southern Low Countries. They will be discussed in Chapter 2. As Walter Simons has recently argued, it is important to emphasize the diversity of this movement organizationally, as well as in status and function. Although more fully organized, enclosed, and incorporated in the southern Low Countries—hence enabling its survival after the decrees against errant beguines issued by the Council of Vienne—the movement was diverse even there. See Walter Simons, "The Beguine Movement in the Southern Low Countries: A Reassessment," *Bulletin de l'Institut Historique Belge de Rome* (1990): 63–105. See also Joseph Greven, *Die Anfänge der Beginen: Ein Beitrag zur Geschichte der Volksfrömmigkeit und des Ordenswesens im Hochmittelalter* (Munster: Aschendorff, 1912); L. J. M. Philippen, *De Begijnhoven, Oorsprong. Geschiedenis, Inrichting* (Antwerp: n.p., 1918); Herbert Grundmann, *Religiöse Bewegungen im Mittelalter: Untersuchungen über die geschichtlichen Zusammenhänge zwischen der Ketzerei, den Bettelorden und der religiösen Frauenbewegung im 12. und 13. Jahrhundert* (1935; reprint ed., Hildesheim: Georg Olms Verlagsbuchhandlung, 1961); Ernest W. McDonnell, *The Beguines and Beghards in Medieval Culture* (New Brunswick: Rutgers University Press, 1954); Frederic M. Stein, "The Religious Women of Cologne: 1120–1320" (Ph.D. diss., Yale University, 1977); Lester K. Little, *Religious Poverty and the Profit Economy in Medieval Europe* (Ithaca: Cornell University Press, 1978); Bernard Delmaire, "Les béguines dans le Nord de la France au première siècle de leur histoire (vers 1230–vers 1350)," in *Les Religieuses en France au XIIIe siècle*, ed. Michel Parisse (Nancy: Presses Universitaires de Nancy, 1985), pp. 121–62; and Johanna Ziegler, "The *curtis* beguinages in the Southern Low Countries and art patronage," *Bulletin de l'Institut Historique Belge de Rome* (1987): 31–70.

Debate still continues about the derivation and original meanings of the term "beguine," although evidence suggests it was originally used in a derogatory sense, hence its absence from many early beguine lives and documents. Jacques of Vitry, in the prologue to his *Life of Marie of Oignies*, alludes to the "new names" (*nova nomina*) with which jealous men were caluminating the "holy women" (*mulieres sanctae*) of whom he writes. Unfortunately, he does not deign to repeat the names, so we can not be sure if "beguine" was one of them. Jacques of Vitry, *Vita Mariae Oignacensis*, in Acta Sanctorum, ed. J. Bolland, G. Henschenius, et al. (1643–1940; reprint ed., Brussels: Culture et civilisation, 1965–70), 23: 637; *Life of Marie d'Oignies*, trans. Margot H. King (Toronto: Peregrina, 1989), p. 18 (hereafter I will use the abbreviation *VMO* for this *Life*). In a later sermon, however, he says that "men of the world" call these holy women *beguinae*. For the reference to the sermon, see J. Greven, "Der Ursprung des Beginenwesens," *Historisches Jahrbuch* 35 (Munich, 1914), pp. 47–48. For more on the history of the term and its early appearances, see J. Van Mierlo, "Béguins, Béguines, Béguinages," *Dictionnaire de Spiritualité, ascétique et mystique, doctrine et histoire*, ed M. Viller et al. (Paris: Beauchesne, 1937–) (hereafter cited as *DS*) 1: 1341–43; Simone Roisin, "L'efflorescence cistercienne et le courant féminin de piété au XIIIe siècle," *Revue d'histoire ecclésiastique* 39 (1943): 342–43; A. Mens, "Les béguines et béghards dans le cadre de la culture médiévale," *Moyen Âge* 64 (1958): 305–15.

2. "Dis waren dú waffen miner sele, [súfzen, weinen, bihten, vasten, wachen, besmenschlege und betten steteklichen an] da ich den lip mit úberwant also sere, da bi zwenzig jaren nie die zit wart, ich were mude, siech und krank allererst von rúwen und von leide, da nach von guter gerunge und von geistlicher arbeit und dar zu manig swere siechtag von nature. Hie zu kam dú gewaltige minne und beschaste mich so sere mit disen wundern, das ich es nit getorste verswigen; alleine do wart mir an miner einvaltekeit vil leide." Mechthild of Magdeburg, *Mechthild von Magdeburg 'Das fliessende Licht der Gottheit': Nach der Einsiedler Handschrift in kritischem Vergleich mit der gesamten Überlieferung*, ed. Hans Neumann (Munich: Artemis Verlag, 1990), Bk. IV, Ch. 2, p. 113 (Hereafter I will use the abbreviation *FL* for this work; unless otherwise noted, all translations are my own).

3. "ein tore, ein súndig und arm mensche bin an libe und an sele." Ibid.

4. See Peter Dronke, *Women Writers of the Middle Ages: A Critical Study of Texts from Perpetua (d. 203) to Marguerite Porete (d. 1310)* (Cambridge: Cambridge University Press, 1984), pp. 66, 82, for similar moves in Hrotsvitha of Gandersheim. For a fuller exposition of this dialectic in Mechthild, see Chapter 3.

5. On this authorizing dynamic in the work of Mechthild, see Ursula Peters, *Religiöse Erfahrung als literarisches Faktum: Zur Vorgeschichte und Genese frauenmystischer Texte des 13. und 14. Jahrhunderts* (Tubingen: Niemeyer, 1988), pp. 116–29.

6. "Herre, din wunder hat mich verwunden, din gnade hat mich verdruket." *FL*, Bk. 1, Ch. 14, p. 14.

7. Song of Songs 4:9. See *FL*, Bk. I. Ch. 22, p. 17; Bk. 2, Ch. 20, pp. 52–53; and Bk. 2, Ch. 24, pp. 58–62. For wound imagery and its Christological role in Mechthild, see Margit Sinka, "Christological Mysticism in Mechthild von Magdeburg's *Das Fliessende Licht der Gottheit*: A Journey of Wounds," *The Germanic Review* 60 (1985): 123–28. For the centrality of the wound and wounding imagery in twelfth- and thirteenth-century spirituality, see Peter Dinzelbacher, "Das Christusbild der heiligen Lutgard von Tongeren im Rahmen der Passionsmystik und der Frauenmystik und Bildkunst des 12. und 13. Jahrhunderts," *Ons Geestelijk Erf* 56 (1982): 217–77; and Jeffrey Hamburger, *The Rothschild Canticles: Art and Mysticism in Flanders and the Rhineland circa 1300* (New Haven: Yale University Press, 1990), pp. 72–77.

8. "Do sprach aber únser herre: 'Du solt mir an disen dingen volgen und getrúwen, und du solt och lange siech wesen, und ich wil din selber pflegen; und alles, des du bedarft an lip und an sele, das will ich dir geben.' " *FL*, Bk. IV, Ch. 2 , p. 114.

9. There is some debate as to whether Porete was a beguine. The canon lawyers who came together to discuss Porete referred to her as a *beguina*. See H. C. Lea, *A History of the Inquisition in the Middle Ages* (Manchester: 1888), 2: 578. She is also referred to as a beguine by the chroniclers who record her story. See *Les grandes chroniques de France*, ed. Jules Viard (Paris, 1934), 8: 273; and Jean d'Outremeuse, *Chronique*, in Paul Fredericq, *Corpus documentorum inquisitionis haereticae pravitatis neerlandicae* (Ghent: The Hague, 1889–1906), 2: 64 n. 39. See Robert Lerner, *The Heresy of the Free Spirit in the Later Middle Ages* (Berkeley: University of California Press, 1972), p. 71; and Ursula Peters, *Religiöse Erfahrung*, pp. 71–72. Peters makes much of the fact that an explicit connection between Marguerite's apparent status as a beguine and her heretical teachings is lacking in the official judgment against her. Yet the connection *is* made, as Peters herself concedes, by contemporary commentators, in particular the canon lawyers mentioned above. While it is impossible to demonstrate that Marguerite's audience was only or even primarily beguines, it is clear that they made up an important part of that audience and were perceived, rightly or wrongly, as central proponents of such teachings. See Peters, *Religiöse Erfahrung*, pp. 67–81. The royalist continuator of the chronicle of Nangis may have wished to

avoid identifying Marguerite as a beguine (perhaps this in part sparked his reference to her as a *pseudomulier*) because of the king's support of other, more enclosed beguine communities. He uses the same appelation in his discussion of a beguine from Metz who ran afoul of Philip IV. See Lerner, *Free Spirit*, p. 70.

10. "Et quant elle vit que ceste amour loingtaigne, qui luy estoit si prouchaine ou dedans d'elle, estoit si loing dehors, elle se pensa que elle conforteroit sa masaise par ymaginacion d'aucune figure de son amy dont elle estoit souvent au cueur navree. Adonc fist elle paindre ung ymage qui representoit la semblance du roy, qu'elle amoit, au plus pres qu'elle peut de la presentacion dont elle l'amoit et en l'affection de l'amour dont elle estoit sourprinse, et par le moyen de cest ymage avec ses autres usages songa le roy mesmes." Marguerite Porete, *Le Mirouer des simples ames anienties et qui seulement demourent en vouloir et desir d'amour*, ed. Romana Guarnieri and Paul Verdeyen, in Corpus Christianorum: Continuatio Mediaevalis, vol. 69 (Turnhout: Brepols, 1986) Ch. 1, p. 12.

11. For more, see Chapter 4.

12. See Michael Sells, *Mystical Languages of Unsaying* (Chicago: University of Chicago Press, 1994), pp. 180–205.

13. "Der gerehte ensuochet niht in sînen werken; wan die iht suochent in irn werken, die sint knehte und mietlinge, oder die umbe einic warumbe würkent. Dar umbe, wilt dû în- und übergebildet werden in die gerehticheit, sô enmeine niht in dînen werken und enbilde kein warumbe in dich, noch in zît noch in êwicheit, noch lôn noch saelicheit, noch diz not daz; wan disiu werk sind alliu waerlîche tôt. Jâ, und bildest dû got in dich swaz dû werke dar umbe würkest, diu sint alliu tôt, und dû verderbest guotiu werk; und niht aleine verderbest dû guotiu werk, mêr; dû tuost ouch sünde." Ser. 39: DW 2: 253–54. All references are to *Meister Eckhart. Die deutschen und lateinischen Werke*, ed. Josef Quint and Josef Koch (Stuttgart and Berlin: W. Kohlhammer, 1936–), which will be abbreviated as DW and LW followed by a volume number. When possible, translations will be from *Meister Eckhart: The Essential Sermons, Commentaries, Treatises and Defense*, trans. Edmond Colledge and Bernard McGinn (New York: Paulist Press, 1981), and *Meister Eckhart: Teacher and Preacher*, trans. Bernard McGinn with Frank Tobin and Elvira Borgstädt (New York: Paulist Press, 1986). For important parallels in Porete, see Chapter 7.

14. Grundmann, *Religiöse Bewegungen*, pp. 430–31.

15. Although feminist critics have increasingly attempted to undermine "the influence paradigm," a mode of history writing that has consistently worked to marginalize women, we would participate in that marginalization by refusing to acknowledge those moments of influence which

have occurred. Moreover, in these moments of women's "influence," the philosophical concepts of authority, mastery, and originality on which the paradigm rests are themselves subverted. For the critique, see Karma Lochrie, *Margery Kempe and Translations of the Flesh* (Philadelphia: University of Pennslyvania Press, 1991), p. 205.

16. Luce Irigaray provides another frame within which the present study can be read. See Luce Irigaray, *Speculum of the Other Woman*, trans. Gillian C. Gill (Ithaca: Cornell University Press, 1985), pp. 191–92. Although Irigaray's comments about mysticism have been dismissed as ahistorical, they become more interesting when read in their philosophical context. We can then appreciate that she is speaking to a specific, albeit broad, historical, theological, and philosophical tradition, its assumptions, and self-contradictions. While operating on a level of philosophical generality, therefore, her discussion is not without interest for historians of spirituality. For the criticisms, see Sarah Beckwith, "A Very Material Mysticism: The Medieval Mysticism of Margery Kempe," in *Medieval Literature: Criticism, Ideology, and History*, ed. David Aers (New York: St. Martin's, 1986), pp. 34–57; and Laurie Finke, *Feminist Theory, Women's Writing* (Ithaca: Cornell University Press, 1992), p. 76. For a reading of Irigaray on mysticism that includes such criticisms while trying to show the importance of her work, see Amy Hollywood, "Beauvoir, Irigaray, and the Mystical," *Hypatia* 9:4 (1994): 158–85.

17. Although scholars have demonstrated the influence of Porete on Eckhart, detailed textual study of the relationship between the mysticism of the women's movement and that of Eckhart is only beginning to be done. See note 19 below.

18. McDonnell, *Beguines and Beghards*, pp. 355–61.

19. On the inadequacy of the terms traditionally used to distinguish women's and men's mystical texts, see Louis Bouyer, Preface, *Gertrude of Helfta: The Herald of Divine Love*, trans. Margaret Winkworth (New York: Paulist Press, 1993), p. 2.

20. On Porete's *Mirror* and Eckhart, see Herbert Grundmann, "Ketzerverhöre des Spätmittelalters als quellenkritisches Problem," *Deutsches Archiv für Erforschung des Mittelalters* 21 (1965): 519–75; Edmund Colledge and J. C. Marler, "'Poverty of the Will': Ruusbroec, Eckhart and *The Mirror of Simple Souls*," in *Jan van Ruusbroec: The Sources, Content and Sequels of His Mysticism*, ed. P. Mommaers and N. de Paepe (Leuven: Leuven University Press, 1984), pp. 14–57; Sells, *Mystical Languages of Unsaying*, Chaps. 5–7; and Emilie zum Brunn, "Une source méconnue de l'ontologie eckhartienne," in *Métaphysique, Histoire de la philosophie, Hommage à Fernand Brunner* (Neuchâtel, 1981), pp. 111–18. For Mechthild's *Flowing Light* and Eckhart, see Oliver Davies,

Meister Eckhart: Mystical Theologian (London: SPCK, 1991), pp. 37–45. Moving in a somewhat different direction is Otto Langer's study of the relationships between Eckhart's thought and the spirituality of contemporary German Dominican convents, represented, perhaps inadequately, by the convent chronicles, particularly those of Ötenbach and Töss. See Otto Langer, *Mystische Erfahrung und spirituelle Theologie. Zu Meister Eckharts Auseinandersetzung mit der Frauenfrömmigkeit seiner Zeit*, Münchener Texte und Untersuchungen zur deutschen Literatur des Mittelalters, 91 (Munich: Artemis, 1987) and the review by Frank Tobin in *Speculum* 64 (1989): 995–97. For the general argument, grounded in Grundmann's study, see Bernard McGinn's studies of Eckhart, particularly "Meister Eckhart: An Introduction," in *An Introduction to the Medieval Mystics of Europe*, ed. Paul Szarmach (Albany: State University of New York Press, 1984), pp. 242–44. See also Kurt Ruh, "Meister Eckhart und die Spiritualität der Beginen," *Perspektiven der Philosophie* 8 (1982): 322–34; "Meister Eckhart und die Beginenspiritualität," in *Kleine Schriften*, 2 vols. (Berlin: n.p., 1984), 2: 327–36; Kurt Ruh, *Meister Eckhart: Theologe, Prediger, Mystiker* (Munich: C. H. Beck, 1985), pp. 95–114; Jean Leclercq, François Vandenbroucke and Louis Bouyer, *A History of Christian Spirituality*, vol. 2: *The Spirituality of the Middle Ages* (Minneapolis: Seabury Press, 1968), pp. 384–88; and Davies, *Meister Eckhart*. This evidence will be discussed further in Chapter 2. Two sessions held at the 1993 International Conference of Medieval Studies in Kalamazoo, Michigan, including papers on Eckhart and Hadewijch, Mechthild, Marguerite Porete, and Hadewijch II give evidence for growing interest in the topic.

21. The only other substantial body of work authored by a woman generally agreed to be a beguine are the letters, poems, and visions of Hadewijch. Her central theological agenda is strikingly similar to that of Mechthild of Magdeburg. The comparison with Eckhart has recently been taken up by Saskia Murk Jansen in a paper presented at Kalamazoo, 1993. See Hadewijch, *The Complete Works*, trans. Mother Columba Hart (New York: Paulist Press, 1980).

22. See, for example, two works by Caroline Walker Bynum, *Holy Feast and Holy Fast: The Religious Significance of Food to Medieval Women* (Berkeley: University of California Press, 1987), and *Fragmentation and Redemption: Essays on Gender and the Human Body in Medieval Religion* (New York: Zone Books, 1991), both of which rely on hagiographical sources as well as women's writings. Others place even more emphasis upon the hagiographical sources. For example, Brenda Bolton, "*Mulieres sanctae*" in *Women in Medieval Society*, ed. Susan Mosher Stuard (Philadelphia: University of Pennsylvania Press, 1976),

pp. 141–58; Bolton, "*Vitae Matrum*: A further aspect of the *Frauenfrage*" in *Medieval Women*, ed. Derek Baker (Oxford: Basil Blackwell, 1978), pp. 253–73; Brenda Bolton, "Some Thirteenth Century Women in the Low Countries," *Nederlands Archief voor Kerkgeschiedenis* 61 (1981): 7–29; Michael Goodich, "Contours of Female Piety in Later Medieval Hagiography," *Church History* 50 (1981): 20–32; and Carol Neel, "The Origins of the Beguines," *Signs* 14 (1989):321–41. There are of course a host of recent studies of saint's lives, from perspectives ranging across the disciplines. For discussion of hagiography as a distinct genre or type of text, and bibliographies, see Hippolyte Delehaye, *The Legends of the Saints*, trans. V. M. Crawford (Notre Dame: University of Notre Dame Press, 1961); Michel de Certeau, "Hagiographie," *Encyclopedia Universalis* (Paris: n.p., 1968), 8: 207–9; Alison Goddard Elliot, *Roads to Paradise: Reading the Lives of the Early Saints* (Hanover: University Press of New England, 1987); Thomas J. Heffernan, *Sacred Biography: Saints and their Biographers in the Middle Ages* (Oxford: Oxford University Press, 1988); Renate Blumenfeld-Kosinski and Timea Szell, eds., *Images of Sainthood in Medieval Europe* (Ithaca: Cornell University Press, 1991); and Jo Ann McNamara and John E. Halborg with E. Gordon Whatley, eds., *Sainted Women of the Dark Ages* (Durham: Duke University Press, 1992).

23. This claim has important implications for feminist theory and its current preoccupation with differences between women. I hope to explore these implications further in another work.

24. For a discussion of the problem of authorship and gender, see E. Jane Burns, *Bodytalk: When Women Speak in Old French Literature* (Philadelphia: University of Pennslyvania Press, 1993), pp. 9–12. It is crucial to ask who is writing, from what social position, and with benefit to whom. On these issues in contemporary feminist literary criticism, see Nancy K. Miller, *Subject to Change: Reading Feminist Writing* (New York: Columbia University Press, 1988); Rachel Blau DuPlessis, *The Pink Guitar: Writing as Feminist Practice* (New York: Routledge, 1990); and Tania Modleski, *Feminism Without Women: Culture and Criticism in a "Postfeminist" Age* (New York: Routledge, 1991).

25. Many of the hagiographers themselves possessed great theological sophistication and education, yet as *hagiographers* their work was geared towards more general audiences and concerns. For example, Jacques of Vitry's life of the early beguine Mary of Oignies was concerned with presenting a picture of lay female sanctity to battle the spread of heresy, particularly among women in southern France. See *VMO*, 23: 630–66.

26. See Bynum, *Holy Feast*, pp. 87–88; Michael Goodich, *Vita Perfecta: The Ideal of Sainthood in the Thirteenth Century* (Stuttgart: Anton

Hiersemann, 1982), pp. 1–20; Siegfried Ringler, "Die Rezeption mittelalterlicher Frauenmystik als wissenschaftliches Problem, dargestellt am Werk der Christine Ebner," in *Frauenmystik im Mittelalter*, ed. Peter Dinzelbacher and Dieter R. Bauer (Ostfildern bei Stuttgart: Schwabenverlag, 1985), pp. 178–200; Jane Tibbetts Schulenburg, "Saints Lives as a Source for the History of Women, 500–1100" in *Medieval Women and the Sources of Medieval History*, ed. Joel Rosenthal (Athens: University of Georgia Press, 1990), pp. 285–320; and Miri Rubin, *Corpus Christi: The Eucharist in Late Medieval Culture* (Cambridge: Cambridge University Press, 1991), pp. 168–69.

27. Throughout the study I will be concerned with the ways in which women writers respond to and attempt to negotiate with cultural inscriptions of femininity and female sanctity. As Rachel Blau DuPlessis argues, the woman writer is "a power in her own work, but an artifact in most of the traditions of meaning on which she draws." DuPlessis, *The Pink Guitar*, p. viii.

28. Bernard McGinn, "St. Bernard and Meister Eckhart," *Cîteaux* 31 (1980): 373–86.

29. While it might be objected that this is making too much of the vagaries of a gendered language, the deliberateness with which gendered nouns and images are used suggest their intentional deployment by the authors. Furthermore, gendered language has effects that override its self-conscious use. On this issue, see Roman Jakobson, "On Linguistic Aspects of Translation," in *Theories of Translation: An Anthology of Essays from Dryden to Derrida*, ed. Rainer Schulte and John Biguenet (Chicago: University of Chicago Press, 1992), pp. 144–51.

30. I will follow the usages of the texts with regard to gendered language for the divine and the soul. While there are clear problems with this practice, in that the gendering of nouns does not occur in English and thus the use of gendered pronouns for God and the soul is given greater weight and significance in the translation than they have in the original, to elide these differences entirely through the use of masculine or neuter pronouns is clearly inadequate.

31. Kurt Ruh, "Beginenmystik: Hadewijch, Mechthild von Magdeburg, Marguerite Porete," *Zeitschrift für deutsches Altertum und deutsche Literatur* 106 (1977): 265–77.

32. This most clearly formulated by Hadewijch, although Mechthild has remarkably similar accounts. From Hadewijch, two passages from Letter 6 are particularly pertinent: "Metter menscheit gods suldi hier leuen in aerbeide ende in ellenden, Ende metten moghenden ewekelen god suldi Minnen ende Jubileren van binnen met enen sueten toeuerlate."

("With the Humanity of God you must live here on earth, in the labors and sorrows of exile, while within your soul you love and rejoice with the omnipotent and eternal Divinity in sweet abandonment.") "Wi willen alle wel god met gode wesen; Mer, wet god, luttel es onser die mensche met siere minscheit will leuen Ende sijn cruce met hem willen draghen Ende met hem are den crucen willen staen. Ende die scout der menscheit volghelden." ("We all indeed wish to be God with God, but God knows there are few of us who want to live as men with his Humanity, or want to carry his cross with him, or want to hang on the cross with him and pay humanity's debt to the full.") Hadewijch, *Brieven*, ed. J. Van Mierlo (Antwerp: Standaard, 1947), vol. 1, pp. 58, 64 (Hadewijch, *Complete Works*, pp. 59, 61). For Mechthild, see *FL*, Bk. VII, Ch. 47, pp. 292–93.

33. "Got leitet sinú kint, dú er userwelt hat, wunderliche wege. Das ist ein wunderlich weg und ein edel weg und ein helig weg, den got selber gieng, das ein mensche pine lide ane súnde und ane schulde. . . . wan er wil si sinem lieben sune gelichen, der an libe und an sele wart gepinget." *FL*, Bk. I, Ch. 25, p. 20.

34. Ruh, "Beginenmystik," pp. 273–74.

35. Caroline Walker Bynum, *Jesus as Mother: Studies in the Spirituality of the High Middle Ages* (Berkeley: University of California Press, 1982), p. 230.

36. "Je fu jadis enclose/ ou servage de prison,/ Quant desir m'en chartra/ en vouloir d'affeccion./ La me trouva la lumiere/ d'ardour de divine amour,/ Laquelle tantost occist mon desir,/ mon vouloir et mon affection/ Qui m'enpeschoient l'entreprise/ du plain de divine amour." *Mirouer*, Ch. 122, p. 344.

37. "Je le tiens, dit elle, car c'est le mien. Je ne le lesseray mie aler. Il est en ma voulenté. Adviengne ce qu'il peut advenir, puis qu'il est avec moy. Ce seroit donc faulte a moy, se je me esmaioie." Ibid., Ch. 86, p. 246.

38. See Ser. 2, *DW* 1: 24–45 (*Essential*, pp. 177–81).

39. See Ser. 83, *DW* 3: 437–48 (*Essential*, pp. 206–8).

40. Although for another movement in Mechthild's text, allied more closely to Eckhart's thought, see Chapter 3.

41. For the dialectic, see *Commentary on Wisdom* nn. 144–57, *LW* 2: 481–94 (*Teacher*, pp. 166–71). Bernard McGinn, "Meister Eckhart on God as Absolute Unity," in *Neoplatonism and Christian Thought*, ed. Dominic J. O'Meara (Norfolk, Va.: International Society for Neoplatonic Studies, 1982), pp. 128–39.

42. See Dietmar Mieth, *Die Einheit von Vita Activa und Vita Contemplativa in den deutschen Predigten und Traktaten Meister Eckharts und bei Johannes Tauler* (Regensburg: Friedrich Pustet Verlag, 1969), pp. 173–85; Dietmar Mieth, "Die theologische Transposition der Tugendethik

bei Meister Eckhart," in *Abendländische Mystik im Mittelalter*, ed. Kurt Ruh (Stuttgart: Metzlersche Verlagsbuchhandlung, 1986), p. 63; Bernard McGinn, "The God Beyond God: Theology and Mysticism in the Thought of Meister Eckhart," *Journal of Religion* 61 (1981): 18; and Richard Kieckhefer, "Meister Eckhart's Conception of Union with God," *Harvard Theological Review* 71 (1978): 203–25. Reiner Schürmann makes a related claim for Eckhart's "inner-worldly" mysticism. See Reiner Schürmann, *Meister Eckhart: Mystic and Philosopher*, (Bloomington: University of Indiana Press, 1978), p. 108–10; and Reiner Schürmann, "The Loss of Origin in Soto Zen and in Meister Eckhart," *The Thomist* 42 (1978): 303, 305–12.

43. "Eya min allerliebste gevengnisse, da ich inne gebunden bin, ich danken dir alles, des du hast gevolget mir; alleine ich dike betrubet bin von dir, so bistu doch mir ze helfe komen; dir wirt noch alle din not benomen an dem jungesten tage." *FL*, Bk. VII, Ch. 65, p. 310.

44. Here we see the enormous difference between the thought of Mechthild, Porete, and Eckhart and contemporary understandings of the body. As Susan Bordo points out, while modern American society is obsessed with the body, the desire is to demonstrate and inscribe the power of the will upon it. Contemporary culture shares features with early Christianity and later Christian hagiographical traditions, in which the "athletes" of Christ exhibit the strength of their will through acts of asceticism and, at times, self-mutilation. Porete and Eckhart, in particular, argue paradoxically that the will must surpass itself, thereby *freeing* the body and the soul. In fact, we might question whether such a dualism is capable of describing their thought. See Chapter 7 and, for the discussion of contemporary culture, Susan Bordo, *Unbearable Weight: Feminism, Western Culture, and the Body* (Berkeley: University of California Press, 1993).

45. Eckhart was tried for heresy in Cologne and for error in Avignon. A final bull of condemnation, "In agro dominico" was issued on March 27, 1329. The statements condemned included those pointing to an uncreated aspect of the soul and extended to the consequences of this teaching. For the text of the bull, see *Essential*, pp. 77–81; and M.-H. Laurent, ed., "Autour du procès de Maître Eckhart. Les documents des Archives Vaticanes," *Divus Thomas* (Piacenza), ser. III, 13 (1936): 435–46. For fuller discussion of the trials and condemnation, see Bernard McGinn, "Eckhart's Condemnation Reconsidered," *The Thomist* 44 (1980): 390–414; Trusen, *Der Prozess*; and the review of that volume by Robert Lerner, *Journal of Ecclesiastical History* 41 (1990): 152–53. See also, Chapter 5.

46. Mechthild records the suspicion cast on her because of her suggestion that humans are God's children by nature as well as by grace. See

FL, Bk. VI, Ch. 31, pp. 238–40; and Chapter 3 above. Porete's work was condemned twice, at Valenciennes in 1306 and again in Paris in 1310. She refused to speak in her own defense in Paris and was burned at the stake as a relapsed heretic. Although her book was ordered to be destroyed, anonymous manuscripts survived until the rediscovery of their author in the twentieth century. See Romana Guarnieri, "Il movimento del Libero Spirito," *Archivio Italiano per la storia della pietà* 4 (1965): 351–708. The articles extracted from Porete's work are remarkably similar to those enumerated by the Council of Vienne as teachings of the so-called heresy of the Free Spirit. As Robert Lerner has shown, however, the only significant evidence for this "heresy" before the council is the work of Porete. The association of beguines with heresy and general lack of discipline seems, then, to have been exacerbated by Porete and given institutional sanction by the council. See Lerner, *Free Spirit*. For the documents relative to Porete's trial, see Paul Verdeyen, "Le procès d'Inquisition contre Marguerite Porete et Guiard de Cressonessart (1309–10)," *Revue d'histoire ecclésiastique* 81 (1986): 47–94. For the decrees of the Council of Vienne, see Fredericq, *Corpus documentorum*, vol. 1, nn. 170–72. For evidence of increased persecution of beguines and other religious women after the promulgation of the decrees, see Lerner, *Free Spirit*, Chaps. 4–6; McDonnell, *Beguines and Beghards*, Part 6; and Richard Kieckhefer, *Repression and Heresy in Medieval Germany* (Philadelphia: University of Pennsylvania Press, 1979), Ch. 3.

47. Elaine Scarry, *The Body in Pain: The Making and Unmaking of the World* (Oxford: Oxford University Press, 1985).

48. Drew Leder, *The Absent Body* (Chicago: University of Chicago Press, 1990). Leder's account is a phenomenology of the lived body. While recognizing the historicity of conceptions and experiences of the body, he argues that there are certain structures of bodily experience which remain constant. His work is an analysis of these structures.

49. Leder argues that it is *most* consistently present in such experience, a claim I would dispute. It is not true for many women to the same extent as it may be for most men. Those women who experience menstruation, pregnancy, lactation, and menopause are made conscious of their bodies, not by the body's dysfunction, but by its healthy working order. Not surprisingly, male medical establishments have generally insisted on describing and treating these healthy conditions *as if* they were signs of disease and dysfunction. Although many women may have incorporated such views of their bodies, these descriptions are clearly not adequate to a phenomenological account. Leder attempts to sidestep the issue by arguing that while such experiences are not dysfunctional, they are "problematic." Leder, *The Absent Body*, pp. 89–90; Iris Marion

Young, "Pregnant Embodiment: Subjectivity and Alienation," *The Journal of Medicine and Philosophy* 9 (1984): 45–62; and Emily Martin, *The Woman in the Body: A Cultural Analysis of Reproduction* (Boston: Beacon Press, 1987).

50. Leder, *Absent Body*, pp. 90–91.

51. Scarry, *The Body in Pain*, p. 256. Wounds may be said to mark and communicate the body in pain, but the need for such external signs to validate physical suffering supports Scarry's point. This might help explain the tendency, to be demonstrated in Chapter 2, for medieval hagiographers to externalize accounts of internal bodily experiences.

52. For this understanding of the relationship between suffering and language, see Simone Weil, "The Love of God and Affliction," in *Waiting for God*, trans. Emma Craufurd (New York: Putnam, 1951); Dorothee Soelle, *Suffering*, trans. Everett R. Kalin (Philadelphia: Fortress Press, 1975), pp. 13–16, 61–86; and Scarry, *Body in Pain*, pp. 3–19, 161–80. While Weil and Soelle are discussing suffering or affliction in its sociological, psychological, and physical dimensions, Scarry points to recent medical research that argues for the importance of language as a diagnostic tool and partial alleviation for physical pain.

53. Scarry, *Body in Pain*, p. 304.

54. See, for example, *A History of Private Life*, vol. 2, *Revelations from the Medieval World*, ed. Georges Duby (Cambridge: Harvard University Press, 1987), pp. 268–72 and 592–93.

55. Scarry implies that this is a primary cause of such suffering in the premodern Western world. Her reading of Marx as a central modern theorist of work and the powers of the imagination suggest that, for the modern world, the central crisis takes the form of alienation from the product of one's own imagination and labor. As attention to the Feuerbachian roots of Marx's (and Scarry's) atheism demonstrate, for these thinkers the problems are essentially the same. The alienation of the believer from that Artifact who is God necessitates his or her wounding. What Scarry is unable to explain, leaving an odd lacuna in her study, is *why* many (not only in the premodern, but also in the modern world) want so desperately to believe that this artifact is not only real (as is any created artifact, however fictitious) but independent of human creativity. Is it because if God is our creation, he cannot protect us from suffering and pain? Does Scarry, in positing the creative imagination as that which mitigates our suffering and pain, replace God with the imagination? In its transcending moments, Eckhart might agree. As subject to limitation, he attempts to transcend even imagination.

56. Scarry, *Body in Pain*, pp. 233–41.

57. Ibid., pp. 210–21.

58. This formulation of Scarry's arguments points to the similarities between them and those of contemporary feminist theorists of the body, particularly those influenced by the work of Michel Foucault. However, the possibility and importance of transcendence is often either undermined or exaggerated. For the debates, see Bordo, *Unbearable Weight*, pp. 36–42, 215–44, and 277–300; Sandra Bartky, "Foucault, Feminism and Patriarchal Power," in *Feminism and Foucault: Reflections on Resistence*, ed. Irene Diamond and Lee Quinby (Boston: Northeastern University Press, 1988); Lois McNay, *Foucault and Feminism: Power, Gender, and the Self* (Boston: Northeastern University Press, 1992); Judith Butler, *Gender Trouble: Feminism and the Subversion of Identity* (New York: Routledge, 1990); and Donna Haraway, *Simians, Cyborgs, and Woman: The Reinvention of Nature* (New York: Routledge, 1991), pp. 149–82 and 203–33.

59. See Friedrich Ohly, *Hohelied-Studien: Grundzüge einer Geschichte der Hoheliedauslegung des Abendlandes bis um 1200* (Wiesbaden: Franz Steiner, 1958); and E. Ann Matter, *"The Voice of My Beloved": The Song of Songs in Western Medieval Christianity* (Philadelphia: University of Pennsylvania Press, 1990).

60. As Ellen Ross points out, early Christian accounts of martyrdom do not dwell on suffering but on the transfiguration of the believer's suffering into joy. See Ellen Ross, " 'She Wept and Cried Right Loud for Sorrow and for Pain': Suffering, the Spiritual Journey, and Women's Experience in Late Medieval Mysticism," in *Maps of Flesh and Light: The Religious Experience of Medieval Women Mystics*, ed. Ulrike Wiethaus (Syracuse: Syracuse University Press, 1993), p. 45. For the importance of Christ's suffering in late medieval religiosity, see also Rubin, *Corpus Christi*, pp. 302–16.

61. For the ubiquity of descriptions of female spirituality as affective and visionary, see the references in Bynum, *Jesus as Mother*, pp. 172–73; 182–84. For attempts to supersede and problematize these dichotomies, see, for example, Bouyer, Preface; and Hamburger, *Rothschild Canticles*. For the reassertion of these distinctions and attempts to question their meanings from a feminist perspective, see Lochrie, *Translations*; Elizabeth Robertson, "The Corporeality of Female Sanctity in *The Life of Saint Margaret*," in *Images of Sainthood in Medieval Europe*, ed. Renate Blumenfeld-Kosinski and Timea Szell (Ithaca: Cornell University Press, 1991), pp. 285–86; Elizabeth Robertson, "Medieval Medical Views of Women and Female Spirituality in the *Ancrene Wisse* and Julian of Norwich's *Showings*," in *Feminist Approaches to the Body in Medieval Literature*, ed. Linda Lomperis and Sarah Stanbury (Philadelphia: University of Pennsylvania Press, 1993), p. 166; and Kathleen Biddick, "Genders,

Bodies, Borders: Technologies of the Visible," *Speculum* 68 (1993): 389–418. Robertson's readings of Middle English mystical and spiritual texts in light of contemporary medical texts on sexual difference are particularly informative and convincing, although they cannot be generalized without contextualized readings like that offered here.

62. In this light Grundmann's work, despite its continued association of women with the realm of unmediated experience and textual naivité, is radical in its assertion of female influence on what were generally seen to be the greatest (and, not surprisingly, most "speculative") of medieval mystical writers. Furthermore, Grundmann recognized that medieval women's texts could not be subsumed under the category of "bridal or nuptial mysticism," marked by its affective and erotic language.

63. See Augustine, *De Genesi ad litteram*, in *Patrologia cursus completus: Series latina*, ed. J.-P. Migne (Paris: Garnier, 1844–64), vol. 34, Bk. 12; Bernard of Clairvaux, *Sermones super Cantica canticorum*, in *Sancti Bernardi Opera*, ed. J. Leclerq and H. M. Rochais, 8 vols. (Rome: Editiones Cisterciensis, 1957–77), ser. 31; and Bernard of Clairvaux, *On the Song of Songs II*, trans. Kilian Walsh (Kalamazoo: Cistercian Publications, 1976), ser. 31, pp. 124–33; and ser. 16a, *DW* I: 264.

64. For the place of imagination in medieval philosophy, see Murray W. Bundy, *The Theory of the Imagination in Classical and Medieval Thought* (Champaign: University of Illinois Press, 1927); and, more briefly, Eva T. H. Brann, *The World of the Imagination: Sum and Substance* (Savage, Md.: Rowman and Littlefield, 1991), pp. 57–64. For the Aristotelians of the thirteenth century imagination has a slightly higher status, given the claim that all knowledge is mediated by the senses. Eckhart is, once again, turning away from Aquinas here. For Avicenna's psychological theory and its influence on Aquinas, see E. Ruth Harvey, *The Inward Wits: Psychological Theory in the Middle Ages and the Renaissance* (London: The Warburg Institute, 1975).

65. See Hamburger, *Rothschild Canticles*, p. 302, n. 110.

66. *DW* I: 264.

67. This relationship continues despite claims by the visionary that what is being apprehended does *not* come through the senses, either externally or internally, but is purely spiritual, given that the vision or locution is *reported* using the language of the senses. Apophasis is the movement against and beyond such analogical usage.

68. Hamburger gives evidence the woman is a dominican nun; the evidence for a female audience is summarized in his *Rothschild Canticles*, p. 296, n. 1. In a review of Hamburger's book, Barbara Newman argues that the woman must have been wealthy and against talking about a "popular" audience. See *Mystics Quarterly* 18: 4 (1992): 138–41. On

the beguines as art patrons in the fourteenth century, see Zeigler, "The *curtis* beguinages," and Johanna Zeigler, "Reality as Imitation: The Role of Religious Imagery Among the Beguines of the Low Countries," in *Maps of Flesh and Light: The Religious Experience of Medieval Women Mystics*, ed. Ulrike Wiethaus (Syracuse: Syracuse University Press, 1993), pp. 112–26.

69. Ernst Benz and W. Blank argue that there is no connection between art and mysticism. Ernst Benz, "Christliche Mystik und christliche Kunst: Zur theologischen Interpretation mittelalterlichen Kunst" *Deutsche Vierteljahrschrift für Literaturwissenschaft und Geistesgeschichte* 12 (1934): 22–48; and W. Blank, "Dominikanische Frauenmystik und die Enstehung des Andachtsbildes um 1300," *Alemannisches Jahrbuch* (1964–65): 67–68. See Hamburger, *Rothschild Canticles*, p. 302, n. 103. Hamburger also points to exceptions to this tendency.

70. The Eucharist and other sacraments can serve a similar function. See, for example, the Eucharistic vision of Hadewijch in her *Complete Works*, pp. 280–82.

71. "Habebat enim in suo psalterio crucifixi depictam imaginem, cuius cum intenta mentis acie cicatrices vulnerum scissurasque verberum, spinarum aculeos et ipsum vulnus lateris gemebunda revolverat, mox tota liquescens in lacrimas, tam acerbis afficiebatur plena doloribus, ut se non ferens, doloris anxietas ipsam prorumpere compelleret in haec verba: Memoria memor ero et tabescit in me anima mea." *Vitae B. Odiliae Viduae Leodiensis*, in *Analecta Bollandiana* 13 (1844), n. 11, pp. 214–15.

72. See, for example, Denise Despres, *Ghostly Sights: Visual Meditation in Late Medieval Literature* (Norman, Okla.: Pilgrim Press, 1989).

73. Such images are both imagistic and apophatic, although Eckhart moves beyond even Trinitarian language.

74. "Videbat nihilominus stellam lucidissimam in altari descendere, quae se in tres dividens particulas, tanta erat in qualibet, quanta et primo fuerat, cum minime partiretur; separatis particulis non habebat minui, nec simul redeuntibus augmentari poterat, una manens et eadem quantitas claritatis. Sic innotescere ancillae suae voluit in figura huiusmodi summae et individaue unitas Trinitatis." *Vita Odilia*, n. 13, p. 217. See also n. 17, p. 223. Hamburger points to the Trinitarian vision of Marguerite of Oingt as the closest parallel to the images of the *Rothschild Canticles*. See Marguerite of Oingt, *Les Oeuvres de Marguerite d'Oingt*, ed. Antonin Duraffour, Pierre Gardette, and Paulette Durdilly (Paris: Belles Lettres, 1965), p. 94. For the comparison of visions to works of art or the use of images in stimulating them, see pp. 120, 136. Hamburger, *Rothschild Canticles*, p. 134.

75. *FL*, Bk.2, Ch. 44, pp. 27–32; and Hadewijch, *Complete Works*, pp. 280–82.

76. This raises important issues of women's literacy and their access to biblical and liturgical culture. Clearly, many beguines were educated and could read and write in the vernacular. Some also had access to Latin culture. There is evidence, as well, that beguines were among those in the thirteenth century who began to translate the Bible into the vernaculars and to produce commentaries. Such activity, however, was always subject to suspicion. The Franciscan Gilbert of Tournai, from whom we know of such activity, uses it as a complaint against the beguines and claims that their work was full of unspecified errors. The error, one could argue, was merely in the activity itself, evidenced by the condemnation of the Waldensians and Humiliati in the south for similar activities. As Innocent IV's rapprochement with the Humiliati shows, preaching might be undertaken by lay people only if it was an exhortation to penance and not concerned with issues of doctrine. Preaching on doctrine could be undertaken only by the clergy. As Thomas Aquinas reiterates, following the Pauline injunction of 1 Corinthians 14: 34–35, although women might have gifts of the spirit, their weakness, lack of wisdom, and subordinate status barred them from the priesthood and from public preaching (although the latter prohibition was abrogated on occasion when the gifts of the spirit warranted). For medieval women's literacy, see Joan Ferrante, "The Education of Women in the Middle Ages in Theory, Fact and Fantasy," in *Beyond Their Sex: Learned Women in the European Past*, ed. Patricia H. Labalme (New York: New York University Press, 1980), pp. 9–45; Shulamith Shahar, *The Fourth Estate: A History of Women in the Middle Ages*, trans. Chaya Galai (London: Methuen, 1983), pp. 50–56, 154–65; Eileen Power, *Medieval Women*, ed. M. M. Postan (Cambridge: Cambridge University Press, 1975), pp. 76–80; and Suzanne Wemple, "Sanctity and Power: The Dual Pursuit of Early Medieval Women," in *Becoming Visible: Women in European History*, ed. Renate Bridenthal, Claudia Koonz, and Susan Stuard (Boston: Houghton Mifflin, 1987, 2nd ed.), p. 138–39. For the account of beguines translating the Bible into French and reading vernacular commentaries in public, see Grundmann, *Religiöse Bewegungen*, p. 240; and Lerner, *Free Spirit*, p. 46. On the Waldensians and the Humiliati, see R. I. Moore, *The Origins of European Dissent* (Oxford: Blackwell, 1977), pp. 227–28; and Malcolm Lambert, *Medieval Heresy: Popular Movements from the Gregorian Reform to the Reformation* (Oxford: Blackwell, 1982, 2nd ed.), pp. 60–95.

For Aquinas on women, Holy Orders, and prophecy, see *STh* II–II, q. 177, a. 2, concl.; III, q. 27, a. 5; III, Supplement, q. 39, a. 1; Kari

Elisabeth Børresen, *Subordination et équivalence: Nature et rôle de la femme d'après Augustin et Thomas d'Aquin.* Oslo: Universitetsforlaget, 1968, 2nd ed.), pp. 183–88; and Eleanor Commo McLaughlin, "Equality of Souls, Inequality of Sexes: Woman in Medieval Theology," in *Religion and Sexism: Images of Woman in the Jewish and Christian Traditions*, ed. Rosemary Radford Ruether (New York: Simon and Schuster, 1974), pp. 235–36.

77. These kinds of arguments have been contested recently by contextualist readings of mysticism such as those of Stephen Katz. Others, represented in a recent collection edited by Robert Forman, wish to return to more traditional readings. See Stephen Katz, ed., *Mysticism and Philosophical Analysis* (Oxford: Oxford University Press, 1978); *Mysticism and Religious Traditions* (Oxford: Oxford University Press, 1983); and Robert Forman, *The Problem of Pure Consciousness: Mysticism and Philosophy* (Oxford: Oxford University Press, 1990). The contextualist arguments have demonstrated the dangers in generalizing claims about mysticism. What I say here is meant to refer only to late medieval Christian texts and shows the importance of tradition to even the most apophatic among them. Analysis of this interplay may help resolve the contemporary dilemma in theories of mysticism.

78. This is not to say that all experience is linguistic, and hence linguistic experience alone has reality, but merely an assertion of the mediating role of language with regard to human consciousness.

79. Thus Porete and Eckhart subvert the referential understanding of the relationship between speech and experience. See Chapter 6.

80. See Michel de Certeau, *La fable mystique* (Paris: Gallimard, 1982), and Lochrie, *Translations*, pp. 56–88.

81. There are, however, historical problems with using Certeau's analysis to describe medieval texts, given that the term "mysticism" gained currency as a substantive only in the sixteenth century. Certeau argues for late medieval texts as precursors to this trend in post-nominalist writings. See his *"Mystique* au XVIIe siècle: Le problème du langage mystique," in *L'Homme devant Dieu: Mélanges de Lubac*, 2 vols. (Paris: Aubier, 1968), vol. 2, pp. 267–81, and *Heterologies: Discourse on the Other*, trans. Brian Massumi (Minneapolis: University of Minnesota Press, 1986).

82. For the use of the Song of Songs, see Hamburger, *Rothschild Canticles*, pp. 70–87; and Ann W. Astell, *The Song of Songs in the Middle Ages* (Ithaca: Cornell University Press, 1990).

83. For further examples, see Hamburger, *Rothschild Canticles*.

84. See the opening to the lives of the sisters in the convent of Engelthal, where it is made clear that God's special gifts are given freely through his grace. Karl Schröder, *Der Nonne von Engelthal Büchlein von der*

Genaden Überlast (Tübingen: Literarischer Vereins in Stuttgart, 1871). The gratuitousness of grace, as we will see, is problematized by Mechthild, Porete, and Eckhart, all of whom argue that the humble or detached soul *compels* God. See Chapter 7.

85. Julian of Norwich, *A Book of Showings to the Anchoress Julian of Norwich*, ed. Edmund Colledge and James Walsh (Toronto: Pontifical Institute of Medieval Studies, 1978), Long Text, Chapter 2; *Showings*, trans. Edmund Colledge and James Walsh (New York: Paulist Press, 1978), pp. 177–78.

86. See Bynum, *Fragmentation*, p. 194.; Robertson, "Corporeality"; and Robertson, "Medieval Medical Views."

87. Almost all of the medieval women's religious texts I am aware of are so-grounded. Exceptions are Clare of Asissi's occasional writings, Beatrice of Nazareth's "On the Seven Manners of Loving," and Porete's *Mirror*. In the first two cases, visionary grounding was supplied immediately after their deaths by hagiographers. Porete and her work were condemned. For more on the importance of visionary authorization, see Chapter 7.

CHAPTER 2

1. On the sources for the beguines in the northern Rhineland, see Jean-Claude Schmitt, *Mort d'une hérésie: l'Église et les clercs face aux béguines et aux béghards du Rhin supérieur du XIVe et XVe siècle* (Paris: Mouton, 1978), pp. 12–18; and the critical review by Robert Lerner in *Speculum* 54 (1979): 842–44. For the sources specifically instructive with regard to spirituality, see Peters, *Religiöse Erfahrungen*.

2. Christocentrism and visionary-mystical qualities are emphasized by Roisin, *L'Hagiographie cistercienne*; Roison, "L'efflorescence"; Bolton, "*Mulieres sanctae*"; Bolton, "*Vitae Matrum*"; and Bynum, *Jesus as Mother*. Bodiliness has been more recently emphasized by Bynum, *Holy Feast*; Bynum, *Fragmentation*; Vauchez, *La Sainteté*; Donald Weinstein and Rudolph Bell, *Saints and Society: The Two Worlds of Western Christendom, 1000–1700* (Chicago: University of Chicago Press, 1982), pp. 220–38; Rudolph Bell, *Holy Anorexia* (Chicago: University of Chicago Press, 1985); and Lochrie, *Translations of the Flesh*.

3. Bynum, *Fragmentation*, p. 194. The argument, not surprisingly, has been put forward in many modern studies of medieval sanctity whose primary sources are hagiographical texts. See ibid., n. 3.

4. See Joan Ferrante, *Woman as Image in Medieval Literature* (New York: Columbia University Press, 1975), 17–35. On medieval models of sex, see Thomas Laqueur, *Making Sex: Body and Gender from the Greeks*

to Freud (Cambridge: Harvard University Press, 1990). Joan Cadden complicates Laqueur's "one-sex" model and demonstrates the complexity of medieval medical traditions. See Joan Cadden, *Meanings of Sex Difference in the Middle Ages* (Cambridge: Cambridge University Press, 1993), p. 3. See also Vern Bullough, "Medieval Medical and Scientific Views of Women," *Viator* 4 (1973): 485–501; and, more generally, Nancy Tuana, *The Less Noble Sex: Scientific, Religious, and Philosophical Conceptions of Woman's Nature* (Bloomington: Indiana University Press, 1993).

5. In discussing these historically grounded and contingent views of sexual difference it is important to underline the historicity of the bodies under discussion. Against those who assume that the body is closed, self-sufficient, and untouched by culture, recent theorists argue that human bodies are themselves historical. While embodiment may be phenomenologically described in its essential structures, these include that of transcendence through which bodies constitute and are shaped by history and culture. Laqueur, for example, argues that medieval medical views stressed the "oneness" of the sexed body. Although in the early Christian and medieval periods gender is not fluid—reason is male and always superior to the female and the body (despite their redeemability)—the *bodies* to which these genders are ascribed sometimes are. Through chastity, fasting, prayer, and other disciplines, the frail flesh of the woman might be transformed into the redemptive male flesh of Christ; just as the body of Christ, in its *bodiliness*, is associated with woman. So, as Gail Corrington points out, excessive fasting leads to the loss or diminishment of female secondary sex characteristics, including menstruation. See Laqueur, *Making Sex*, pp. 4–8; Gail Paterson Corrington, "Anorexia, Asceticism, and Autonomy," *Journal of Feminist Studies in Religion* 2 (1986): 53; and Gail Paterson Corrington, "The Defense of the Body and the Discourse of Appetite: Continence and Control in the Greco-Roman World," *Semeia* 57 (1992): 70. For a problematizing and complication of Laqueur's views, see Gail Kern Paster, *The Body Embarassed: Drama and Disciplines of Shame in Early Modern England* (Ithaca: Cornell University Press, 1993), pp. 16–17, 82–83; and Cadden, *Meanings*, p. 3. The desire to "enclose" the body is crucial here, as Paster contends. Yet the presence of "good" emissions in medieval hagiographical and Christological texts blurs the distinction—taken from Mikhail Bakhtin—between the grotesque and classical body. I am not sure that this distinction, perhaps important in the Renaissance, does justice to medieval texs. For the original distinction, see Mikhail Bakhtin, *Rabelais and His World*, trans. Helene Iswolsky (Bloomington: Indiana University Press, 1984). For a cogent example of distinction between good and bad emissions in medieval hagiography, see *Vie de Douceline*; and Claude Carozzi, "Douceline et les autres," in *La*

Religion populaire en Langeudoc du XIIIe siècle à la moitié du XIVe siècle (Toulouse: Privat, 1976), pp. 251–67.

6. See Chapter 3 on the hagiographical body.

7. Angela of Foligno is the one notable, and often-cited, exception. See Ludger Thier and Abele Calufetti, eds. *Il Libro della Beata Angela da Foligno (Edizione critica)* (Calufetti: Grottaferrata, 1985); and Angela of Foligno, *Complete Works*, trans. Paul Lachance (New York: Paulist Press, 1993). Without being able to demonstrate the claim here, I would argue that this text, like the fifteenth-century *Book* of the Englishwoman Margery Kempe, represents a new genre, the "autohagiography." See Margery Kempe, *The Book of Margery Kempe*, ed. Sanford Meech and Hope Emily Allen (London: Oxford University Press, 1940).

8. Bynum points to the importance of recognizing that most of our sources for late medieval women's lives are male-authored. Arguing for sensitivity to this fact, she goes on to accept fairly unproblematically their accounts of women's lives, experiences, and practices. She claims not to be concerned about whether hagiographical accounts of paramystical and other activities are "true." Yet in assuming that they tell us something about medieval women and not just about what the men who wrote these texts projected onto and thought *about* medieval women, she effectively accepts their truth. We cannot assume an acquiescent female audience for these texts *from* the texts themselves. See Bynum, *Holy Feast*, pp. 8, 28–29, 82–84. Although she separates her discussion of the hagiographical evidence and that taken from women's mystical writings, she does not elaborate on the important differences between these texts. These differences are obscured by her tendency to use hagiographical sources even for those women whose writings she discusses. See *Holy Feast*, Ch. 5. This conflation is prominent in more recent work on the body in late medieval women's piety. For two examples, see Finke, *Feminist Theory*, Ch. 3; and Lochrie, *Translations of the Flesh*, Ch. 1. In both cases, women's somatic spirituality is read as disruptive of clerical culture in ways that are undermined when we recognize that members of this clerical elite often produced the texts in which these "fissured" bodies appear.

9. See Michel Foucault, *The History of Sexuality*, 1: 11.

10. On Beatrice's life, see Roisin, *L'hagiographie cistercienne*, pp. 61–65; McDonnell, *Beguines and Beghards*, pp. 71; and Roger DeGanck, trans. and annot., *The Life of Beatrice of Nazareth* (Kalamazoo: Cistercian Publications, 1991), xiii–xix.

11. *Life of Beatrice*, Chapter 20, pp. 24–25.

12. For the text, in both Latin and English, together with manuscript information and speculations about authorship, see DeGanck, *Life of*

Beatrice. For the critical edition, see Leonce Reypens, *Vita Beatricis: De Autobiografie van de Z. Beatrijs van Tienen O. Cist., 1200–680* (Antwerp: Ruusbroec Genootschap, 1964).

13. *Life of Beatrice*, Prologue, n. 4, pp. 4–5; and Conclusion, n. 273, pp. 340–43.

14. See Roisin, *L'hagiographie*, pp. 64–65; and DeGanck, *Life of Beatrice*, pp. xix, xxvii–xxix. Ursula Peters has recently questioned the attestation of "The Seven Manners" to Beatrice of Nazareth, arguing that the differences between it and Book 4 of the *Life* are too great for the latter to be considered a translation of the former, but the similarities in structure, metaphors, and images are too strong to be explained in any other way and clearly override their divergences. See Peters, *Religiöse Erfahrung*, pp. 32–33.

15. Compare *Life of Beatrice*, Bk. 1, n. 5, pp. 36–37; and *Vita Arnulfi*, *AASS* (June 30) 24: 612–16. See DeGanck, *Life of Beatrice*, x.

16. *Life of Beatrice*, Chapter 5, pp. 36–37.

17. Angela of Foligno, *Il Libro.*

18. André Vauchez and others have demonstrated that in the later Middle Ages asceticism became intrinsic to conceptions of sanctity not only for female but also for many male saints (especially nonclerical and lowerclass men, like Arnulph himself). See Vauchez, *La Sainteté*, pp. 450–55; and Weinstein and Bell, *Saints and Sanctity*, pp. 123–37, 153–57, 236–37. See also Giles Constable, *Attitudes Toward Self-inflicted Suffering in the Middle Ages* (Brookline, Mass.: Hellenic College Press, 1982).

19. Asceticism becomes increasingly important for all saints, but it is a *central* mark of and means to sanctity for women, whereas there are many other roads to sainthood opened for men. See Vauchez, *La Sainteté*, pp. 450–55; and Weinstein and Bell, *Saints and Society*, pp. 123–27, 153–57, 236–37.

20. On the problems with using such dualistic terms to discuss medieval experience, see Bynum, *Fragmentation*, pp. 190–91.

21. "Seuen manieren sijn van minnen, die comen uten hoegsten ende [keren] weder ten ouersten." L. Reypens and J. van Mierlo, eds. *Seven manieren van minne* (Leuven: S. V. de Vlaamsche Boekenhalle, 1926), p. 3; and Beatrice of Nazareth, "There Are Seven Manners of Loving," trans. Eric Colledge, in Elizabeth Alvilda Petroff, *Medieval Women's Visionary Literature* (Oxford: Oxford University Press, 1986), p. 200.

22. "Sunt igitur hij dilectionis gradus sive status septem numero; per quos ad dilectum suum, non equalibus quidem passibus, sed nunc ut pedibus incedendo, nunc cursu velocissimo properando, nonnumquam etiam, sumptis agilitatis pennis, pernicius evolando, pervenire promeruit." *Life of Beatrice*, pp. 288–89.

23. As we will see, women often speak indirectly about mystical and visionary experience. The acquisition of first-person narrative voice requires authority, and confidence in that authority. For the dynamic in modern literature, where despite the perception that women's writing is "autobiographical," women only rarely engage in first-person narration before the mid-nineteenth century (and then only for a short time), see Susan Sniader Lanser, *Fictions of Authority: Women Writers and Narrative Voice* (Ithaca: Cornell University Press, 1992).

24. There is an implicit hierarchy of manners, and the metaphor of ascent is used, but the dialectic of presence and absence running through and between the seven manners disrupts any easily identified pattern. There is a parallel here with Marguerite Porete's seven states of the soul, which operate in a similar dialectical manner. See Chapter 4, and Sells, *Languages of Unsaying*, pp. 116–45.

25. As Else Marie Wiberg Pedersen points out, these are the only two instances in which Beatrice uses female imagery to describe the soul. Paper presented at the International Conference of Medieval Studies, Kalamazoo, 1993.

26. The similarity with Mechthild of Magdeburg will become obvious. See Chapter 3.

27. "te vercrigene ende te wesene in die puerheit ende in die vriheit ende in die edelheit daer si in ghemaket es van haren sceppere na sijn beelde ende na sijn ghelikenesse" *Seven Manieren*, p. 4; "Seven Manners," p. 201.

28. "pro hac de qua mentionem fecimus libertate spiritus obtinenda." *Life of Beatrice*, pp. 290–91.

29. "corporales etiam languores solebat incurrere; quibus aliquotiens adeo gravabatur in corpore, quod mortem sibi [crederet] imminere." Ibid., pp. 292–93.

30. Ibid., pp. 294–97.

31. "Alse aldus har seluen gevuelt in die oueruloedicheit van waelheit ende in die grote volheit van herten, soe wert hare geest altemale in minnen versinkende ende hore lichame hare ontsinkende hare herte versmeltende, ende al hare macht verderuende. Ende [so] seere wert si verwonnen met minnen, datsi cumelike hare seluen can gedragen ende datsi dicwile ongeweldich wert haerre lede ende al hare sinne.

"Ende also gelijc also i vat dat vol es, alsment ruret, haesteleke oueruloyt ende vutwelt also wert hi haestelec sere gerenen, ende al verwonnen van der groter uolheit hars herten, so datsi dicwile hars ondanx vut moet breken." *Seven Manieren*, pp. 15–16; "Seven Manners," p. 202 (translation modified).

32. "Fuit etiam in hoc statu tam delicatus sancte mulieris affectus, ut, liquefacto corde, frequentissime lacrimarum imbre madesceret, et, pre

nimia spiritualis copia delectationis, interdum, virium deficiente presidio, languens et egrotans in lectulo decubaret. . . . frequentier accidit ut, ad vasis similitudinem quod, cum plenum liquoris fuerit, impulsum vel modice, mox quod continent eiciendo refundit, et ipsa, per plurima sancti amoris indicia, quod sentiebat intrinsecus, velut impulsa, refunderet; aut certe paraliticum quodammodo tremorem incurreret, aut alia queque languoris incommoda sustineret." *Life of Beatrice*, pp. 304–7. The hagiographer here also follows a familiar topos of the genre—tears as a mark of compunction and mystical fervor. See, for example, *VMO*, n. 18.

33. "Ondertusschen so wert minne so onghemate ende so ouerbrekende in der sielen also har seluen so starkeleke ende so verwoedelike [berurt] int herte, dat hare dunct, dat har herte menichfoudeleke wert seere gewont ende dat die wonden dagelix veruerschet werden ende verseert, in smerteliker weelicheiden ende in nuer iegenwordicheiden. Ende so dunct hare dat har adren ontpluken ende hare bloet verwalt ende hare march verswijnt ende hare been vercrencken, ende [hare] borst verbrent ende hare kele verdroget, so dat hare anscijn ende al har ede gevuelen der hitten van binnen ende des orwoeds van minnen." *Seven Maniernen*, pp. 19–20; "Seven Manners," p. 203.

34. This movement can be traced in texts involving the stigmata. In the early texts describing this phenomenon, the visibility of the markings was unimportant, but in later ones it takes precedence. See Herbert Thurston, *The Physical Phenomena of Mysticism* (Chicago: Regnery, 1952); and Antoine Imbert-Gourbeyre, *La Stigmatisation: L'Extase divine et les miracles de Lourdes: Réponse aux libres-penseurs*, 2. vols. (Clermont-Ferrand: Librairie Catholique, 1894).

35. "Siquidem ipsum cor, ad illius invasionem viribus destitutum, frequenter, ipsa sentiente simul et a foris audiente, quasi vas quod confringitur [sonitum] fractionis emisit; ipse quoque sanguis, per corporalia membra diffusus, apertis venis exiliens, ebulliut, ossibusque contractis ipsa quoque medulla disparuit, pectoris siccitas ipsius gutturis raucitatem induxit, et, ut paucis multa concludam, ipse fervor sancti desiderii et amoris omnia membra corporea, mirum in modum sensibiliter estuanti, incendio conflagravit." *Life of Beatrice*, pp. 308–311.

36. See Chapter 1.

37. "Fuit enim huius desiderii tam vehemens insolentia, quod, pre nimia importunitate [vel sensum sui] se putaret interdum amittere vel etiam vite sue dies, pre magna lesione vitalium et cordis angustia, breviare." *Life of Beatrice*, pp. 324–35.

38. "Also ontsegt si allen troest dicwile van gode selue ende van sinen creaturen want alle die rasten die hare daer af mogen gescien dat sterket meer hare minne, ende trecket har begerte in een hoger wesen, ende dat

uernuwet hare verlancnisse der minnen te plegene ende int gebruken der minnen te wesene ende sonder genuechte in ellenden te leuene." *Seven Manieren*, pp. 34–35; "Seven Manners," p. 205. This portion of the text is not included in the *Life*, the hagiographer having lost the meaning of the treatise at this point; he writes that "they can be conceived only by experience, not by a flood of words" ("sola mentis experientia, non autem verborum affluentia possunt concipi"). *Life of Beatrice*, pp. 324–25.

39. Although there are important exceptions, asceticism and paramystical phenomena clearly are more prominent in the hagiographies of women than in those of men. See, for example, Bynum, *Holy Feast*; Vauchez, *La Sainteté*, pp. 450–55; and Weinstein and Bell, *Saints and Sanctity*, pp. 123–27, 153–57, 236–37. Francis and Suso are two famous exceptions, but they remain just that—exceptional. For more on Suso, see Chapter 7. The importance of this trend can be seen in Bolton's reading of the hagiographies of the *mulieres sanctae* as "desert mothers"—early Christian male models of ascetic heroism are transformed in the later Middle Ages into women. See Bolton, "*Mulieres Sanctae*."

40. Elizabeth Castelli's comments about the movement between the visionary and the object of vision in *The Martyrdom of Perpetua and Felicitas* helped me to clarify this point. See Elizabeth Castelli, "Mortifying the Body, Curing the Soul: Beyond Ascetic Dualism in *The Life of Saint Syncletica*," *differences* 4 (1992): 151, n. 17.

41. Verdeyen, "Le procès," p. 89.

42. This is one interpretation of the meaning of the appellation. Others might be put forward.

43. Much has been written on the authorizing function of visionary experience, in particular in discussions of Hildegard of Bingen. For the theological warrant, see Thomas Aquinas, *STh* III, Supplement, q. 39, a. 1. On Hildegard, see, for example, Dronke, *Women Writers*, pp. 144–201, and Barbara Newman, *Sister of Wisdom: Saint Hildegard's Theology of the Feminine* (Berkeley: University of California Press, 1987). For a general discussion, see Petroff, *Visionary Literature*, pp. 3–59.

44. As Bynum notes, the semi-sacerdotal functions some religious women were able to carry out in the early Middle Ages were increasingly restricted in the twelfth and thirteenth centuries, making visionary sources of authority even more central. See Bynum, *Jesus as Mother*, pp. 247–62. For women's restriction from interpreting the biblical texts and various methods by which they eluded these strictures, see Patricia Demers, *Women as Interpreters of the Bible* (New York: Paulist Press, 1992), pp. 25–71.

45. See Thomas Aquinas, *STh* II–II, q. 177, a. 2, concl.; III, q. 27, a. 5; III, Supplement, q. 39, a. 1.

46. Experience, as I indicated in Chapter 1, is not a simple category. My point here is simply that the body as experienced by itself and the body as seen by another are analytically distinct. The distinction between literal and metaphorical language, with which this problem has often been approached, is inadequate to convey the central distinction. While Beatrice might have "really" felt heat throughout her body, that does not mean she necessarily glowed perceptibly.

47. Hence the need to include such externally visible phenomena within one's account. See, for example, Angela of Foligno, *Il Libro*; and Kempe, *Book*. Both Angela and Margery, furthermore, were married women. This could have contributed to their need to demonstrate the sanctity of their bodies, given the stress laid on chastity in female sanctity. Mystical and hagiographical tropes increasingly interpenetrate in the fourteenth century and beyond. In saying this, I do not mean to imply a denigration or trivialization of the later materials, but merely to point to differences in self-presentation and textual construction that need to be noted and explained.

48. See Burns, *Bodytalk*, pp. 1–18.

49. See Gertrude of Helfta, *Gertrude d'Helfta: Oeuvres spirituelles II: Le Heraut (I et II*, ed. Pierre Doyère (Paris: Editions du Cerf, 1968); and *The Herald of God's Loving-Kindness: Books One and Two*, trans. Alexandra Barratt (Kalamazoo: Cistercian Publications, 1991). Book I is the *Life*, written by a member of her community.

50. Marguerite of Oingt, *Les Oeuvres*, pp. 106–15.

51. See J. H. Albanés, ed., *La Vie de Sainte Douceline* (Marseilles: Camoin, 1879), pp. 50–51.

52. See, for example, Jeanne Ancelet-Hustache, ed., "Les 'Vitae Sororum' d'Unterlinden. Edition critique du Manuscrit 508 de la Bibliothèque de Colmar," *Archives d'histoire doctrinale et littéraire du moyen âge* 5 (1930): 317–509; Elsbet Stagel, *Das Leben der Schwestern zu Töss beschrieben von Elsbet Stagel*, ed. Ferdinand Vetter (Berlin: Weidmannsche Buchhandlung, 1906); Karl Schröder, ed., *Der Nonne von Engelthal Büchlein von der Genaden Überlast* (Tübingen: Literarischen Vereins in Stuttgart, 1871); and J. Bächtold, ed., "Die Stiftung des Klosters Ötenbach und das Leben der seligen Schwestern daselbt," *Zürcher Taschenbuch* N. F. 12 (1889): 213–76. For further examples and discussion, see Louis Cognet, *Introduction aux mystiques rhéno-flamands* (Paris: Desclée de Brouwer, 1968), pp. 196–201; Langer, *Mystische Erfahrung*; and Otto Langer, "Zur dominikanischen Frauenmystik im spätmittelalterlichen Deutschland," in Peter Dinzelbacher and Dieter R. Baur, eds., *Frauenmystik im Mittelalter* (Ostfildern: Schwabenverlag, 1985), pp. 341–46.

53. As Bynum points out, women's lives record their suffering, illness, and food abstinences as themselves sanctifying; men are more often shown being healed by such holy persons. *Holy Feast*, pp. 199–200. See, for just

a few of the many possible examples, *VMO*, nn. 6–7, pp. 668–69; and *Vie de Douceline*, pp. 211–14.

54. The Council took place in 1311–12, although due to the death of Pope Clement V and a long vacancy, the decrees were not published until 1317. Two were of particular relevance to the beguines. *Cum de quibisdam mulieribus* forbids the beguine way of life, although an escape clause protects those women who follow the semireligious life with true piety. Enclosure and control seem to have been primarily at issue, as evidenced by the survival of the *curtis* beguinages in the southern Low Countries. *Ad nostrum* is against the heresy of the free spirit, said explicitly to be the heresy of the beguines. The only clear antecedent for any of the condemned teachings—including the claims that one can take leave of the virtues, give to nature what it demands, and that the free soul can do without divine consolations—is Porete. On the Council and its decrees, see Lerner, *Free Spirit*, pp. 47, 81–84; McDonnell, *Beguines and Beghards*, pp. 521–38; Jacqueline Tarrant, "The Clementine Decrees on the Beguines: Conciliar and Papal Versions," *Archivum Historiae Pontificiae* 12 (1974): 300–308; Simons, "Beguine Movement;" and Fredericq, I, nn. 170–72. On the activity against beguines leading up to the Council, see Grundmann, *Religiöse Bewegungen*, pp. 330–43.

55. On the desire to enclose medieval religious women in order to protect their chastity and control their religiosity, see Schulenburg, "Strict Active Enclosure and its Effects on the Female Monastic Experience (500–1100)" in *Distant Echoes: Medieval Religious Women*, ed. John A. Nichols and Lillian Thomas Shank (Kalamazoo: Cistercian Publications, 1984), pp. 51–86; and Simons, "Beguine Movement." For the medical claim that women were less able to maintain their chastity, see Danielle Jacquart and Claude Thomassett, *Sexuality and Medicine in the Middle Ages*, trans. Matthew Adamson (Princeton: Princeton University Press, 1988), p. 81; and Robertson, "Medieval Medical Views of Women," p. 147.

56. On the relationship between mendicant men and holy women, see John Coakley, "Friars as Confidants of Holy Women in Medieval Dominican Hagiography," in *Images of Sainthood in Medieval Europe*, ed. Renate Blumenfeld-Kosinski and Timea Szell (Ithaca: Cornell University Press, 1991), pp. 222–46; and John Coakley, "Gender and the Authority of Friars: The Significance of Holy Women for Thirteenth-Century Franciscans and Dominicans," *Church History* 60 (1991): 445–60. Coakley is in part concerned to show why mendicant men were so fascinated with and willing to grant authority to women.

57. Despite the apparent language barriers between Mechthild, Porete, and the holy women in the Dutch-speaking Low Countries, scholars

point to the interchanges between these vernaculers in the thirteenth century. See, for example, J. B. Porion, *Hadewijch d'Anvers* (Paris, 1954), pp. 147–48.

58. This parallels Jacques of Vitry's description of these women in a letter to a friend in Flanders from 1216 in which he records Honorius III's verbal approbation of their way of life. Jacques also points to the commonalities between the northern movement and those of the south. See Grundmann, *Religiöse Bewegungen*, pp. 170–71.

59. Herbert Grundmann, "Die Frauen und die Literatur," pp. 129–61. Peters contends with this thesis, although in ways which ultimately reaffirm the basic argument that the women's religious movement served as the grounds out of which a vernacular mystical tradition arose. In collapsing the distinction between beguinel and Cistercian writings (seemingly in order to reaffirm the existence of a female form of piety not overly dependent on male, clerical direction), she ignores the rather obvious point that most of the thirteenth-century convent literature is in Latin, in particular the work of Gertrude of Helfta and Mechthild of Hackeborn. See Peters, *Religiöse Erfahrung*. While I agree with her stress on the women writers' relative independence and the highly literary quality of their works, I do think distinctions can and should be made between beguine and Cistercian, mystical and hagiographical, vernacular and Latin writings. See also the two reviews of Peters, by D. H. Green in *Modern Language Review* 85 (1990): 129–30; and Rosemary Hale in *Speculum* 68 (1993): 350–51.

60. Ruh, "Meister Eckhart"; and McGinn, "*Unio mystica*." Peters argues with the attestation of this characteristic as specifically beguine, but without offering any convincing evidence of these mystical themes in non-beguine texts. See Peters, *Religiöse Erfahrung*, esp. pp. 1–8.

61. Among the beguines or semireligious women of whom lives survive are Marie of Oignies (d. 1213), Odilia (d. 1220), Christina the Astonishing (d. 1234), Ivetta of Huy (d. 1228), Margaret of Ypres (d. 1237), Douceline (d. 1274), and Gertrude van Oosten (d. 1358). Other women who had strong interactions with beguines are Lutgard of Aywières (d. 1246), Juliana of Mont-Cornillon (d. 1257/58), Ida of Nivelles (d. 1231/32), Ida of Léau (d. ca. 1260), Ida of Louvain (d. ca. 1255), and Beatrice of Nazareth (d. 1268). I do not discuss the documents gathered by Peter of Dacia about the beguine Christine of Stommeln (1242–1312). All of the women I discuss who had interactions with the beguines were Cistercians at some point in their lives. All except Douceline are from the Low Countries. In the following, I will show that certain elements recur only in the beguine hagiographies, while others can be seen in both sets of texts.

62. Hugh of Floreffe, *Vita Ivetta Reclusa*, AASS 1: 863–87. Hereafter *VIR*.

63. "Inter haec tamen sedulae officia servitutis, & lippitudines Liae, non obliviscebatur Racheliticae pulchritudinis: sed velut Moyses nunc in castris populi sollicitudinem gerens, nunc in tabernaculo foederis Dei expectans responsa, quidquid ageret foris, intro tamen semper ipsa eadem perseverans, non diebus, neque noctibus vacabat a colloquis divinis & oratione." *VIR*, p. 870, n. 37.

64. "omissoque ministerio Marthae, in partem Mariae, quae optima est." *VIR*, p. 871, n. 42.

65. For example, *Vita Idae Lovaniensis*, AASS 10: nn. 18, 36, pp. 163, 181. Ida of Louvain lived alone in a cell and was in close contact with a community of beguines (referred to by that name in the life, which suggests a date in the later part of the thirteenth century for the text), before entering the Cistercian order. While living as a solitary, she performed manual labor and acted as a "Martha" on behalf of the poor around her. It is perhaps noteworthy that in the chapter before her decision to enter the Cistercian order, she is shown saying the office for Mary Magdalene, commonly associated with Mary who took the better part.

66. *VMO*, n. 38, p. 646.

67. Ibid., p. 647.

68. Thomas of Cantimpré, *Vita Margarete de Ypris*, ed. by G. Meersseman in "Les Frères Prêcheurs et le Mouvement Dévot en Flandre au XIIIe Siècle," *Archivium Fratrum Praedicatorum* 17 (1947), Chaps. 14–15, pp. 113–14. Margaret, apparently in a state of spiritual distraction, throws some eggs out of the window. When her mother comes home and finds their meal missing, the eggs miraculously reconstitute themselves.

69. *Vita Iulianae*, AASS, 9: n. 14, p. 448. This explicit usage is particularly interesting given that the life has its antecedents in a vernacular life written by the recluse Eva of St. Martin (d. 1264/65). See G. Lambot, "Un precieux manuscrit de la Vie de S. Julienne du Mont-Cornillon," in *Miscellanea historica in honorem Alberti de Meyer*, 2 vols. (Louvain, 1946), vol. 1, pp. 603ff.

70. For the place of this theme in Bernard's work, see Jean Leclercq, *Saint Bernard Mystique* (Bruges: De Brouwes, 1948), pp. 393–94; and Bernard of Clairvaux, *On the Song of Songs III*, trans. Kilian Walsh and Irene Edmunds (Kalamazoo: Cisterican Publications, 1979), ser. 49–51, pp. 21–48.

71. On Thomas's career as a hagiographer, see Simone Roisin, "La Méthode hagiographique de Thomas de Cantimpré," in *Miscellanea historica in honorem Alberti de Meyer*, 2 vols. (Louvain: Bibliothèque de l'Université, 1946), vol. 1, pp. 546–57.

72. Thomas de Cantimpré, *Vita Lutgardis, AASS* 22: 234–62. Trans. Margot King, *The Life of Lutgard of Aywières* (Toronto: Peregrina Publishing, 1991).

73. *VMO*, Bk. 2, n. 45, pp. 618–19.

74. Thomas of Cantimpré, *Vita Christinae Mirabilis, AASS* 31: nn. 22–24, pp. 654–65. Trans. Margot King, *The Life of Christina Mirabilis* (Toronto: Peregrina Publishing, 1986). Hereafter *VCM*. King points out that the author of the Middle English translation of the life, more shocked by this activity than Thomas, appends to the chapter title ("How she was driven by the spirit to live by begging") "like a man" ("*et quasi homo*"). King, *Life of Christina*, p. 45, n. 13.

75. *Vita Margarete*, Ch. 22, p. 117.

76. See Greven, "Der Ursprung," pp. 57–58; and Bolton, "Some Thirteenth Century Women," pp. 7–29. Bolton argues that this theme appears in only "one or two early beguine lives" and is not a general or particularly important feature. I think that I have shown this not to be the case. In fact the only early beguine lives I read in which mendicancy or concern for the source of money plays *no* role are those of Odilia and Ivetta. Because she was the mother of a local prelate, such activity would certainly have been suppressed in Odilia. Both, furthermore, are very concerned about how to get rid of the money left them by their husbands. See *Vita Ivetta*; *Vita Odilia*.

77. *Vie de Douceline*, Ch. 5, pp. 38–47. Although she does not beg in the streets, she survives on the alms contributed to her community.

78. *Vita Gertrudis ab Oosten, AASS*, 1: n. 8, p. 350. The appearance of such a scene of "youthful indiscretion" in a late beguine *vita* points to the perception of mendicancy as a specifically beguine temptation. The only possibly non-beguine example I found is in the life of the former Augustinian, Juliana of Mont-Cornillon, who did have close contacts with beguines and may herself be described as one. After having been forced out of her convent by detractors, she tells her companions that they will survive by begging if necessary. See *Vita Iuliana*, Bk. 2, n. 31, p. 469.

79. See Grundmann, *Religiöse Bewegungen*, 172.

80. The gendered nature of this distrust can be clearly seen in the case of Clare of Assisi, who wished to follow Francis's poverty. She had first to submit to enclosure, thereby curtailing her poverty and that of the community; they would own only what was necessary for the maintenance of an enclosed community. After her death, even this concession was denied. See Rosalind B. Brooke and Christopher N. L. Brooke, "St. Clare," in *Medieval Women*, ed. Derek Baker (Oxford: Basil Blackwell, 1978), pp. 275–88.

81. Robert Grosseteste (d. 1253) was a Franciscan and bishop of Lincoln from 1235 to 1253. See Grundmann, *Religiöse Bewegungen*, p. 322; and Bolton, "Some Thirteenth Century Women," pp. 7–8.

82. McDonnell, *Beguines and Beghards*, pp. 270–77.

83. *VMO*, n. 38.

84. See, for example, Neel, "The Origins of the Beguines," pp. 321–41; and Janet I. Summers, "'The Violent Shall Take It By Force': The First Century of Cistercian Nuns, 1125–1228" (Ph.D. diss., University of Chicago, 1986).

85. See Philip of Harvengt, *Vita beatae Odae* in *PL* 203, cols. 1359–74.

86. The humility and abjection of the victim of the disease or diseases named as the biblical affliction of leprosy seems to have been behind the ubiquity of such acts in the hagiographies. To see Christ in the leper is to see him in the lowest and most outcast group of society, those often understood as suffering for sexual sin. As a mark of abjection, it was even better to *be* a leper. Alice of Schaarbeck's patience and humility when afflicted with leprosy is a central mark of her sanctity, although in this context the cause of the disease is not raised. See *VIR*, nn. 36–37, p. 871; and *Vita Aleydis de Scarembecanae*, *AASS* 21: 476–83. On a practical level, there must have been a dearth of volunteers to take care of those afflicted with such stigmatized diseases. See also, Françoise Beriac, *Histoire des lépreux au moyen âge: un société d'exclus* (Paris: Imago, 1989). For the relationship between sexuality and leprosy, see Stephen R. Ell, "Blood and Sexuality in Medieval Leprosy," *Janus: Revue Internationale de l'Histoire des Sciences, de la Médecine, de la Pharmacie et de la Technique* 71 (1984): 156–63; Jacquart and Thomasset, *Sexuality and Medicine*, pp. 177–97.

87. On the move from "corporeal charity" to "spiritual almsgiving" in the lives, see Jo Ann McNamara, "The Need to Give: Suffering and Female Sanctity in the Middle Ages," in *Images of Sainthood in Medieval Europe*, ed. Renate Blumenfeld-Kosinski and Timea Szell (Ithaca: Cornell University Press, 1991), pp. 199–221.

88. See, for example, Finke, *Feminist Theory*, Ch. 3. The best recent study of Christina's life is Robert Sweetman "Christine of Saint-Trond's Preaching Apostolate: Thomas of Cantimpré's Hagiographical Method Revisited," *Vox Benedictina* 60 (1992): 67–97.

89. *VMO*, Prologue, n. 7, pp. 637–38.

90. "Revera, inquit, dulcissima mea, hic mecum eris; sed nunc tibi duorum optionem propono; aut nunc scilicet permanere mecum; aut ad corpus reverti, ibique [agere poenas] immortalis animae per mortale corpus sine detrimento sui, omnesque illas animas, quas in illo purgatorii loco miserata es, ipsis tuis poenae eripere: homines vero viventes exemplo

poenae & vitae tuae converti ad me, & a sceleribus resilire, peractisque omnibus, ad me tandem multorum praemiorum mercede te cumulatam reverti." *VCM*, n. 7, p. 652. King, *Life of Christina*, pp. 13–14. Translation modified.

91. Bynum describes this aspect of women's asceticism with extreme sympathy and insight. See *Holy Feast*, pp. 120–21.

92. Heinrich Suso, with no claims to possessing a miraculous body, is described as undergoing some astonishing asceticisms. See "The Life of the Servant," in Heinrich Suso, *Heinrich Seuse: Deutsche Schriften im Auftrag der Wurttembergischen Kommission für Landesgeschichte*, ed. Karl Bihlmeyer (Stuttgart: Kohlhammer, 1907), and *The Exemplar with Two Sermons*, trans. Frank Tobin (New York: Paulist Press, 1989).

93. "Qui Symeonis vermes ex vulneribus scaturientes; qui B. Antonii ignem, quo pedes incendit, venerando admirantur; cur non etiam in sexu fragili tantam mulieris fortitudinem obstupescant, quae caritate vulnerata, & Christi vulneribus vegetata, proprii corporis neglexit vulnera?" *VMO*, n. 22, pp. 642. King, *Life of Marie D'Oignies*, p. 37. Translation modified.

94. "Cumque non solum in mente, sed quod mirabilius est, sensibiliter doleret in pedibus, quibus loca praedicta calcaverat; vix tandem, cum multotiens pedes ad terram collisisset, potuit quiescere." *VMO*, n. 67, p. 654. King, *Life of Marie D'Oignies*, p. 83.

95. These passages are read by Bynum as evidence of self-inflicted stigmata. For the association, see also *VMO*, n. 103, p. 664.

96. Bynum, *Fragmentation*, pp. 234–35.

97. Dante's account is only the most famous. For the possible relationship between Dante's poem and the visionary literature of the Middle Ages, including that of Mechthild of Magdeburg, see Peter Dronke, *Dante and Medieval Latin Traditions* (Cambridge: Cambridge University Press, 1986), p. 126, n. 8.

98. Thomas of Cantimpré, *Vita Mariae Oigniancensis. Supplementum*, *AASS* 23: n. 20, p. 674. For another among many examples, while Marie was alive, touching a few strands of her hair cured a man and his son from illness and injury. Ibid., nn. 6–7, pp. 668–69.

99. Lochrie argues that in the Middle Ages women were identified not with the body but with the flesh, understood in its Pauline sense as fallen humanity. While she is correct to point out that the "flesh" so understood is heterogeneous, neither purely body nor soul, her desire to read Kempe and other women's somatic mysticisms in terms of a redemption of the flesh may be untenable. Given the Pauline and Augustinian usages, the flesh is by definition fallen. The *body* is not, despite Augustine's unfortunate tendency to conflate the two. See Lochrie, *Translations*, pp. 12–27. I would argue that the will and its dispositions are, implicitly,

also heterogeneous and thus capable of deciding the fate of both body and soul. The continued suspicion of the *body* as leading to or causing *fleshliness* (i.e., placing oneself before God) obscures this fact in many medieval texts.

100. It should be remembered furthermore, that Christina's body has died once already, thereby having achieved a first level of sanctification. Perhaps in dying, the elision between body and flesh is viewed as being partially undone. On this move in Augustine, see Peter Brown, *The Body and Society: Men, Women, and Sexual Renunciation in Early Christianity* (New York: Columbia University Press, 1988), pp. 387–427.

101. Bynum, *Fragmentation*, p. 234. See also, *Holy Feast*, pp. 120–21.

102. See Hadewijch, "Letter Six," in *Complete Works*, pp. 59–61; Hadewijch, *Brieven*, pp. 58–64; and, for Mechthild, Chapter 3.

103. Together with the questionable hagiographical evidence, Robert Lerner describes inquisitorial documents that suggest some beguine communities were radically ascetic. See Lerner, *Free Spirit*, pp. 112–19.

104. Juliana of Mont-Cornillon was instrumental in establishing the feast of Corpus Christi, and Lutgard's visions are a central source for devotion to the Sacred Heart. See Bynum, *Holy Feast*, p. 77. For more on the origins of this movement and late medieval Eucharistic devotions, see Rubin, *Corpus Christi*.

105. Bynum, *Holy Feast*, pp. 117–19, and Rubin, *Corpus Christi*.

106. VMO, Bk. 2, n. 12; *Vita Idae Lewensis, AASS* 60: Chaps. 2–3, nn. 18–26; *Vita Margarete*, Ch. 40, p. 122.

107. See, for example, *Vita Idae Lovaniensis*, Bk. 2, n. 3; *Vita Lutgardis*, Bk. 1, nn. 1–2. See Bynum, *Feast*, pp. 227–32.

108. *FL*, Bk. II, Ch. 4, pp. 41–44. Mechthild's critics claimed this was impossible, as John the Baptist had not been a priest. See *FL*, Bk. VI, Ch. 36, pp. 244–45.

109. VMO, n. 22 is taken by some as a self-inflicted stigmata; *Life of Ida of Louvain*, Bk. 1, n. 3; and *Vita Gertrudis*.

110. Roisin, *L'hagiographie cistercienne*.

111. Bynum has also emphasized this aspect of the beguine life. See *Fragmentation*, pp. 68–72.

112. See Chapter 3.

113. See *FL*, Bk. IV, Ch. 2, p. 110, where Mechthild describes how she went to a place where she knew almost no one in order to share in Christ's suffering, exile, and loneliness. Peters argues that these remarks cannot be read as autobiographical since they involve hagiographical commonplaces. Yet Peters ignores the ways in which Mechthild's text departs from standard hagiographical forms in its detail (its mention of the one person in Magdeburg she feared would befriend her) and *lack* of

emphasis on physical suffering as a means of imitating Christ. See Peters, *Religiöse Erfahrung*, pp. 53–67.

114. Bolton, "*Vitae Matrum*"; and Thomas of Cantimpré, *Vita Lutgardis*.

115. See *FL*, Bk. V, Ch. 8, pp. 161–62.

116. See, for example, *FL*, Bk. VI, Ch. 31, pp. 238–40.

117. For Dietrich's life of Saint Dominic, see Thierry of Apolda, *Acta Ampliora S. Dominici Confessoris*, *AASS* 34: 562–632. One of the citations from Mechthild's work found in the *vita* makes its way into Dante's *Divine Comedy*, leading to speculation—since disproved—of an identification between Mechthild of Magdeburg and Dante's Matilda. See Dante, *The Divine Comedy. Paradise: Text and Commentary*, trans. Charles C. Singleton (Princeton: Princeton University Press, 1975), Canto 12, lines 37–45. Mechthild's work was originally composed in a Low German dialect which has been lost. A Latin translation was made early, probably around 1285, and an Alemannic version in 1343–45 by Heinrich of Nordlingen. The latter is the text on which the Morel edition and the critical edition are based.

118. For this information, see Davies, *Meister Eckhart*, pp. 37–45.

119. See my arguments in this chapter, and Bynum, *Holy Feast*; Bynum, *Fragmentation*, Ch. 3; Jeffrey Hamburger, "Visual and Visionary: The Image in Late Medieval Monastic Devotions," *Viator* 20 (1989): 161–82; and Hamburger, *Rothschild Canticles*.

120. The Dominican order undertook, albeit reluctantly, the pastoral care of many religious women in northern Europe, particularly Germany. While many were incorporated into the Dominican order during the middle years of the thirteenth century, others remained beguines. It is almost certain that Eckhart was involved in the *cura monialium* for nuns and beguines after 1314 in Strassbourg and later Cologne, where his preaching was attended by religious and laypeople. The vernacular sermons themselves offer strong evidence that Eckhart was addressing religious women and laypeople. For the Dominican involvement with religious women, see Grundmann, *Religiöse Bewegungen*; and John B. Freed, "Urban Development and the *Cura Monialium* in Thirteenth-Century Germany," *Viator* 3 (1972): 311–27. On Eckhart's ties to women, see Langer, *Mystische Erfahrung*, pp. 35–46; Josef Koch, "Kritische Studien zum Leben Meister Eckharts," *Archivium Fratrum Praedicatorum* 30 (1960): 5–16; and Trusen, *Der Prozess gegen Meister Eckhart*, pp. 19–61. Trusen argues for the importance of this context by declaring that Eckhart sought to avoid the twin dangers of ecstatic mysticism and the so-called heresy of the free spirit. While the argument structurally parallels my own, I am less concerned with defending Eckhart's

"orthodoxy" (and denigrating that of his female influences and audiences) and more concerned with showing his *positive* links to beguine traditions.

121. Bynum, *Fragmentation*, Ch. 6. Further examples of such extreme asceticism and the dimension of holiness it adds to the woman's life can be seen in Thomas of Cantimpré, *Vita Lutgardis*, Bk. 2, Ch. 1, and Bk. 3, Ch. 4; *Vita Margarete*; and Hugh of Floreffe, *VIR*, 1: 863–67.

122. Bolton, "*Vitae Matrum*"; Bynum, *Holy Feast*, pp. 208–18, 246–51; Bynum, *Fragmentation*, pp. 38-40, 131–34, 181–238; McDonnell, *Beguines and Beghards*, p. 445.

123. Lerner tells of the radical asceticism of the beguines of Schweidnitz in Silesia (1332) among others; see his *Free Spirit*, pp. 112–19.

124. As Bynum points out, the hierarchy also attempted to curtail such activity insofar as it was seen to threaten discipline and male authority. See *Holy Feast*, pp. 237–51.

125. For full discussion, see Chapter 7.

126. See Grundmann, "Ketzerverhöre des Spätmittelalters," pp. 519–75; and Colledge and Marler, " 'Poverty of the Will'," p. 15.

127. Colledge and Marler, " 'Poverty of the Will'," p. 15, cite evidence given by Thomas Kaeppeli that suspect or condemned materials could remain in orthodox houses for this period of time. The large number of translations and manuscripts of the *Mirror* make it clear that the text was not destroyed. See Lerner, *Free Spirit*.

128. The growing suspicion of the beguines might also explain the absence of any reference to them or to their work in Eckhart's writings. Such direct references are rare in the Sermons (when there, they are often to his own texts and even more often subverted by later discussion), but any references to his female influences and auditors would be even less likely to appear in the climate surrounding the Council of Vienne. While the decrees of the Council were not published until 1317, about three years after the beginning of his preaching in Strasbourg, his presence in the Dominican house at Paris from 1311 to 1312 would have made him aware of the general attitudes toward the beguines and heresy.

CHAPTER 3

1. Margot Schmidt, for example, writes that Mechthild's language is "so spontaneous and so independent of all genre and of all rhetorical figures, that the work furnishes 'the phenomenology of the experience of God in a pure state' (Haas)." Margot Schmidt, "Mechtilde de

Magdeburg," *Dictionnaire de spiritualité, ascétique et mystique, doctrine et histoire*, ed. M. Viller et al. (Paris: Garnier, 1937–), vol. 10, col. 878.

2. Heinz Tillman, "Studien zum Dialog bei Mechthild von Magdeburg" (Ph.D. diss., Marburg, 1933), p. 1.

3. Hans Robert Jauss, "Theories of Genres and Medieval Literature," in *Toward an Aesthetic of Reception*, trans. Timothy Bahti (Minneapolis: University of Minnesota Press, 1982).

4. Kathryn L. Lynch, *The High Medieval Dream Vision: Poetry, Philosophy and Literary Form* (Stanford: Stanford University Press, 1988), p. 5.

5. Kurt Ruh, "Beginenmystik," p. 269; and Alois Haas, *Sermo mysticus. Studien zu Theologie und Sprache der deutschen Mystik* (Freiburg, Universitätsverlag, 1979), p. 105.

6. As a partial autobiography, see Wolfgang Mohr, "Darbietungsformen der Mystik bei Mechthild von Magdeburg," in *Märchen, Mythos, Dichtung: Festschrift zum 90. Geburtstag Friedrich von der Leyens am 19. August 1963*, ed. H. Kuhn and K. Schier (Munich: n.p., 1963), pp. 375–99. Mohr is intent on showing the varieties of genres and literary conceits reflected in *The Flowing Light*. This may well be a more accurate way of describing the text; my reading would then be one that focuses on its confessional character, which, I believe, is overarching. As veiled, see Margot Schmidt, " 'Die spilende minnevluot? Der Eros als Sein und Wirkkraft in der Trinität bei Mechthild von Magdeburg," in *"Eine Höhe, über die nichts geht." Spezielle Glaubenserfahrung in der Frauenmystik?*, ed. Dieter R. Bauer and Margot Schmidt (Stuttgart-Bad Cannstatt: Fromann-holzboog, 1986), p. 71. Schmidt does recognize the reflective quality of Mechthild's text, yet her use of the phrase "veiled autobiography" seems redundant and inappropriate in the light of contemporary theories of autobiography. Certainly these theories recognize and stress the constructed nature of autobiographies. See, for example, James Olney, ed., *Autobiography: Essays Theoretical and Critical* (Princeton: Princeton University Press, 1980); Domna Stanton, ed., *The Female Autograph* (Chicago: University of Chicago Press, 1987); Sidonie Smith, *A Poetics of Women's Autobiography: Marginality and the Fictions of Self-Representation* (Bloomington: Indiana University Press, 1987); and Sidonie Smith, *Subjectivity, Identity, and the Body: Women's Autobiographical Practices in the Twentieth Century* (Bloomington: Indiana University Press, 1993).

7. It should be said, however, that I do not believe that experience and rhetorical strategies can be easily disentangled, or that the former always should be given priority.

8. See Robert McMahon, *Augustine's Prayerful Ascent: An Essay on the Literary Form of the Confessions* (Athens: University of Georgia Press, 1989), pp. xi–xxii.

9. See Karl Joachim Weintraub, *The Value of the Individual* (Chicago: University of Chicago Press, 1978), esp. Chaps. 2–3, and 9, for an account of the classical conception of autobiography and why medieval and early modern Christian texts, often by women, are found lacking. For the problematizing of such conceptions in contemporary theory, see the works cited in n. 6 above.

10. In addition to McMahon, see Peter Brown, *Augustine of Hippo: A Biography* (Berkeley: University of California Press, 1967), pp. 158–81; Marcia Colish, *The Mirror of Language: A Study in the Medieval Theory of Language* (Lincoln: University of Nebraska Press, 1983), Ch. 1; Eugene Vance, "Augustine's *Confessions* and the Grammar of Selfhood," *Genre* 6 (1973): 1–28; Vance, "Le Moi comme langage: Saint Augustin et l'autobiographie," *Poétique* 42 (1980): 139–55; and Vance, *Mervelous Signals: Poetics and Sign Theory in the Middle Ages* (Lincoln: University of Nebraska Press, 1986), Ch. 1.

11. On dialogic character, see McMahon, *Prayerful Ascent*; Tillman, "Dialog;" and Walter Haug, "Das Gespräch mit dem unvergleichlichen Partner. Der mystiche Dialog bei Mechthild von Magdeburg als Paradigma für eine personale Gesprächstruktur," in *Das Gespräch*, ed. K. Stierle and R. Warning (Munich: W. Fink, 1984), pp. 251–79.

12. *FL*, Bk. IV, Ch. 2, p. 110. This parallels the distinction made by Bynum between the structures of male and female life-narratives in the Middle Ages. See Bynum, *Fragmentation*, pp. 27–51.

13. Augustine, *Confessions*, trans. R. S. Pine-Coffin (London: Penguin Books, 1961), pp. 197–98. "Et dum loquimur et inhiamus illi, attingimus eam modice toto ictu cordis; et suspiravimus, et reliquimus ibi religatas primitias spiritus, et remeavimus ad strepitum oris nostri, ubi verbum et incipitur et finitur. et quid simile verbo tuo, domino nostro, in se permanenti sine vetustate atque innovanti omnia?" Augustine *Confessions*, 2 vols., Loeb Classical Library, (Cambridge: Harvard University Press, 1989), Bk. 9, Ch. 10, 2: 48–50.

14. Vance, *Mervelous Signals*, p. 24.

15. Mechthild tells us that she knows no Latin (*FL*, Bk. II, Ch. 3, p. 40), although phrases from the liturgy and scriptural citations used in the liturgy are found in Latin in her text.

16. On Hildegard and the source of her authority, see Peter Dronke, *Women Writers*; and Barbara Newman, *Sister of Wisdom*.

17. Bynum, *Jesus as Mother*, p. 230.

18. See Marianne Heimbach, *"Der ungelehrte Mund" als Autorität. Mystische Erfahrung als Quelle kirchlich-prophetischer Rede im Werk*

Mechthilds von Magdeburg (Stuttgart-Bad Cannstatt: Frommann-holz-boog, 1989), on the unity of the mystical and prophetic poles in Mechthild's work.

19. See Vance, *Mervelous Signal*, p. 5; and Joseph Ratzinger, "Originalität und Ueberlieferung in Augustins Begriff der Confessio," *Revue des études augustiniennes* 3 (1957): 375–82.

20. On the centrality of linguistic and rhetorical practices to mystical writings, see Michel de Certeau, "Mystic Speech," in *Heterologies*, trans. Brian Massumi (Minneapolis: University of Minnesota Press, 1986); Certeau, "*Mystique* au XVIIe siècle;" Certeau, *Fable mystique*; and Marguerite Harl, "Le Langage de l'Expérience Religieuse chez Pères Grecs," *Rivista di Storia e Letteratura Religiosa* 5 (1977): 5–34.

21. See especially, Augustine, *Confessions*, Bk. 13, Ch. 32–38. For a discussion of whether the *Confessions* is better read as a dialogue or a monologue, see Lynn Poland, "Invocation as Interruption in Augustine's *Confessions*," in *Morphologies of Faith: Essays in Religion and Culture in Honor of Nathan A. Scott, Jr.*, ed. Mary Gerhart and Anthony C. Yu (Atlanta, Ga.: Scholars Press, 1990), pp. 343–58.

22. See Vance, *Mervelous Signals*, Ch. 1; and Vance, "Le Moi."

23. This tradition is briefly discussed with reference to Marguerite and her use of allegory in Chapter 4.

24. Ancelet-Hustache, *Mechtilde*, pp. 65–87; and Neumann, "Beiträge," pp. 27–80.

25. *FL*, Bk. I, Ch. 1, pp. 5–7.

26. "Der ware gottes grus, der da kumet von der himelschen flut us dem brunnen der fliesenden drivaltekeit, der hat so grosse kraft, das er dem lichamen benimet alle sin maht, und machet die sele ir selben offenbar, das si sihet sich selben den heligen gelich und enpfahet denne an sich gotlichen schin. So scheidet dú sele von dem lichamen mit aller ir maht, wisheite, liebin und gerunge, sunder das minste teil irs lebendes belibet mit dem lichamen als in eime sussen schlaffe." Ibid., Bk. I, Ch. 2, p. 7. The description is very similar to those found in Beatrice's "Seven Manners of Loving." See Chapter 2.

27. "ein spil, das der lichame nút weis," Ibid.

28. "So swebent si fúrbas an ein wunnenriche stat, da ich nút von sprechen wil noch mag. Es ist ze notlich, ich engetar, wan ich bin ein vil súndig monsche." Ibid., p. 8.

29. Ibid., Bk. I, Ch. 1, pp. 5–7.

30. "Wenne das spil allerbest ist, so mus man as lassen." Ibid., Bk. I, Ch. 2, p. 8.

31. "So sprichet der licham: 'Eya frowe, wa bist du nu gewesen? Du kumest so minnenklich wider, schone und creftig, fri und sinnenrich. Din wandelen hat mir benomen minen smak, rúchen, varwe und alle min

maht.' So sprichet si: 'Swig, morder, la din klagen sin! Ich wil mich iemer hutten vor dir. Das min vient verwundert si, das wirret uns nút, ich frowe mich sin.'" Ibid.

32. Ibid., Bk. I, Ch. 5, p. 11.

33. There is some debate over the authorship of the chapter titles. Neumann suggests that they were supplied by her Dominican confessor, Heinrich of Halle. I am not convinced that this was the case throughout, yet in any event my arguments hold, the original absence of chapter titles simply enhancing the ambiguities of voice. See Neumann, "Beiträge"; and Neumann, *Untersuchungen*, pp. 201–6.

34. *FL*, Bk. I, Ch. 12–20, pp. 14–15.

35. Ibid., Bk. I, Ch. 34–37, pp. 24–25.

36. "So man dir ere bútet, so solt du dich schamen; so man dich pineget, so solt du dich vrowen; so man dir gut tut, so solt du dich vorhten; so du súnde wider mich tust, so solt du dich betruben von herzen. Maht du dich nit betruben, so sich, wie sere und wie lange ich dur dich betrubet was." Ibid., Bk. I, Ch. 32, p. 24.

37. "Dis buch das sende ich nun ze botten allen geistlichen lúten beidú bosen und guten, wand wenne die súle vallent, so mag das werk nút gestan, und ez bezeichent alleine mich und meldet loblich mine heimlichkeit." Ibid., Prologue, p. 4. There has been much written on this passage. See Eberhard Nellmann, "*Dis buch . . . bezeichent alleine mich*—Zum Prolog von Mechthilds 'Fliessendem Licht der Gottheit'," in *Gotes und der Werlde Hulde: Literatur in Mittelalter und Neuzeit: Festschrift für Heinz Rupp*, ed. Rüdiger Schnell (Stuttgart: Francke, 1989), pp. 200–205; and Neumann, *Untersuchungen*, p. 3. The attitude expressed here constrasts sharply with that of Marguerite Porete. See Chapter 4.

38. *FL*, Bk. V, Ch. 34, p. 195.

39. Margot Schmidt, "Elemente der Schau bei Mechthild von Magdeburg und Mechthild von Hackeborn. Zur Bedeutung der geistlichen Sinne," in *Frauenmystik im Mittelalter*, ed. Peter Dinzelbacher and Dieter R. Bauer (Ostfildern bei Stuttgart: Schwabenverlag, 1985), p. 124; Heimbach, *Mund*, p. 173; and Haas, *Sermo*, p. 107.

40. This is in contrast with Marguerite Porete's claim that she does not write her book, God does.

41. "'Wa von bist du gemachet, sele, das du so hohe stigest úber alle creaturen, und mengest dich in die heligen drivaltekeit unde belibest doch gantz in dir selber?' . . . Ich bin in der selben stat gemachet von der mine, darumbe mag mich enkein creature noch miner edelen nature getrosten noch entginnen denne allein die minne." Ibid., Bk. I, Ch. 22, pp. 18.

42. See Ibid., Bk. II, Ch. 20, p. 52; Bk. II, Ch. 25, p. 63; Bk. IV, Ch. 1–2, pp. 109, 113–14; and Bk. V, Ch. 12, p. 166.

43. See Petrus W. Tax, "Die grosse Himmelsschau bei Mechthild von Magdeburg and ihre Höllenvision. Aspekte des Erfahrungshorizontes, der Gegenbildlichkeit und der Parodierung," in *Zeitschrift für deutsches Altertum und deutsche Literatur* 108 (1979): 112–37.

44. Ruh, "Beginenmystik," p. 271, argues that the chapter is the genetic basis for the text, yet many sequences of chapters clearly belong together and form larger units.

45. On the importance of this oscillating movement from the Song of Songs for Bernard of Clairvaux, see Michael Casey, *Athirst for God: Spiritual Desire in Bernard of Clairvaux's Sermons on the Song of Songs* (Kalamazoo: Cistercian Publications, 1988). The theme is also crucial for Bernard's friend and fellow Cistercian, William of St. Thierry, who wrote sermon commentaries on the Song of Songs.

46. Ancelet-Hustache, *Mechthilde*, pp. 1–28; and Schmidt, "Eros," p. 71–72.

47. See Colledge and Walsh, eds. *Showings*; and Julian of Norwich, *Showings*.

48. Heimbach, *Mund*, pp. 11–12.

49. See esp. *FL*, Bk. I, Ch. 2, p. 7; Bk. VI, Ch. 20, pp. 229–31; and Bk. VI, Ch. 23, pp. 232–33.

50. See Augustine, *De Genesi ad litteram*, Bk XII; and *Epistolae*, in *Patrologia cursus completus: Series latina*, ed. J.-P. Migne (Paris: Garnier, 1844–64), vol. 33, Epistle 146. For a brief discussion of this aspect of Augustine's thought, see Eugene TeSelle, "Augustine," in *An Introduction to the Medieval Mystics of Europe*, ed. Paul Szarmach (Albany: State University of New York Press, 1984), p. 25.

51. Neumann, "Beiträge"; and Hans-Georg Kemper, "Allegorische Allegorese. Zur Bildlichkeit und Struktur mystischer Literatur," in *Formen und Funktionen der Allegorie*, ed. Walter Haug (Stuttgart: Metzler, 1979), pp. 96–97.

52. "Dis buch ist begonnen in der minne, es sol och enden in der minne, wand es ist niht also wise noch also helig noch also schone noch also stark noch also vollekomen als die minne. Do sprach únser herre Jhesus Christus: 'Sprich, vatter, ich wil nu swigen alse du swigest in dem munde dins sunes albrimmende dur die krankheit der lúten, und alse min menscheit sprach albibende durch die valschheit der welte, wan si lonete mir mit dem bitteren tode.' " *FL*, Bk. IV, Ch. 28, p. 148–49.

53. "Das ich dich sere minne, das han ich von miner nature, wan ich selbe bin die minne." Ibid., Bk. I, Ch. 24, p. 20.

54. For the place of sexual and gender imagery in Mechthild's text, see Ulrike Wiethaus, "Sexuality, Gender, and the Body in Late Medieval Women's Spirituality: Cases from Germany and the Netherlands," *Journal of Feminist Studies in Religion* 7 (1991): 35–52.

55. "spilende minnevlut." Ibid., Bk. VII, Ch. 45, p. 291.

56. Schmidt, "Eros," p. 74.

57. For other examples of this Trinitarian mysticism, see the works of the Cistercian William of St. Thierry, especially *Lettre aux Frères du Mont-Dieu*, ed. Jean Dechanet, in Sources chrétienne 223 (Paris: Editions du Cerf, 1985); and *The Golden Epistle*, trans. Theodore Berkeley (Kalamazoo: Cistercian Publications, 1980). Also see Hadewijch, *The Complete Works*.

58. In Eckhart, the soul will be the mother of the divine Son alongside the divine Father. See Chapter 6.

59. " 'Wir wellen fruhtbar werden, uf das man úns wider minne und das man únser grossen ere ein wenig erkenne. Ich wil mir selben machen ein brut, dú sol mich grussen mit irem munde und mit irem ansehen verwunden, denne erste gat es an ein minnen.' " *FL*, Bk. III, Ch. 9, p. 87. For the image of the wounding glance, see Song of Songs 4:9.

60. *FL*, Bk. I, Ch. 22, p. 18.

61. Ibid., Bk. III, Ch. 4, pp. 82–83. See Heimbach, *Mund*, p. 80; and Bynum, *Jesus as Mother*, pp. 229–30, 233–34.

62. *FL*, Bk. III, Ch. 9, p. 88.

63. "O gebenedicte minne, das was sunder beginne din ambaht und ist noch, das du got und des menschen sele zesamene bindest; das sol din ambaht sunder ende sin." Ibid., Bk. IV, Ch. 19, p. 135. See also, Bk. II, Ch. 1, p. 37; Bk. VI, Ch. 30, p. 238; and Bk. VII, Ch. 17, pp. 268–70.

64. See Margot Schmidt, " 'minne du gewaltige kellerin.' On the Nature of minne in Mechthild of Magdeburg's 'fliessende licht der gottheit,' " *Vox benedictina* 4 (1987): 104; and Heimbach, *Mund*, p. 67.

65. "Ich habe gesehen ein stat, ir namme ist der ewige has; si ist gebuwen in dem nidersten abgrúnde von manigerleie steinen der grossen hoptsúnden. Dú hoffart was der erste stein, als es an Lucifer wol schein." *FL*, Bk. III, Ch. 21, p. 100.

66. Ibid.

67. Ibid., Bk. IV, Ch. 12, p. 123.

68. Ibid., Bk. I, Ch. 1, pp. 5–7.

69. "Swenne ich iht des gesach, das schone was oder mir lieb was, so begonde ich ze súfzenne, da nach ze weinende, und da nach begonde ich ze denkende, ze klagende und ze sprechende alsus ze allen dingen: 'Eya nein, nu hute dich, wan dis ist din lieber nit, der din herze gegrusset hat und dine sinne erlúhtet hat und dine sele also wunnenklich gebun-

den hat, das dise manigvaltige sussekeit irdenischer dingen dich nit von ime dringet; mere die edelkeit der creaturen, ir schoni und ir nutz, da wil ich got inne meinen und nit mich selben.'" Ibid., Bk. VI, Ch. 5, p. 211.

70. Ibid., Bk. I, Ch. 22, p. 19.

71. See Ruh, "Beginenmystik," pp. 273–74; and Bernard McGinn, "Love, Knowledge and *Unio mystica* in the Western Christian Tradition," in *Mystical Union and Monotheistic Faith: An Ecumenical Dialogue*, ed. Moshe Idel and Bernard McGinn (New York: Macmillan, 1989), pp. 72–73. For a critique of the language of essential or substantial union, based on the fact that for Eckhart and others the soul is striving to get beyond essences and substance, see the response by Michael Sells in *Mystical Union*, ed. Idel and McGinn, pp. 163–74. I will discuss this distinction further in the chapters on Porete and Eckhart, where the critique has more bearing.

72. See Chapter 4.

73. On Mechthild's relationship to the courtly tradition and the motifs of courtly poetry, see Francis Gooday, "Mechthild of Magdeburg and Hadewijch of Antwerp: A Comparison," *Ons Geestelijk Erf* 48 (1974): 305–62; Elizabeth Wainwright-de Kadt, "Courtly Literature and Mysticism: Some Aspects of their Interaction," *Acta Germanica* 12 (1980): 41–60; and Mohr, "Darbietungsformen."

74. "loptanz," and "lobetantz," *FL*, Bk. I, Ch. 44, pp. 28–29.

75. "Ich mag nit tanzen, herre, du enleitest mich. Wilt du, das ich sere springe, so must du selber vor ansingen; so springe ich in die minne, von der minne in die bekantnisse, von der bekantnisse in die gebruchunge, von der gebruchunge über alle monschliche sinne. Da wil ich bliben und wil doch fúrbas crisen." Ibid.

76. "Das ist ein kintlich liebi, das man kint soge und wiege. Ich bin ein vollewahsen brut, ich wil gan nach minem trut." Ibid., p. 30. This follows, of course, the Bernardine theme that bridal love is always the highest form of love. See Bernard of Clairvaux, *Sermones super Cantica canticorum*, in *Sancti Bernardi Opera*, ed. J. Leclercq and H. M. Rochais, 8 vols. (Rome: Editiones Cistercienses, 1957–77), ser. 83, n. 5, 2: 301; and Bernard of Clairvaux, *On the Song of Songs IV*, trans. Irene Edmonds (Kalamazoo: Cistercian Publications, 1980), ser. 83, n. 5, pp. 184–85. The passage also supports Johanna Ziegler's claim that there is a disjunction between thirteenth-century beguine mystical thought and more popular forms of beguine piety in the fourteenth-century. Artworks designed for beguine contexts include the *Christuskindje*, intended to inspire just such a desire to suckle the infant Christ. See Ziegler, "Reality as Imitation," pp. 112–26.

77. "Der visch mag in dem wasser nit ertrinken, der vogel mag in dem lufte nit versinken, das gold mag in dem fúre nit verderben, wan es enpfat da sin klarheit und sin lúhtende varwe. Got hat allen creaturen das gegeben, das si ir nature pflegen, wie mohte ich denne miner nature widerstan? Ich muste von allen dingen in got gan, der min vatter ist von nature, min bruder von siner monscheit, min brútegom von minnen und ich sin brut ane anegenge." *FL*, Bk. I, Ch. 44, pp. 30–31.

78. "ir sint so sere genatúrt in mich, das zwúschent úch und mir nihtes nit mag sin." Ibid., p. 31.

79. Ibid., Bk. III, Ch. 1, p. 72.

80. "hat si gebildet nach im selber; er hat si gepflanzet in im selber; er hat sich allermeist mit ir vereinet under allen creaturen; er hat si in sich besclossen und hat siner gotlichen nature so vil gegossen, das si anders nit gesprechen mag, denne das er mit aller einunge me denne ir vatter ist." Ibid., Bk. VI, Ch. 31, p. 239. Despite the arguments of Ancelet-Hustache, who in her study of Mechthild consistently attempts to read her as a Thomist, Mechthild is decidedly not Thomistic here. See her *Mechthilde*, pp. 153–87.

81. "Rehte ze glicher wis als er ein clot und allú ding waren in gotte besclossen ane sclos und ane túr." *FL*, Bk. VI, Ch. 31, p. 239.

82. "Swenne aber kumt din ostertag und din lichame enpfat den totschlag, so wil ich dich alumbe van und wil dich aldurch gan und wil dich dime lichamen stelen und wil dich dime liebe geben." *FL*, Bk. I, Ch. 3, p. 10.

83. "Ich vluche dir: Din lichame musse sterben, din wort musse verderben, din ogen mussen sich sliessen, din herze musse vliessen, din sele musse stigen, din licham musse bliben, din monschliche sinne mussin vergan, din geist musse vor der heligen drivaltekeit stan." Ibid., Bk. I, Ch. 7, p. 12.

84. Grete Lüers points to the metaphorical equivalence between the heart and the soul in Mechthild's work and that of the later German mystics when she demonstrates that the term "heart" is used as a synecdoche for the Godhead and for the innermost part of the soul. The soul and the divine are said to be unified in the divine heart (*FL*, Bk. I, Ch. 4, p. 11) and the "heart of the soul" is torn in two by the arrow of divine love (*FL*, Bk. III, Ch. 2, p. 79). While *geist* is not used as frequently as *sele*, they are closely linked terms for Mechthild, as the quotation above shows. See Grete Lüers, *Die Sprache der deutschen Mystik des Mittelalters im Werke der Mechthild von Magdeburg* (Munich: Ernst Reinhardt, 1926), pp. 196–97.

85. *FL*, Bk. I, Ch. 2, pp. 7–9; and Bk. I, Ch. 5, p. 11.

86. Ibid., Bk. III, Ch. 3, pp. 80–81.

87. For more on the role of suffering in Mechthild, see Ulrike Weithaus, "Suffering, Love and Transformation in Mechthild of Magdeburg," *Listening* 22 (1987): 139–51.

88. For the classical formulation, see Anselm, *Cur Deus Homo*, in *Sancti Anselmi Cantuariensis Archiepiscopi Opera Omnia*, ed. F. S. Schmitt, 5 vols. (Edinburgh, 1946–51), 2: 42–133; and "Why God Became Man," in *A Scholastic Miscellany: Anselm to Ockham*, ed. Eugene R. Fairweather (Philadelphia: Westminster Press, 1956), pp. 100–183.

89. See Haas, *Sermo*, pp. 117–18; and Heimbach, *Mund*, pp. 63–66.

90. "Got leitet sinú kint, dú er userwelt hat, wunderliche wege. Das ist ein wunderlich weg und ein edel weg und ein helig weg, den got selber gieng, das ein mensche pine lide ane súnde und ane schulde. In disem wege frowet sich dú sele, dú nach got jamerig ist, wan si vrowet sich von nature ze irem herren, der dur sine woltat manige pine gelitten hat." *FL*, Bk. I, Ch. 25, p. 20.

91. "Do hatte ich lange vor gegert, das ich ane mine schulde wúrde versmahet. Do fur ich dur gottes liebi in ein stat, da nieman min frúnt was denne ein mensche alleine. Vor dem selben hatte ich angest, das mir die helige smacheit und dú luter gottes liebe wúrde mitte entteilet. Do lies mich got niergen eine und brachte mich in so minnenkliche sussekeit, in so helige bekantheit und in so unbegriflich wunder, dc ich irdenscher dingen wenig gebruchen konde." Ibid., Bk. IV, Ch. 2, p. 110.

92. "Do hup únser herre zwene guldin kopffe in sinen henden, die waren bede vol lebendiges wines; in der linggen hant waz der rote win der pine und in der vordren hant der wisse win des úberheren trostes. Do sprach únser herre: 'Selig sint, die disen roten win trinkent; wand alleine ich bede schenke von gotlicher liebi, so ist doch der wisse win edeler in im selber; und alleredlest sint die, die beide trinkent, wissen und roten.'" Ibid., Bk. II, Ch. 7, pp. 45–46.

93. "Si habent die vrien willekúr, das si mogent varen ze himmelriche oder zu der helle oder in das lange vegevúr; das ist úch ein swerú burdin." Ibid., Bk. VII, Ch. 17, p. 269.

94. See ibid., Bk. VI, Ch. 19, pp. 228–29.

95. As Barbara Gist demonstrates in an unpublished seminar paper given at the University of Chicago Divinity School, the same point is made by Hadewijch.

96. "Dis ist menschlich: hunger, turst, hitze, vrost, pine, jamer, bekorunge, sclafen, mudekeit; das sint die ding, die Christus an ime leit, der ein ware mensche was dur úns und mits úns. Mere were dú súnde alleine menschlich, so solte er och gesúndet han, wan er ein warer mensche was an dem vleische und ein gerehte mensche an der wisheit und ein steter

mensche an den tugenden und ein vollekomen monsche an dem heiligen geiste, und da úber was er ein ewig got in der ewigen warheit und nit ein súnder." *FL*, Bk. V, Ch. 16, p. 168.

97. This hope for the body is reflected in the closing dialogue of the book (*FL*, Bk. VII, Ch. 65, p. 310). It is further reflected in passages such as Mechthild's vision of the body of St. John, which has become fully enclosed and bounded while awaiting the final resurrection. See *FL*, Bk. IV, Ch. 23, pp. 139–40. As Wiethaus suggests, Mechthild shares her culture's distaste for the emissions and fluidity of the human (particularly the female) body. See Wiethaus, "Gender and the Body," p. 48.

98. "Ich enkan noch mag nit schriben, ich sehe es mit den ogen miner sele und hore es mit den oren mines ewigen geistes und bevinde in allen liden mines lichamen die kraft des heiligen geistes." *FL*, Bk. IV, Ch. 13, p. 127.

99. Ibid., Bk. VII, Ch. 50, p. 297.

100. Ibid., Bk. VI, Ch. 7, p. 263.

101. "Alsust sprichet der gepineget licham zu der ellendigen sele: 'Wenne wiltu vliegen mit den vedern diner gerunge in die wunneklichen hohi zu Jhesu, dime ewigen liebe? Danke im da, vrowe, fúr mich, alleine ich snode und unwirdig si, das er doch min wolte sin, do er in dis ellende kam und únser menscheit an sich nam; und bit, das er mich ane schult behalte in sinen [lutern] hulden untz in ein helig ende, wenne du, vil liebú sele, von mir wendest.'" *FL*, Bk. VII, Ch. 65, p. 310.

102. See Jon Whitman, *Allegory: The Dynamics of an Ancient and Medieval Technique* (Boston: Harvard University Press, 1987), esp. Introduction and Ch. 1.

103. Ibid., and the discussion of allegory in Chapter 4.

104. "Eya min allerliebste gevengnisse, da ich inne gebunden bin, ich danken dir alles, des du hast gevolget mir; alleine ich dike betrubet bin von dir, so bistu doch mir ze helfe komen; dir wirt noch alle din not benomen an dem jungesten tage. So wellen wir nit me clagen, so sol es úns alles wol behagen, das got mit úns hat getan, wiltu nu vaste stan und susse hoffunge han." *FL*, Bk. VII, Ch. 65, p. 310.

105. See Bernard of Clairvaux, *Liber de diligendo Deo*, in *Sancti Bernardi Opera*, n. 30, 3: 144–45; and "The Book on Loving God," in *Treatises II* (Kalamazoo: Cistercian Publications, 1980), n. 30, pp. 121–22.

106. For free will ("vrien willekúr") and the power of the good will ("guten willen") see *FL*, Bk. VII, Ch. 17, p. 269; and Bk. VI, Ch. 19, p. 228. Mechthild's use of language is not at all systematic. One cannot distinguish the will from the desires in any strict way, nor can one distinguish between

different terms used for love or for the soul or spirit. See Lüers, *Die Sprache.*

107. *FL*, Bk. I, Ch. 2, pp. 7–9; Bk. I, Ch. 4, pp. 10–11; and Bk. VII, Ch. 25, pp. 275–76.

108. "Du solt minnen das niht,/du solten vliehen das iht. . . ." Ibid., Bk. I, Ch. 35, p. 24.

109. Ibid., Bk. I, Ch. 5, p. 11.

110. "uf in den himmel und zúhet si in das abgrúnde wider, si leitet die sele zu allen creaturen sunderlich und sprichet: 'Nu sich, dis ist alles besser, denne du bist!' und bringet si denne an die stat, da si nit fúrbas mag, das ist under Lucifers zagel. Mohte si denne in der gerunge nach irem willen gotte zu eren da wesen, da wolte si nút fúr nemen." Ibid., Bk. V, Ch. 4, pp. 157–58.

111. Ibid., p. 158.

112. "Mere der arme licham mus sich vor vinsternisse sines herzen und vor krankheit siner uswendigen sinne beide vorhten und schemmen, wan er noch unverwandelt ist vom tode. Aber die sele ist also schone in irme lichamen als in dem himmelriche, si ist aber also gewis nit. . . ." Ibid.

113. "Eya herre, als du mir hast alles enzogen, das ich von dir habe, / so la mir doch von gnade die selben gabe, / die du von nature einem hunde hast gegeben, / das ist, das ich dir getrúwe si in miner not / ane allerleie verdrutz; / des gere ich sicherliche / serer denne des himmelriches." Ibid., Bk. II, Ch. 25, p. 63.

114. "Min gotlichú wisheit ist so sere úber dir,/das ich an dir also ordene alle mine gaben,/ als du si an dinem armen libe maht getragen. . . . / Dines seren herzen súfzen und biben/ hat min gerehtekeit von dir vertriben./ Das ist vil rehte dir als mir:/ ich mag nit eine von dir sin:/ wie wite wir geteilet sin,/ wir mogen doch nit gescheiden sin. . . . / Solte ich mich dir ze allen ziten geben nach diner ger,/so muste ich meiner sussen herbergen in dem ertrich an dir enbern,/Wan tusent lichamen mohtin nit einer minnenden sele ire ger vollewern./Darumbe ie hoher minne, ie heliger marterer." Ibid, pp. 63–64.

115. See also references to "constant union" with God, ibid., Bk. IV, Ch. 15, p. 130; and Bk. VII, Ch. 7, pp. 262–63.

116. "Maria únser vrowe sprach mit iren gedenken únserm herren zu, als dikke si wolte, und so antwúrte ir etteswenne sin gotheit, da von trug si gezogenlich ir herzeleit; und das was Marie Magdalenen vil unbereit, wene si únsern herren mit vleischlichen ogen nit sach, so was si ungetrostet und ir herze trug die wile grossen jamer und ungemach. Si brante sere in einvaltiger minne sunder hohe bekantnisse himelscher dingen untz an die stunde, do die apposteln enpfiengen den heligen geist; do allererste wart ir sele verwundet mit der gotheit. Aber únser vrowe was vil stille, do únser

herre von dem tode uferstunt also erliche, doch hette ir herze an gotlicher bekantnisse vor allen menschen den tiefosten grunt." Ibid., Bk. V, Ch. 23, pp. 180–81.

117. "Minne, din scheiden und din komen das ist gliche willekomen der wolordeneten sele." Ibid., Bk. V, Ch. 30, p. 190.

118. See ibid., Bk. VII, Ch. 6, pp. 261–62; and Bk. VII, Ch. 38, p. 287.

119. Ibid., Bk. VII, Ch. 6, pp. 261–62. This parallels the moves made by Meister Eckhart described in this study, Chapter 6.

120. For the intellectual history of this conflict, see Nikolaus Lobkowicz, *Theory and Practice: The History of a Concept from Aristotle to Marx* (Notre Dame: University of Notre Dame Press, 1967).

121. "Du solt minnen das niht,/ du solt vliehen das iht,/ du solt alleine stan/ und solt zu nieman gan./ Du solt nit sere unmussig sin/ und von allen dingen wesen vri./ Du solt die gevangenen enbinden,/ und die vrien twingen./ Du solt die siechen laben/ und solt doch selbe nit haben./ Du solt das wasser der pine trinken/ und das fúr der minne mit dem holtz der tugende entzúnden:/ So wonestu in der waren wustenunge." *FL*, Bk. I, Ch. 35, pp. 24–25.

122. For a similar idea, see Franz-Josef Schweitzer, ed., "Schwester Katrei," in *Der Freiheitsbegriff der deutschen Mystik* (Frankfort am Main: Peter Lang, 1981), pp. 322–70; and "The 'Sister Catherine' Treatise," trans. by Elvira Borgstädt, in *Teacher and Preacher*, pp. 349–87.

123. Jo Ann McNamara argues that ecclesiastical restrictions on women's activities in the world led to a situation in which "spiritual almsgiving" replaced "corporal charity." See her essay, "The Need to Give."

124. *FL*, Bk. II, Ch. 8, pp. 46–47; and Bk. III, Ch. 15, pp. 94–97. The same occurs in Gertrude of Helfta, *Oeuvres spirituelles*, vol. 1: *Le Héraut I and II*, ed. Pierre Doyère, Sources chrétiennes, vol. 139 (Paris: Editions du Cerf, 1968); and *Oeuvres spirituelles*, vol. 2: *Le Héraut III*, ed. Pierre Doyère, Sources chrétiennes, vol. 143 (Paris: Editions du Cerf, 1968). See especially Books 2 and 3.

125. *FL*, Bk. V, Ch. 8, pp. 161–62.

126. This is similar to Porete's self-understanding of her mission and that of her books, although Mechthild includes a much larger audience.

127. See *FL*, Bk. III, Ch. 8, pp. 85–86; and Bk. III, Ch. 14, pp. 93–94.

128. The earliest known apocalypse is the "Book of Watchers" found in the compilation of texts known as 1 Enoch, pointing to the ancient association of Enoch with last times. Augustine is among the first to name Elias as the great prophet who will proceed the Anti-Christ, an association taken up by Joachim of Fiore in the twelfth century. It is probably due to Joachim's indirect influence that Mechthild has associated the two

witnesses in Apocalypse 11: 3–12 with Enoch and Elias. See Joachim of Fiore, *Expositio de prophetia ignota*, ed. by Bernard McGinn in "Joachim and the Sibyl," *Cîteaux* 24 (1973): 136, lines 263–88. See also Bernard McGinn, *The Calabrian Abbot: Joachim of Fiore in the History of Western Thought* (New York: Macmillan, 1985), pp. 74–75, 106, 112.

129. See *FL*, Bk. VI, Ch. 15, pp. 222–25.

130. " . . . wa ich ie sunderliche gnade gap, da suchte ich ie zu die nidersten, minsten, heimlichosten stat; die irdenschen hohsten berge mogent nit enpfan die offenbarunge miner gnaden, wan die vlut mines heligen geistes vlússet von nature ze tal. Man vindet manigen wisen meister an der schrift, der an im selber vor minen ogen ein tore ist. Und ich sage dir noch me: Das ist mir vor inen ein gros ere und sterket die heligen cristanheit an in vil sere, das der ungelerte munt die gelerte zungen von minem heligen geiste leret." Ibid., Bk. II, Ch. 26, p. 69. This move is similar to that made by the twelfth-century visionary Hildegard of Bingen. On this justification of her work, see Newman, *Sister of Wisdom*, pp. 34–41. For more on this, see Chapter 7.

131. "husvrowe." *FL*, Bk. VII, Ch. 3, p. 260.

132. See Ruh, "Beginenmystik," pp. 273–74. For the tradition of the two loves, see Bernard, *Sermones super Cantica canticorum, Sancti Bernardi Opera*, ser. 49–50, 2: 72–83; and *On the Song of Songs III*, trans. Kilian Walsh and Irene M. Edmonds (Kalamazoo: Cistercian Publications, 1979), ser. 49–50, pp. 21–38.

133. See *FL*, Bk. VII, Ch. 47, pp. 292–93. There are a number of late passages that stress the suffering of God's friends, even as Mechthild argues that God is always present to the soul. See *FL*, Bk. VII, Ch. 31, p. 279; Bk. VII, Ch. 56, p. 302; Bk. VII, Ch. 7, pp. 262–63.

134. See Ruh, "Beginenmystik," pp. 273–74.

135. *FL*, Bk. VII, Ch. 47, pp. 292–93.

136. See Ibid., Bk. II, Ch. 2, pp. 37–38; Bk. II, Ch. 4, p. 44; Bk. V, Ch. 32, pp. 192–93; Bk. VI, Ch. 6, pp. 211–13; Bk. VI, Ch. 26–28, pp. 234–36; Bk. VI, Ch. 37–38, pp. 245–48; Bk. VII, Ch. 8, p. 264; Bk. VII, Ch. 16, p. 268; Bk. VII, Ch. 39, pp. 287–88; Bk. VII, Ch. 42, p. 290; Bk. VII, Ch. 63, pp. 308–9; and Bk. VII, Ch. 65, pp. 310–11.

137. See Chapter 2. These issues will be discussed further in Chapter 7.

CHAPTER 4

1. "*Le Mirouer des simples ames anienties et qui seulement demourent en vouloir et desir d'amour.*" *Mirouer*, p. 1.

2. Margot Schmidt, "Miroir," *Dictionnaire de spiritualité, ascétique et mystique, doctrine et histoire*, ed. M. Viller et al. (Paris: Beauchesne, 1937–), vol. 10, col. 1297.

3. *Webster's New World Dictionary of the American Language* (New York: Simon and Schuster, 1980). The dictionary also defines mirror as (1) a true representation or description; (2) something to be emulated; (3) a crystal used by fortune-tellers.

4. See Herbert Grabes, *The Mutable Glass: Mirror-Imagery in Titles and Texts of the Middle Ages and English Renaissance* (Cambridge: University of Cambridge Press, 1982), p. 73, on the switch from metal to glass for mirrors in the Renaissance. Although the use of glass was known in antiquity, it did not come into general use until the sixteenth century.

5. See Frederick Goldin, *The Mirror of Narcissus in the Courtly Love Lyric* (Ithaca: Cornell University Press, 1967). For an interesting discussion of the Narcissus myth in Plotinus, see Julia Kristeva, *Tales of Love*, trans. Leon S. Roudiez (New York: Columbia University Press, 1987).

6. See Grabes, *Mutable Glass*, Part 1.

7. "quant elle vit que ceste amour loingtaigne, qui luy estoit si prouchaine ou dedans d'elle, estoit si loing dehors, elle se pensa que elle conforteroit sa masaise par ymaginacion d'aucune figure de son amy dont elle estoit souvent au cueur navree." *Mirouer*, Ch. 1, p. 12.

8. Emilie zum Brunn and Georgette Epiney-Burgard, *Women Mystics in Medieval Europe*, trans. Sheila Hughes (New York: Paragon House, 1989), p. 153. Zum Brunn argues that Marguerite uses Alexander as a symbol of the gratuitous nature of Divine Love.

9. See Goldin, *Mirror of Narcissus*, pp. 67, 79, 196–97, 241. As Goldin shows, public reputation is seen as intrinsic to identity in the courtly poetic tradition.

10. Kurt Ruh argues that there is no need to suppose Marguerite had firsthand knowledge of the secular courtly literature. He points to the existence within the beguine context of texts that take up the courtly language and claims that they are sufficient as sources for Marguerite's images and language. See " 'Le Miroir des simples ames' der Marguerite Porete," *Verbum et Signum. Festschrift für Friedrich Ohly*, ed. H. Fromm, W. Harms and U. Ruberg (Munich: W. Fink, 1975), pp. 365–87 and also the beguine rule to which Ruh alludes, " 'La regle des fins amans.' Eine Beginenregal aus dem Ende des XIII Jahrhunderts," in K. Christ, ed., *Festschrift für K. Voretzsch* (Halle: n.p., 1927): 173–213, text 192–206. Peter Dronke, on the other hand, argues that Marguerite shows evidence of a knowledge of secular poetry that cannot be explained by this beguine context, for example, her use of lyric poetic forms, the Prologue to the text being a canzone and the Song of the Soul in Chapter 122 a rondeau.

See Dronke, *Women Writers*, p. 318, note 48. For further claims about Marguerite's influence by courtly poetry, see Babinsky, "A Beguine at the Court," Ch. 2.

11. "d'ung roy de grant puissance, qui estoit par courtoisie et par tres grant courtoisie de noblece et largesse ung noble Alixandre." *Mirouer*, Ch. 1, p. 12.

12. "mais si loing estoit de moy et moy de luy, que je ne savoie prandre confort de moy mesmes, et pour moy souvenir de lui il me donna ce livre qui represente en aucuns usages l'amour de lui mesmes." Ibid.

13. See Dronke, *Women Writers*, p. 219.

14. On the identification of God and love, see *Mirouer*, Ch. 112, p. 304, where it is first made explicit.

15. "Mais non obstant que j'aye son ymage, n'est il pas que je ne soie en estrange païs et loing du palais ouquel les tres nobles amis de ce seigneur demourent, qui sont tous purs, affinés et franchix par les dons de ce roy, avec lequel ilz demourent." *Mirouer*, Ch. 1, pp. 12–14. Babinsky reads the lines to mean precisely the opposite, indicating that the soul is at the palace despite having an image or mediator. In either case, the soul indicates the *tension* between the book as mediator and the desire for union without mediation. See Marguerite Porete, *The Mirror of Simple Souls*, trans. Ellen Babinsky (New York: Paulist Press, 1993), pp. 80–81.

16. "Et pource nous vous dirons comment Nostre Seigneur n'est mie du tout enfranchi d'Amour, mais Amour l'est de Lui pour nous, affin que les petis le puissent oïr a l'occasion de vous: /car Amour peut tout faire sans a nully meffaire." Ibid., p. 14.

17. "Entre vous enfans de Saincte Eglise, dit Amour, pour vous ay je fait ce livre, affin que vous oyez pour mieulx valoir la parfection de vie et l'estre de paix, ouquel creature peut venir par la vertu de parfaicte charité, a qui ce don est donné de toute la Trinité; lequel don vous orrez diviser en ce livre par l'Entendement d'Amour aux demandes des de Raison." Ibid.

18. The central passages dealing with the authorship of the work are those discussed above, ibid., Ch. 37, pp. 118–20; Ch. 97, pp. 268–70; and Ch. 119, pp. 332–34. See also Ch. 75, pp. 208–10; and Ch. 121, pp. 336–40. While the authorial soul writes the book, Love or God causes it to be written.

19. This tendency is seen most clearly in Dronke, *Women Writers*; and Elizabeth Alvida Petroff, "Introduction," pp. 3–59. See also Chapter 7.

20. On the distinctions between continuous and discontinuous use of allegory, see Michael Murrin, *The Allegorical Epic* (Chicago: University of Chicago Press, 1980).

21. W. T. H. Jackson, "Allegory and Allegorization," in *The Challenge of the Medieval Text* (New York: Columbia University Press, 1985), p. 170.

22. Whitman, *Allegory*, p. 2. See the discussion of this issue with regard to Mechthild of Magdeburg, Chapter 3.

23. Whitman, *Allegory*, pp. 247–48.

24. Ibid., p. 249.

25. Robert Lamberton argues that the personification allegory represented most clearly by the *Psychomachia* is only one strand of constructive allegory, although the most clearly defined. See Robert Lamberton, *Homer the Theologian: Neoplatonist Allegorical Reading and the Growth of the Epic Tradition* (Berkeley: University of California Press, 1986), Chaps. 4 and 6, particularly pp. 282–97.

26. Charles Muscatine, "The Emergence of Psychological Allegory in Old French Romance," *Proceedings of the Modern Language Association* 68 (September–December, 1953): 1160–72.

27. See this chapter, n. 10, for references to the scholarly debate on this topic.

28. There is a higher understanding or higher intellect in Porete's scheme, putting her in the Gregorian tradition of those who argue that love itself is a species of understanding. On this tradition and Marguerite's place within it, see McGinn, "*Unio mystica*" and further in this chapter. I do not think that this idea is adequate to explain the fact that Reason, by which Marguerite clearly means the lower Reason, does not die in the text. This Reason is differentiated from the higher Intellect precisely by the fact that it must ask questions and receive discursive explanations of the nature of the simple souls and their union with the divine. Reason and the explanations it requires must die in order for Love to become Understanding.

29. For an interesting argument about why *The Romance of the Rose*, an allegorical text somewhat similar to the *Mirror*, should be read as autobiographical, see Evelyn Birge Vitz, *Medieval Narrative and Modern Narratology: Subjects and Objects of Desire* (New York: New York University Press, 1989), Ch. 2.

30. See Dronke, *Women Writers*, pp. x-xi, and more recently Frances Beer, *Women and Mystical Experience in the Middle Ages*.

31. Michael Sells suggests that the text may have been intended as a drama, hence references to its "hearers." This may refer to practices of reading aloud in beguine and other religious communities. See Sells, *Languages of Unsaying*, p. 119.

32. This is possibly a mnemonic device, which would point to its being intended for the devotional use of beguines and others.

33. "[Amour]. Or y a il une autre vie, que nous appellons paix de charité en vie adnientie. De ceste vie, dit Amour, voulons nous parler, en demandant que l'en puisse trouve i. une ame, ii. qui se saulve de foy sans oevres, iii. qui soit seulement en amour, iv. qui ne face rien pour Dieu, v. qui ne laisse rien a faire pour Dieu, vi. a qui l'en ne puisse rien aprandre, vii. a qui l'en ne puisse rien toullir, viii. ne donner, ix. et qui n'ait point de voulenté." *Mirouer*, Ch. 5, pp. 18–20.

34. For the distinction between Holy Church the Little and Holy Church the Great, the visible church and the invisible fellowship of simple souls, see ibid., Ch. 19, pp. 74–76; and Ch. 43, pp. 132–36.

35. I would argue against Edmund Colledge and J. C. Marler, who imply that these two developmental schemes are not in agreement with each other. See their " 'Poverty of the Will'," pp. 25–27. For a full treatment of the interlocking nature of these two schemes, see Max Huot de Longchamp's introduction to his modern French translation of the *Mirror, Marguerite Porete: Le Miroir des âmes simples et anéanties* (Paris: Albin Michel, 1984); and Babinsky, "A Beguine at the Court," Ch. 4.

36. *Mirouer*, Ch. 118, p. 318, lines 8–25.

37. Ibid., pp. 318–20, lines 27–37.

38. Ibid., pp. 320–22, lines 39–64.

39. "Le quart estat est que l'Ame est tiree par haultesse d'amour en delit de pensee par meditacion, et relenquie de tous labours de dehors et de obedience d'aultruy par haultesse de contemplacion; . . . Adonc tient l'Ame que il n'est point de plus haulte vie, que de ce avoir, dont elle a seigneurie; car Amour l'a de ses delices si grandement resasié, que elle ne croit point que Dieu ait plus grant don a donner a ame ycy bas, qu'est telle amour que Amour a par amour dedans elle espandue." Ibid., p. 322.

40. Ibid., pp. 322–24, lines 66–92.

41. Ibid., Ch. 55, pp. 158–60.

42. Ibid., Ch.63, p. 184.

43. Ibid., Ch. 57, pp. 164–66.

44. Ibid., Ch. 118, pp. 324–32, lines 94–203.

45. Ibid., p. 332, lines 204–6.

46. The use of this phrase—"opening of the aperture"—points again to the importance of gender and sexual imagery in her work, despite their ultimate apophasis. See ibid., Ch. 61, p. 178.

47. "Il ne tient pas a elle, dit l'Espoux de ceste Ame mesmes; je vous ay par mon Loingprés les erres envoiees, mais nul me demande qui est ce Loingprés, ne ses oeuvres qu'i<l> fait et oeuvre quant il monstre la gloire de l'Ame, car l'en peut rien dire, sinon: Le Loingprés est la Trinité mesmes, et luy monstre sa demonstration, que nous nommons "mouvement," non

mye pource que l'Ame se meuve ne la Trinité, mais la Trinité oeuvre a ceste Ame la monstre de sa gloire." Ibid.

48. Babinsky, "A Beguine at the Court," Ch. 5.

49. In this, Marguerite's language more closely resembles the more traditional language of Bonaventure. See Ewert Cousins, *Bonaventure and the Coincidence of Opposites* (Chicago: Franciscan Herald Press, 1978), Ch. 4. For further discussion of Marguerite's Trinitarian language, see Babinsky, "A Beguine at the Court," Ch. 5.

50. See Sells, *Languages of Unsaying*, p. 136.

51. See Wiethaus, "Sexuality, Gender, and the Body."

52. See Lerner, *Free Spirit*, Chaps. 2, 4–6, for accounts of the apparent rigorism of many beguinages.

53. Also important in supporting this thesis is the advice given by the Soul and Love against feeling anxiety over sinfulness. They argue that the simple soul need have no shame or anxiety over sin, using figures in scripture as models. See *Mirouer*, Ch. 41, pp. 128–30; and Ch. 76, pp. 210–12.

54. "Mais je vous diray, dit ceste Ame, en quoy je me appaseray de telz gens. En ce, dame Amour, que ilz sont hors mis de la court de voz secrez, ainsi comme seroit ung villain de la court d'ung gentil homme en jugement de pers, ou il n'en peut nul avoir, se il n'est de lignage,—au moins en court de roy." *Mirouer*, Ch. 63, pp. 183–84.

55. "les despiz et les pouvretez et les tourmens non suffrables." Ibid., p. 184.

56. "[*La Saincte Trinité*] Je vous prie, chere fille, / Ma seur et la moye amye, / Par amour, se vous voulez, / Que vous ne vueillez plus dire les secrez, / Que vous savez: / Les aultres s'en dampneroient, / La ou vous / vous sauverez, / Puisque Raison et Desir les gouvernent, / Et Crainte et Voulenté. / Sachez pourtant mon eslite fille, / Que paradis leur est donné.

"*L'Ame Esleue.*—Paradis? dit ceste eslite, ne leur octroiez vous aultrement. Aussi bien l'auront les murtriers, se ilz veulent mercy crier. Mais non pour tant je m'en vueil taire, puisque vous le voulez." Ibid., Ch. 121, p. 340.

57. See Verdeyen, "Procès," p. 51. Also this work, Chaapter 2.

58. "Vertuz, je prens congé de vous / a tousjours,
Je en auray le cueur plus franc/ et plus gay;
Voustre service est troup coustant, / bien la sçay.
Je mis ung temps mon cueur en vous, / sans nulle dessevree;
Vous savez que je estoie a vous trestoute / habandonnee;
Je estoie adonc serve de vous, / on en suis delivree." *Mirouer*, Ch. 6, p. 24.

59. "*Amour.*—Quant Amour demoure en elles, et que les Vertuz servent a elles sans nul contredit et sans travail de telles Ames. . . . Hee, sans faille,

Raison . . . telles Ames qui sont si franches devenues, ont sceu mainte journee ce que Danger seult faire; et qui leur demenderoit le plus grant tourment que creature puisse souffrir, elles diroient que ce seroit demourer en Amour et estre en l'obedience des Vertuz. Car il convient donner aux Vertuz tout ce qu'elles demandent, que qu'il couste a Nature. Or est il ainsi que les Vertuz demandent honneur et avoir, cueur et corps et vie; c'est a entendre que telles Ames laissent toutes chouses, et encoures dient les Vertuz a ceste Ame qui tout ce leur a donné ne n'a rien retenu pour conforter Nature, que *a grant paine est le just saulvé.* Et pource dit telle lasse Ame qui encores sert aux Vertuz, que elle vouldroit estre demenee par Crainte, et en enfer tourmentee jusques au jugement, et aprés qu'elle deust estre saulvee." Ibid., Ch. 8, pp. 28–30.

60. See Romana Guarnieri, who argues that a central tenet of the supposed heresy of the free spirits is the desire to return to an Adamic state of innocence. Although many of her arguments about the supposed heretical sect have been convincingly challenged, particularly by Lerner, I believe that this characterization is true to Marguerite's text, taken by Guarnieri as a central source for the heresy. See her "Frères du Libre Esprit," *Dictionnaire de spiritualité, ascétique et mystique, doctrine et histoire,* ed. M. Viller et al. (Paris: Beauchesne, 1937–), vol. 5, col. 1263. See *Mirouer,* Ch. 29, pp. 96–98, for a discussion of the soul's absolute innocence.

61. See Ruh, "Le Miroir," p. 378, who argues that it is this aspect of Porete's work rather than the nature of union that led to her condemnation. The surpassing of the physical world and the physical church and the nature of union in Porete are intimately related.

62. "donne a Nature tout ce qu'il luy fault, sans remors de conscience." *Mirouer,* Ch. 9, p. 32.

63. "ne desire ne ne desprise pouvr[e]té ne tribulation, ne messe ne sermon, ne jeune ne oraison." Ibid.

64. "nature est si bien ordonnee . . . que la nature ne demande chose qui soit deffendue." Ibid. See Jean Orcibal, "Le 'Miroir des simples âmes' et la 'secte' du Libre Esprit," *Revue de l'histoire des religions* 175 (1969): 35–60; E. C. McLaughlin, "The Heresy of the Free Spirit and Late Medieval Mysticism," *Medievalia et Humanistica* 4 (1973): 37–54; and Lerner, *Heresy,* p. 204. Some of these statements may be later interpellations. They accord, however, with the theological implications of the text.

65. *Mirouer,* Ch. 103–5, pp. 280–88.

66. The place of such works and the necessity of surpassing them is succintly expressed in ibid., Ch. 113, pp. 304–6. Marguerite does occasionally refer to Christ's suffering, although always as a *stage* on the path to freedom. Just as Christ's divinity does not feel what the humanity

suffers, so stand simple souls in relation to those at stages three and four. See *Mirouer*, Ch. 34, p. 112; Ch. 39, p. 124; Ch. 63, pp. 182–84; Ch. 79, p. 224; Chaps. 126–27, pp. 362–68.

67. Ibid., Ch. 13, pp. 52–60.

68. Ibid., Ch. 19–20, pp. 74–78.

69. Other passages pointing to the necessity of apophatic language to refer to God and the soul are in *Mirouer*, Ch. 11, p. 42; Ch. 20, pp. 76–78; Ch. 30, pp. 98–100; and Ch. 95, pp. 264–66. We see a similar teaching in Hadewijch, and of course, in Eckhart.

70. This dialectic parallels and intensifies the play of ascension and descension in Mechthild of Magdeburg. In both, the fall is given a new, positive valuation. For this in Porete, see Sells, *Languages of Unsaying*, pp. 127–31.

71. *Mirouer*, Ch. 51, pp. 150–52.

72. "*[Amour]*.—Il convient, dit Amour, que ceste Ame soit semblable a la Deité car elle est muee en Dieu, dit Amour, par quoy elle a sa vraye forme detenue; laquelle luy est sans commancement octroiee et donnee de ung seul, qui l'a tousjours de sa bonté amee.

L'Ame.—Hee, Amour, dit ceste Ame, le sens de ce qui est dit m'a fait nulle, et le nient de ce seul m'a mis en abysme / dessoubs moins que nient sans mesure. Et la cognoissance de mon nient, dit ceste Ame, m'a donné le tout, et le nient de ce tout, dit ceste Ame, m'a tollu oraison et priere, et ne prie nient." Ibid., Ch. 51, p. 150.

73. For the fire metaphor, see ibid., Ch. 25, pp. 90–92; Ch. 52, p. 152; Ch. 83, p. 236; and Ch. 85, p. 242. The sea metaphor is found in Ch. 28, p. 96; and Ch. 82, pp. 234–36. For the distinction between essential union and the union of wills in Marguerite and others, see McGinn, "*Unio mystica*," pp. 71–81. For a critique of the use of the terms "substantial" or "essential" to describe this radical union, see the response by Michael Sells in *Mystical Union*, pp. 169–73. As Sells argues, Porete and Eckhart both claim to pass beyond substance or essence, making the use of these terms to describe the union problematic. For this reason the phrase "union without distinction" is used here.

74. *Mirouer*, Ch. 25, p. 92.

75. Ibid., Ch. 83, p. 236.

76. Babinsky sees the fire analogy as descriptive of the fifth stage of union with the Holy Spirit as Love, which in turn is union with the entire Trinity, whereas the water images describe the union of the sixth stage, in which the soul is united with its virtual existence in the Father, who is the source of the Trinity. See Babinsky, "A Beguine at the Court," Ch. 5.

77. See *Mirouer*, Ch. 52, pp. 152–54, and Babinsky, "A Beguine at the Court," Chaps. 4–5. She argues that Porete wants to show that the simple

soul retains its created faculties although it abandons the human use of them. Babinsky goes on to point out that, despite Porete's affirmation of the difference in nature between the soul and God, the difference carries little weight in her theology.

78. "Car ceste Ame a en elle la maitresse des Vertuz, que l'en nomme Divine Amour, laquelle l'a muee du tout en elle, et unie a elle, par quoy ceste Ame n'est mie a elle ne aux Vertuz.

Raison.—A qui donc? dit Raison.

Amour.—A la voulenté de moy, dit Amour, qui l'ay muee en moy.

Raison.—Et qui estes vous, Amour? dit Raison. N'estes vous pas une des Vertuz avec nous, pouse que vous soiez dessus nous?

Amour.—Je suis Dieu, dit Amour, car Amour est Dieu, et Dieu est amour, et ceste Ame est Dieu par condicion d'amour, et je suis Dieu par nature divine, et ceste Ame l'est par droicture d'amour."

Mirouer, Ch. 21, pp. 80–82. Also see Ch. 77, p. 218.

79. "*L'Ame.*—Voire, dit ceste Ame, mon corps est en foiblesse, et mon ame en crainte. Car j'ay souvent soing, dit elle, vueille ou non, de ces deux natures, que les frans n'ont mie, ne ne pevent avoir." *Mirouer*, Ch. 77, p. 218. For other important references to the body, see Chaps. 93–94, pp. 260–64; Chaps. 102–5, pp. 280–88; Ch. 124, pp. 352–54; Ch. 126, pp. 362–66; and Ch. 128, pp. 368–70.

80. Ibid., Ch. 74, pp. 206–8.

81. "Et quant tel soleil est en l'ame, et tel raiz et telz resplendisseurs, le corps n'a plus foiblece, ne/ l'ame crainte; car le vray Soleil de Justice ne sana ne garit oncques ame sans garir le corps, quant il fasoit ses miracles en terre; et souvent encore le fait il, mais il ne le fait a nully qui n'a foy de ce mesmes." Ibid., Ch. 78, p. 220.

82. "Et qui courtois seroit, il n'ameroit que ce qu'il devroit. Oncques n'ama L'Umanité, qui ama temporalité. Oncques n'ama divinement, qui rien ama corporelment; et ceulx qui ament la Deité sentent pou de l'Umanité. Oncques ne fut joinct ne uny ne divinement rempli, qui corporelment sentist." Ibid., Ch. 79, p. 224.

83. *Mirouer*, Ch. 15, pp. 62–64.

84. See Bernard of Clairvaux, *Liber de diligendo Deo*, in *Sancti Bernardi Opera*, n. 23, 3: 138–39; *On Loving God*, in *Treatises II*, trans. Robert Walton (Kalamazoo: Cistercian Publications, 1980), n. 23, pp. 115–17; William of Saint Thierry, *Lettre*, nn. 42–90; and *Golden Epistle*, nn. 42–90, pp. 25–42.

85. *Mirouer*, Ch. 93, pp. 260–61.

86. See Chapter 2; and Lerner, *Free Spirit*.

87. See *Mirouer*, Ch. 75, pp. 208–10; Ch. 97, pp. 268–72; Ch. 119, pp. 332–34; Ch. 121, pp. 338–40.

88. Ibid., Ch. 89, pp. 252–54; and Ch. 93–95, pp. 260–66.

89. Ibid., Ch. 98, pp. 272–74.

90. On the way the appearance of a mirror or portrait in a text often points to the difficulties inherent in all representational language, see Lucien Dallenbach, *The Mirror in the Text* (Chicago: University of Chicago Press, 1989), and Françoise Meltzer, *Salome and the Dance of Writing* (Chicago: University of Chicago Press, 1987).

91. "Or cognois je, pour vostre pais et pour le vray, qu'il est de bas. Couardise l'a mainé, qui a Raison a rendue l'entente par response d'Amour aux demandes de Raison; et si a esté fait par humaine raison et humain sens; et humaine science et humain sens ne scevent rien d'amour denentraine, ne denentraine amour de divine science. Mon cueur est tiré si hault et avalé si bas, que je n'y puis actaindre; car tout ce que l'en peut de Dieu dire ne escrire, ne que l'en peut penser, qui plus est que n'est dire, est assez mieulx mentir que ce n'est vray dire." *Mirouer*, Ch. 119, p. 334.

92. "J'ay dit, dit ceste Ame, que Amour l'a fait escrire par humaine science, et par le vouloir de la mutacion de mon entendement, dont j'estoie encombree, comme il appert par ce livre; car Amour l'a fait, en descombrant mon esperit parmy ces trois dons, dont nous avons parlé. Et pource dis je que il est de bas et tres petit, combien que grant il me semblast au commencement / de la monstre de cest estre." Ibid.

93. This is in contrast to the position held by Mechthild. For both beguines this "work" is necessary to salvation and to the attainment of union without distinction, but for Mechthild it is part of the dialectic of ascent and descent and hence part of the coming to union in a way it is not for Porete.

94. *Mirouer*, Ch. 121, p. 340.

95. "Et aprés ce, regarday en pensant, comme se il me demendroit comment je me contendroie, se je savoie qu'il luy peust mieulx plaire que j'amasse aultruy mieulx que luy; et adonc me faillit le sens, et ne sceu que respondre, ne que voulloir, ne que escondire, mais je / respondi que je m'en conseilleroie.

Et aprés, me demenda comment comment je me contendroie, se il povoit estre qu'il peust mieulx aultruy amer que moy. Et ycy me faillit le sens, et ne sceu que respondre, ne que vouloir, ne que escondire.

Oultre plus, me demenda que je feroie et comment je me contendroie, se il povoit estre qu'il peust vouloir que ung aultre que luy me amast mieulx que luy. Et pareillement me faillit le sens, et ne sceu que respondre, nientplus que devant, mais je dis tousjours que je m'en conseilleroie." *Mirouer*, Ch. 131, p. 384.

96. "Se j'avoye ce mesmes que vous avez, avec la creacion que vous m'avez donnee; et ainsi, sire, que je seroie egal a vous, excepté en ce

point, que je pourroye ma voulenté changer pour aultruy que pour moy, / —laquelle chose vous ne faites mie—puisque vous vouldriez, sans nul si, ces trois choses qui m'ont esté si grefves a porter et a octroyer. . . . Et ainsi, sire, ma voulenté prent sa fin en ce dire; et pource est mon vouloir martir, et mon amour martire: vous les avez a martire amenez; leur cuider est bien a declin alez. Mon cueur cuidoit jadis tousdis vivre d'amour par desirer de bonne voulenté. Or maintenant sont ces deux choses en moy finees, que m'ont fait hors de mon enffance yssir." Ibid., pp. 386–88.

97. The phrase "without a why" is used by Porete to describe both God and the soul. It is first found in Beatrice of Nazareth and was taken up by Eckhart. See ibid., ch. 81, pp. 232–34; Ch. 89, p. 252; Ch. 91, pp. 256–58; Ch. 111, p. 302; and Ch. 134, p. 394.

98. The term "quietism" was first used in the seventeenth century to name a mystical heresy in which the soul was said to be so united to God that it surpassed all "works," including the sacramental and mediating rites of the Church. The charge was allied with the claim that such mystical writings condoned the active breaking of moral laws, or antinomianism. Historically the heresy is associated with the condemnation of Molinos's *Spiritual Guide* in 1687 and the persecutions of Madame Guyon and Père La Combe in the late seventeenth and early eighteenth centuries. Some have taken the term to name a much more wide spread mystical phenomenon, and thus have associated it with the so-called heresy of the Free Spirit. See P. Pourrat, "Quiétisme," in *Dictionnaire de spiritualité, ascétique et mystique, doctrine et histoire*, ed. M. Viller et al., vol. 13:2, cols. 1547–81. There are, in fact, interesting parallels between Marguerite's work and that of Madame Guyon. For some of these parallels, particularly with regard to their relationship to the established church, see Franz-Josef Schweitzer, "Von Marguerite von Porete (d. 1310) bis Mme. Guyon (d. 1717): Frauenmystik im Konflikt mit der Kirche," in *Frauenmystik im Mittelalter*, ed. Dınzelbacher and Bauer, pp. 256–74.

99. "Et s'aucune chose avoient telles Ames . . . et elles sceussent que aultres en eussent plus grant besoing que elles, telles Ames jamais ne le re-tendroient, et feussent elles ores certaines que jamais ne deust croiste en terre ne pain ne ble ne aultre soustenance." *Mirouer*, Ch. 17, p. 70.

100. "Mais se ceste Ame, qui est si hault assise, povoit aider a ses proesmes, elle leur aideroit de tout son povoir a leur besoing. Mais les pensees de telles Ames sont si divines, que elles ne se arrestent mie tant es choses passees ne cree[e]s, qu'elles conçoivent mesaise dedans elle, puisque Dieu est bon sans comprennement." Ibid., Ch. 16, p. 68.

101. See the soul's song, ibid., Ch. 122, pp. 340–46.

102. See Chapter 3.

103. Reason, of course, takes umbrage at this claim. See *Mirouer*, Ch. 35, pp. 114–16; and Ch. 87, pp. 246–48.

104. "Or ceste Ame en l'estre de ce premier estre qui est son estre, et si a laissé trois, et a fait de deux ung. Mais quant est cest ung? Cest ung est, quant l'Ame est remise en celle simple Deité, qui est ung simple Estre d'espandue fruiction, en plain savoir, sans sentement, dessus la pensee. Ce simple Estre fait par charité en l'Ame quanque l'Ame fait, car le vouloir est simple devenue;" Ibid., Ch. 138, pp. 400–2. See also Ch. 107, pp. 290–92.

105. Ibid., Ch. 107, pp. 290–92.

106. See, for example, Ruh, " 'Le Miroir' " and "Beginenmystik."

107. On Porete's formulation of an agency without essence, see Sells, *Languages of Unsaying*, pp. 123–27.

CHAPTER 5

1. See D. L. D'Avray, *The Preaching of the Friars: Sermons Diffused from Paris before 1300* (Oxford: Clarendon Press, 1985). For the history of the relationship between the German and Latin works as seen by modern Eckhart scholarship, see Kurt Ruh, *Altdeutsche Mystik* (Bern: n. p., 1950), p. 136; Mieth, *Einheit*, pp. 120–23; and Frank Tobin, *Meister Eckhart: Thought and Language* (Philadelphia: University of Pennsylvania Press, 1986), pp. 21–23.

2. Evidence that women transcribed texts and sermons can be found in D'Avray, *Preaching*, p. 2.

3. This constancy of theme was, in fact, a major test of authenticity for the editor of the German sermons, Josef Quint. See his introduction to the German works, *DW* 1: v–xv.

4. See D'Avray, *Preaching*, p. 256, on the preaching tradition and singularity of the German mystical tradition beginning with Eckhart.

5. Jeanne Ancelet-Hustache, *Master Eckhart and the Rhineland Mystics*, trans. Hilda Graef (New York: Harper, 1957), p. 144.

6. For an exemplary study, see Joan Ferrante, *Woman as Image in Medieval Literature from the Twelfth Century to Dante* (New York: Columbia University Press, 1975). Medievalists have been at the forefront of feminist historiography. For historical perspective and important recent work, see Susan Mosher Stuard, ed., *Women in Medieval History and Historiography* (Philadelphia: University of Pennsylvania Press, 1987); *Signs* 14 (1989); and *Speculum* 68:2 (1993). On the importance of gender as a category of historical analysis, see Natalie Zemon Davis, " 'Women's History' in Transition: The European Case," *Feminist Studies* 4 (1976): 83–103; and Joan Scott, *Gender and the Politics of History* (New York: Columbia University Press, 1988), pp. 28–50.

7. For this argument with regard to Bernard of Clairvaux, see Jean Leclercq, *Women and Saint Bernard of Clairvaux*, trans. Marie-Bernard Saïd (Kalamazoo: Cistercian Publications, 1989).

8. The historicization of sex has, in many ways, eroded and made less necessary the sex/gender distinction, as both are recognized to be culturally coded (if not entirely "constructed") categories. This does not, however, mean the elision of those "sexed" and "gendered" as women as a historical, analytic, and political category. See, for example, Moira Gatens, "A Critique of the Sex/Gender Distinction," in *A Reader in Feminist Knowledge*, ed. Sneja Gunew (New York: Routledge, 1990), pp. 139–57; Judith Butler, *Gender Trouble: Feminism and the Subversion of Identity* (New York: Routledge, 1990); Judith Butler, *Bodies That Matter* (New York: Routledge, 1993); Modleski, *Feminism Without Women*, pp. 3–22.

9. Penny Shine Gold, *The Lady and the Virgin: Image, Attitude and Experience in Twelfth-Century France* (Chicago: University of Chicago Press, 1985), pp. 145–52.

10. This conflict has primarily come out in debates among Anglo-American feminists with and about French feminisms, particularly the work of Luce Irigaray and Hélène Cixous. See, for example, Hélène Cixous and Catherine Clément, *The Newly Born Woman*, trans. Betsy Wing (Minneapolis: University of Minnesota Press, 1986); Irigaray, *Speculum*; Luce Irigaray, *This Sex Which Is Not One*, trans. Catherine Porter with Carolyn Burke (Ithaca: Cornell University Press, 1985); Toril Moi, *Sexual/Textual Politics: Feminist Literary Theory* (New York: Methuen, 1985), pp. 121–26; and Margaret Whitford, *Luce Irigaray: Philosophy in the Feminine* (New York: Routledge, 1991), pp. 9–25.

11. For a similar reading of a medieval woman's religious ideals as "utopian," see Elizabeth Petroff, "A Medieval Woman's Utopian Vision: The Rule of St. Clare of Assisi," in *Feminism, Utopia, and Narrative*, ed. Libby Falk Jones and Sarah Webster Goodwin (Knoxville: University of Tennessee Press, 1990), pp. 174–90.

12. This scheme is implied in many ways in Elaine Showalter's typology of feminist literary criticism—feminist criticism, gynocritics, and gynesis—and in the threefold understanding of feminity put forward by the German feminist Sigrid Weigel. See Elaine Showalter, "Feminist Criticism in the Wilderness" in *The New Feminist Criticism: Essays on Women, Literature, and Theory*, ed. Elaine Showalter (New York: Pantheon, 1985), pp. 243–70; "Women's Time, Women's Space: Writing the History of Feminist Criticism," in *Feminist Issues in Literary Scholarship*, ed. Shari Benstock (Bloomington: Indiana University Press, 1987), pp. 30–34; Sigrid Weigel, "Double Focus: On the History of Women's Writing," in *Feminist Aesthetics*, ed. Gisela Ecker (Boston: Beacon Press, 1985),

pp. 59–80; and the longer German article from which this is taken, "Der schielende Blick: Thesen zur Geschichte weiblicher Schreibpraxis," in *Die verborgene Frau: Sechs Beiträge zu einer feministischen Literatur- wissenschaft*, Inge Stephan and Sigrid Weigel (Berlin: Argument, 1983), pp. 83–137.

13. On the diversity of late medieval Europe and the tendency falsely to "essentialize" it, see David Aers, "A Whisper in the Ear of Early Modernists: or, Reflections on Literary Critics Writing the 'History of the Subject,'" in *Culture and History 1350–1600: Essays on English Communities, Identities and Writing*, ed. David Aers (Detroit: Wayne State University Press, 1992), pp. 177–202.

14. Ser. 43, *DW* 2: 316–30. The other is Ser. 42, *DW* 2: 301–9.

15. There is some debate as to the proper translation of *sêle* and its meaning for Eckhart. Schürmann argues that the term is interchangeable with the Latin *mens* and *animus*, signifying the mind or intellectual center, rather than *anima*, understood as the animating principle of the body. Regardless, the grammatical dichotomy is essential to Eckhart's meaning in this Sermon and, I would argue, in his mystical theology as a whole. See Reiner Schürmann, *Meister Eckhart: Mystic and Philosopher* (Bloomington: Indiana University Press, 1978), p. xiv.

16. " 'Witewe' sprichet in einer andern wîse als vil als: der 'verlâzen ist' und verlâzen hat. Alsô muezen wir alle crêatûren läzen und abescheiden." Ser. 43, *DW* 2: 319.

17. See M. O'C. Walshe, *Meister Eckhart: German Sermons and Trea- tises*, 3 vols. (London and Dulverton: Watkins, 1979–83), Ser. 43, 2: 233.

18. See Ser. 2, *DW* 1: 25–45 (*Essential*, pp. 177–81); Ser. 13, *DW* 1: 211–22; and Ser. 22, *DW* 1: 375–83 (*Essential*, pp. 192–96) for the major discussions.

19. See Tobin, *Meister Eckhart*, pp. 24–25.

20. For a different reading of the use of such female imagery by men, based on Victor Turner's theory of liminality, see Bynum, *Fragmentation*, Ch. 1. She argues that while images of femininity mark a reversal for men, and women themselves are a site of liminality for the dominant male group, a parallel reversal does not occur in texts by women. Furthermore, because the female image marks a reversal for the male author, it functions in a markedly different way than it would for a woman. Yet if women's symbols are marked by continuity, and if Eckhart was often addressing his words to a female audience, it could be argued that he was attempting to speak to his audience out of these images.

21. For the central sermon in which this image is developed, see Ser. 2, *DW* 1: 25–45 (*Essential*, pp. 177–81). The sermon will be discussed in Chapter 6, and is the subject of an interesting discussion by Schürmann, *Mystic and Philosopher*, pp. 9–47.

22. Augustine, *On Christian Doctrine*, trans. D. W. Robertson (Indianapolis: Bobbs-Merrill, 1958), Bk. 1, Ch. 6, pp. 10–11. "Diximusne aliquid et sonuimus aliquid dignum Deo? Imo vero nihil me aliud quam dicere voluisse sentio: si autem dixi, mon hoc est quod dicere volui. Hoc unde scio, nisi quia Deus ineffabilis est; quod autem a me dictum est, si ineffabilis esset, dictum non esset? Ac per hoc ne ineffabilis quidem dicendus est Deus, quia hoc cum dicitur, aliquid dicitur: Et fit nescio quae pugna verborum, quoniam si illud est ineffabile, quod dici non potest, non est ineffabile quod vel ineffabile dici potest. Quae pugna verborum silentio cavenda potius quam voce pacanda est. Et tamen Deus, cum de illo nihil digne dici possit, admisit humanae vocis obsequium, et verbis nostris in laude." Augustine, *De Doctrina Christiana*, in *Patrologia cursus completus: Series latina*, ed. J.-P. Migne (Paris: Garnier, 1844–64) vol. 34, Bk. 1, Ch. 6, col. 21.

23. See Chapter 3.

24. Bernard McGinn, "Introduction," in *Teacher*, p. 16; and Harry A. Wolfson, *Studies in the History of Philosophy and Religion*, ed. Isadore Twersky and George H. Williams, 2 vols. (Cambridge: Harvard University Press, 1973, 1977), 2: 497–524.

25. *Teacher*, p. 53. "Primo quid philosophi quidam de hoc senserint et quidam Hebraeorum de his attributionibus, quibus deus nominatur, puta cum dicitur deus substantia, deus bonus, pius, largus et huiusmodi. . . . Secundo sumendum breviter quid sentiendum sit de talibus praedicationibus sive nominibus secundum catholicos tractatores. Tertio quid est quod secundum Boethium et doctores communiter tantum duo genera praedicamenti, puta substantia et relatio, admittuntur in divinis? Quarto vero de nomine magis proprio deo et specialiter separato, quod est tetragrammaton, dicetur infra vicesimo capitulo super illo: 'non assumes nomen dei tui in vanum.' " *Commentary on Exodus* n. 34, *LW* 2: 40–41.

26. *Teacher*, pp. 56–57. "Unde omnia positive dicta de deo, quamvis sint perfectiores in nobis, in deo tamen non plus sunt nec perfectiones sunt quam horum oppposita. Verbi gratia: misericordia, pietas et huiusmodi perfectiones sunt nobis, ira, odium et similia sunt imperfectiones. Sicut autem dicitur deus irasci vel odire, cum talia nihil sint nec ponant prorsus in deo, sed quia deus operatur quaedam foris, quae in nobis ex ira vel odio procedunt, similiter et de horum oppositis." *Comm. Ex.* n. 44, *LW* 2: 48.

27. *Teacher*, p. 64. "Nulla igitur in ipso deo distinctio esse potest aut intelligi." *Comm. Ex.* n. 60, *LW* 2: 66.

28. *Comm. Ex.* n. 65, *LW* 2: 69–70 (*Teacher*, p. 20).

29. *Teacher*, pp. 20–21.

30. *Comm. Ex.* n. 73, *LW* 2: 75–76 (*Teacher*, p. 67).

31. *Comm. Ex.* n. 73, *LW* 2: 76–77 (*Teacher*, p. 68).

32. *Teacher*, p. 68. "Nulla ergo negatio, nihil negativum deo competit, nisi negatio negationis, quam significat unum negative dictum: 'deus unus est', Deut. 6; Gal. 3. Negatio vero negationis purissima et plenissima est affirmatio: 'ego sum qui sum.'" *Comm. Ex.* n. 74, *LW* 2: 77. Other important texts on the "negation of negation" are Ser. 21 *DW* 1: 357–70; *Commentary on Ecclesiasticus* n. 60, *LW* 2: 288–89; *Comm. Wis.* n. 148, *LW* 2: 485–86; and *Commentary on John* n. 556, *LW* 3: 485–86 (*Teacher*, pp. 281, 181, 167–68, 185).

33. McGinn, *Teacher*, p. 25.

34. *Comm. Ex.* n. 78, *LW* 2: 81–82 (*Teacher*, p. 70). For Thomas on the subject, see *Summa Theologiae*, Blackfriars ed., 61 vols. (New York: McGraw-Hill, 1964–81), Part Ia, q. 13, a. 3.

35. *Teacher*, p. 99. "Igitur perfectiones in rebus extra non verae perfectiones sunt. Ipsas igitur attribuere deo est ipsum apprehendere imperfectum et ipsum non esse intellectum se toto purum, sed esse rem extra, saltem aliquo sui, sicut in intellectibus creatis." *Comm. Ex.* n. 176, *LW* 2: 152.

36. *Teacher* p. 101. "perfectior enim est ille in cognitione dei et qui fortiori ratione removet huiusmodi attributiones a deo, et iterum ille, qui plura scit removere talia ab ipso, quae remotio fit per nomina negativa." *Comm. Ex.* n. 183, *LW* 2: 158.

37. *Comm. Ex.* n. 184, *LW* 2: 158.

38. Aquinas, *STh*, Part I, q. 13, a. 2.

39. *Teacher*, p. 25. On Aquinas as apophatic thinker, see David B. Burrell, *Knowing the Unknowable God: Ibn-Sina, Maimonides, Aquinas* (Notre Dame: University of Notre Dame Press, 1986).

40. *Comm. Ex.* n. 35, 78, 178, *LW* 2: 41–42, 81–82, 153–54.

41. *Comm. Ex.* n. 36, 44, 51, 161–69, *LW* 2: 42–43, 48–50, 54–55, 142–48.

42. *Comm. Jn.* n. 564, *LW* 3: 492.

43. For Eckhart's understanding of analogy, see McGinn, "God as Absolute Unity"; Josef Koch, "Zur Analogielehre Meister Eckharts," in *Mélanges offerts à Etienne Gilson* (Paris: Vrin, 1959), pp. 327–50; Fernand Brunner, "L'analogie chez Maître Eckhart," *Freiburger Zeitschrift für Philosophie und Theologie* 16 (1969): 333–49; Schürmann, *Mystic and Philosopher*, pp. 176–80 and 185–92; Alain de Libera, *Le problème de l'être chez Maître Eckhart: Logique et métaphysique de l'analogie* (Geneva: Cahiers de la revue de théologie et de philosophie 4, 1980); and Alain de Libera and Emilie zum Brunn, *Maître Eckhart: Métaphysique du Verbe et théologie négative* (Paris: Beauchesne, 1984).

44. For Aquinas on this distinction, see *Sententia super Peri hermenias II*, in *Sancti Thomae Aquinatis Opera Omnia* (Parma: Fiaccadori, 1865), vol. 18, lectio 2, nos. 2–5, commenting on Aristotle's

Peri hermenias 10 (19b20–25). See McGinn, "God as Absolute Unity," pp. 130–31.

45. On *esse simpliciter* and *esse hoc et hoc*, see *Prologues*. n. 3, *LW* 1: 166–67; *Comm. Jn.* n. 60 *LW* 3: 49–50; *Collatio in Libros Sententiarum* n. 3, *LW* 5: 20.

46. Translated by Bernard McGinn in "God as Absolute Unity," p. 131. "Cum igitur dico aliquid esse, aut unum, verum seu bonum praedico, et in praedicato cadunt tamquam secundum adiacens praemissa quattuor et formaliter accipiuntur et substantive. Cum vero dico aliquid esse hoc, puta lapidum, et esse unum lapidum, verum lapidum aut bonum hoc, scilicet lapidum, praemissa quattuor accipiuntur ut tertium adiacens propositionis nec sunt praedicata, sed copula vel adiacens praedicati." *LW* 1: 167.

47. See McGinn, "God as Absolute Unity," p. 132. Other important commentators upon Eckhart's dialectic are Vladimir Lossky, *Théologie négative et connaissance de Dieu chez Maître Eckhart* (Paris: Vrin, 1960), esp. pp. 254–65; and M. de Gandillac, "La 'dialectique' de Maître Eckhart," in *Le mystique rhénane: Colloque de Strasbourg 1961* (Paris: Presses Universitaires de France, 1963), pp. 59–94.

48. *Teacher*, p. 166. "Est igitur sciendum quod li unum idem est quod indistinctum. Omnia enim distincta sunt duo vel plura, indistincta vero omnia sunt unum." *Comm. Wis.* n. 144, *LW* 2: 482.

49. *Teacher*, p. 166. "Dicens ergo deum esse unum vult dicere deum esse indistinctum ab omnibus, quod est proprietas summi esse et primi et eius bonitas exuberans." *Comm. Wis.* n. 144, *LW* 2: 482–83.

50. *Teacher*, p. 167. "Adhuc autem unum se toto descendit in omnia, quae citra sunt, quae multa sunt, quae numerata sunt. In quibus singulis ipsum unum non dividitur, sed manens unum incorruptum profundit omnem numerum et sua unitate informat. Adhuc autem ante quaelibet duo aut plura necessario et in re et in omni apprehensione prius cadit unum. Iterum etiam li unum nihil addit super esse, nec secundum rationem quidem, sed secundum solam negationem; non sic verum et bonum. Propter quod immediatissime se tenet ad esse, quin immo significat puritatem et medullam sive apicem ipsius esse, quam nec li esse significat." *Comm. Wis.* n. 148, *LW* 2: 485–86.

51. *Teacher*, p. 169. "nihil tam distinctum a numero et numerato sive numerabili, creato scilicet, sicut deus, et nihil tam indistinctum." *Comm. Wis.* n. 154, *LW* 2: 489.

52. *Teacher*, p. 169. "omne quod indistinctione distinguitur, quanto est indistinctius, tanto est distinctius; distinguitur enim ipsa indistinctione. Et e converso, quanto distinctius, tanto indistinctius, quia distinctione sua distinguitur ab indistincto. Igitur quanto distinctius, tanto indistinctius; et quanto indistinctius, tanto distinctius, ut prius." *Comm. Wis.* n. 154, *LW* 2: 490.

53. See McGinn, "God as Absolute Unity," p. 157.

54. See Lossky, *Théologie négative*, pp. 340–50.

55. Michael Sells gives a reading of the main passages dealing with *bullitio* in his dissertation, "The Metaphor and Dialectic of Emanation in Plotinus, John the Scot, Meister Eckhart, and Ibn Arabi" (Ph.D. diss., University of Chicago, 1982), pp. 150–94. The main passages are the Latin sermon, *Cuius Imago Est*, Ser. XLIX, *LW* 3: 425–26; *Comm. Ex.* n. 16, *LW* 3: 21–22; and the commentary on John's prologue discussed above.

56. *Essential*, pp. 122–23. "In cuius verbi expositione et aliorum quae sequuntur, intentio est auctoris, sicut et in omnibus suis edition-ibus, ea quae sacra asserit fides christiana et utriusque testamenti scrip-tura, exponere per rationes naturales philosophorum." *Comm. Jn.* n. 2, *LW* 3: 4.

57. Sells, "Dialectic," p. 157.

58. On the influence of Boethius, see Alain de Libera, "A propos de quelques théories logiques de Maître Eckhart: existe-t-il une tradi-tion médiévale de la logique néo-platonicienne?" *Revue de théologie et philosophie* 113 (1981): 1–24.

59. *Essential*, p. 123. "sic se habet quod productum sive procedens ab aliquo prius est in illo"; "praeest in illo sicut semen in suo principio." *Comm. Jn.* n. 4, *LW* 3: 5–6.

60. *Essential*, p. 124. "in univocis autem semper est aequale, eandem naturam non participans, sed totam simpliciter, integraliter et ex aequo a suo principio accipiens.

Et propter hoc sexto sic: procedens est filius producentis. Filius est enim qui fit alius in persona, non aliud in natura." *Comm. Jn.* n. 5, *LW* 3: 7.

61. *Essential*, p. 124. "sicut fuit a principio, antequam arca fieret." *Comm. Jn.* n. 7, *LW* 3: 8.

62. *Essential*, p. 124. "quae non est cum motu nec in tempore, sed est finis et terminus motus. . . . Propter quod consequenter non transit in non-esse nec labitur in praeteritum." *Comm. Jn.* n. 8, *LW* 3: 8.

63. *Essential*, p. 125. "semper nascitur, semper generatur; aut enim nunquam aut semper, quia principium sive *in principio* est semper." *Comm. Jn.* n. 8, *LW* 3: 9.

64. The importance of this aspect of Eckhart's thought was first em-phasized by Tobin, *Meister Eckhart*, pp. 59–62.

65. *Essential*, p. 187. "Ist mîn leben gotes wesen, sô muoz das gotes sîn mîn sîn und gotes isticheit mîn isticheit, noch minner noch mêr." Ser. 6, *DW* 1: 106.

66. On the crucial distinction between *bullitio* and *ebullitio*, see *Book of the Parables of Genesis* nn. 9–15, *LW* 1: 479–86.

67. See McGinn, "Theological Summary," in *Essential*, p. 38.

68. *Essential*, p. 128. "Nam omne habens principium operationis suae ab alio, ut aliud, non proprie vivit." *Comm. Jn.* n. 19, *LW* 3: 16.

69. For the preexistence of things in their ideas, *Comm. Jn.* nn. 9, 12, 54, *LW* 3: 10, 11–12, 45–46 (*Essential*, pp. 125, 126, 141); *Comm. Gen.* n. 25, *LW* 1: 204 (*Essential*, p. 91). For the virtual existence of all things as Word in the Father, see *Comm. Jn.* nn. 44–45, *LW* 3: 36–38 (*Essential*, pp. 137–38); *Comm. Gen.* nn. 77–78, *LW* 1: 238–40; *Comm. Ex.* n. 121, *LW* 2: 114–15 (*Teacher*, p. 83); and Ser. 52 *DW* 2: 486–506 (*Essential*, pp. 199–203).

70. On this discussion and the debate around various terms used to describe this type of union, see the discussion in Chapters 3 and 4.

71. *Essential*, p. 127. "iustus procedens et genitus a iustitia, hoc ipso ab illa distinguitur. Nihil enim se ipsum gignere potest." *Comm. Jn.* n. 16, *LW* 3: 14.

72. For the importance of the *inquantum* principle in Eckhart's work, see Koch, "Analogielehre;" and Hans Hof, *Scintilla animae: Eine Studien zu einem Grundbegriff in Meister Eckharts Philosophie* (Lund: Gleerup, 1952).

73. Eckhart put forward this principle as one of three by which he attempted to justify and explain his work to his critics. See Eckhart's written defense of forty-nine articles drawn from his works by the inquisitors in Cologne (September 26, 1326), edited by Gabriel Théry, "Édition critique des pièces relatives au procès d'Eckhart contenues dans le manuscrit 33b de la Bibliothèque de Soest," *Archives d'histoire littéraire et doctrinal du moyen âge* 1 (1926): 186–87; and *Essential*, pp. 72–73. Also see McGinn, "Theological Summary," p. 54; and Bernard McGinn, "Eckhart's Condemnation Reconsidered," *The Thomist* 44 (1980): 406.

74. *Essential*, pp. 127–28. Translation modified. "Adhuc nono constat quod iustitia, sed nec iustus ut sic non cadunt sub motu et tempore, sicut nec vita nec lux. Et propter hoc iustus sic semper nascitur ab ipsa iustitia, sicut a principio, quo iustus, natus est, sicut est de generatione luminis in medio et eius conservatione: eo ipso continue, quia non continue." *Comm. Ex.* n. 18 *LW* 3: 15.

75. *Essential*, p. 128. "Iustitia vero genita ipsa est verbum iustitiae in principio suo, parente iustitia." *Comm. Jn.* n. 19, *LW* 3: 16.

76. *Essential*, p. 128. Translation modified. "iustus in ipsa iustitia iam non est genitus nec genita iustitia, sed est ipsa iustitia ingenita." *Comm. Jn.* n. 19, *LW* 3: 16.

77. For more on God as the principle of all existence and what it means that God exists without principle, see C. F. Kelley, *Meister Eckhart on Divine Knowledge* (New Haven: Yale University Press, 1977), esp. 87–93, 114–16.

78. *Essential*, p. 128. "Hoc enim proprie vivit quod est sine principio. Nam omne habens principium operationis suae ab alio, ut aliud, non proprie vivit." *Comm. Jn.* n. 19, *LW* 3: 16.

79. Eckhart also uses related expressions, such as "little town" (*bürgelîn*), "the noble" or "highest" (*daz edele, oberste*), and the "innermost" (*daz innigeste*). See the Middle High German glossary in *Teacher*, pp. 402 and 404. See also Benno Schmoldt, *Die deutsche Begriffsprache Meister Eckharts* (Heidelberg: Quelle and Meyer, 1954).

80. *Essential*, p. 85. "Simul enim et semel quo deus fuit, quo filium sibi coaeternum per omnia coaequalem deum genuit, etiam mundum creavit." *Comm. Gen.* n. 7, *LW* 1: 190. The second article also deals with this teaching, and is drawn from *Comm. Jn.* n. 216, *LW* 3: 181–82. For the text of the bull, see M.-H. Laurent, "Autour du procès de Maître Eckhart. Les documents des Archives Vaticanes," *Divus Thomas* (Piacenza), ser. III, 13 (1936): 435–46; and *Essential*, pp. 77–81.

81. Eckhart cites passages from the eleventh book of the *Confessions* in support of his teachings about the eternal aspect of creation. See *Comm. Jn.* nn. 217–8, *LW* 3: 182–84. In the defense, he cites the first book, again to support the teaching that God creates in the now of eternity even though it is also true that the world was created in time. See Théry, "Édition critique," p. 206; *Essential*, p. 75.

82. Eckhart made this argument both in his written defense at Cologne, and, it appears, at Avignon. On the first, see Théry, "Édition critique," p. 194. The documentary evidence from Eckhart's defense at Avignon comes from the one surviving report given by the investigators to Pope John XXII, known as the *Gutachten*. The document states each of the suspect articles (at this point the number had been pared down to twenty-eight), gives reasons for the view being in error, a summary of Eckhart's defense and the investigating theologians' rebuttals of that defense. From these documents we know that Eckhart again made his Neoplatonic argument and was misread by his critics due to certain philosophical misunderstandings. See Franz Pelster, ed., "Ein Gutachten aus dem Eckehart-Prozess in Avignon," *Aus der Geisterwelt des Mittelalters. Festgabe Martin Grabmann (Beiträge Supplement III)* (Munster, 1935), pp. 1109–10 for the summary of Eckhart's argument and pp. 1110–11 for the rebuttal of the investigators. For the nature of the documentary evidence, see McGinn, "Eckhart's Condemnation," pp. 395–98.

83. See Ser. XV. 2, *LW* 4: 147–48.

84. See *Comm. Gen.* nn. 10–13, *LW* 1: 193–97; and *Comm. Wis.* nn. 35–7, *LW* 2: 355–59.

85. On the three levels of creation, see *Comm. Jn.* nn. 63–64, 83 and

89, *LW* 3: 51–53, 71–72, 77 (*Essential*, pp. 144–45, 153, 155–56); and *Par. Gen.* n. 151, *LW* 1: 621 (*Essential*, p. 115).

86. Ser. XXIX, *LW* 4: 263–70 (*Teacher*, pp. 223–7).

87. *Comm. Ex.* n. 265, *LW* 2: 213–14 (*Teacher*, p. 125); *Comm. Jn.* nn. 673, 697, *LW* 3: 587–88, 612; Ser. XI.2 *LW* 4: 110–15; and Ser. 9 *DW* 1: 152–54 (*Teacher*, pp. 255–61). The primacy of the intellect is also the subject of one of the few extant questions argued by Eckhart during his academic years at Paris. Although early, it suggests the continuity of this theme in his thought and its interest to his contemporaries. See *Parisian Questions* q. 3, *LW* 5: 55–71. There is a translation available by Armand Maurer, *Master Eckhart. Parisian Questions and Prologues* (Toronto: Pontifical Institute of Medieval Studies, 1974), pp. 55–67.

88. See Ser. XXIX *LW* 4: 263–70 (*Teacher*, pp. 223–27).

89. Ser. 69, *DW* 3: 159–180 (*Teacher*, pp. 311–16).

90. See Chapter 6.

91. See Ser. 2 *DW* 1: 24–45 (*Essential*, p. 177–81); Ser. 69 *DW* 3: 159–80 (*Teacher*, pp. 311–16); and Ser. 76 *DW* 3: 310–29 (*Teacher*, pp. 327–32).

92. *Essential*, p. 80. "Aliquid est in anima, quod est increatum et increabile; si tota anima esset talis, esset increata et increabilis; et hoc est intellectus." Laurent, "Autour du procès," p. 442. The statement can be found in Ser. 13 *DW* 1: 220, although the last phrase, "et hoc est intellectus," does not appear there.

93. *Comm. Gen.* n. 7, *LW* 1: 190 (*Essential*, p. 85); and *Comm. Jn.* n. 216, *LW* 3: 181–82 (*Essential*, p. 187).

94. For the most direct parallels, see Ser. 13 cited above and also Ser. 48, *DW* 2: 418 (*Essential*, p. 198).

95. Such denials are found throughout the written defense. See Théry, "Édition critique," pp. 188, 191, 201, 211, 214–15. He repeated his claim that such statements were false in his public sermon and defense in Cologne on February 13, 1327, and before the Avignon commission. For the former, see Laurent, "Autour du procès," p. 345. For Avignon, see Pelster, "Ein Gutachten," pp. 1111–12.

96. As McGinn argues, it is the language of "piece" or "part" that troubles Eckhart in his public statement of defense in the Dominican church at Cologne on February 13, 1327, and the same themes recur at Avignon. For the former, see M.-H. Laurent, "Autour du procès," p. 345, and for Avignon, Pelster, "Ein Gutachten," pp. 1111–12. See McGinn, "Theological Introduction," in *Essential*, p. 52.

97. Again compare Laurent, "Autour du procès," p. 442, with Ser. 13, *DW* 1: 220.

98. McGinn, "Theological Summary," in *Essential*, p. 42.

CHAPTER 6

1. *Essential*, p. 177. "von allen vremden bilden ledic ist, alsô ledic, als er was, dô er niht enwas." Ser. 2, *DW* 1: 25.

2. *Essential*, p. 177. Translation modified. "Waere ich alsô vernünftic, daz alliu bilde vernünyticlîche in mir stüenden, diu alle menschen ie enpfiengen und diu in gote selber sint, waere ich der âne eigenschaft, daz ich enkeinez mit eigenschaft haete begriffen in tuonne noch in lâzenne, mit vor noch mit nâch, mêr: daz ich in disem gegenwertigen nû vrî und ledic stüende nâch dem liebesten willen gotes und den ze tuonne âne underlâz, in der wârheit sô waere ich juncvrouwe âne hindernisse aller bilde als gewaerlîche, als ich was, dô ich niht enwas." Ser. 2, *DW* 1: 25–26.

3. *Essential*, p. 177. "vrî ist und megetlich" Ser. 2, *DW* 1: 26.

4. *Essential*, p. 186. "enhânt zemâle keinen willen; waz got wil, daz ist in allez glîch, swie grôz daz ungemach sî." Ser. 6 *DW* 1: 102.

5. Schürmann, *Mystic and Philosopher*, pp. 9–13. Also see Sells, "Dialectic," pp. 183–98; Bernard Welte, "Meister Eckhart als Aristoteliker," *Philosophisches Jahrbuch der Görres Gesellschaft* 69 (1961): 64–74; and McGinn, "Theological Summary," p. 48.

6. See Chapter 4.

7. *Essential*, p. 187. "Götlich wesen enist niht glîch, in im enist noch bilde noch forme." Ser. 6, *DW* 1: 107.

8. *Essential*, p. 288. "Und dû solt wizzen: laere sîn aller crêatûre ist gotes vol sîn, und vol sin aller crêatûre ist gotes laere sîn." *On Detachment*, *DW* 5: 413.

9. Colledge and Marler suggest this chronology, which is taken further by Sells. See Colledge and Marler, "Poverty of the Will"; and Sells, *Languages of Unsaying*, p. 183.

10. See Chapter 5.

11. See Ser. 52, *DW* 2: 493. For the debates around this text and its meaning, see Quint's note in the critical edition. Sells has many useful comments on the problems with the textual editing and interpellating of Eckhart's work. Sells, *Languages of Unsaying*, pp. 1–2, 180–205.

12. *Essential*, p. 200. "Her umbe sô biten wir got, daz wir gotes ledic werden und daz wir nemen die wârheit und gebrûchen der êwiclîche, dâ die obersten engel und diu vliege und diu sêle glîch sint in dem, dâ ich stuont und wolte, daz ich was, und was, daz ich wolte. Alsô sprechen wir: sol der mensche arm sîn von willen, sô muoz er als lützel wellen und begern, als er wolte und begerte, dô er niht enwas. Und in dirre wîse ist der mensche arm, der niht enwil." Ser. 52, *DW* 2: 493–94.

13. See the General Prologue to the Opus Tripartium, n. 12, *LW* 1: 156–58. There is an English translation in Armand A. Maurer, trans.,

Master Eckhart: Parisian Questions and Prologues (Toronto: Pontifical Institute of Medieval Studies, 1974), pp. 85–86.

14. *Essential*, p. 201. Translation modified. "Sô sprechen wir: got enist niht wesen noch vernünftic noch enbekennet niht diz noch daz. Her umbe ist got ledic aller dinge, und her umbe ist er alliu dinc. Der nû arm sol sîn des geistes, der muoz arm sîn alles sînes eigenen wizzennes, daz er niht enwizze dehein dinc, weder got noch crêatûre noch sich selben. Her umbe sô ist ez nôt, daz der mensche begernde sî, daz er niht enmüge wizzen noch bekennen diu werk gotes. In dirre wîse sô mac der mensche arm sîn sînes eigenen wizzenes." Ser. 52, DW 2: 497–98.

15. *Essential*, p. 202. Translation modified. "wan daz ist diu armuot des geistes, daz er alsô ledic stâ gotes und aller sîner werke, welle got würken in der sêle, daz er selbe sî diu stat, dar inne er würken wil,—und diz tuot er gerne." Ser. 52, DW 2: 500–1.

16. *Essential*, p. 202. Translation modified. "Her umbe sô bite ich got, daz er mich ledic mache gotes" Ser. 52, DW 2: 502.

17. *Essential*, p. 203. "ich blîben sol nû und iemermê." Ser. 52, DW 2: 505.

18. *Essential*, p. 208. "Dú solt in minnen, als er ist Ein nit-got, Ein nit-geist, Ein nit-persone, Ein nút-bilde, Mer: als er ein luter pur clar Ein ist, gesundert von aller zweiheite, und in dem einen súlen wir ewiklich versinken von nite zu núte." Ser. 83, DW 3: 448. The translation has been modified, although it still misses the full meaning of *Ein* in the original, which stresses the unity of the divine.

19. On some of the central criticisms against Eckhart in the accusations and condemnations, see McGinn, "Theological Summary;" and McGinn, "Eckhart's Condemnation." Also see the bull *In agro dominico* (1329) in Laurent, "Autour du procès," pp. 435–46; and *Essential*, pp. 77–81.

20. Porete makes similar claims about the free soul. See Chapter 4.

21. Ser. 6, DW 2: 114–15 (*Essential*, p. 189).

22. *Essential*, p. 189. "Alsô werden wir in got verwandelt, daz wir in bekennen suln, als er ist." DW 2: 115. Eckhart here follows Paul. See 1 Cor. 13:12.

23. John Caputo, *The Mystical Element in Heidegger's Thought* (Athens, Ohio: Ohio University Press, 1978), Ch. 3.

24. *Essential*, p. 188. "Sumlîche einveltige liute waenent, sie süln got sehen, als er dâ stande und sie hie. Des enist niht. Got und ich wir sint ein. Mit bekennenne nime ich got in mich, mit minnenne gân ich in got." Ser. 6, DW 1: 113.

25. See Chapter 4.

26. See Chapters 3 and 4.

27. On the formal emanation of the Son and Spirit from the Father, see *Comm. Ex.* n. 16, *LW* 2: 21–22; and Serm. XLIX, *LW* 4: 421–28 (*Teacher*, pp. 234–38).

28. For the history of this theme, see Hugo Rahner, "Die Gottesgeburt: Die Lehre der Kirchenväter von der Geburt Christi aus dem Herzen der Kirche und der Glaübigen," *Zeitschrift für katholische Theologie* 59 (1933): 33–418.

29. See Chapter 5.

30. *Essential*, p. 186. "Dû solt dînes eigenen willen alzemâle ûzgân." Ser. 6, *DW* 1: 102.

31. For detachment as self-abandonment, see *Detach.*, *DW* 5: 400–434 (*Essential*, pp. 285–94); and *Counsels on Discernment*, nn. 3–4, 23, *DW* 5: 191–98, 290–309 (*Essential*, pp. 249–50, 280–85).

32. On the compulsion of the divine, see especially, *Detach.*, *DW* 5: 402–3, 411 (*Essential*, pp. 286, 288). Mechthild and Porete make similar claims about the power of the humble or free soul.

33. *Essential*, p. 187. Translation modified. "Niht aleine ist si bî im noch er bî ir glîch, sunder er ist in ir, und gebirt der vater sînen sun in der sêle in der selben wîse, als er in der êwicheit gebirt, und niht anders. Er muoz ez tuon, ez sî im liep oder leit. Der vater gebirt sînen sun âne underlâz, und ich spriche mêr: er gebirt mich sînen sun and den selben sun. Ich spriche mêr: er gebirt mich niht aleine sînen sun, mêr: er gebirt mich sich und sich mich und mich sîn wesen und sîn nâture." Ser. 6, *DW* 1: 109. The parentheses are added. While "as" is necessary for clarity, its insertion disrupts the immediacy of Eckhart's language.

34. See, for example, Ser. 6, *DW* 1: 109 (*Essential*, p. 187); and Ser. 15, *DW* 1: 245 (*Essential*, p. 189).

35. See Sells, "Dialectic," pp. 30–33, 181–203.

36. The directness of these claims makes it difficult to understand the assertion that Eckhart's writings are distanced and impersonal, and the questions as to whether he claims to have the experiences or consciousness that he describes. It seems clear that he does. See, for example, Tobin, *Meister Eckhart*.

37. See, for example, Ser. 5b *DW* 1: 85–96 (*Essential*, pp. 181–85); Ser. 24 *DW* 1: 414–23 (*Teacher*, pp. 284–86); and Ser. 39. *DW* 2: 251–66 (*Teacher*, pp. 296–98).

38. *Essential*, pp. 178–79. "Ein juncvrouwe, diu ein wîp ist, diu ist vrî und ungebunden âne eigenschaft, diu ist gote und ir selber alle zît glîch nâhe. Diu bringet vil vrühte und die sint grôz, minner noch mêr dan got selber ist. Dise vruht und dise geburt machet disiu juncvrouwe, diu ein wîp ist, geborn und bringet alle tage hundert mâl oder tûsent mal vruht joch âne zal gebernde und vruhtbaere werdende ûz dem aller edelsten grunde;

noch baz gesprochen: jâ, ûz dem selben grunde, dâ der vater ûz gebernde ist sîn êwic wort, dar ûz wirt si vruhtbaere mitgebernde." Ser. 2, *DW* 1: 30–31.

39. Sells, *Languages of Unsaying*, pp. 146–79.

40. *Teacher*, p. 323. "wie ez swanger würde von nihte als ein vrouwe mit einem kinde, und in dem nihte wart got geborn" Ser. 71, *DW* 3: 224. See Bernard McGinn, "The God Beyond God: Theology and Mysticism in the Thought of Meister Eckhart," *Journal of Religion* 61 (1981): 1–19.

41. Sells argues that this is not an appropriative gesture but rather subverts the appropriation of female creativity by a male God central to the Christian tradition. See Sells, *Languages of Unsaying*, pp. 146–79.

42. See, for example, Caputo, *Mystical Element*, pp. 127–34.

43. John Caputo, "Fundamental Themes in Meister Eckhart's Mysticism," *The Thomist* 42 (1978): 224. Caputo's reading, which is repeated in *Mystical Element*, pp. 132–34, is indebted to the study by Shizutera Ueda, *Die Gottesgeburt in der Seele und der Durchbruch zur Gottheit: Die mystische Anthropologie Meister Eckharts und ihre Konfrontation mit der Mystik Zen-Buddhismus* (Gütersloh: G. Mohn, 1965).

44. Eckhart makes this traditional distinction in Ser. XXV.1, *LW* 4: 237–38. See Lossky, *Théologie négative*, pp. 182–84.

45. This parallel is brought out more fully in the mystical theology of John Ruusbroec, which was deeply indebted to the thought of Meister Eckhart. See his "Spiritual Espousals," found in both the original Dutch and English translation in Jan van Ruusbroec, *De ornatu spiritalium nuptiarum/Die Geestelike Brulocht*, ed. J. Alaerts and trans. H. Rolfson, in Corpus Christianorum Continuatio Medievalis, vol. 103 (Turnhout: Brepols, 1988).

46. On the redeeming power of grace, see Ser. II.2, *LW* 4: 16–20; and *Sermon for the Feast of St. Augustine* n. 11, *LW* 5: 97–98. For the Incarnation as the central work of grace and the source of divine sonship, see Laurent, "Autour du procès," pp. 229–31; *Comm. Jn.* nn. 102, 106, 117–20, *LW* 3: 88, 90–91, 101–5 (*Essential*, pp. 161–62, 167–69); and Ser. 22, *DW* 1: 375–89 (*Essential*, pp. 192–93). Also see McGinn, "Theological Summary," pp. 45–46.

47. *Essential*, pp. 284–85. "er hât sie gemachet nâch im selber, jâ, nâch allem dem, daz er ist, nâch natûre, nach wesene und nâch sînem ûzvliezenden inneblîbenden werke und nâch dem grunde, dâ er in im selber blîbende ist, dâ er gebernde ist sînen eingebornen sun, dâ von der heilige geist ûzblüejende ist: nâch disem ûzvliezenden inneblîbenden werke sô hât got die sêle geschaffen." Ser. 24, *DW* 1: 415.

48. See Beverly Lanzetta, "Three Categories of Nothingness in Eckhart," *Journal of Religion* (1992): 248–68.

49. There has been extensive feminist commentary and criticism of the paradoxical nature of Mary as an impossible ideal for women; for example, Marina Warner, *Alone of All Her Sex: The Myth and Cult of the Virgin Mary* (London: Weidenfeld and Nicolson, 1976). Eckhart's mystical reading of this Christian theme potentially subverts such impossible patriarchal imperatives through his revaluation of the wifely figure. For comments on the soul as divine feminine in Eckhart, see Sells, *Languages of Unsaying*, pp. 180–205.

50. See Chapter 5.

51. *Essential*, p. 208. "Dú solt in bekennen ane bilde, ane mittel und ane glichnis. Sol aber ich also got bekennen ane mittel, so mus vil bi ich er werden und er ich werden. Me sprich ich: Got mus vil bi ich werden und ich vil bi got, alse gar ein, das dis 'er' und dis 'ich' Ein 'ist' werdent und sint und in dér istikeit ewiklich ein werk wirkent; wande vil nüzze sint dis 'er' und dis 'ich', dc ist got und die sel." Ser. 83 *DW* 3: 447.

52. See Chapter 5.

53. See Chapter 5.

54. On Eckhart's concept of justice and the just act, see Meith, *Einheit*, pp. 157–81. Also Chapter 7.

55. On the influence of Aristotelian epistemology on these mystical ideas, see Sells, "Dialectic," pp. 183–98; Schürmann, *Mystic and Philosopher*, pp. 12–13; and Welte, "Meister Eckhart als Aristoteliker," pp. 64–74.

56. See *Comm. Ex.* n. 74, *LW* 2: 78 (*Teacher*, p. 68); *Comm. Wis.* n. 148, *LW* 2: 485 (*Teacher*, p. 167–68); *Comm. Jn.* n. 556, *LW* 3: 484 (*Teacher*, p. 185); and Ser. 21, *DW* 1: 360–62 (*Teacher*, p. 281).

57. Again, see especially, *Comm. Ex.* n. 74, *LW* 2: 78 (*Teacher*, p. 68).

58. *Essential*, p. 207. Translation modified. "Sprich ich och: 'Got ist wise'—es ist nit war: Ich bin wiser den er. Sprich ich och: 'Got ist ein wesen'—es ist nit war: Er ist ein uber swebende wesen und ein uber wesende nitheit." Ser. 83, *DW* 3: 441–42.

59. See *Comm. Wis.* n. 282, *LW* 2: 614–15 (*Teacher*, p. 172); *Comm. Ecc.* n. 46, *LW* 2: 274–75 (*Teacher*, p. 176); and *Comm. Jn.* n. 44, 52, *LW* 3: 36–37, 43–44 (*Essential*, pp. 137, 140).

60. See Lossky, *Théologie négative*, pp. 255–60.

61. Alois Haas, "Seinsspekulation und Geschöpflichkeit in der Mystik Meister Eckharts," in *Sein und Nichts in der Abendländischen Mystik*, ed. Walter Stolz (Freiburg: Herder, 1984), pp. 33–58.

62. *Teacher*, p. 250. "Dû suochest etwaz mit gote und tuost rehte als dû von gote eine kerzen machtest, daz man etwaz dâ mite suoche; und sô man diu dinc vindet, diu man suochet, sô wirfet man die kerzen enwec. Alsô tuost dû: swaz dû mit gote suochest, daz enist

niht, swaz ez joch sî, ez sî nutz oder lôn oder innerkeit oder swaz ez joch sî; dû suochest niht, dar umbe envindest dû ouch niht." Ser. 4, *DW* 1: 69.

63. *Teacher*, p. 250. "Alle crêatûren sint ein lûter niht. Ich spriche niht, daz sie kleine sîn oder iht sîn: sie sint ein lûter niht. Swaz niht wesens enhât, daz enist niht. Alle crêatûren hânt kein wesen, wan ir wesen swebet an der gegenwerticheit gotes. Kêrte sich got ab allen crêatûren einen ougenblik, sô würden sie ze nihte." Ser. 4, *DW* 1: 69–70.

64. "collatio esse," *Comm. Gen.* n. 160, *LW* 1: 197.

65. *Teacher*, p. 250. "Ich sprach etwenne und ist ouch wâr; der alle die werlt naeme mit gote, der enhaete niht mê, dan ob er got aleine haete. Alle crêatûren hânt niht mê âne got, dan ein mücke haete âne got, rehte glîch noch minner noch mê." Ser. 4, *DW* 1: 70.

66. See Chapter 4.

67. *Teacher*, pp. 296–97. "Jâ, und bildest dû got in dich, swaz dû werke dar umbe würkest, diu sint alliu tôt, und dû verderbest guotiu werk; . . . Und dar umbe, wilt dû leben und wilt, daz dîniu werk leben, sô muost dû allen dingen tôt sîn und ze nihte worden sîn. Der crêatûre eigen ist, daz si von ihte iht mache; aber gotes eigen ist, daz er von nihte iht mache; und dar umbe, sol got iht in dir oder mit dir machen, sô muost dû vor ze nihte worden sîn." Ser. 39, *DW* 2: 254–56.

68. *Teacher*, p. 297. "Und dar umbe ganc in dînen eigenen grunt, und dâ würke, und diu werk, diu dû dâ würkest, diu sint alliu lebendic." Ser. 39, *DW* 2: 256.

69. See especially *Book of "Benedictus"* 2, *DW* 5: 109–19 (*Essential*, pp. 240–47).

70. "Alle crêatûren enrüerent got niht nâch der geschaffenheit, und daz geschaffen ist, daz muoz gebrochen sîn, sol daz guot her ûz komen." Ser. 13, *DW* 1: 212.

71. "Got minnet niht wan sich selben und als vil er sîn glîch vindet in mir und mich in im." Ser. 41, *DW* 2: 285.

72. "Der gote daz benaeme, daz er uns minnet, der benaeme im sîn wesen und sîne gotheit, wan sîn wesen swebet dar ane, daz er mich minnet." Ibid., p. 287.

73. See *FL*, Bk. III, Ch. 9, p. 87.

74. For the parallels with Mechthild, see Chapters 3 and 7.

75. This has been the implicit assertion of those commentators who have seen a marked similarity between Eckhart's thought and Zen Buddhism. For example, see Ueda, *Gottesgeburt*; and Schürmann, "The Loss of Origin."

76. See Chapter 4.

77. See Sells, *Languages of Unsaying*, pp. 1–2.

78. See esp. Ser. 2, *DW* 1: 24–45 (*Essential,* pp. 177–81); Ser. 69, *DW* 3: 159–80 (*Teacher,* pp. 311–16); and Ser. 76, *DW* 3: 310–29 (*Teacher,* pp. 327–32).

79. See Chapter 5.

80. See Serm. 23, *DW* 1: 251–66 (*Teacher,* pp. 296–300); and Ser. 39, *DW* 1: 521–23.

81. *Teacher,* pp. 285–86. Translation modified. "Die meister sprechent, daz menschlich natûre mit der zît niht habe ze tuonne und daz si zemâle unberüerlich sî und dem menschen vil inniger und naeher sî dan er im selber. Und dar umbe nam got menschlîche natûre an sich und einigete sie sîner persônen. Dâ wart menschlich natûre got, wan er menschlîche natûre blôz und keinen menschen an sich nam. Dar umbe, wilt dû der selbe Krist sîn und got sîn, sô ganc alles des abe, daz daz êwige wort an sich niht ennam. Daz êwige wort nam keinen menschen an sich; dar umbe ganc abe, swaz menschen an dir sî und swaz dû sîst, und nim dich nâch menschlîcher natûre blôz, sô bist dû daz selbe an dem êwigen worte, daz menschlich natûre an im ist. Wan dîn menschlîche natûre und diu sîne enhât keinen underscheit: si ist ein, wan, swaz si ist in Kristô, daz ist si in dir." Ser. 24, *DW* 1: 420. See also Ser. 5b, *DW* 1: 86 (*Essential,* p. 182); and Ser. 46, *DW* 2: 380 (*Teacher,* p. 304).

82. See Ser. 25, *DW* 2: 14–16.

83. See Théry, "Édition critique," pp. 233–34.

84. See Ser. 12, *DW* 1: 192–203 (*Teacher,* pp. 267–71).

85. Characteristically, Eckhart speaks more of the positive than the negative. All of his discussions of the primacy of the One posit, implicitly or explicitly, the "fallenness" of multiplicity just as the emphasis on the eternal now shows that temporality is creaturely and secondary. For the One in distinction from multiplicity, see *Comm. Gen.* n. 12, *LW* 1: 195–96; and *Comm. Jn.* n. 114, *LW* 3: 99–100. For the eternal now distinguished from temporality, see Ser. 1, *DW* 1: 11 (*Teacher,* p. 241); Ser. 4, *DW* 1: 74 (*Teacher,* p. 251); Ser. 9, *DW* 1: 144 (*Teacher,* p. 256); Ser. 10, *DW* 1: 166–74 (*Teacher,* p. 263–65); Ser. 14, *DW* 1: 238–40 (*Teacher,* p. 273); Ser. 30, *DW* 2: 94–96 (*Teacher,* p. 292); Ser. 39, *DW* 2: 261–63 (*Teacher,* pp. 297–98); and Ser. 69, *DW* 3: 170 (*Teacher,* p. 313).

86. See Ser. 47 *DW* 2: 394–409; and Ser. 57, *DW* 2: 594–606.

87. See Ser. 4, *DW* 1: 70 (*Teacher,* p. 250).

88. *Teacher,* p. 338. Translation modified. "Genuoc sîn nâch sinnelicheit, daz ist, daz uns got gibet trôst, lust und genüegede; und hie inne verwenet sîn, daz gât abe den lieben vriunden gotes nâch den nidern sinnen. Aber redelîchiu genüegede, daz ist nâch dem geiste. Ich spriche dem redelîche genüegede, daz von allem luste daz oberste wipfelîn der sêle niht enwirt geneiget her abe, daz az niht ertrinke in dem luste, ez

enstande gewalticlîche ûf im. Danne ist er in redelîcher genüegede, sô liep und leit der crêatûre daz oberste wipfelîn niht geneigen enmac her abe. 'Crêatûre' heize ich allez, daz man enpfindet und sihet under got." Ser. 86, DW 3: 482.

89. *Teacher*, p. 344. "Nû wellent etelîche liute dar zuo komen, daz sie werke ledic sîn. Ich spriche: ez enmac niht gesîn. Nâch der zît, dô die jünger enpfiengen den heiligen geist, dô viengen sie êrste ane, tugende zu würkenne." Ser. 86, DW 3: 492.

90. This will be discussed further in Chapter 7.

91. *Teacher*, p. 344. "Nû waenent unser guoten liute erkriegen, daz gegenwürticheit sinnelîcher dinge den sinnen niht ensî. Des engât in niht zuo. Daz ein pînlich gedoene mînen ôren als lustic sî als ein süezez seitenspil, daz erkriege ich niemer. Aber daz sol man haben, daz ein redelich gotgeformeter wille blôz stande alles natûrlîchen lustes, swenne ez bescheidenheit aneschouwet, daz si dem willen gebiete, sich abe ze kêrenne, und der wille spreche: ich tuon ez gerne." Ser. 86, DW 3: 491–92.

92. *Teacher*, p. 341. "Der eine ist: mit manicvaltigem gewerbe, mit brinnender minne in allen crêatûren got suochen." Ser. 86, DW 3: 486.

93. *Teacher*, p. 341. "wec âne wec, vrî und doch gebunden, erhaben und gezucket vil nâch über sich und alliu dinc âne willen und âne bilde, swie aleine ez doch weselîche niht enstâ." Ser. 86, DW 3: 486.

94. *Teacher*, p. 341. "Der dritte wex heizet wec und ist doch heime, daz ist: got sehen âne mittel in sînesheit." Ser. 86, DW 3: 487.

95. *Teacher*, p. 340. "bî den dingen und niht in den dingen." Ser. 86, DW 3: 485. And also, "dû stâst bî den dingen, und diu dinc enstânt niht in dir." Ibid.

96. *Teacher*, p. 344. "Kein glit was an sînem lîbe, ez enüebete sunderlîche tugent." Ser. 86, DW 3: 492.

97. On the traditional reading of the text as a statement of the superiority of the contemplative to the active life, see D. A. Csányi, " 'Optima Pars:' Die Auslegungsgeschichte von Lk. 10, 38–42 bei den Kirchenvätern der ersten vier Jahrhunderte," *Studia Monastica* 2 (1960): 5–78.

98. See Mieth, *Einheit*, pp. 173–85; Mieth, "Transposition der Tugendethik," p. 63; and McGinn, "God Beyond God," p. 18.

99. See Ser. 5b, DW 1: 90 (*Essential*, p. 183); Ser. 29, DW 2: 77, 80 (*Teacher*, pp. 288–89); Ser. 39, DW 2: 253–54, 266 (*Teacher*, pp. 296, 298); Ser. 41, DW 2: 289; and Ser. 59, DW 2: 625–26 (*Teacher*, p. 307).

100. Ser. 59, DW 2: 625–26 (*Teacher*, p. 307).

101. *Teacher*, p. 296. Translation modified. "Der gerehte ensuochet niht in sînen werken; wan die iht suochent in irn werken, die sint knehte und mietlinge, oder die umbe einic warumbe würkent. Dar umbe, wilt du în- und übergebildet werden in die gerehticheit, sô enmeine niht in

dînen werken und enbilde kein warumbe in dich, noch in zît noch in êwicheit, noch lôn noch saelicheit, noch diz noch daz; wan disiu werk sint alliu waerlîche tôt. Jâ, und bildest dû got in dich, swaz dû werke dar umbe würkest, diu sint alliu tôt, und dû verderbest guotiu werk." Ser. 39, *DW* 2: 253–55. Also see Schürmann, *Mystic and Philosopher*, pp. 63–65.

102. See Ser. 39, *DW* 2: 271 (*Teacher*, p. 298). Eckhart might be seen as offering a response to Nietzsche's critique of Christian ethics. Insofar as we are willing, we are not doing works of justice.

103. See Mieth, *Einheit*, pp. 219–22.

104. Aquinas, *STh* IIaIIae, q. 182, aa. 1–4.

105. For the sermon in question, see Franz Pfeiffer, Ser. III, in *Deutsche Mystiker des vierzehnten Jahrhunderts*, vol. 2: *Meister Eckhart, Predigten und Traktate* (Leipzig: n. p., 1857 and Aalan: n. p., 1962), pp. 18–19. Also see the *Couns.*, n. 23, *DW* 5: 290–309 (*Essential*, pp. 280–85).

106. See *Par. Gen.* n. 165, *LW* 1: 634–36 (*Essential*, p. 121); *Comm. Jn.* n. 646, *LW* 3: 561; and *Comm. Wis.* n. 226, *LW* 2: 561. These are the sources for articles 16–19 condemned in the bull *In agro*. See *Essential*, p. 79. See also Ser. 4, *DW* 1: 71 (*Teacher*, p. 250); and Ser. 25, *DW* 2: 17. To compare with Mechthild's claims, see Chapter 3.

107. At Cologne he cites Aquinas, *STh* IaIIae. q. 20 a. 4. See Théry, "Édition critique," p. 195.

108. *Par. Gen.* n. 165, *LW*, 1: 634–36 (*Essential*, p. 121). See McGinn, "Theological Summary," p. 58.

109. For more on this, see Chapter 7.

110. See Théry, "Édition critique," p. 202, 233–34; and McGinn, "Theological Summary," p. 46.

111. See, for example, *Couns.* 19 and 21, *DW* 5: 260–62, 274–76 (*Essential*, pp. 270, 274).

112. "Der hundert mark goldes durch got gaebe, daz waere ein grôzes werk . . . aber . . . hân ich einen willen, haete ich hundert mark ze gebenne, ist eht der wille ganz, in der wârheit, sô hân ich gote bezalt, und er muoz mir antwürten, als ob ich im hundert mark bezalt haete." Ser. 25 *DW* 2: 17.

113. On the ideal state, in which the exterior and the interior acts would coincide, see *Counc.* n. 23, *DW* 5: 290–309 (*Essential*, pp. 280–85).

114. This is where Eckhart's thought is still distant from twentieth-century assumptions, in which the body is increasingly seen as the source and ground for our transcending activity. Perhaps the differing *experience* of the body in the medieval period, particularly among Eckhart's beguine audiences, is in part responsible for this. For Mechthild, the body is a source of transcendence only through pain; it is this move which Eckhart seeks to avoid. See Scarry, *Body in Pain*.

CHAPTER 7

1. "Adoncques ne veult lame nient, dit Amour, puis quelle est franche, car cil nest mie franc qui veult aucune chose de la voulenté de son dedans, quelque chose quil vieulle. Car de tant est il serf a luy mesmes, et cil qui ce veult ne le veult sinon pour la voulenté de dieu acomplir tant seulement en luy et en aultruy. Pour telle gent, dit Amour, refusa dieu son royaulme." *Mirouer*, Ch. 48, p. 144.

2. Ser. 39: *DW* 2: 253.

3. *Essential*, p. 200. Translation modified. "als lange als der mensche daz hât, daz daz sîn wille ist, daz er wil ervüllen den allerliebesten willen gotes, der mensche enhât niht armuot, von der wir sprechen wellen; wan dirre mensche hât einen willen, mit dem er genuoc wil sîn dem willen gotes, und daz enist niht rehtiu armuot. Wan, sol der mensche armuot haben gewaerlîche, sô sol er sînes geschaffenen willen alsô ledic stân, als er tete, dô er niht enwas. Wan ich sage iu bî der êwigen wârheit: als lange als ir willen hât, ze ervüllenne den willen gotes, und begerunge hât der êwicheit und gotes, als lange ensît ir niht arm; wan daz ist ein arm mensche, der niht enwil und niht enbegert." Ser. 52, *DW* 2: 491–92.

4. See Colledge and Marler, " 'Poverty of Will'," p. 30. For a typical expression of this threefold proposition, see *Mirouer*, Ch. 42, pp. 130–32.

5. *Essential*, p. 85. "noch guot noch êre noch gemach noch lust noch nuz noch innicheit noch heilicheit noch lôn noch himelrîche." Ser. 6, *DW* 1: 100.

6. See *Mirouer*, Ch. 136–37, pp. 398–400.

7. "Or l'a maintenant, sans nul pourquoy, en tel point comme il l'avoit, ains que telle en fust dame. Ce n'est nul fors qu'il; nul n'ayme fors qu'il, car nul n'est fors que luy, et pource ayme tout seul et se voit tout seul, et loe tout seul de son etre mesmes." *Mirouer*, Ch. 91, p. 258. For similar texts see Ch. 11, pp. 46–48; Ch. 27, p. 94; Ch. 45, pp. 138–40; Ch. 51, pp. 150–52; Ch. 64, pp. 184–86; Ch. 70, pp. 196–98; Ch. 82, pp. 232–36; Ch. 89, p. 284; Ch. 104, p. 300; Ch. 110, pp. 298–300; Ch. 111, pp. 302–4; and Ch. 133, pp. 390–94. Also see McGinn, "*Unio mystica*," p. 74.

8. See *FL*, Bk. I, Ch. 22, pp. 18–19; Bk. I, Ch. 44, pp. 30–32; Bk. VI, Ch. 31, pp. 238–40 and *Mirouer* Ch. 35, pp. 114–15; Ch. 78, pp. 218–20; Ch. 107, pp. 290–92; and Ch. 138, pp. 400–2.

9. See *Mirouer*, Ch. 8, p. 30.

10. See ibid., Ch. 35, pp. 114–16; Ch. 87, pp. 246–48; Ch. 107, pp. 290–92.

11. See ibid., Ch. 91, pp. 256–58; and Eckhart, Ser. 5b, *DW* 1: 83–96.

12. For this somewhat anachronistic use of the term "quietism," see Chapter 4.

13. See Chapter 3.

14. Thus contrast *FL*, Bk. I, Ch. 44, pp. 27–32, with *FL*, Bk. V, Ch. 23, pp. 180–81.

15. Bynum points out the importance of this unity between the active and contemplative to the spirituality of the women's movement. See Bynum, *Fragmentation*, Ch. 2 and my discussion in Chapter 2.

16. See *FL*, Bk. I, Ch. 25, p. 20; Bk. V, Ch. 3, p. 155; Bk. V, Ch. 16, p. 168; Bk. VI, Ch. 4, pp. 209–11; and Bk. VII, Ch. 53, pp. 299–300.

17. Ibid., Bk. VII, Ch. 6, p. 262; Bk. VII, Ch. 17, pp. 268–70; and Bk. VII, Ch. 38, p. 287.

18. Ibid., Bk. VII, Ch. 54, pp. 300–1. For similar ideas in Eckhart, see Chapter 6. The term does not appear in Lüers's compendia of central words in the mystical vocabulary of the German mystics, pointing, perhaps, to its oddity and hence augmenting the argument for influence.

19. See, for example, Ibid., Bk. IV, Ch. 19, pp. 135–36; Bk. V, Ch. 4, pp. 156–58; Bk. V, Ch. 12, p. 166 and Eckhart, *Detach.*, DW 5: 402–4 (*Essential*, p. 286).

20. The sermon appears to have been preached at a Cistercian convent, thereby accounting for the Bernardine language. Similar themes appear in Sermons 10–15. For the evidence, see *Essential*, p. 339, n. 13; and DW 1: 372–74.

21. *Essential*, p. 194. Translation modified. "Waere ich hie oben und spraeche ich ze einem: 'kum her ûf!' daz waere swaere. Mêr: spraeche ich: 'sitz hie nider!' daz waere lîht. Alsô tuot got. Swenne sich der mensche dêmüetiget, sô enmac sich got niht enthalten von sîner eigenen güete, er enmüeze sich senken und giezen in den dêmüetigen menschen, und dem allerminsten dem gibet er sich in dem allermeisten und gibet sich im alzemâle. Daz got gibet, daz ist sîn wesen, und sîn wesen daz ist sîn güete, und sîn güete daz ist sîn minne." Ser. 22, DW 1: 385.

22. See, for example, *FL*, Bk. VII, Ch. 62, pp. 306–7.

23. Ser. 22, DW 1: 377–79.

24. See *Essential*, 234–35. Eckhart's discussions of suffering frequently turn on the identification of the divine and the soul in such experiences, thereby stressing the ways in which God takes on human pain. This allows both consolation to those who *are* suffering, as well as undercutting religious demands that one *imitate* the suffering of Jesus Christ. Some attention should also be given to possible changes in Eckhart's thought, particularly given the probable date of his introduction to Porete's work. See Donald Duclow, " 'My Suffering is God': Meister Eckhart's *Book of Divine Consolation*," *Theological Studies* 44 (1983): 570–86; and Jean Malherbe, *"Souffrir Dieu": La prédication de Maître Eckhart* (Paris: Cerf, 1992), pp. 35–42.

25. See Chapter 2.

26. On women's religious experience as somatic and the experiential quality of their writings, see Bynum, *Fragmentation*, pp. 190–95. Bynum warns against absolute contrasts, but is willing to entertain explanations of these differences ranging from educational and linguistic differences to biological ones. For more on the experiential nature of women's writing, see Dinzelbacher, "Überblick," in *Frauenmystik im Mittelalter*, ed. Dinzelbacher and Bauer; Peter Dinzelbacher, "Rollenverweigerung, religiöser Aufbruch und mystisches Erleben mittelalterlicher Frauen," in *Religiöse Frauenbewegung und mystische Frömmigkeit im Mittelalter*, ed. Peter Dinzelbacher and Dieter R. Bauer (Cologne and Vienna: Bohlau, 1988), pp. 1–5; and Danielle Régnier-Bohler, "Voix littéraire, voix mystique," in *Histoire des Femmes en Occident*, vol. 2, *Le Moyen Âge*, ed. Christiane Klapisch-Zuber (Paris: Plon, 1991). Translated in *A History of Women in the West*, vol. 2, *The Middle Ages* (Cambridge: Belknap Press, 1992), pp. 427–82. Dronke, *Women Writers*, pp. xx–xxi, argues for the greater "immediacy" of women's writings, claiming that an "extrinsic" relationship toward writing was impossible for most women, given the cultural constraints on them. Meg Bogin makes a similar claim about the women troubadours, claiming their writings are "direct, unambiguous and personal," having the quality of journals because of their "urgency." See Meg Bogin, *The Women Troubadours: An Introduction to the Women Poets of 12th-century Provence and a Collection of Their Poems* (New York: Norton, 1980), pp. 67–68. The problem with such claims, as I attempted to show in Chapters 1 and 2, and as Joan Ferrante and others show with relationship to the trobairitz, is that they dilute the rhetorical artistry and conceptual complexity of women's writings. See the essays by Joan M. Ferrante, H. Jay Siskin, and Julie A. Storme in William D. Paden, ed., *The Voice of the Trobairitz: Perspectives on the Women Troubadours* (Philadelphia: University of Pennsylvania Press, 1989). Elizabeth Alvilda Petroff makes similar claims for the experiential and autobiographical nature of women's writings, yet points to the rhetorical uses to which such claims to experience are put. See her "Introduction," pp. 3–59. For a study which pays close attention to these issues, see Alison Weber, *Teresa of Avila and the Rhetoric of Femininity* (Princeton: Princeton University Press, 1990).

27. For the denigration of women's "emotionalism," see the discussion and references in Bynum, *Jesus as Mother*, pp. 172–73, 182–84. On the critique of somatic forms of spirituality, see André Vauchez, *Les laïcs au Moyen Âge: Pratiques et expériences religieuses* (Paris: Édition du Cerf, 1987), pp. 273–75; and Lochrie, *Translations of the Flesh*, pp. 13–16.

28. *Mirouer*, Ch. 8, p. 144.

29. See Bynum, *Fragmentation*, Chaps. 6–7; Caroline Walker Bynum, "Bodily Miracles and the Resurrection of the Body in the High Middle Ages," in *Belief in History*, ed. Thomas Kselman (Notre Dame: University of Notre Dame Press, 1990), pp. 68–106; Piero Camporesi, *The Incorruptible Flesh: Bodily Mutation and Mortification in Religion and Folklore*, trans. Tania Croft-Murray (Cambridge: Cambridge University Press, 1988); and Lochrie, *Translations of the Flesh*, pp. 13–55.

30. See Chapter 2.

31. This phenomenon can be seen, for example, in Beatrice of Nazareth and Mechthild. See Chapters 2 and 3.

32. For many examples, see Bynum, *Fragmentation*, Chaps. 6–7; and "Bodily Miracles."

33. See *FL*, Bk. IV, Ch. 23, pp. 139–40.

34. See Patrick J. Geary, *Furta Sacra: Thefts of Relics in the Central Middle Ages* (Princeton: Princeton University Press, 1978); E. A. R. Brown, "Death and the Human Body in the Later Middle Ages: The Legislation of Boniface VIII on the Division of Corpses," *Viator* 12 (1981): 221–70; and Bynum, *Fragmentation*, pp. 11–13, 183–85. Bynum discusses in particular the concern expressed by Guibert of Nogent that the fragmentation of the holy person's body (and in particular Christ's) somehow endangered or denied its future integrity. See Guibert of Nogent, *De pignoribus*, in *Patrologiae cursus completus: Series latina*, ed. J.-P. Migne (Paris: Garnier, 1844–64), vol. 156, cols. 607–80.

35. See, among others, *Summa contra Gentiles*, Bk. 4, Ch. 88; *STh* IIIa, q. 54, a. 4; and Bynum, *Fragmentation*, p. 230. In these texts, as Bynum points out, Aquinas argues that the resurrected body will have all defects repaired, although the marks of martyrdom and of sexual difference will remain.

36. Eckhart, at times, also makes this argument. See Ser. 47, *DW* 2: 407–8; and Ser. 57, *DW* 2: 598–600. This should be contrasted with those places in which the body is seen as secondary to human nature, i.e., Ser. 35, *DW* 2: 173–83. Eckhart would clearly be aligned with the more traditional "Platonic" tradition, as opposed to the "hylomorphic" position of Thomas and the Aristotelians. Yet, as Bynum has shown, both maintain the necessity of the body and the soul to full personhood, the more traditional, Platonic position perhaps even more so in that there is a plurality of forms and thus an independently subsisting body. See Bynum, *Fragmentation*, pp. 253–65.

37. Bynum, *Fragmentation*, pp. 239–97.

38. Philippe Ariès, *Western Attitudes toward Death from the Middle Ages to the Present*, trans. Patricia M. Ranum (Baltimore: Johns Hopkins University Press, 1974), pp. 27–52.

39. See, in particular, *FL*, Bk. VII, Ch. 65, pp. 310–11.

40. Bynum writes: "Because preachers, confessors and spiritual directors assumed the person to be a psychosomatic unity, they not only read unusual bodily events as expressions of soul, but also expected body itself to offer a means of access to the divine. Because they worshiped a God who became incarnate and died for the sins of others, they viewed all bodily events—the hideous wounds of martyrs or stigmatics as well as the rosy-faced beauty of virgins—as possible manifestations of grace. Because they associated the female with the fleshly, they expected somatic expressions to characterize women's spirituality." Clearly these conclusions are about male cultural perceptions more than about women's experience. Bynum, *Fragmentation*, p. 235.

41. See Margaret R. Miles, *Carnal Knowing: Female Nakedness and Religious Meaning in the Christian West* (Boston: Beacon Press, 1989), Introduction.

42. In an earlier study, Bynum is quite clear about the way in which this occurs, demonstrating that while men often see and image women as "liminal," a parallel situation does not exist for women. For this reason, symbolic reversal is important for men, but not, according to Bynum, for women, who stress continuity in their use of symbols and in their narratives. See *Fragmentation*, Ch. 1; and *Holy Feast*, Ch. 7. The centrality of paradoxical reversals between high and low, all and nothing, and named and nameless in Mechthild and Porete temper the extension of the argument, although the claims with regard to *gender* imagery continue to hold.

43. See *FL*, Bk. I, Ch. 25, p. 20; Bk. V, Ch. 3, p. 155; Bk. V, Ch. 16, p. 168; Bk. VI, Ch. 4, pp. 209–10; and Bk. VII, Ch. 53, pp. 299–300.

44. I have again taken over language used by Hadewijch in Letter 6, which succintly states the central theological point made by both beguine theologians. See Hadewijch, *Complete Works*, p. 59; and *Brieven*, p. 58; and *FL*, Bk. VII, Ch. 47, pp. 292–93. It is, moreover, a standard pattern found in the Cistercian mystics, although without the same emphasis on participating in the suffering of Christ.

45. It is also important that Mechthild tells this story from within the experience of the wounded soul, rather than in the external narrative modes of hagiography, with its emphasis on the visible actions and markings of the body. See Chapter 2.

46. See especially *FL*, Bk. I, Ch. 44, pp. 27–32; and Bk. VI, Ch. 31, pp. 238–40.

47. See, for example, *FL*, Bk. II, Ch. 25, pp. 63–64; and Bk. VI, Ch. 5, p. 211.

48. Ibid., Bk. VII, Ch. 50, pp. 297–98. Furthermore, it will clearly share in the joy of the resurrected soul. See Bk. VI, Ch. 35, pp. 243–44; and Bk. VII, Ch. 65, pp. 310–11.

49. Ibid., Bk. V, Ch. 23, p. 174; Bk. V, Ch. 30, pp. 189–90; Bk. VII, Ch. 6, pp. 261–62; Bk. VII, Ch. 38, p. 287; and Bk. VII, Ch. 56, p. 302.

50. See, for example, Porete's critique of those who remain in the life of the Spirit, *Mirouer*, Ch. 118, pp. 320–22, and Eckhart's comments about Mary in Ser. 86, *DW* 3: 481–92 (*Teacher*, pp. 327–31).

51. For the place of rapture in Eckhart's thought, see Robert K. C. Forman, "Eckhart, *Gezücken*, and the Ground of the Soul," in *The Problem of Pure Consciousness: Mysticism and Philosophy*, ed. Robert K. C. Forman (Oxford: Oxford University Press, 1990), pp. 98–120. The argument is made in the context of the collective volume's attempt to demonstrate the philosophical and textual evidence for experiences of pure consciousness against contextualist or constructivists such as Stephen Katz. While this is not the place to enter the debate, it should be noted that many of the experiences recorded by Mechthild in her work would not be considered "proper" mystical experiences according to Forman's definition. Thus, Forman does not pay adequate attention to the differences between Eckhart's discussion of Paul's rapture, which is given a reading in alignment with Eckhart's understanding of detachment, and the ecstasies and visions of his contemporaries. See Forman, "Introduction: Mysticism, Constructivism and Forgetting," in *Problem of Pure Consciousness*, pp. 3–49; and Stephen T. Katz, "Language, Epistemology and Mysticism," in *Mysticism and Philosophical Analysis*, ed. Stephen T. Katz (Oxford: Oxford University Press, 1978), pp. 22–74. For the few references in Eckhart to what might be understood as a rapturous or ecstatic state, see McGinn, "God Beyond God," pp. 16–17. Moreover, Eckhart clearly warns against such experiences and stresses the importance of the inner over external or sensible manifestations of the divine. See *On Detach.*, nn. 10, 15, 20, *DW* 5: 215–24, 240–44, 262–74; Ser. 86, *DW* 3: 482; Ser. 16b, *DW* 1: 272; and Ser. 66, *DW* 3L 113–114.

52. I am not claiming that Porete knew Mechthild's work, nor is it necessary to do so. I am tracing the development of a theological problematic, one of which there is every reason to believe Porete was aware and to which she responded.

53. On this issue, see Chapter 4.

54. *Mirouer*, Ch. 6, p. 24; and Ch. 8–9, pp. 28–34.

55. See Chapter 4.

56. *Mirouer*, Ch. 8, p. 30. Readers have commented that there seems to be a contradiction between Porete's and Eckhart's call for the soul to live without a why and my argument that they thereby desire to free humans from suffering. I think I have shown there is ample textual warrant for my claim. The tension lies within the texts, as we see here.

57. See *Mirouer*, Ch. 16–17, pp. 64–68; and this work, Chapter 4.

58. Despite the centrality of the body in the later Middle Ages, there is another strand of the Christian tradition in which the body is given a different and less important role. In this group of texts, beginning with Clement and Origen, thinkers have sought to use Middle Platonic and Neoplatonic philosophical categories to explain and elucidate the Christian faith. Eckhart clearly is located within this tradition, one that in the works of Origen, Pseudo-Dionysius, John the Scot, and others provides him with historical warrants for his relative neglect of both the bodily aspect of the Incarnation and the resurrection of the body. Allusions to a precreated aspect of the soul also raise the possibility of Porete's secondhand knowledge of or familiarity with certain aspects of Christian Neoplatonism. Yet, despite this philosophical background, I would argue that the attitudes of both Porete and Eckhart toward corporeality are much more the result of their responses to the spiritual climate in which they lived than of theological or literary influences. Neoplatonic traditions could function as warrants for mystical teachings, but they are not sufficient to explain their genesis, significance, or meaning. For Porete's possible ties, see Colledge and Marler, " 'Poverty of the Will.' "

59. See Schürmann, *Mystic and Philosopher*, pp. 108–10, and "Loss of Origin," pp. 303, 305–12.

60. See Mieth, *Einheit*, pp. 173–85; "Die theologische Transposition der Tugendethik," p. 63; McGinn, "God Beyond God," p. 18; and Kieckhefer, "Eckhart's Conception of Union," pp. 203–25.

61. See Eckhart, Ser. 4, *DW* 1: 71 (*Teacher*, p. 250); Ser. 25, *DW* 2: 17; *Par. Gen.*, n. 165, *LW* I: 634–36 (*Essential*, p. 121); *FL*, Bk. VII, Ch. 6, pp. 261–62; and Bk. VII, Ch. 38, p. 253.

62. Ser. 66, *DW* 3: 113–14.

63. See Ser. 16b, *DW* 1: 270–74 (*Teacher*, pp. 277–78); Ser. 29, *DW* 2: 109 (*Teacher*, p. 295); and *Detach.*, *DW* 5: 436–37 (*Essential*, p. 294).

64. Thus the widespread use of exempla and books of exempla as preaching manuals.

65. Schürmann, *Mystic and Philosopher*, p. 85.

66. See the Middle High German Glossary, *Teacher*, p. 403, for a full list of places in which Eckhart discusses the now or "*nû*".

67. See Chapter 2.

68. See Lerner, *Free Spirit*, pp. 112–19. Similar accounts were elicited from other beguines and beghards; see in particular John of Brunn's testimony against the beghards at Cologne. Ibid., pp. 108–9.

69. See Bynum, *Fragmentation*, pp. 38–40, 131–34, and Ch. 6; *Holy Feast*, pp. 208–18, 246–51; Roisin, *L'Hagiographie cistercienne*; McDonnell, *Beguines and Beghards*, pp. 299–339; Weinstein and Bell, *Saints*, pp. 233–35; Bolton, "*Mulieres Sanctae*"; Bolton, "*Vitae Matrum*";

Kieckhefer, *Unquiet Souls*, Ch. 3–5 and pp. 189–96; Vauchez, *Sainteté*, pp. 243–56, 426–27; Goodich, "*Vita Perfecta*," pp. 173–85; and this study, Chapter 2. Bynum shows, furthermore, the evidence for hostility to this asceticism among authorities and laypeople. See *Holy Feast*, pp. 84–87, 103–4, 237–49.

70. See, for examples, Schröder, *Engelthal*; Stagel, *Töss*; Ancelet-Hustache, "Unterlinden." Ascetic activities include group flagellations at Töss and binding themselves with nail-studded chains at Unterlinden. See also Otto Langer, "Zur dominikanische Frauenmystik im spätmittelalterlichen Deutschland," in *Frauenmystik im Mittelalter*, ed. Dinzelbacher and Bauer, pp. 341–46; Langer, *Mystische Erfahrung*, pp. 70–104; and Peter Ochsenbein, "Leidensmystik im dominikanische Frauenklöstern des 14. Jahrhunderts am Beispiel der Elsbeth von Oye," in *Religiöse Frauenbewegung*, ed. Dinzelbacher and Bauer, pp. 353–72. For a brief description of these lives, see Valerie Lagorio, "The Medieval Continental Women Mystics: An Introduction," in *Medieval Mystics*, pp. 172–73. Also Langer, *Mystische Erfahrungen*, pp. 47–155. McGinn is one of the most recent commentators to make the claim that Eckhart's position was a response to the proliferation of visions and bodily phenomena among beguines and nuns. He does not specifically mention their asceticism, but bodily phenomenan and asceticism go together in the lives. See McGinn, "Meister Eckhart: An Introduction," in *Medieval Mystics*, p. 248.

71. See this study, chapters 4 and 6.

72. Ser. 86, *DW* 3: 481–92 (*Teacher*, pp. 327–32); *Couns*. nn. 1–4, 11, 19, *DW* 5: 185–98, 224–31, 260–62 (*Essential*, pp. 247–51, 259–61, 270); and *Detach.*, *DW* 5: 400–434 (*Essential*, pp. 285–94).

73. *Mirouer*, Ch. 118, p. 322.

74. See *FL*, Bk. V, Ch. 5, pp. 159–60.

75. See also Trusen, *Der Prozess gegen Meister Eckhart*, pp. 19–61.

76. For other, more direct references, see the early *Counsels on Discernment* in which the spiritual nature of the imitation of Christ is stressed over its physical expression. *Couns, DW* 5: 185–309 (*Essential*, pp. 247–85).

77. This is made explicit in the *Couns*, nn. 16, 19, 21, 23, *DW* 5: 244–48, 260–62, 274–84, 290–309 (*Essential*, pp. 265–66, 270, 274–77, 280–85).

78. Again, this is not to claim a theological "victory" for Eckhart, but merely to try to show why he might have moved away from an aspect of the theological position found in Mechthild's text, a position to which he was otherwise deeply indebted. In my attempt to do justice to the theological richness of women's writings in the Middle Ages, it is important not to minimize certain areas of ambivalence that they themselves felt and with which they grappled.

79. It could be argued that Eckhart is attempting to save humanity from suffering itself, and in a number of sermons this seems to be the explicit claim. Thus in Sermon 76 he claims that the truly detached soul feels joy in suffering. The claim, however, is explicitly contradicted in Latin Sermon 45, the treatises, and in the very understanding of detachment itself, which is not a form of impassivity. Like Mechthild, Eckhart desires the soul to feel joy in suffering because it is the will of God, not in order to pervert human emotions. As Eckhart explains, the detached soul is able to feel sorrow and other painful emotions, but in its detachment it is not moved by them. See Ser. 76, DW 3: 329 (*Teacher*, p. 330); and Ser. XLV, LW 4: 374–87 (*Teacher*, pp. 227–34).

80. Ser. 86, DW 3: 481–92 (*Teacher*, pp. 327–32).

81. See Herbert Grundmann, "Die geschichtliche Grundlagen der deutschen Mystik," in *Altdeutsche und altniederländische Mystik*, ed. Kurt Ruh (Darmstadt: Wissenschaftliche Buchgesellschaft, 1964), pp. 72–99.

82. Ibid., p. 85. I have borrowed the English translation from McGinn, "Meister Eckhart," p. 243.

83. See Mieth, *Einheit*, pp. 198–207, where he makes similar points, although differently formulated.

84. This points to the problematic of grace and free will in Eckhart's work. Grace, for Eckhart, operates within the apophatic movements and is similarly paradoxical. For discussions of Eckhart on grace, see Tobin, *Meister Eckhart*, pp. 105–15; Lossky, *Théologie négative*, pp. 182–92; Caputo, "Fundamental Themes"; and Konrad Weiss, "Meister Eckhart der Mystiker," in *Freiheit und Gelassenheit. Meister Eckhart heute*, ed. Udo Kern (Munich: Kaiser, 1980), pp. 113–14.

85. See again Ser. 86, DW 3: 481–92 (*Teacher*, pp. 327–32) in which the nature of such activity is made explicit. See Chapter 6.

86. Ser. 6, DW 1: 248 (*Essential*, p. 187).

87. See Mieth, *Einheit*, pp. 173–75.

88. See Théry, "Édition Critique," p. 247.

89. The reference books for the use of confessors disseminated by the preaching orders were related to, yet markedly different in character from, the early medieval penitentials, in which punishments were prescribed in accordance with the seriousness of the sin. The confessors' books were more intent on deciding the seriousness of sins and giving justifications for these decisions and punishments. A popular example of such a book is the *Summa de casibus poenitentiae* by Raimundo de Penafort, master general of the Dominican order from 1237 to 1245. It was often included in *vade mecum* books used by traveling preachers and confessors. See D'Avray, *Preaching*, p. 51; and Albert R. Jonsen and Stephen Toulmin, *The*

Abuse of Casuistry: A History of Moral Reasoning (Berkeley: University of California Press, 1988), p. 255.

90. See Vernon J. Bourke, "Aquinas" in *Ethics in the History of Western Philosophy*, ed. Robert J. Cavalier, James Gouinlock, and James P. Sterba (New York: St. Martin's Press, 1989), p. 101.

91. See Bourke, "Aquinas."

92. See Chapter 6.

93. See Bourke, "Aquinas," p. 101. For an understanding of Aquinas's thought as a theoretical grounding for casuistry, see Jonsen and Toulmin, *Abuse*, pp. 135–36.

94. Aquinas, *STh* I-II. q. 18 aa. 10–11.

95. Carol Gilligan, *In a Different Voice* (Boston: Harvard University Press, 1982); and Carol Gilligan, Janie Victoria Ward, and Jill McLean Taylor, with Betty Bardige, *Mapping the Moral Domain* (Cambridge: Harvard University Graduate School of Education, 1988).

96. For a selection of the many philosophical applications, see Eva Feder Kittay and Diana T. Meyers, eds., *Women and Moral Theory* (Savage, Md.: Rowman and Littlefield, 1987); and Mary Jeanne Larrabee, ed., *An Ethic of Care: Feminist and Interdisciplinary Perspectives* (New York: Routledge, 1993). For a cogent philosophical critique of Gilligan's position, see Michele M. Moody-Adams, "Gender and the Complexity of Moral Symbols," in *Feminist Ethics*, ed. Claudia Card (Lawrence: University Press of Kansas, 1991), pp. 195–212. For one of many recent defenses of the importance of her research for contemporary women and girls, see Gayle Greene, "Looking at History," in *Changing Subjects: The Making of Feminist Literary Criticism*, ed. Gayle Greene and Coppélia Kahn (New York: Routledge, 1993), pp. 13–14.

97. Gilligan's arguments are in large part directed against the account of moral maturity given by Lawrence Kohlberg in such studies as *The Philosophy of Moral Development* (San Francisco: Harper and Row, 1981). Kohlberg was primarily indebted to Jean Piaget and John Rawls for his account of morality, and hence can be said to represent a Kantian position that stresses an ideal of rational morality grounded in disinterestedness. Again, this might sound much like Eckhart, and at least one recent philosopher has attempted to show the similarities between Kant and certain forms of mystical thought on the basis of Kant's "negative theology" with regard to the concept of God. It is easier, however, to see the enormous differences between the two, given what Eckhart could only have viewed as the Kantian idolatry of reason and Kant's own distaste for all things "mystical." The central point in this context is that important differences are elided when we refuse to distinguish between various philosophical and ethical positions. See Kevin Hart, *The Trespass of the*

Sign: Deconstruction, Theology, and Philosophy (Cambridge: Cambridge University Press, 1990), pp. 207–36.

98. In fact, he devotes uncharacteristic attention in one sermon to the probable state of the *body* after death, suggesting further affinities with Mechthild. See Ser. 57, *DW* 2: 594–606.

99. See Ariès, *Death*, pp. 40–46.

100. See Chapter 2.

101. Although it is possible to see the attractiveness of the ideal of detachment for medieval women as much, if not more, than for men, there is no way of knowing to what extent such a position was more difficult for them to sustain. My point in the following pages will be that we can find clear reasons why women would continue advancing positions like those found in Mechthild.

102. For more on the ways in which Eckhart subverts his own authority, see Sells, *Languages of Unsaying*, Chaps. 6–7.

103. Prophecy was explicitly open to women as a charismatic role, with ample biblical warrant, and separated out as such from the office of priesthood. See Aquinas, *STh* III, Supplement, q. 39, a. 1; and Ch. 1, above, n. 44.

104. See *FL*, Prologue, p. 5; and Bk. V, Ch. 34, p. 195. Also see her account of the way in which she came to write the book. *FL*, Bk. IV, Ch. 2, pp. 109–10.

105. The same is true of many other women. For a discussion of the way in which visions grant authority for Hildegard of Bingen and Elizabeth of Schönau, see Newman, *Sister of Wisdom*, pp. 34–41. For a more general discussion, see Bynum, *Fragmentation*, pp. 195–96; and Petroff, "Introduction."

106. For example, *FL*, Bk. II, Ch. 26, pp. 68–70; Bk. III, Ch. 1, pp. 78–79; Bk. V, Ch. 12, p. 166; and Bk. VI, Ch. 15, pp. 222–25.

107. On these claims, and Porete's continued ambivalence about them and about her book, see Chapter 4.

108. See Verdeyen, "Le Procès," p. 89; and Sells, *Languages of Unsaying*, p. 117.

109. For example, the validity of Mechthild's visions were questioned insofar as they seemed to disagree with theological orthodoxy. She was criticized for saying that John the Baptist said mass for her, as he was not a priest. She responds, defending her vision and its content. See *FL*, Bk. II, Ch. 4, pp. 40–44; and Bk. VI, Ch. 36, pp. 244–45.

110. This tendency is seen in Petroff, "Introduction"; Emilie Zum Brunn and Georgette Epiney-Burgard's introduction to their collection, *Women Mystics in Medieval Europe*, trans. Sheila Hughes (New York: Paragon House, 1989); and Régnier-Bohler, "Voix littéraires, voix mys-

tiques." The tendency is also found in Bynum's work, particularly *Holy Feast*, Ch. 10 and *Fragmentation*, Chaps. 1 and 6, although she makes other claims that work toward historical, cultural, and sociological explanations for certain characteristics seen to be peculiar to many women's writings. The position is allied with attempts, by some contemporary feminist literary critics, to discover a "feminist aesthetics." Generally grounded in psychological accounts of the nature of female or human development such as those of Carol Gilligan and Nancy Chodorow, as well as those of the so-called "French Feminists," these accounts argue for a particular type of feminine writing practice grounded in the particular nature of female psychology. As I shall argue, they are inadequate in dealing with medieval texts, which in fact call into question many contemporary assumptions about gender differentiation. Gilligan and Chodorow, moreover, both show the constructed nature of gender identity, thereby implicitly problematizing the ahistorical use of their theories. Many of the literary critics associated with "feminist aesthetics" also recognize this problem. See, for example, Gilligan, *In A Different Voice*; Nancy Chodorow, *The Reproduction of Mothering: Psychoanalysis and the Sociology of Gender* (Berkeley: University of California Press, 1978); Showalter, "Feminist Criticism in the Wilderness," pp. 243–70; Margaret Homans, *Bearing the Word: Language and Female Experience in Nineteenth-Century Women's Writing* (Chicago: University of Chicago Press, 1986), esp. Ch. 1; and Sandra M. Gilbert and Susan Gubar, *No Man's Land: The Place of the Woman Writer in the Twentieth Century*, vol. 1: *The War of the Words* (New Haven: Yale University Press, 1988), esp. pp. 227–71. For an interesting critique of this position and of the somewhat different ones associated with French feminist thought, see Rita Felski, *Beyond Feminist Aesthetics: Feminist Literature and Social Change* (Cambridge: Harvard University Press, 1989).

111. See "Schwester Katrei," in Franz-Josef Schweitzer, *Der Freiheitsbegriff der deutschen Mystik* (Frankfort am Main: Peter Lang, 1981), pp. 322–70. For a discussion of the text and a translation by Elvira Borgstadt, see *Teacher*, pp. 10–14 and 349–87. Other post-Eckhartian texts that stress these themes are the poems ascribed to Hadewijch II. See Saskia Murk Jansen, *The Measure of Mystic Thought: A Study of Hadewijch's Mengedichten* (Goppingen: Kummerle, 1991).

112. See Suso, "Life of the Servant"; and *Exemplum*, pp. 63–204. The text tells us that the bulk of it was written by Elsbet Stagel from conversations with Suso. Portions, however, were clearly also written by Suso himself and some argue for his strong editorial hand in the whole. The text is, moreover, clearly hagiographical. See *Exemplum*, pp. 38–40, 41–50.

113. See Bynum, *Holy Feast*, pp. 102–5.

114. *FL*, Bk. V, Ch. 12, p. 166. See also Bk. VI, Ch. 36, pp. 244–45. In a later book, Mechthild defends a criticized theological point on the basis of her experience of mystical relation to the divine rather than direct visionary counsel. See Bk. VI, Ch. 31, pp. 238–40. Yet in these last two books, God continues to speak in order to comfort the lamenting soul who is fearful about her constancy and desires a good end, and she records her condemnatory visions of the last days. He also directly reconfirms her writing mission. See Bk. VII, Ch. 36, p. 284.

115. See Hildegard of Bingen, *Scivias*, ed. Adelgundis Führkötter in Corpus christianorum: continuatio medievalis, vol. 43–43a (Turnhout: Brepols, 1978), "Protestificatio," pp. 3–6; Mechthild of Hackeborn, *Revelationes Gertrudianae ac Mechtildianae 2: Sancta Mechtildis virginis ordinis sancti Benedicti Liber specialis gratiae*, ed. monks of Solesmes (Paris, 1877), Bk. 1, Prologue, pp. 5–7; and Gertrud of Helfta, *Oeuvres spirituelles*, vol. 3: *Héraut III*, Prologue and Ch. 1, pp. 12–16.

116. See Ignatius Brady, *The Legend and Writings of Saint Clare of Assisi* (St. Bonaventure, N. Y.: The Franciscan Institute, 1953). Also see Chapter 2.

117. On his use of these strategies and their mystical significance, see Tobin, *Meister Eckhart*, pp. 158–92.

118. Ser. 6, DW 1: 244–53 (*Essential*, pp. 185–89).

119. See Schürmann, "Loss of Origin," pp. 305–12.

BIBLIOGRAPHY

MECHTHILD OF MAGDEBURG

Editions

Neumann, Hans, ed. *Mechthild von Magdeburg, 'Das fliessende Licht der Gottheit': Nach der Einsiedler Handschrift in kritischem Vergleich mit der gesamten Überlieferung*. 2 vols. Munich: Artemis Verlag, 1990–1993.

Modern Translations

Galvani, Christiane Mesch, trans. *Mechthild von Magdeburg: Flowing Light of the Divinity*. New York: Garland Publishing, 1991.

Menzies, Lucy, trans. *The Revelations of Mechthild of Magdeburg (1210–1297) or The Flowing Light of the Godhead*. London: Longmans, Green, 1953.

Schmidt, Margot, trans. *Das fliessende Licht der Gottheit*. Einsiedeln, Zurich, Cologne: Benziger, 1955.

Secondary Literature

Ancelet-Hustache, Jeanne. *Mechtilde de Magdebourg: Étude de psychologie religieuse*. Paris: Librairie Ancienne Honore Champion, 1926.

Balthasar, Hans Urs von. "Mechthilds kirchlicher Auftrag." In *Das fliessende Licht der Gottheit*. Trans. by Margot Schmidt. Einsiedeln, Zurich, Cologne: Benziger, 1955. Pp. 19–45.

Beer, Frances. *Women and Mystical Experience in the Middle Ages*. Rochester, N.Y.: Boydell, 1992.

Gooday, Francis. "Mechthild of Magdeburg and Hadewijch of Antwerp: A Comparison." *Ons Geestelijk Erf* 48 (1974): 305–62.

297

Haas, Alois. "Mechthild von Magdeburg—Dichtung und Mystik." In *Sermo mysticus. Studien zu Theologie und Sprache der deutschen Mystik.* Freiburg: Universitätsverlag, 1979. Pp. 67–103.

Haas, Alois. "Die Struktur der mystischen Erfahrung nach Mechthild von Magdeburg." In *Sermo mysticus. Studien zu Theologie und Sprache der deutschen Mystik.* Freiburg: Universitätsverlag, 1979. Pp. 104–35.

Haug, Walter. "Das Gespräch mit dem unvergleichlichen Partner. Der mystische Dialog bei Mechthild von Magdeburg als Paradigma für eine personale Gesprächsstruktur." In *Das Gespräch.* Ed. K. Stierle and R. Warning. Munich: W. Fink, 1984. Pp. 251–79.

Heimbach, Marianne. *"Der ungelehrte Mund" als Autorität. Mystische Erfahrung als Quelle kirchlich-prophetischer Rede im Werk Mechthilds von Magdeburg.* Stuttgart-Bad Cannstatt: Frommann-holzboog, 1989.

Kemper, Hans-Georg. "Allegorische Allegorese. Zur Bildlichkeit und Struktur mystischer Literatur (Mechthild von Magdeburg und Angelus Silesius)." In *Formen und Funktionen der Allegorie.* Ed. Walter Haug. Stuttgart: Metzler, 1979. Pp. 90–125.

Lüers, Grete. *Die Sprache der deutschen Mystik des Mittelalters im Werke der Mechthild von Magdeburg.* Munich: Ernst Reinhardt, 1926.

Mohr, Wolfgang. "Darbietungsformen der Mystik bei Mechthild von Magdeburg." In *Märchen, Mythos, Dichtung: Festschrift zum 90. Geburtstag Friedrich von der Leyens am 19. August 1963.* Ed. Hugo Kuhn and K. Schier. Munich: Beck, 1963. Pp. 375–99.

Nellmann, Eberhard. "*Dis buch . . . bezeichent alleine mich*—Zum Prolog von Mechthilds 'Fliessendem Licht der Gottheit." In *Gotes und der Werlde Hulde: Literatur in Mittelalter und Neuzeit: Festschrift für Heinz Rupp.* Ed. Rüdiger Schnell. Stuttgart: Francke, 1989. Pp. 200–205.

Neumann, Hans. "Beiträge zur Textgeschichte des 'Fliessende Lichts der Gottheit,' und zur Lebensgeschichte Mechthilds von Magdeburg." *Nachrichten der Akademie der Wissenschaften in Göttingen, Philologisch-historische Klasse* (1954): 27–80.

Neumann, Hans. "Mechthild von Magdeburg und die mittelniederländische Frauenmystik." *Medieval German Studies Presented to Frederick Norman.* London: Institute of Germanic Studies, 1965. Pp. 231–46.

Ruh, Kurt. "Beginenmystik. Hadewijch, Mechthild von Magdeburg, Marguerite Porete." *Zeitschrift für deutsches Altertum und deutsche Literatur* 106 (1977): 265–77.

Schmidt, Margot. "Elemente der Schau bei Mechthild von Magdeburg und Mechthild von Hackeborn. Zur Bedeutung der geistlichen Sinne."

In *Frauenmystik im Mittelalter*. Ed. Peter Dinzelbacher and Dieter R. Bauer. Ostfildern: Schwabenverlag, 1985. Pp. 123–51.

Schmidt, Margot. "Mechtilde de Magdebourg." *Dictionnaire de spiritualité, ascétique et mystique, doctrine et histoire*. Ed. M. Viller et al. Paris: Beauchesne, 1937– . Vol. 10: cols. 877–85.

Schmidt, Margot. " 'minne dú gewaltige kellerin.' On the nature of minne in Mechthild of Magdeburg's 'fliessende lieht der gotheit.' " *Vox Benedictina* 4 (1987): 100–125.

Schmidt, Margot. " 'Die spilende minnevluot.' Der Eros als Sein und Wirkkraft in der Trinität bei Mechthild von Magdeburg." In *"Eine Höhe, über die nichts geht." Spezielle Glaubenserfahrung in der Frauenmystik?* Ed. Dieter R. Bauer and Margot Schmidt. Stuttgart-Bad, Connstatt: Fromann-holzboog, 1986. Pp. 71–133.

Sinka, Margit. "Christological Mysticism in Mechthild von Magdeburg's *Das Fliessende Licht der Gottheit*: A Journey of Wounds." *The Germanic Review* 60 (1985): 123–28.

Tax, Petrus. "Die grosse Himmelsschau bei Mechthild von Magdeburg und ihre Höllenvision. Aspekte des Erfahrungshorizontes, der Gegenbildlichkeit und der Parodierung." *Zeitschrift für deutsches Altertum und deutsche Literatur* 108 (1979): 112–37.

Tillmann, Heinz. "Studien zum Dialog bei Mechthild von Magdeburg." Ph. D. dissertation, Marburg, 1933.

Wainwright-de Kadt, Elizabeth. "Courtly literature and mysticism: some aspects of their interaction." *Acta Germanica* 12 (1980): 41–60.

Wiethaus, Ulrike. "Sexuality, Gender, and the Body in Late Medieval Women's Spirituality: Cases from Germany and the Netherlands." *Journal of Feminist Studies in Religion* 7 (1991): 35–52.

Wiethaus, Ulrike. "Suffering, Love and Transformation in Mechthild of Magdeburg." *Listening* 22 (1987): 139–51.

MARGUERITE PORETE

Editions

Guarnieri, Romana and Paul Verdeyen, eds. *Le Mirouer des simples ames anienties et qui seulement demourent en vouloir et desir d'amour*. In Corpus Christianorum: Continuatio Mediaevalis. Vol. 69. Turnhout: Brepols, 1986.

Modern Translations

Babinsky, Ellen, trans. *Marguerite Porete: The Mirror of Simple Souls.* New York: Paulist Press, 1993.

Longchamp, Max Huot de, trans. *Marguerite Porete. Le Miroir des âmes simples et anéanties.* Paris: Albin Michel, 1984.

Secondary Literature

Babinsky, Ellen. "A Beguine at the Court of the King: The Relation of Love and Knowledge in the *Mirror of Simple Souls* by Marguerite Porete." Ph. D. dissertation, University of Chicago, 1991.

Colledge, Edmund. "Liberty of Spirit: 'The Mirror of Simple Souls.'" In *Theology of Renewal.* Ed. L. K. Shook. 2 vols. Montreal: Palm Publishers, 1968. 2: 100–17.

Colledge, Edmund and Romana Guarnieri. "The Glosses by 'M.N.' and Richard Methley to 'The Mirror of Simple Souls.'" *Archivio Italiano per la storia della pietà* 5 (1968): 357–82.

Guarnieri, Romana. "Frères du Libre Esprit." *Dictionnaire de spiritualité, ascétique et mystique, doctrine et histoire.* Ed. M. Viller et al. Paris: Beauchesne, 1937–. Vol. 5: cols. 1241–1268.

Guarnieri, Romana, ed. "Il movimento del Libero Spirito." *Archivio Italiano per la storia della pietà* 4 (1965): 351–708. The text of the *Mirouer* is given in pp. 513–635.

Lerner, Robert. *The Heresy of the Free Spirit in the Later Middle Ages.* Berkeley: University of California Press, 1972.

McLaughlin, E. C. "The Heresy of the Free Spirit and Late Medieval Mysticism." *Medievalia et Humanistica* 4 (1973): 37–54.

Mommaers, P. "La transformation d'amour selon Marguerite Porete." *Ons Geestelijk Erf* 65 (1991): 89–107.

Orcibal, Jean. "'Le Miroir des simples ames' et la 'secte' du Libre Esprit." *Revue de l'histoire des religions* 175 (1969): 35–60.

Ruh, Kurt. "'Le Miroir des Simples Ames' der Marguerite Porete." In *Verbum et Signum: Festschrift für Friedrich Ohly.* Ed. H. Fromm, W. Harms, and U. Ruberg. Munich: W. Fink, 1975. Pp. 365–87.

Schweitzer, Franz-Josef. "Von Marguerite von Porete (d. 1310) bis Mme. Guyon (d. 1717): Frauenmystik im Konflikt mit der Kirche." In *Frauenmystik im Mittelalter.* Ed. Peter Dinzelbacher and Dieter R. Bauer. Ostfildern: Schwabenverlag, 1985. Pp. 256–74.

Sells, Michael. *Mystical Languages of Unsaying.* Chicago: University of Chicago Press, 1994.

Verdeyen, Paul. "Le Procès d'Inquisition contre Marguerite Porete et Guiard de Cressonessart (1309–1310)." *Revue d' Histoire Ecclésiastique* 81 (1986): 47–94.

MEISTER ECKHART

Editions

Koch, Josef and Josef Quint, eds. *Meister Eckhart. Die deutschen und lateinischen Werke.* Stuttgart and Berlin: W. Kohlhammer, 1936–.

Laurent, M.-H., ed. "Autour du procès de Maître Eckhart. Les documents des Archives Vaticanes." *Divus Thomas* (Piacenza). Ser. III, 13 (1936): 331–48, 430–47.

Pelster, Franz, ed. "Ein Gutachten aus dem Eckehart-Prozess in Avignon." *Aus der Geisteswelt des Mittelalters. Festgabe Martin Grabmann (Beiträge Supplement III)*. Munster: n. p., 1935. Pp. 1099–1124.

Pfeiffer, Franz, ed. *Deutsche Mystiker des vierzehnten Jahrhunderts.* Vol. 2: *Meister Eckhart, Predigten und Traktate.* Leipzig: Göshen, 1857, and Aalen: Scientia Verlag, 1962.

Théry, Gabriel. "Édition critique des pièces relatives au procès d'Eckhart contenues dans le manuscrit 33b de la Bibliothèque de Soest." *Archives d'histoire littéraire et doctrinal du moyen âge* 1 (1926): 129–268.

Modern Translations

Colledge, Edmund and Bernard McGinn, trans. *Meister Eckhart: The Essential Sermons, Commentaries, Treatises and Defense.* New York: Paulist Press, 1981.

McGinn, Bernard with Frank Tobin and Elvira Borgstädt, trans. *Meister Eckhart: Teacher and Preacher.* New York: Paulist Press, 1986.

Maurer, Armand, trans. *Master Eckhart. Parisian Questions and Prologues.* Toronto: Pontifical Institute of Medieval Studies, 1974.

Schürmann, Reiner. *Meister Eckhart. Mystic and Philosopher.* Bloomington: Indiana University Press, 1978. Includes translations of eight sermons.

Walshe, M. O'C., trans. *Meister Eckhart: German Sermons and Treatises.* 3 vols. London and Dulverton: Watkins, 1979–83.

Secondary Literature

Ancelet-Hustache, Jeanne. *Master Eckhart and the Rhineland Mystics.* Trans. Hilda Graef. New York: Harper, 1957.

Brunner, Fernand. "L'analogie chez Maître Eckhart." *Freiburger Zeitschrift für Philosophie und Theologie* 16 (1969): 333–49.

Caputo, John. "Fundamental Themes in Meister Eckhart's Mysticism." *The Thomist* 42 (1978): 197–225.

Caputo, John. *The Mystical Element in Heidegger's Thought*. Athens, Ohio: Ohio University Press, 1978.

Caputo, John. "Mysticism and Transgression: Meister Eckhart and Derrida." In *Derrida and Deconstruction*. Ed. Hugh J. Silverman. New York: Routledge, 1989. Pp. 4–39.

Caputo, John. "The Nothingness of the Intellect in Meister Eckhart's 'Parisian Questions.'" *The Thomist* 39 (1975): 85–115.

Colledge, Edmund and J. C. Marler. "'Poverty of the Will': Ruusbroec, Eckhart and *The Mirror of Simple Souls*." In *Jan van Ruusbroec: The Sources, Content, and Sequels of His Mysticism*. Ed. P. Mommaers and N. de Paepe. Leuven: Leuven University Press, 1984. Pp. 14–57.

Davies, Oliver. *Meister Eckhart: Mystical Theologian*. London: SPCK, 1991.

Duclow, Donald. "'My Suffering is God': Meister Eckhart's *Book of Divine Consolation*." *Theological Studies* 44 (1983): 570–86.

Forman, Robert K. C. "Eckhart, *Gezücken*, and the Ground of the Soul." In *The Problem of Pure Consciousness*. Ed. Robert K. C. Forman. Oxford: Oxford University Press, 1990. Pp. 98–120.

Gandillac, M. de. "La 'dialectique' de Maître Eckhart." In *La mystique rhénane. Colloque de Strasbourg 1961*. Paris: Presses Universitaires de France, 1963. Pp. 59–94.

Haas, Alois. *Geistliches Mittelalter*. Freiburg: Universitätsverlag, 1984.

Haas, Alois. "Seinsspekulation und Geschöpflichkeit in der Mystik Meister Eckharts." In *Sein und Nichts in der Abendländischen Mystik*. Ed. by Walter Strolz. Freiburg: Herder, 1984. Pp. 33–58.

Haas, Alois. *Sermo mysticus. Studien zu Theologie und Sprache der deutschen Mystik*. Freiburg: Universitätsverlag, 1979.

Hof, Hans. *Scintilla animae: Eine Studien zu einem Grundbegriff in Meister Eckharts Philosophie*. Lund: Gleerup, 1952.

Imbach, Ruedi. *Deus ist Intelligere: Das Verhältnis von Sein und Denken in seiner Bedeutung für das Gottesverständnis bei Thomas von Aquin und in den Pariser Quaestionen Meister Eckharts*. Freiburg: Universitätsverlag, 1976.

Kelley, C. F. *Meister Eckhart on Divine Knowledge*. New Haven: Yale University Press, 1977.

Kieckhefer, Richard. "Meister Eckhart's Conception of Union with God." *Harvard Theological Review* 71 (1978): 203–25.

Koch, Josef. "Kritische Studien zum Leben Meister Eckharts." *Archivium Fratrum Praedicatorum* 29 (1959): 5–51; 30 (1960): 5–52.

Koch, Josef. "Zur Analogielehre Meister Eckharts." In *Mélanges offerts à Etienne Gilson*. Paris: Vrin, 1959. Pp. 327–50.

Langer, Otto. *Mystische Erfahrung und spirituelle Theologie. Zu Meister Eckharts Auseinandersetzung mit der Frauenfrömmigkeit seiner Zeit.* Münchener Texte und Untersuchungen zur deutschen Literatur des Mittelalters 91. Munich: Artemis, 1987.

Lanzetta, Beverly. "Three Categories of Nothingness in Eckhart." *Journal of Religion* (1992): 248–68.

Libera, Alain de. "A propos de quelques théories logiques de Maître Eckhart: existe-t-il une tradition médiévale de la logique néo-platonicienne." *Revue de théologie et philosophie* 113 (1981): 1–24.

Libera, Alain de. *Le problème de l'être chez Maître Eckhart: Logique et métaphysique de l'analogie*. Geneva: Cahiers de la revue de théologie et de philosophie 4, 1980.

Libera, Alain de and Emilie zum Brunn. *Maître Eckhart: Métaphysique du Verbe et théologie négative*. Paris: Beauchesne, 1984.

Lossky, Vladimir. *Théologie négative et connaissance de Dieu chez Maître Eckhart*. Paris: Vrin, 1960.

McGinn, Bernard. "Eckhart's Condemnation Reconsidered." *The Thomist* 44 (1980): 390–414.

McGinn, Bernard. "The God Beyond God: Theology and Mysticism in the Thought of Meister Eckhart." *Journal of Religion* 61 (1981): 1–19.

McGinn, Bernard. "Meister Eckhart: An Introduction." In *An Introduction to the Medieval Mystics of Europe*. Ed. Paul Szarmach. Albany: State University of New York Press, 1984. Pp. 237–57.

McGinn, Bernard. "Meister Eckhart on God as Absolute Unity." In *Neoplatonism and Christian Thought*. Ed. Dominic J. O'Meara. Norfolk, Va.: International Society for Neoplatonic Studies, 1982. Pp. 128–39.

McGinn, Bernard. "St. Bernard and Meister Eckhart." *Cîteaux* 31 (1980): 373–86.

Malherbe, Jean-François. *"Souffrir Dieu": La prédication de Maître Eckhart*. Paris: Cerf, 1992.

Mieth, Dietmar. *Die Einheit von Vita Activa und Vita Contemplativa in den deutschen Predigten und Traktaten Meister Eckharts und bei Johannes Tauler*. Regensburg: Verlag Friedrich Pustet, 1969.

Mieth, Dietmar. "Meister Eckhart: Authentische Erfahrung als Einheit von Denken, Sein und Leben." In *Das "einig Ein": Studien zu Theorie und Sprach der deutschen Mystik*. Ed. Alois Haas and Heinrich Stirnimann. Freiburg: Universitätsverlag, 1980. Pp. 11–61.

Mieth, Dietmar. "Die theologische Transposition der Tugendethik bei Meister Eckhart." In *Abendländische Mystik im Mittelalter.* Ed. Kurt Ruh. Stuttgart: J. B. Metzlersche Verlagsbuchhandlung, 1986. Pp. 63–79.

Ruh, Kurt. "Meister Eckhart und die Beginenspiritualität." In *Kleine Schriften.* 2 vols. Berlin: W. de Gruyter, 1984. 1: 327–36.

Ruh, Kurt. "Meister Eckhart und die Spiritualität der Beginen." *Perspektiven der Philosophie* 8 (1982): 322–34.

Ruh, Kurt. *Meister Eckhart: Theologe, Prediger, Mystiker.* Munich: C. H. Beck, 1985.

Schmoldt, Benno. *Die deutsche Begriffsprache Meister Eckharts.* Heidelberg: Quelle and Meyer, 1954.

Schürmann, Reiner. "The Loss of Origin in Soto Zen and in Meister Eckhart." *The Thomist* 42 (1978): 281–312.

Sells, Michael. "The Metaphor and Dialectic of Emanation in Plotinus, John the Scot, Meister Eckhart, and Ibn Arabi." Ph. D. dissertation, University of Chicago, 1982.

Tobin, Frank. "Eckhart's Mystical Use of Language: The Contexts of *eigenschaft.*" *Seminar* 8 (1972): 160–68.

Tobin, Frank. *Meister Eckhart: Thought and Language.* Philadelphia: University of Pennsylvania Press, 1986.

Trusen, Winfried. *Der Prozess gegen Meister Eckhart: Vorgeschichte, Verlauf und Folgen.* Paderborn: Schöningh, 1988.

Ueda, Shizuteru. *Die Gottesgeburt in der Seele und der Durchbruch zur Gottheit. Die mystische Anthropologie Meister Eckharts und ihre Konfrontation mit der Mystik des Zen-Buddhismus.* Gütersloh: Mohn, 1965.

Weiss, Konrad. "Meister Eckhart der Mystiker." In *Freiheit und Gelassenheit; Meister Eckhart heute.* Ed. Udo Kern. Munich: Kaiser, 1980.

Welte, Bernard. "Meister Eckhart als Aristoteliker." *Philosophisches Jahrbuch der Görres Gesellschaft* 69 (1961): 64–74.

Welte, Bernard. "Rückblick auf die Metaphysik. Thomas von Aquin und Heideggers Gedanke von der Seinsgeschichte." *Wort und Wahrheit* 22 (1967): 747–57.

Zum Brunn, Emilie. "Une source méconnue de l'ontologie eckhartienne." In *Métaphysique, Histoire de la philosophie, Hommage à Fernand Brunner.* Neuchâtel: Édition de la Baconniére, 1981. Pp. 111–18.

OTHER PRIMARY SOURCES

Albanés, J. H., ed. *La Vie de Sainte Douceline.* Marseilles: Camoin, 1879.

Ancelet-Hustache, Jeanne, ed. "Les '*Vitae Sororum*' d'Unterlinden. Edition critique du Manuscrit 508 de la Bibliothèque de Colmar." *Archives d'histoire doctrinale et littéraire du moyen âge* 5 (1930): 317–509.

Angela of Foligno. *Il libro della Beata Angela da Foligno (Edizione critica)*. Ed. Ludger Thier and Abele Calufetti. Grottaferrata: Editiones Collegii S. Bonaventurae ad Claras Aquas, 1985. *Angela of Foligno: Complete Works*. Trans. Paul Lachance. New York: Paulist Press, 1993.

Anselm of Canterbury. *Cur Deus Homo*. In *Sancti Anselmi Cantuariensis Archiepiscopi Opera Omnia*. Ed. F. S. Schmitt. 5 vols. Edinburgh: Nelson, 1946–51. 2: 42–133. Trans. Eugene R. Fairweather. In *A Scholastic Miscellany: Anselm to Ockham*. Philadelphia: Westminster Press, 1956. Pp. 100–183.

Augustine of Hippo. *Confessions*. 2 vols. Loeb Classical Library. Cambridge: Harvard University Press, 1989. Trans. R. S. Pine-Coffin. London: Penguin Books, 1961.

Augustine of Hippo. *De Doctrina Christiana*. In *Patrologiae cursus completus: Series latina*. Ed. J.-P. Migne. Paris: Garnier, 1844–64. Vol. 34: cols. 15–122. *On Christian Doctrine*. Trans. D. W. Robertson. Indianapolis: Bobbs-Merrill, 1958.

Augustine of Hippo. *De Genesi ad litteram*. In *Patrologiae cursus completus: Series latina*. Ed. J.-P. Migne. Paris: Garnier, 1844–64. Vol. 34: cols. 245–486.

Augustine of Hippo. *Epistolae*. In *Patrolgiae cursus completus: Series latina*. Ed. J.-P. Migne. Paris: Garnier, 1844–64. Vol. 33.

Bächtold, J., ed. "Die Stiftung des Klosters Ötenbach und das Leben der seligen Schwestern daselbt." *Zürcher Taschenbuch* N.F. 12 (1889): 213–76.

Beatrice of Nazareth. *Seven Manieren van Minne*. Ed. L. Reypens and J. Van Mierlo. Leuven: S.V. de Vlaamsche Boekenhalle, 1926. "There Are Seven Manners of Loving." Trans. Eric Colledge. In *Medieval Women's Visionary Literature* Ed. Elizabeth Alvilda Petroff. Oxford: Oxford University Press, 1986. Pp 200–206.

Beatrice of Nazareth. *Vita Beatricis: De Autobiografie van de Z. Beatrijs van Tienen O. Cist. 1200–68*. Ed. L. Reypens. Antwerp: Ruusbroec-Genootschap, 1964. *The Life of Beatrice of Nazareth*. Trans. and annotated by Roger DeGanck. Kalamazoo: Cistercian Publications, 1991.

Bernard of Clairvaux. *Liber de diligendo Deo*. In *Sancti Bernardi Opera*. Ed. J. Leclercq and H. M. Rochais. 8 vols. Rome: Editiones Cistercienses, 1957–77. Vol. 3. Trans. Robert Walton. In *Treatises II*. Kalamazoo: Cistercian Publications, 1973.

Bernard of Clairvaux. *Sermones super Cantica canticorum.* In *Sancti Bernardi Opera.* Ed. J. Leclercq and H. M. Rochais. 8 vols. Rome: Editiones Cistercienses, 1957–77. Vols. 1 and 2.

On the Song of Songs I. Trans. Kilian Walsh. Kalamazoo: Cistercian Publications, 1971. *On the Song of Songs II.* Trans. Kilian Walsh. Kalamazoo: Cistercian Publications, 1976. *On the Song of Songs III.* Trans. Kilian Walsh and Irene Edmunds. Kalamazoo: Cistercian Publications, 1979. *On the Song of Songs IV.* Trans. Irene Edmunds. Kalamazoo: Cistercian Publications, 1980.

Brady, Ignatius, ed. and trans. *The Legend and Writings of Saint Clare of Assisi.* St. Bonaventure, N.Y.: The Franciscan Institute, 1953.

Christ, Karl, ed. "La regle des fins amans. Eine Beginen-regal aus dem Ende des XIII Jahrhunderts." In *Philologische Studien aus dem romanisch-germanischen Kulturkreise. Festschrift für K. Voretzsch.* Halle: n. p., 1927. Pp. 192–206.

Dante Alighieri. *The Divine Comedy. Paradise: Text and Commentary.* Trans. Charles C. Singleton. Princeton: Princeton University Press, 1975.

Dietrich of Apolda. *Acta Ampliora S. Dominici Confessoris.* In *Acta Sanctorum.* Ed. J. Bolland, G. Henschenius et al. Brussels: Culture et civilisation, 1965–70. Originally published 1643–1940. Hereafter, *AASS.* August 1. Vol. 34. Pp. 562–632.

Fredericq, Paul. *Corpus documentorum inquisitionis haereticae pravitatis neerlandicae.* 2 vols. Ghent: The Hague, 1889–1906.

Fry, Timothy, ed. *The Rule of Saint Benedict: 1980.* Collegeville, Minn.: The Liturgical Press, 1980.

Gertrude of Helfta. *Oeuvres spirituelles.* Vol. I: *Les Exercices.* Ed. Jacques Hourlier and Albert Schmitt. In Sources chrétiennes, vol. 127. Paris: Cerf, 1967. *Oeuvres spirituelles.* Vol. II: *Le Héraut I and II.* Ed. Pierre Doyère. In Sources chrétiennes, vol. 139. Paris: Cerf, 1968. *Oeuvres spirituelles.* Vol. III: *Le Héraut III.* Ed. Pierre Doyère. In Sources chrétiennes, vol. 143. Paris: Cerf, 1968.

Gertrude the Great of Helfta: Spiritual Exercises. Trans. Gertrud Jaron Lewis and Jack Lewis. Kalamazoo: Cistercian Publications, 1989. *The Herald of God's Loving-Kindness: Books One and Two.* Trans. Alexandra Barratt. Kalamazoo: Cistercian Publications, 1991. *Gertrude of Helfta: The Herald of Divine Love.* Trans. Margaret Winkworth. New York: Paulist Press, 1993.

Guibert of Nogent. *De pignoribus.* In *Patrologiae cursus completus: Series latina.* Ed. J.-P. Migne. Paris: Garnier, 1844–64. Vol. 156. Cols. 607–80.

Guillaume de Lorris and Jean de Meun. *Le Roman de la Rose*. Ed. Daniel Porion. Paris: Garnier-Flammarion, 1974. *The Romance of the Rose*. Trans. Harry W. Robbins. New York: E. P. Dutton, 1962.

Hadewijch. *Brieven*. Ed. Jozef Van Mierlo. 2 vols. Antwerp: Standaard, 1947.

Hadewijch: *The Complete Works*. Trans. Mother Columba Hart. 1 vol. New York: Paulist Press, 1980.

Hildegard of Bingen. *Scivias*. Ed. Adelgundis Führkötter. In Corpus Christianorum: Continuatio Medievalis. Vols. 43–43a. Turnhout: Brepols, 1978. Trans. Mother Columba Hart and Jane Bishop. New York: Paulist Press, 1990.

Hugh of Floreffe. *Vita Ivetta Reclusa Huyi*. AASS. Jan. 1. Vol. 1: 863–87.

Jacques of Vitry. *Vita Mariae Oignacensis*. AASS. June 4. Vol. 23: 630–66. *The Life of Marie d'Oignies*. Trans. Margot H. King. Toronto: Peregrina Publishing, 1989. Rev. ed.

Joachim of Fiore. *Expositio de prophetia ignota*. Ed. Bernard McGinn. In "Joachim and the Sibyl." *Cîteaux* 24 (1973): 129–38.

Julian of Norwich. *A Book of Showings to the Anchoress Julian of Norwich*. Ed. Edmund Colledge and James Walsh. Toronto: Pontifical Institute of Medieval Studies, 1978. *Showings*. Trans. Edmund Colledge and James Walsh. New York: Paulist Press, 1978.

Kempe, Margery. *The Book of Margery Kempe*. Ed. Sanford Meech and Hope Emily Allen. EETS, o.s. 212. London: Oxford University Press, 1940. Trans. Barry A. Windeatt. New York: Penguin, 1985.

Marguerite of Oingt. *Les Oeuvres de Marguerite d'Oingt*. Ed. and trans. Antonin Duraffour, Pierre Gardette, and Paulette Durdilly. Paris: Belles Lettres, 1965.

Mechthild of Hackeborn. *Revelationes Gertrudianae ac Mechtildianae 2: Sancta Mechtildis virginis ordinis sancti Benedicti Liber specialis gratiae*. Ed. monks of Solesmes. Paris: Oudin, 1877.

Petroff, Elizabeth Alvilda, ed. *Medieval Women's Visionary Literature*. Oxford: Oxford University Press, 1986.

Philip of Harvengt. *Vita beatae Odae*. Patrologiae cursus completus: Series latina. Ed. J.-P. Migne. Paris: Garnier, 1844–64. Vol. 203: cols. 1359–74.

Ruusbroec, John. *De ornatu spiritalium nuptiarum/ Die Geestelike Brulocht*. Ed. J. Alaerts. Trans. H. Rolfson. In Corpus Christianorum: Continuatio Medievalis. Vol. 103. Turnhout: Brepols, 1988.

Schröder, Karl, ed. *Der Nonne von Engelthal Büchlein von der Genaden Überlast*. Tübingen: Literarischer Verein in Stuttgart, 1871.

Schweitzer, Franz-Josef, ed. "Schwester Katrei." In *Der Freiheitsbegriff der deutschen Mystik*. Frankfort am Main: Peter Lang, 1981. Pp. 322–70. "The Sister Catherine Treatise." Trans. by Elvira Borgstädt. In *Meister Eckhart: Teacher and Preacher*. Trans. Bernard McGinn with Frank Tobin and Elvira Borgstädt. New York: Paulist Press, 1986. Pp. 349–87.

Stagel, Elsbet. *Das Leben der Schwestern zu Töss beschrieben von Elsbet Stagel*. Ed. Ferdinand Vetter. Berlin: Weidmannsche Buchhandlung, 1906.

Suso, Heinrich. *Heinrich Seuse: Deutsche Schriften im Auftrag der Wurttenbergischen Kommission für Landesgeschichte*. Ed. Karl Bihlmeyer. Stuttgart: Kohlhammer, 1907. *The Exemplar with Two German Sermons*. Trans. Frank Tobin. New York: Paulist Press, 1989.

Thomas Aquinas. *Sententia super Peri hermenias II*. In *Sancti Thomae Aquinatis Opera Omnia*. Parma: Fiaccadori, 1865. 18: 1–83.

Thomas Aquinas. *Summa Theologiae*. Blackfriars ed. 61 vols. New York: McGraw-Hill, 1964–81.

Thomas of Cantimpré. *Vita Mariae Oigniacensis Supplementum, AASS*. June 4. Vol. 23: 666–84. *Supplement to the Life of Marie d'Oignies*. Trans. by Hugh Feiss. Toronto: Peregrina Publishing, 1990. 2d ed.

Thomas of Cantimpré. *Vita S. Christinae Mirabilis. AASS*. July 5. Vol. 31: 637–60. *The Life of Christina Mirabilis*. Trans. Margot H. King. Toronto: Peregrina Publishing, 1986.

Thomas of Cantimpré. *Vita Lutgardis Virgine. AASS*. July 3. Vol 22: 234–62. *The Life of Lutgard of Aywières*. Trans. Margot H. King. Toronto: Peregrina Publishing, 1991. Rev. ed.

Thomas of Cantimpré. *Vita Margarete de Ypris*. In "Les Fréres Prêcheurs et le Mouvement Dévot en Flandre au XIIIe Siècle." Ed. G. Meersseman. *Archivium Fratrum Praedicatorum* 17 (1947): 106–130. *The Life of Margaret of Ypres*. Trans. Margot H. King. Toronto: Peregrina Publishing, 1990.

Viard, Jules. *Les grandes chroniques de France*. Paris, 1934.

Vita Aleydis de Scarembecanae. AASS. June 2. Vol. 21: 476–83.

Vita Arnulfu. AASS. June 30. Vol. 24: 606–31.

Vita Gerdrudis ab Oosten virginis. AASS. Jan. 1. Vol. 1: 348–53.

Vita Idae Lewensis. AASS. Oct. 13. Vol. 60: 100–124.

Vita Idae Lovaniensis. AASS. April 2. Vol. 10: 155–89.

Vita Idae Nivellensis. Prologue and excerpts. In *Catalogus Codicum Hagiographorum Bibliothecae Regiae Bruxellensis*. 2 vols. Vol. 2: 222–28.

Vita Iulianae Corneliensis. AASS. April 1. Vol. 9: 437–77. *The Life of the Blessed Juliana of Mont-Cornillon*. Trans. Barbara Newman. Toronto: Peregrina Publishing, 1989.

Vita Venerabilis Lukardis. Analecta Bollandiana 18 (1899): 303–67.
Vitae B. Odiliae. Analecta Bollandiana 13 (1844): 197–287.
William of Saint Thierry. *Lettre aux Frères du Mont-Dieu (Lettre d'or).*
  Ed. Jean Déchanet. In Sources chrétiennes. Vol. 223. Paris: Editions du
  Cerf, 1985. *The Golden Epistle.* Trans. Theodore Berkeley. Kalama-
  zoo: Cistercian Publications, 1980.
Zum Brunn, Emilie and Georgette Epinay-Burgard, eds. *Women Mystics
  in Medieval Europe.* Trans. Sheila Hughes. New York: Paragon House,
  1989.

OTHER SECONDARY SOURCES CITED

Aers, David. "A Whisper in the Ear of Early Modernists: or, Reflections
  on Literary Critics Writing the 'History of the Subject'." In *Culture
  and History 1350–1600: Essays on English Communities, Identities
  and Writing.* Ed. David Aers. Detroit: Wayne State University Press,
  1992. Pp. 177–202.
Ariès, Philippe. *Western Attitudes toward Death from the Middle Ages
  to the Present.* Trans. Patricia M. Ranum. Baltimore: Johns Hopkins
  University Press, 1974.
Astell, Ann W. *The Song of Songs in the Middle Ages.* Ithaca: Cornell
  University Press, 1990.
Baker, Derek, ed. *Medieval Woman.* Oxford: Basil Blackwell, 1978.
Bakhtin, Mikhail. *Rabelais and His World.* Trans. Hélène Iswolsky.
  Bloomington: Indiana University Press, 1984.
Bartky, Sandra. "Foucault, Femininity and the Modernization of Patriar-
  chal Power." In *Feminism and Foucault.* Ed. Irene Diamond and Lee
  Quinby. Boston: Northeastern University Press, 1988.
Beckwith, Sarah. "A Very Material Mysticism: The Medieval Mysticism
  of Margery Kempe." In *Medieval Literature: Criticism, Ideology, His-
  tory.* Ed. David Aers. New York: St. Martin's, 1986. Pp. 34–57.
Bell, Rudolph. *Holy Anorexia.* Chicago: University of Chicago, 1985.
Benz, Ernst. "Christliche Mystik und christliche Kunst: Zur theologischen
  Interpretation mitteralterlichen Kunst." *Deutsche Vierteljahrschrift für
  Literaturwissenschaft und Geistesgeschichte* 12 (1934): 22–48.
Beriac, Françoise. *Histoire des lépreux au moyen âge: un société d'exclus.*
  Paris: Imago, 1988.
Blank, W. "Dominikanische Frauenmystik und die Enstehung des An-
  dachtsbildes um 1300." *Alemannisches Jahrbuch* (1964–65): 57–86.
Blumenfeld-Kosinski, Renate and Timea Szell, eds. *Images of Sainthood
  in Medieval Europe.* Ithaca: Cornell University Press, 1991.

Bogin, Meg. *The Women Troubadours: An Introduction to the Women Poets of 12th-century Provence and a Collection of Their Poems*. New York: Norton, 1980.

Bolton, Brenda. "*Mulieres sanctae*." In *Women in Medieval Society*. Ed. Susan Mosher Stuard. Philadelphia: University of Pennsylvania Press, 1976. Pp. 141–58.

Bolton, Brenda. "Some Thirteenth Century Women in the Low Countries: A Special Case?" *Nederlands Archief voor Kerkgeschiedenis* 61 (1981): 7–29.

Bolton, Brenda. "*Vitae Matrum*: A Further Aspect of the *Frauenfrage*." In *Medieval Woman*. Ed. Derek Baker. Oxford: Basil Blackwell, 1978. Pp. 253–73.

Bordo, Susan. *Unbearable Weight: Feminism, Western Culture, and the Body*. Berkeley: University of California Press, 1993.

Børresen, Kari Elisabeth. *Subordination et équivalence: Nature et rôle de la femme d'après Augustin et Thomas d'Aquin*. Oslo: Universitetsforlaget, 1968. 2d edition.

Bourke, Vernon J. "Aquinas." In *Ethics in the History of Western Philosophy*. Ed. Robert J. Cavalier, James Gouinlock, and James P. Sterba. New York: Saint Martin's Press, 1989. Pp. 98–122.

Brann, Eva T. H. *The World of the Imagination: Sum and Substance*. Savage, Md.: Rowman and Littlefield, 1991.

Brooke, Rosalind B. and Christopher N. L. Brooke. "St. Clare." In *Medieval Woman*. Ed. Derek Baker. Oxford: Basil Blackwell, 1978. Pp. 275–88.

Brown, E. A. R. "Death and the Human Body in the Later Middle Ages: The Legislation of Boniface VIII on the Division of Corpses." *Viator* 12 (1981): 221–70.

Brown, Peter. *Augustine of Hippo: A Biography*. Berkeley: University of California Press, 1967.

Brown, Peter. *The Body and Society: Men, Women, and Sexual Renunciation in Early Christianity*. New York: Columbia University Press, 1988.

Bullough, Vern L. "Medieval Medical and Scientific Views of Women." *Viator* 4 (1973): 485–501.

Bundy, Murray W. *The Theory of the Imagination in Classical and Medieval Thought*. Champaign: University of Illinois Press, 1927.

Burns, E. Jane. *Bodytalk: When Women Speak in Old French Literature*. Philadelphia: University of Pennsylvania Press, 1993.

Burrell, David. *Knowing the Unknowable God: Ibn-Sina, Maimonides, Aquinas*. Notre Dame: University of Notre Dame Press, 1986.

Butler, Judith. *Bodies That Matter*. New York: Routldege, 1993.

Butler, Judith. *Gender Trouble: Feminism and the Subversion of Identity.* New York: Routledge, 1990.

Bynum, Caroline Walker. "Bodily Miracles and the Resurrection of the Body in the High Middle Ages." In *Belief in History.* Ed. by Thomas Kselman. Notre Dame: University of Notre Dame Press, 1990. Pp. 68–106.

Bynum, Caroline Walker. *Fragmentation and Redemption: Essays on Gender and the Human Body in Medieval Religion.* New York: Zone Books, 1991.

Bynum, Caroline Walker. *Holy Feast and Holy Fast: The Religious Significance of Food to Medieval Women.* Berkeley: University of California Press, 1987.

Bynum, Caroline Walker. *Jesus as Mother: Studies in the Spirituality of the High Middle Ages.* Berkeley: University of California Press, 1982.

Cadden, Joan. *Meanings of Sex Difference in the Middle Ages: Medicine, Science, and Culture.* Cambridge: Cambridge University Press, 1993.

Camporesi, Piero. *The Incorruptible Flesh: Bodily Mutation and Mortification in Religion and Folklore.* Trans. Tania Croft-Murray. Cambridge: Cambridge University Press, 1988.

Carozzi, Claude. "Douceline et les autres." In *La Religion populaire en Languedoc du XIIIe siècle à la moitié du XIVe siècle.* Toulouse: Privat, 1976. Pp. 251–67.

Casey, Michael. *Athirst for God: Spiritual Desire in Bernard of Clairvaux's Sermons on the Song of Songs.* Kalamazoo: Cistercian Publications, 1988.

Castelli, Elizabeth. "Mortifying the Body, Curing the Soul: Beyond Ascetic Dualism in *The Life of Saint Syncletica.*" *differences* 4 (1992): 134–53.

Certeau, Michel de. *La fable mystique, XVIe–XVIIe siècle.* Paris: Gallimard, 1982.

Certeau, Michel de. "Hagiographie." *Encyclopedia Universalis.* Paris: n. p., 1968. 8: 207–9.

Certeau, Michel de. *Heterologies: Discourse on the Other.* Trans. Brian Massumi. Minneapolis: University of Minnesota Press, 1986.

Certeau, Michel de. "*Mystique* au XVIIe siècle: Le problème du langage mystique." In *L'Homme devant Dieu: Mélanges de Lubac.* 2 vols. Paris: Aubier, 1964. 2: 267–91.

Chodorow, Nancy. *The Reproduction of Mothering: Psychoanalysis and the Sociology of Gender.* Berkeley: University of California Press, 1978.

Cixous, Hélène and Catherine Clément. *The Newly Born Woman.* Trans. Betsy Wing. Minneapolis: University of Minnesota Press, 1986.

Coakley, John. "Friars as Confidants of Holy Women in Medieval Dominican Hagiography." In *Images of Sainthood in Medieval Europe*. Ed. Renate Blumenfeld-Kosinski and Timea Szell. Ithaca: Cornell University Press, 1991. Pp. 222–46.

Coakley, John. "Gender and the Authority of Friars: The Significance of Holy Women for Thirteenth-Century Franciscans and Dominicans." *Church History* 60 (1991): 445–60.

Cognet, Louis. *Introduction aux mystiques rhéno-flamands*. Paris: Descleé de Brouwer, 1968.

Colish, Marcia. *The Mirror of Language: A Study of the Medieval Theory of Language*. Lincoln: University of Nebraska Press, 1983.

Constable, Giles. *Attitudes Toward Self-Inflicted Suffering in the Middle Ages*. Brookline, Mass.: Hellenic College Press, 1982.

Corrington, Gail Paterson. "Anorexia, Asceticism, and Autonomy." *Journal of Feminist Studies in Religion* 2 (1986): 51–63.

Corrington, Gail Paterson. "The Defense of the Body and the Discourse of Appetite: Continence and Control in the Greco-Roman World." *Semeia* 57 (1992): 65–74.

Cousins, Ewert. *Bonaventure and the Coincidence of Opposites*. Chicago: Franciscan Herald Press, 1978.

Csányi, D. A. " '*Optima Pars:*' Die Auslegungsgeschichte von Lk. 10, 38–42 bei den Kirchenvätern der ersten vier Jahrhunderte." *Studia Monastica* 2 (1960): 5–78.

Dallenbach, Lucien. *The Mirror in the Text*. Chicago: University of Chicago Press, 1989.

Davis, Natalie Zemon. "Women's History in Transition: The European Case." *Feminist Studies* 4 (1976): 83–103.

D'Avray, D. L. *The Preaching of the Friars: Sermons Diffused from Paris before 1300*. Oxford: Clarendon Press, 1985.

DeGanck, Roger. *Beatrice of Nazareth in Her Context*. 2 vols. Kalamazoo: Cistercian Publications, 1991.

Delehaye, Hippolyte. *The Legends of the Saints*. Trans. V. M. Crawford. Notre Dame: University of Notre Dame Press, 1961.

Delmaire, Bernard. "Les béguines dans le Nord de la France au première siècle de leur histoire (vers 1230–vers 1350)." In *Les Religieuses en France au XIIIe siècle*. Ed. Michel Parisse. Nancy: Presses Universitaires de Nancy, 1985. Pp. 121–62.

Demers, Patricia. *Women as Interpreters of the Bible*. New York: Paulist Press, 1992.

Despres, Denise. *Ghostly Sights: Visual Meditation in Late Medieval Literature*. Norman, Okla.: Pilgrim Press, 1989.

Dinzelbacher, Peter. "Das Christusbild der heiligen Lutgard von Tongeren im Rahmen der Passionsmystik und der Frauenmystik und Bildkunst des 12. und 13. Jahrhunderts." *Ons Geestelijk Erf* 56 (1982): 217–77.

Dinzelbacher, Peter. "Rollenverweigerung, religiöser Aufbruch und mystisches Erleben mittelalterlichen Frauen." In *Religiöse Frauenbewegung und mystische Frömmigkeit im Mittelalter*. Ed. Peter Dinzelbacher and Dieter R. Bauer. Cologne and Vienna: Bohlau, 1988. Pp. 3–58.

Dinzelbacher, Peter and Dieter R. Bauer, eds. *Frauenmystik im Mittelalter*. Ostfildern: Schwabenverlag, 1985.

Dinzelbacher, Peter and Dieter R. Bauer, eds. *Religiöse Frauenbewegung und mystische Frömmigkeit im Mittelalter*. Cologne and Vienna: Bohlau, 1988.

Dronke, Peter. *Dante and Medieval Latin Traditions*. Cambridge: Cambridge University Press, 1986.

Dronke, Peter. *Women Writers of the Middle Ages: A Critical Study of Texts from Perpetua (d. 203) to Marguerite Porete (d. 1310)*. Cambridge: Cambridge University Press, 1984.

Duby, Georges, ed. *A History of Private Life*. Volume 2: *Revelations of the Medieval World*. Cambridge: Harvard University Press, 1987.

DuPlessis, Rachel Blau. *The Pink Guitar: Writing as Feminist Practice*. New York: Routledge, 1990.

Ell, Stephen R. "Blood and Sexuality in Medieval Leprosy." *Janus: Revue Internationale de l'Histoire des Sciences, de la Médecine, de la Pharmacie et de la Technique* 71 (1984): 153–63.

Elliot, Alison Goddard. *Roads to Paradise: Reading the Lives of the Early Saints*. Hanover: University Press of New England, 1987.

Felski, Rita. *Beyond Feminist Aesthetics: Feminist Literature and Social Change*. Cambridge: Harvard University Press, 1989.

Ferrante, Joan. "The Education of Women in the Middle Ages in Theory, Fact, and Fantasy." In *Beyond Their Sex: Learned Women in the European Past*. Ed. Patricia H. Labalme. New York: New York University Press, 1980.

Ferrante, Joan. *Woman as Image in Medieval Literature from the Twelfth Century to Dante*. New York: Columbia University Press, 1975.

Finke, Laurie. *Feminist Theory, Women's Writing*. Ithaca: Cornell University Press, 1992.

Forman, Robert K. C., ed. *The Problem of Pure Consciousness: Mysticism and Philosophy*. Oxford: Oxford University Press, 1990.

Foucault, Michel. *The History of Sexuality*. Vol. 1. *An Introduction*. Trans. Robert Hurley. New York: Random House, 1978.

Freed, John B. *The Friars and German Society in the Thirteenth Century*. Medieval Academy of American Publications 86. Cambridge: Medieval Academy of America, 1977.

Freed, John B. "Urban Development and the *Cura Monialium* in Thirteenth-Century Germany." *Viator* 3 (1972): 311–27.

Gatens, Moira. "A Critique of the Sex/Gender Distinction." In *A Reader in Feminist Knowledge*. Ed. Sneja Gunew. New York: Routledge, 1990. Pp. 139–57.

Geary, P. J. *Furta Sacra: Thefts of Relics in the Central Middle Ages.* Princeton: Princeton University Press, 1978.

Gilbert, Sandra M. and Susan Gubar. *No Man's Land: The Place of the Woman Writer in the Twentieth Century.* Vol. 1: *The War of the Words.* New Haven: Yale University Press, 1988.

Gilligan, Carol. *In a Different Voice.* Cambridge: Harvard University Press, 1982.

Gilligan, Carol, Janie Victoria Ward and Jill McLean Taylor, with Betty Bardige. *Mapping the Moral Domain.* Cambridge: Harvard University Graduate School of Education, 1988.

Gold, Penny Schine. *The Lady and the Virgin: Image, Attitude and Experience in Twelfth-Century France.* Chicago: University of Chicago Press, 1985.

Goldin, Frederick. *The Mirror of Narcissus in the Courtly Love Lyric.* Ithaca: Cornell University Press, 1967.

Goodich, Michael. "Contours of Female Piety in Later Medieval Hagiography." *Church History* 50 (1981): 20–32.

Goodich, Michael. *Vita Perfecta: The Ideal of Sainthood in the Thirteenth Century.* Stuttgart: Hiersemann, 1982.

Grabes, Herbert. *The Mutable Glass: Mirror-Imagery in Titles and Texts of the Middle Ages and English Renaissance.* Cambridge: Cambridge University Press, 1982.

Gravdal, Katherine. *Ravishing Maidens: Writing Rape in Medieval French Literature.* Philadelphia: University of Pennsylvania Press, 1991.

Greene, Gayle. "Looking at History." In *Changing Subjects: The Making of Feminist Literary Criticism.* Ed. Gayle Greene and Coppélia Kahn. New York: Routledge, 1993.

Greven, Joseph. *Die Anfänge der Beginen: Ein Beitrag zur Geschichte der Volksfrömmigkeit und des Ordenswesens im Hochmittelalter.* Munster: Aschendorff, 1912.

Greven, Joseph. "Der Ursprung des Beginenwesens." *Historiches Jahrbuch* 35 (Munich, 1914): 26–58; 291–318.

Grundmann, Herbert. "Die Frauen und die Literatur im Mittelalter: Ein Beitrag zur Frage nach der Entstehung des Schrifttums in der Volksprache." *Archiv für Kulturgeschichten* 26 (1936): 129–61.

Grundmann, Herbert. "Die geschichtliche Grundlagen der deutschen Mystik." In *Altdeutsche und altniederländische Mystik.* Ed. Kurt

Ruh. Darmstadt: Wissenschaftliche Buchgesellsschaft, 1964. Pp. 72–99.

Grundmann, Herbert. "Ketzerverhöre des Spätmittelalters als quellenkritisches Problem." *Deutschen Archiv für Erforschung des Mittelalters* 21 (1965): 519–75.

Grundmann, Herbert. *Religiöse Bewegungen im Mittelalter: Untersuchungen über die geschichtlichen Zusammenhänge zwischen der Ketzerei, den Bettelorden und der religiösen Frauenbewegung im 12. und 13. Jahrhundert.* 2d ed. Hildesheim: Olms, 1961. 1st ed. 1935.

Hamburger, Jeffrey. *The Rothschild Canticles: Art and Mysticism in Flanders and the Rhineland circa 1300.* New Haven: Yale University Press, 1990.

Hamburger, Jeffrey. "Visual and Visionary: The Image in Late Medieval Monastic Devotions." *Viator* 20 (1989): 161–82.

Haraway, Donna. *Simians, Cyborgs, and Woman: The Reinvention of Nature.* New York: Routledge, 1991.

Harl, Marguerite. "Le Langage de l'Expérience Religieuse chez les Pères Grecs." *Rivista di Storia e Letteratura Religiosa* 15 (1977): 5–34.

Hart, Kevin. *The Trespass of the Sign: Deconstruction, Theology, and Philosophy.* Cambridge: Cambridge University Press, 1989.

Harvey, E. Ruth. *The Inward Wits: Psychological Theory in the Middle Ages and the Renaissance.* London: The Warburg Institute, 1975.

Heffernan, Thomas J. *Sacred Biography: Saints and Their Biographers in the Middle Ages.* Oxford: Oxford University Press, 1988.

Hollywood, Amy. "Beauvoir, Irigaray, and the Mystical." *Hypatia* 9 (1994): 158–85.

Homans, Margaret. *Bearing the Word: Language and Female Experience in Nineteenth-Century Women's Writing.* Chicago: University of Chicago Press, 1986.

Idel, Moshe and Bernard McGinn, eds. *Mystical Union and Monotheistic Faith: An Ecumenical Dialogue.* New York: Macmillan, 1989.

Imbert-Gourbeyre, Antoine. *La Stigmatisation: L'Extase divine et les miracles de Lourdes: Réponse aux libre-penseurs.* 2 vols. Clermont-Ferrand: Librairie Catholique, 1894.

Irigaray, Luce. *Speculum of the Other Woman.* Trans. Gillian C. Gill. Ithaca: Cornell University Press, 1985.

Irigaray, Luce. *This Sex Which is Not One.* Trans. Catherine Porter with Carolyn Burke. Ithaca: Cornell University Press, 1985.

Jackson, W. T. H. *The Challenge of the Medieval Text.* New York: Columbia University Press, 1985.

Jacquart, Danielle and Claude Thomassett. *Sexuality and Medicine in the Middle Ages.* Trans. Matthew Adamson. Princeton: Princeton University Press, 1988.

Jakobson, Roman. "On Linguistics Aspects of Translation." In *Theories of Translation: An Anthology of Essays from Dryden to Derrida.* Ed. Rainer Schulte and John Biguenet. Chicago: University of Chicago Press, 1992. Pp. 144–51.

Jansen, Saskia Murk. *The Measure of Mystic Thought: A Study of Hadewigch's Mengedichlen.* Göppingen: Kummerle, 1991.

Jauss, Hans Robert. *Toward an Aesthetic of Reception.* Trans. Timothy Bahti. Minneapolis: University of Minnesota Press, 1982.

Jonsen, Albert R. and Stephen Toulmin. *The Abuse of Casuistry: A History of Moral Reasoning.* Berkeley: University of California Press, 1988.

Katz, Stephen T., ed. *Mysticism and Philosophical Analysis.* Oxford: Oxford University Press, 1978.

Katz, Stephen T., ed. *Mysticism and Religious Traditions.* Oxford: Oxford University Press, 1983.

Kieckhefer, Richard. *Repression and Heresy in Medieval Germany.* Philadelphia: University of Pennsylvania Press, 1979.

Kieckhefer, Richard. *Unquiet Souls: Fourteenth-Century Saints and Their Religious Milieu.* Chicago: University of Chicago Press, 1984.

Kittay, Eva Feder and Diana T. Meyers, eds. *Women and Moral Theory.* Savage, Md.: Rowman and Littlefield, 1987.

Kristeva, Julia. *Tales of Love.* Trans. Leon S. Roudiez. New York: Columbia University Press, 1987.

Lagorio, Valerie. "The Medieval Continental Women Mystics: An Introduction." In *An Introduction to the Medieval Mystics of Europe.* Ed. Paul Szarmach. Albany: State University of New York Press, 1984. Pp. 161–93.

Lambert, Malcolm. *Medieval Heresy: Popular Movements from the Gregorian Reform to the Reformation.* Oxford: Blackwell, 1992. 2d edition.

Lamberton, Robert. *Homer the Theologian: Neoplatonist Allegorical Reading and the Growth of the Epic Tradition.* Berkeley: University of California Press, 1986.

Lambot, G. "Un précieux manuscrit de la Vie de S. Julienne du Mont-Cornillon." In *Miscellanea historica in honorem Alberti de Meyer.* 2 vols. Louvain: Bibliothèque de l'Université, 1946. Pp. 603–12.

Langer, Otto. "Zur dominikanischen Frauenmystik im spät-mittelalterlichen Deutschland." In *Frauenmystik im Mittelalter.* Ed. Peter Dinzelbacher and Dieter R. Bauer. Ostfildern: Schwabenverlag, 1984. Pp. 341–46.

Lanser, Susan Sniader. *Fictions of Authority: Women Writers and Narrative Voice.* Ithaca: Cornell University Press, 1992.

Laqueur, Thomas. *Making Sex: Body and Gender from the Greeks to Freud.* Cambridge: Harvard University Press, 1990.

Larrabee, Mary Jeanne, ed. *An Ethic of Care: Feminist and Interdisciplinary Perspectives.* New York: Routledge, 1993.

Lea, H. C. *A History of the Inquisition in the Middle Ages.* Manchester, n.p., 1888.

Leclercq, Jean, Francois Vandenbroucke and Louis Bouyer. *A History of Christian Spirituality.* Vol. 2: *The Spirituality of the Middle Ages.* Minneapolis: Seabury Press, 1968.

Leclercq, Jean. *Saint Bernard Mystique.* Bruges: De Brouwes, 1948.

Leclercq, Jean. *Women and Saint Bernard of Clairvaux.* Trans. Marie-Bernard Saïd. Kalamazoo: Cistercian Publications, 1989.

Leder, Drew. *The Absent Body.* Chicago: University of Chicago Press, 1990.

LeGoff, Jacques. *The Birth of Purgatory.* Chicago: University of Chicago Press, 1984.

Little, Lester K. *Religious Poverty and the Profit Economy in Medieval Europe.* Ithaca: Cornell University Press, 1978.

Lobkowicz, Nikolaus. *Theory and Practice: The History of a Concept from Aristotle to Marx.* Notre Dame: University of Notre Dame Press, 1967.

Lochrie, Karma. *Margery Kempe and Translations of the Flesh.* Philadelphia: University of Pennsylvania Press, 1991.

Lomperis, Linda and Sarah Stanbury, eds. *Feminist Approaches to the Body in Medieval Literature.* Philadelphia: University of Pennsylvania Press, 1993.

Lynch, Kathryn L. *The High Medieval Dream Vision: Poetry, Philosophy and Literary Form.* Stanford: Stanford University Press, 1988.

McDonnell, Ernest W. *The Beguines and Beghards in Medieval Culture.* New Brunswick: Rutgers University Press, 1954.

McGinn, Bernard. *The Calabrian Abbot: Joachim of Fiore in the History of Western Thought.* New York: Macmillan, 1985.

McGinn, Bernard. "Love, Knowledge and *Unio mystica* in the Western Christian Tradition." In *Mystical Union and Monotheistic Faith: An Ecumenical Dialogue.* Ed. Moshe Idel and Bernard McGinn. New York: Macmillan, 1989. Pp. 59–86.

McLaughlin, Eleanor Commo. "Equality of Souls, Inequality of Sexes: Woman in Medieval Theology." In *Religion and Sexism: Images of Woman in the Jewish and Christian Traditions.* Ed. Rosemary Radford Ruether. New York: Simon and Schuster, 1974.

McLaughlin, Eleanor. "Les Femmes et l'hérésie médiévale: Un problème dans l'histoire de la spiritualité." *Concilium* 111 (1976): 73–90.

McMahon, Robert. *Augustine's Prayerful Ascent: An Essay on the Literary Form of the Confessions.* Athens: University of Georgia Press, 1989.

McNamara, Jo Ann. "The Need to Give: Suffering and Female Sanctity in the Middle Ages." In *Images of Sainthood in Medieval Europe.* Ed. Renate Blumenfeld-Kosinski and Timea Szell. Ithaca: Cornell University Press, 1991. Pp. 199–221.

McNamara, Jo Ann and John E. Halborg with E. Gordon Whatley, eds. *Sainted Women of the Dark Ages.* Durham: Duke University Press, 1992.

McNay, Lois. *Foucault and Feminism: Power, Gender, and the Self.* Boston: Northeastern University Press, 1992.

Martin, Emily. *The Woman in the Body: A Cultural Analysis of Reproduction.* Boston: Beacon Press, 1987.

Matter, E. Ann. *"The Voice of My Beloved": The Song of Songs in Western Medieval Christianity.* Philadelphia: University of Pennsylvania Press, 1990.

Meltzer, Françoise. *Salome and the Dance of Writing.* Chicago: University of Chicago Press, 1987.

Mens, A. "Les béguines et les béghards dans le cadre de la culture médiévale." *Moyen Âge* 64 (1958): 305–15.

Miles, Margaret. *Carnal Knowing: Female Nakedness and Religious Meaning in the Christian West.* Boston: Beacon Press, 1989.

Miller, Nancy K. *Subject to Change: Reading Feminist Writing.* New York: Columbia University Press, 1988.

Minnis, A. J. *Medieval Theory of Authorship: Scholastic Literary Attitudes.* Philadelphia: University of Pennsylvania Press, 1988. 2nd ed.

Modleski, Tania. *Feminist without Women: Culture and Criticism in a "Postfeminist" Age.* New York: Routledge, 1991.

Moi, Toril. *Sexual/Textual Politics: Feminist Literary Theory.* New York: Methuen, 1985.

Moody-Adams, Michele M. "Gender and the Complexity of Moral Symbols." In *Feminist Ethics.* Ed. Claudia Card. Lawrence: University Press of Kansas, 1991. Pp. 195–212.

Moore, R. I. *The Origins of European Dissent.* Oxford: Blackwell, 1977.

Murrin, Michael. *The Allegorical Epic.* Chicago: University of Chicago Press, 1980.

Muscatine, Charles. "The Emergence of Psychological Allegory in Old French Romance." *PMLA* 68 (Sept.–Dec., 1953): 1160–72.

Neel, Carol. "The Origins of the Beguines." *Signs* 14 (1989): 321–41.

Newman, Barbara. *Sister of Wisdom: Saint Hildegard's Theology of the Feminine.* Berkeley: University of California Press, 1987.

Ochsenbein, Peter. "Leidensmystik im dominikanische Frauenklöstern des 14. Jahrhunderts am Beispiel der Elsbeth von Oye." In *Religiöse Frauenbewegung und mystische Frömmigkeit im Mittelalter*. Ed. Peter Dinzelbacher and Dieter R. Bauer. Cologne and Vienna: Bohlau, 1988. Pp. 353–72.

Ohly, Friedrich. *Hohelied-Studien: Grundzüge einer Geschichte der Hoheliedauslegung des Abendlandes bis um 1200*. Wiesbaden: Franz Steiner, 1958.

Olney, James, ed. *Autobiography: Essays Theoretical and Critical*. Princeton: Princeton University Press, 1980.

Paden, William D., ed. *The Voice of the Trobairitz: Perspectives on the Women Troubadours*. Philadelphia: University of Pennsylvania Press, 1989.

Paster, Gail Kern. *The Body Embarassed: Drama and the Disciplines of Shame in Early Modern England*. Ithaca: Cornell University Press, 1993.

Peters, Ursula. *Religiöse Erfahrung als literarisches Faktum: Zur Vorgeschichte und Genese frauenmysticher Texte des 13. und 14. Jahrhunderts*. Tubingen: Niemeyer, 1988.

Petroff, Elizabeth. "A Medieval Woman's Utopian Vision: The Rule of Saint Clare of Assisi." In *Feminism, Utopia, and Narrative*. Ed. Libby Falk Jones and Sarah Webster Goodwin. Knoxville: University of Tennessee Press, 1990. Pp. 174–90.

Petroff, Elizabeth. "Introduction. The Visionary Tradition in Women's Writing: Dialogue and Autobiography." In *Medieval Women's Visionary Literature*. Ed. Elizabeth Petroff. Oxford: Oxford University Press, 1986. Pp. 3–59.

Philippen, L. J. M. *De Begijnhoven. Oorsprung, Geschiedenis, Inrichting*. Antwerp: n.p., 1918.

Poland, Lynn. "Invocation as Interruption in Augustine's *Confessions*." In *Morphologies of Faith: Essays in Religion and Culture in Honor of Nathan A. Scott, Jr.*. Ed. Mary Gerhart and Anthony C. Yu. Atlanta: Scholars Press, 1990. Pp. 343–58.

Porion, J. B. *Hadewijch d'Anvers*. Paris: 1954.

Pourrat, P. "Quiétisme." *Dictionnaire de spiritualité, ascétique et mystique, doctrine et histoire*. Ed. M. Viller et al. Paris: Beauchesne, 1937–. Vol. 13.2: cols. 1547–81.

Power, Eileen. *Medieval Women*. Ed. M. M. Postan. Cambridge: Cambridge University Press, 1975.

Rahner, Hugo. "Die Gottesgeburt. Die Lehre der Kirchenväter von der Geburt Christi aus dem Herzen der Kirche und der Glaübigen." *Zeitschrift für Katholische Theologie* 59 (1933): 333–418.

Ratzinger, Joseph. "Originalität und Ueberlieferung in Augustins Begriff der Confessio." *Revue des études augustiniennes* 3 (1957): 375–92.

Régnier-Bohler, Danielle. "Voix littéraires, voix mystiques." In *Histoire des Femmes en Occident*. Vol. 2. *Le Moyen Âge*. Ed. Christiane Klapisch-Zuber. Paris: Plon, 1991. Trans. in *A History of Women in the West*, vol. 2, *Silences of the Middle Ages*. Cambridge: Belknap Press, 1992.

Ringler, Siegfried. "Die Rezeption mittelalterlicher Frauenmystik als wissenschaftliches Problem, dargestellt am Werk der Christine Ebner." In *Frauenmystik im Mittelater*. Ed. Peter Dinzelbacher and Dieter R. Bauer. Ostfildern: Schwabenverlag, 1985. Pp. 178–200.

Robertson, Elizabeth. "The Corporeality of Female Sanctity in *The Life of Saint Margaret*." In *Images of Sainthood in Medieval Europe*. Ed. Renate Blumenfeld-Kosinski and Timea Szell. Ithaca: Cornell University Press, 1991. Pp. 268–87.

Robertson, Elizabeth. "Medieval Medical Views of Women and Female Spirituality in the *Ancrene Wisse* and Julian of Norwich's *Showings*." In *Feminist Approaches to the Body in Medieval Literature*. Ed. Linda Lomperis and Susan Stanbury. Philadelphia: University of Pennsylvania Press, 1993. Pp. 142–67.

Roisin, Simone. "L'efflorescence cistercienne et le courant féminin de piété au XIIIe siècle." *Revue d'histoire ecclésiastique* 39 (1943): 342–78.

Roisin, Simone. *L'hagiographie cistercienne dans le diocèse de Liège au XIIIe siècle*. Louvain: Bibliothèque de l'Université, 1947.

Roisin, Simone. "La Méthode hagiographique de Thomas de Cantimpré." *Miscellanea historica in honorem Alberti de Meyer*. 2 vols. Louvain: Bibliothèque de l'Université, 1946. Vol. 1.

Ross, Ellen. " 'She Wept and Cried Right Loud for Sorrow and for Pain': Suffering, the Spiritual Journey, and Women's Experience in Late Medieval Mysticism." In *Maps of Flesh and Light: The Religious Experience of Medieval Women Mystics*. Ed. Ulrike Wiethaus. Syracuse: Syracuse University Press, 1993. Pp. 45–59.

Rubin, Miri. *Corpus Christi: The Eucharist in Late Medieval Culture*. Cambridge: Cambridge University Press, 1991.

Ruh, Kurt, ed. *Abendländische Mystik im Mittelalter*. Stuttgart: Metzler, 1986.

Ruh, Kurt, ed. *Altdeutsche Mystik*. Bern: Francke, 1950.

Scarry, Elaine. *The Body in Pain: The Making and Unmaking of the World*. Oxford: Oxford University Press, 1985.

Schmidt, Margot. "Miroir." *Dictionnaire de spiritualité, ascétique et mystique, doctrine et histoire*. Ed. M. Viller et al. Paris: Beauchesne, 1937–. Vol. 10: cols. 1290–1303.

Schmitt, Jean-Claude. *Mort d'une hérésie: l'Église et les clercs face aux béguines et aux béghards du Rhin supérieur du XIVe au XVe siècle.* Paris: Mouton, 1978.

Schulenburg, Jane Tibbetts. "Saints Lives as a Source for the History of Women, 500–1100." In *Medieval Women and the Sources of Medieval History.* Ed. Joel Rosenthal. Athens: University of Georgia Press, 1990. Pp. 285–320.

Schulenburg, Jane Tibbetts. "Strict Active Enclosure and Its Effects on the Female Monastic Experience (500–1100)." In *Distant Echoes: Medieval Religious Women.* Ed. John A. Nichols and Lillian Thomas Shank. Kalamazoo: Cistercian Publications, 1984. Pp. 51–86.

Scott, Joan. *Gender and the Politics of History.* New York: Columbia University Press, 1988.

Shahar, Shulamith. *The Fourth Estate: A History of Women in the Middle Ages.* Trans. Chaya Galai. London: Methuen, 1983.

Showalter, Elaine. "Feminist Criticism in the Wilderness." In *The New Feminist Criticism: Essays on Women, Literature, and Theory.* Ed. Elaine Showalter. New York: Pantheon, 1985. Pp. 243–70.

Showalter, Elaine. "Women's Time, Women's Space: Writing the History of Feminist Criticism." In *Feminist Issues in Literary Scholarship.* Ed. Shari Benstock. Bloomington: Indiana University Press, 1987. Pp. 30–44.

Signs 14:2 (1989).

Simons, Walter. "The Beguine Movement in the Southern Low Countries: A Reassessment." *Bulletin de l'Institut Historique Belge de Rome.* (1990): 63–105.

Smith, Sidonie. *A Poetics of Women's Autobiography: Marginality and the Fictions of Self-Representation.* Bloomington: Indiana University Press, 1987.

Smith, Sidonie. *Subjectivity, Identity, and the Body: Women's Autobiographical Practices in the Twentieth Century.* Bloomington: Indiana University Press, 1993.

Soelle, Dorothee. *Suffering.* Trans. Everett R. Kalin. Philadelphia: Fortress Press, 1975.

Speculum 68:2 (1993).

Stanton, Domna, ed. *The Female Autograph.* Chicago: University of Chicago Press, 1987.

Stein, Frederic M. "The Religious Women of Cologne: 1120–1320." Ph.D. dissertation, Yale University, 1977.

Stuard, Susan Mosher, ed. *Women in Medieval History and Historiography.* Philadelphia: University of Pennsylvania Press, 1987.

Summers, Janet I. " 'The Violent Shall Take It By Force': The First Century of Cistercian Nuns, 1125–1228." Ph.D. dissertation, University of Chicago, 1986.

Sweetman, Robert. "Christine of Saint-Trond's Preaching Apostolate: Thomas of Cantimpré's Hagiographical Method Revisited," *Vox Benedictina* 60 (1992): 67–97.

Tarrant, Jacqueline. "The Clementine Decrees on the Beguines: Conciliar and Papal Versions." *Archivum Historiae Pontificae* 12 (1974): 300–308.

TeSelle, Eugene. "Augustine." In *An Introduction to the Medieval Mystics of Europe*. Ed. Paul Szarmach. Albany: State University of New York Press, 1984. Pp. 19–35.

Thurston, Herbert. *The Physical Phenomena of Mysticism: A Collection of Studies on Praeternatural Phenomena in the Lives of the Saints and Others*. Chicago: Regnery, 1952.

Tuana, Nancy. *The Less Noble Sex: Scientific, Religious, and Philosophical Conceptions of Woman's Nature*. Bloomington: Indiana University Press, 1993.

Vance, Eugene. "Augustine's *Confessions* and the Grammar of Selfhood." *Genre* 6 (1973): 1–28.

Vance, Eugene. *Mervelous Signals: Poetics and Sign Theory in the Middle Ages*. Lincoln: University of Nebraska Press, 1986.

Vance, Eugene. "Le Moi comme langage: Saint Augustin et l'autobiographie." *Poétique* 42 (1980): 139–55.

Van Mierlo, J. "Béguines." In *Dictionnaire d'histoire et de géographie ecclésiastique*. Ed. Alfred Baudrillart. Paris: Letouzey and Ane, 1934. Vol. 7: 457–73.

Van Mierlo, J. "Béguins, Béguines, Béguinages." *Dictionnaire de Spiritualité, ascétique et mystique, doctrine et histoire*. Ed. M. Viller et al. Paris: Beauchesne, 1937–. Vol. 1: cols. 1341–52.

Vauchez, André. *Les laïcs au Moyen Âge: Pratiques et expérience religieuses*. Paris: Édition du Cerf, 1987.

Vauchez, André. *La Sainteté en Occident aux derniers siècles du moyen âge d'après les procès de canonisation et les documents hagiographiques*. Bibliothèque des écoles françaises d'Athènes et de Rome 241. Paris: Ecole Française de Rome, 1981.

Vitz, Evelyn Birge, *Medieval Narrative and Modern Narratology: Subjects and Objects of Desire*. New York: New York University Press, 1989.

Warner, Marina. *Alone of All Her Sex: The Myth and Cult of the Virgin Mary*. London: Weidenfeld and Nicolson, 1976.

Weber, Alison. *Theresa of Avila and the Rhetoric of Femininity*. Princeton: Princeton University Press, 1990.

Weigel, Sigrid. "Double Focus: On the History of Women's Writing." In *Feminist Aesthetics*. Ed. Gisela Ecker. Boston: Beacon Press, 1985. Pp. 59–80.

Weigel, Sigrid. "Der schielende Blick: Thesen zur Geschichte weiblicher Schriebpraxis." In *Die verboregene Frau: Sechs Beiträge zu einer feministischen Literaturwissenschaft*. Inge Stephan and Sigrid Weigel. Berlin: Argument, 1983. Pp. 83–137.

Weil, Simone. *Waiting for God*. Trans. Emma Craufurd. New York: Putnam, 1951.

Weinstein, Donald and Rudolph Bell. *Saints and Society: The Two Worlds of Western Christendom, 1000–1700*. Chicago: University of Chicago Press, 1982.

Weintraub, Karl Joachim. *The Value of the Individual*. Chicago: University of Chicago Press, 1978.

Wemple, Suzanne F. "Sanctity and Power: The Dual Pursuit of Early Medieval Women." In *Becoming Visible: Women in European History*. Ed. Renate Bridenthal, Claudia Koonz, and Susan Stuard. Boston: Houghton Mifflin, 1987. 2d edition.

Whitford, Margaret. *Luce Irigaray: Philosophy in the Feminine*. New York: Routledge, 1991.

Whitman, Jon. *Allegory: The Dynamics of an Ancient and Medieval Technique*. Cambridge: Harvard University Press, 1987.

Wolfson, Harry A. *Studies in the History of Philosophy and Religion*. 2 vols. Ed. Isadore Twersky and George H. Williams. Cambridge: Harvard University Press, 1973 and 1977.

Young, Iris Marion. "Pregnant Embodiment: Subjectivity and Alienation." *The Journal of Medicine and Philosophy* 9 (1984): 45–62.

Ziegler, Johanna. "The *curtis* beguinages in the Southern Low Countries and art patronage." *Bulletin de l'Institut Historique Belge de Rome* (1987): 31–70.

Ziegler, Johanna. "Reality as Imitation: The Role of Religious Imagery Among the Beguines of the Low Countries." In *Maps of Flesh and Light: The Religious Experience of Medieval Women*. Ed. Ulrike Wiethaus. Syracuse: Syracuse University Press, 1993. Pp. 112–26.

INDEX